FOSTER'S SYSTEMATIC

HIGH POINT
OF OUR SALVATION

An Introduction to Soteriology

J.B. Foster, Th.M, D.Min.

Foreword by **Dr. Samuel Odenyo**

◆ ◆ ◆

ISBN-10: 1530445361
ISBN-13: 978-1530445363
Copyright © 2016
Published by Bell Publishing
All rights reserved.

Printed by CreateSpace, an Amazon.com company.
www.CreateSpace.com
Available from Amazon.com and other retail outlets.
Book design by Larry Smith
www.LarrySmithDesign.com

Dedication

◆ ◆ ◆

Bless the Lord, O my soul:
And all that is within me,
Bless His holy name.
And forget not all His benefits:
Who forgiveth all thine iniquities;
who healeth all thy diseases;
Who redeemeth thy life from destruction;
who crowneth thee with
lovingkindness and tender mercies;
Who satisfieth thy mouth with good things;
so that thy youth is renewed like the eagle's.

Psalm 103:1-5

"In an attempt to be reasonable, man has become irrational.
In an attempt to deify himself, he has defaced himself.
In an attempt to be free, he has made himself a slave.
And like Alexander the Great, he has conquered the world around
him but has not yet conquered himself."

Ravi Zacharias

⊣ CONTENTS ⊢

◆ ◆ ◆

REFLECTIONS

Foreword

◆ ◆ ◆

It has now been nearly ten years since I last saw Joan Foster articulately expressing her points of view in a lecture room at the National Bible College and Seminary.

The book you are holding and the information it contains were once formless ideas residing in a spiritual giant and prayer warrior in the kingdom of God. It was written by someone I have known (personally, as a student) and seen live a practical Christian life for some years.

The High Point of our Salvation comes at a critical time as the world is spiraling out of control and people everywhere are looking for the answer to peace, unity and harmony. The book addresses the single most important question in a person's life: *What must I do to be saved?* Dr. Foster addresses this and goes beyond to answer how we can be saved and what it means. That is a question that bothered the intellectuals in Bible times and has intrigued scholars for years. For instance, Nicodemus was one such person.

The Bible's introduction of him suggests that his encounter with Jesus was a sacred and special appointment. He was a Pharisee, one the three most important societal groups in Bible days with great responsibility and influence over the common Jewish people. The Pharisees were very forthright, religiously teaching the written Word, or what was known as the Old Testament during the times of Christ, as inspired by God. Nicodemus was a public figure with extraordinary knowledge of the law and its divine principles. He was a learned man, held a significantly high position on the Jewish Ruling Council and was held in the utmost regard. Nicodemus was Jerusalem's esteemed Bible teacher of that day. Yet, despite all of his knowledge and priestly years on the Council, Nicodemus could not comprehend the gospel message so he came to Jesus by night. This is where the "Pharisee" in Nicodemus took a back seat and in this instance, he surrendered his own high knowledge. His desire to know the pure unadulterated truth superseded pride and position. He wanted a personal, one on one encounter with Jesus while he sought the Lord in a personal way.

There are many today who want to come and dine at the master's table in hope for a personal encounter with Jesus and to know the truth in a time when our world desperately needs salvation. *The High Point of our Salvation* will open up this topic in a very direct, real life applicable way as the reader studies the high point of salvation and its criticality to man's need. Nicodemus learned that he must be born again and he was. Just as it had a lasting effect on his life (we are able to follow his story through the book of John), this is the promise of salvation for today.

Everyone who has ever pursued the general study of the doctrine of salvation (Soteriology) should realize that it is impossible to produce a completely satisfactory book, as this topic is simply too vast to completely exhaust. However, no matter how many pages are written concerning this subject, the story always sprawls. I would like to personally thank Dr. Foster for her courage and ministry. This book is another shining example of how mightily God is using this bulwark. I am pleased to recommend this book to all students of faith.

– Dr. Samuel Odenyo
National Bible College & Seminary

KEYWORDS and PHRASES

Atonement	Propitiation
Call, *Effectual*	Reconciliation
Call, *General*	Redemption
Compatiblism	Regeneration
Complementarianism	Regeneration, *Synergistic*
Egalitarianism	Regeneration, *Monogistic*
Election, *Conditional*	Repentance
Election, *Unconditional*	Reprobate
Exclusivism	Restrictivism
Fatalism	Salvation
Imputation	Sanctification
Inclusivism	Sin, *Imputed*
Irresistible Grace	Sin, *Inherited*
Justification	Sin, *Mortal*
Liberation	Sin, *Original*
Ordo Salutis	Sin, *Venial*
Pelagianism	Soteriology
Perseverance (Eternal Security)	Theory of the Atonement, *Governmental*
Pluralism	Theory of the Atonement, *Moral Example*
Predestination	Theory of the Atonement, *Ransom to Satan*
Predestination, *Double*	Theory of the Atonement, *Recapitulation*
Predestination, *Single*	Vicarious Substitutionary View of the Atonement

GENERAL ABBREVIATIONS

AD	anno domini (In the Year of our Lord)
AMP	The Amplified Bible (1965)
ASV	American Standard Version (1901)
BC	Before Christ
BCE	Before the Common Era (equivalent to BC)
ca.	approximately (from Latin circa)
CE	Common Era (equivalent to AD = "In the Year of the Lord")
CEV	Contemporary English Version (1995)
cf.	compare (from Latin confer)
ed	editor; edited by; edition
e.g.	for example (from Latin exempli gratia)
Etc.	Etcetera (from Latin phrase meaning 'and the other things, the rest
Gk.	Greek language
Hebr.	Hebrew language
i.e.	that is (from Latin id est)
KJV	King James Version, Authorized Version of the Bible (1611)
NKJV	New King James Version
Lat.	Latin language
LXX	Septuagint (The Greek Old Testament, translated between 250-100 b.c.)
NAB	New American Bible (1970)
NASB	New American Standard Bible (1971; update 1995)
NEB	The New English Bible (1970)
NET	New English Translation
NIV	The New International Version (NT, 1973; OT, 1978)
NLT	New Living Translation (1996)
NRSV	New Revised Standard Version of the Bible
NT	New Testament, Christian scriptures
OT	Old Testament, Hebrew scriptures
RSV	Revised Standard Version of the Bible
viz.	namely (from Latin videlicet)
v.	verse

LIST OF BIBLICAL BOOK ABBREVIATIONS

OLD TESTAMENT BOOKS

Gen., Gn.	Genesis
Ex., Exod.	Exodus
Lev., Le., Lv.	Leviticus
Num., Nu., Nm.	Numbers
Deut., Dt.	Deuteronomy
Josh., Jos., Jsh.	Joshua
Judg., Jdg., Jdgs.	Judges
Rth., Ru.	Ruth
1 Sam.	1 Samuel
2 Sam.	2 Samuel
1 Kgs, 1 Ki, I Ki, 1Ki	1 Kings
2 Kgs, 2 Ki, II Ki, 2Ki	2 Kings
1 Chron., I Chron.	1 Chronicles
2 Chron., II Chron	2 Chronicles
Ezra, Ezr.	Ezra
Neh, Ne.	Nehemiah
Esth., Es.	Esther
Job, Job.	Job
Pslm., Ps., Psa.	Psalm
Prov.	Proverbs
Eccles., Ec., Ecc.	Ecclesiastes
Song of Sol.	Song of Solomon
Isa.	Isaiah
Jer.	Jeremiah
Lam.	Lamentations
Ezek, Eze, Ezk.	Ezekiel
Dan.	Daniel
Hos .	Hosea
Joel.	Joel
Amos, Am.	Amos
Obad., Ob.	Obadiah
Jnh., Jon.	Jonah
Micah., Mic.	Micah
Nah., Na.	Nahum
Hab.	Habakkuk
Zeph.	Zephaniah
Haggai, Hag., Hg.	Haggai
Zech., Zec., Zc.	Zechariah
Mal.	Malachi

NEW TESTAMENT BOOKS

Matt., Mt.	Matthew
Mark., Mk.	Mark
Luk., Lk.	Luke
Jn., Jhn.	John
Acts., Ac.	Acts
Rom., Rm.	Romans
1 Cor., I Cor.	1 Corinthians
2 Cor., II Cor.	2 Corinthians
Gal.	Galatians
Ephes., Eph.	Ephesians
Phil., Php.	Philippians
Col.	Colossians
1 Thess., I Thess.	1 Thessalonians
2 Thess, II Thess.	2 Thessalonians
1 Tim., I Tim.	1 Timothy
2 Tim., II Tim.	2 Timothy
Titus., Tit.	Titus
Philem., Phm.	Philemon
Heb.	Hebrews
Jas.	James
1Pet., I Pet.	1 Peter
2 Pet., II Pet	2 Peter
1 Jn., I Jn, 1 Jhn,	1 John
2 Jn, II Jn. , 2 Jhn.	2 John
3 Jn., III Jn., 3 Jhn	3 John
Jude	Jude
Rev.	Revelation

Salvation Prayer

Heavenly Father, I come to you in the name of Jesus.
I confess that I am a sinner. I am sorry for my sins and ask
your forgiveness.

I believe Jesus Christ is your only begotten Son who died
on the cross at Calvary for my sins but you said in Your Word,
that if we confess with our mouth and believe in our hearts
that God raised Jesus from the dead, we shall be saved.

I believe your Word and I confess Jesus as Lord of my soul
and over my life. With my heart, I believe that Jesus rose from
the dead. I accept Jesus Christ as my personal Savior and that
according to His Word, I am now saved. Please come into my
life and be my Lord. Thank you for saving me from my sins.
Please transform my life so that I may bring glory and honor to
you. Thank you, Jesus, for dying for me and giving me eternal
life. AMEN.

*That if thou shalt confess with thy mouth the Lord Jesus,
and shalt believe in thine heart that God hath raised him
from the dead, thou shalt be saved. For with the heart
man believeth unto righteousness; and with the mouth
confession is made unto salvation.*
Romans 10:9-10

Preface

◆ ◆ ◆

Many people have attended church for years, heard a lot of sermons and watched people "come forward" to heed "the call." They may have even prayed the prayer of salvation themselves. Yet they still do not understand what salvation is or what it means to be converted. Some say it means raising someone from the dead. Others believe it is the act of rescuing and converting people. Skeptics describe it as mind control or a trick used by the preacher to get a parishioner's money.

At one point in my life, I watched a lot of crime scene investigation television programming. The crime detectives almost always wanted to know why the crime was committed. They would examine or trace back through their childhood upbringing and find someone on whom to pin the blame. Why? Because no one wants to believe anyone could really be so evil! The human side of them wants to place the blame on someone or something else in order for the villain to be free. What is at the core of our being that makes us yearn for someone's innocence? One of the most sacred principles in the American criminal justice system is that a defendant is innocent until proven guilty. The prosecution must prove, beyond a reasonable doubt, the crime that is charged. Yet, even after the verdict or after confession, it is often difficult to believe or accept that a human being is capable of committing heinous crimes especially against a fellow human. Lonely women often find friendship, romance, and even true love with inmates on Death Row. So we look for explanation and a way to free the villain. Whether or not we agree, we have this hope predicated on the love of God.

Thinking that salvation means being saved from oneself may sound good to the ears but it is not accurate. All who have sinned against God are under judgment of God. God must punish the sinner. So, being saved from righteous judgment or from the wrath of God is called salvation. Most of us can relate to how, in some instances, a loving father might step forth and confess to a crime that his only daughter committed. It is love for her that would compel him, an innocent man with a good name, to willingly take her place. Immediately the guilt of the crime would be transferred from her to him and according to the law, her guilt would be assuaged and now the penalty would have to be paid by him. He made the choice because of his love for her. Some people have actually given up their lives for others in order to give them a chance at life. Well, God has provided a way of escape for us through Jesus Christ so that we would not have to face His righteous judgment.

Either way, people struggle with the question, "What does it mean to be saved?" Without reading a bunch of books or going to church, they want to understand in plain English, what it is and what they must do. Then there are other questions: *If it is so simple, then why is it so difficult to understand? If salvation is so great, then why is it such a turn off? If it is so free, then why do we feel so pressured?*

At the risk of putting myself on the line here, I must admit that for years, I have wondered what was wrong. It seemed difficult to reconcile our current Christian practices with what Jesus was doing. Growing up Pentecostal was tough; trying to be like Jesus was definitely tough, but being a Preacher's kid was even tougher! There always seemed to be a slight disconnect with the gospel message preached and the life led by Jesus. He made everything seem so simple. A lot of the "insider" language used by church-goers was necessary if we were to have common understanding within the confines of the Church. However, as I ventured out, I discovered that such intimate language belonged to an even smaller group than I had presupposed. It actually created a communication barrier when it came to interacting with other denominations. I did not realize it at first but when the light bulb finally came on and I realized I might be the problem, I began to study the Bible from a different perspective. The simple message of Jesus Christ is sometimes so encumbered with human interpretation and the business of church programming and conditioning, that many people have either no idea or the wrong idea of what the Gospel really is.

Well, the truth of the matter is that among the Christian community, whether intentional or not, there is a tendency to make salvation more difficult to understand than it really is. When we speak about it in our familiar church language, we rightfully feel connected to the body of Christ. However, it can discourage those who are outside of the church family. Common words or phrases like, *"saved"*; *"born again"*; *"redeemed by the blood of the Lamb"*; or *"washed in the blood"* can be overwhelming and disconcerting to those who do not know what they mean. That is not to say that we should change the language – every industry has its own terminology. For example, health care, entertainment, and government industries all have specific terms that are applicable to their environment. However, it does mean we should be sensitive to these kinds of situations and govern our interactions accordingly. In reality, there is nothing confusing, mysterious or hard to understand about salvation. Its doctrine is remarkably simple. God made it that way so that anyone can understand. Also, we should not be too extreme in the opposite direction either. With the help of entertainment network programming over television and radio, people are a lot more savvy today than in years past. The world is far more versed than we realize in certain areas. We are charged to make followers. If we would follow the example of Jesus Christ, who made it very simple, we would be more successful.

Psychology and Salvation

Somehow and somewhere between the time of the apostles and our day, the translation of what salvation means has become distorted.

Life is a manifestation of God's Word and God's works. The apostolic Church of the New Testament practiced the doctrines of Jesus Christ and the Apostles as revealed in the Holy Bible. From the time of the Roman Emperor Constantine, under orders from the emperor and the apostate Church leaders—its bishops and later popes—the civil government of the Roman Empire persecuted, killed and drove the true Christians beyond the bounds of the Empire. The histories written about the scattered members, preserved by Orthodox historians, refer to them as heretics, because they rejected the commandeered ecclesiastical authority of the Roman Church and refused to believe or accept its false teachings and doctrines. The true Church always submitted to the Word of God, believing and practicing its teachings.[1]

Though the flock has been scattered, God's Church has never ceased to exist. Despite the world's hatred and attempts to destroy it, the Church lives on. Since the early Church, there have been a lot of movements in Christianity. In America, the early students of God's works viewed psychology as an appropriate replacement for the Protestant faith of their childhood and as a way to make Christianity scientific. Acting within and through American Protestantism, they spread their ideologies and worked through the cultural structure to advocate macro-secularization through psychology in American Protestantism. It was attractive and plausible because of its ability to provide the proper observation and tools to interpret religious experiences. Through this historical process, religion lost its social and cultural significance. As a result of secularization, the role of religion and its authority in modern societies became restricted. In secularized societies, faith lacks cultural authority, and religious organizations have little social power.[2]

Rev. J. W. D. Smith's synopsis of C. G. Jung's Psychology concludes that psychology offers a particularly subtle and dangerous challenge

1 Fred Coulter, Beliefs and Doctrines of the New Testament Church, The True Teachings and Doctrines of Jesus Christ and His Apostles as Revealed in the Holy Bible. Retrieved from http://www.cbcg.org/beliefs.htm on November 29, 2015.
2 Keith G. Meador. "My Own Salvation": The Christian Century and Psychology's Secularizing of American Protestantism, DOI:10.1525/california/9780520230002.003.0006. Retrieved from http://california.universitypressscholarship.com/view/10.1525/california/9780520230002.001.0001/upso-9780520230002-chapter-6 on November 28, 2015.

to religious belief. While the theologian and psychologist are both interested in the facts of man's spiritual nature, the difference in their approach to these facts inevitably arouses tension between them. The psychologist's approach is totally empirical and he uses descriptive terms which ignore any cosmic significance or faith beliefs of the experiences described. But the experiences of the Christian believer are vitally affected by his beliefs about them. Christian doctrine is part of the total Christian experience and not the result of later reflection on experiences which had no intrinsic meaning.[3] Dr. Jeffrey Mirus, in Salvation for Non-Catholics: Not a New Idea, suggests that, in order to receive eternal punishment for unbelief, people must have heard the teachings of Jesus Christ. Otherwise, they are not responsible and therefore, not culpable, in which case salvation is a non-issue for them. It is true that one will not be damned for rejecting a Gospel he never heard preached in the first place. Without faith it is impossible to please God (*Hebrew 11:6*).[4] Mirus' view disregards the doctrine of original sin and holds that man comes into this world in a state of being saved, or in effect, that man is basically good. However, man came into this world bound for eternal punishment. In order to be delivered from that, the free and unmerited grace of Jesus Christ is necessary. In other words, justification is necessary for salvation; and faith is necessary for justification.

No doubt many of us have become vulnerable to the appeal of generations of cultists, religious competition, the charm of Psychology, and the pervasive attraction of booming mega churches. In other words, we are encumbered with denominational (or non-denominational) perspectives and such varying theological biases, that we have failed to stay singularly focused on the one thing that has and remains the most important concern of all time – the salvation of man.

---

3 J. W. D. Smith (1950). A Study of Sin and Salvation in Terms of C. G. Jung's Psychology. Scottish Journal of Theology, 3, pp 397-408. doi:10.1017/S0036930600057719.

4 Brother André Marie. Psychology and Salvation, Saint Benedict Center, Richmond, New Hampshire August 17, 2010. Retrieved from http://catholicism.org/psychology-and-salvation.html on November 29, 2015.

Modern Science and Technology

Today's quest for more knowledge, influence and global expansion, is evidence that the world is moving at a rapid pace all in the name of modern science and technology advancements. Microbiology and unharnessed aspirations of what biogenetics and micro-robotics engineering may have capacity to produce in our future appears to be fairly unlimited. However, the possibility of imposing limitations, replacing or annihilating humanity as we know it today is a real thought.

Some scientists believe we should eliminate religious faith for the sake of human progress because all ideologies and religions have their own distinct answers for the big questions of life. The argument is that since these answers are bound as a dogma and feature supernatural elements that other faiths cannot accept, religious faith should be destroyed. Their argument is that this would eliminate condescension and anxiety. Agreeing that transcendental searching, *humanity's desire to know whether there is an afterlife*, unites humanity and that these are natural yearnings for answers to important questions, these scientists still believe it is better to leave people hanging, rather than allow religious faith to provide the answers.

If we follow the advice recommended by some renowned scientists in the field and dispense with religious faith, then we are left to wonder what will fill the void. Actually, we have very little commentary from the scientific community on the aspect of life without religious faith. However, concerning the future of mankind, we were able to get some insight from one scientist's perspective. Hannah Osborne reported in the January 28, 2015 issue of the International Business Times, that E.O. Wilson, a noted scientist, and University Research Professor Emeritus at Harvard, said the living world is going to reach a tipping point where it is no longer in equilibrium. "And when that happens, the whole thing collapses – and we collapse with it." How dreadful a prognosis! This would seem to be a perfect time to ask one of those big questions, "Where will we spend eternity?" I would choose to follow the wisdom of Jesus Christ, than a scientist whose solutions are based primarily on what can be witnessed and proven only by the naked eye.

Applied Research and Inventions

We cannot argue that man has been given extraordinary wisdom. I am reminded of it each time we airlift and take a flight somewhere. When we think about the many man-made inventions, we can see it plainly throughout the years. For example, the *wheel* (B.C.) provided humanity with the ability to farm, made us less nomadic and led to the discovery of other great inventions. *Fire* (B.C.) brought warmth and was the basis for energy for years to come. The *magnetic compass* (B.C.) was first invented as a device for divination as early as the Chinese Han Dynasty (since about 206 BC) and was used by the Chinese military for navigational orienteering by 1040 and for maritime navigation by 1111. The *firearm* was originally invented in China during the 13th century AD. Electricity (1752-1882) covers a broad spectrum beginning with lights, communication, travel, and motorized conveniences – the list is infinite. The *printing press* (1450) allowed people freedom to read and make decisions for themselves, and put commoners in position to overthrow governments. The *steam engine* (1792) probably lead to the start of the industrial revolution. The *automobile* (1768-1902) assisted in the growth of private transportation. The *cotton gin* (1793) resulted in the end of Slavery and opened up more time for other discoveries. *Refrigeration* (1850) made a major difference with critical life or death implications. The *telephone* (1876) has been a most remarkable life saver and it continues to save lives. The *airplane* (1903) has made travel times shorter, making the world global without true borders, and more people can see the world. The *television* (1926) introduced a great way to gain knowledge, insight and rapidly influence ways of thinking as well as family and moral values. *Penicillin* (1928) became the cure all for many diseases that once limited our population. *Oil refinement* (1950's) with its pipelines played a major role in the war of engines and octanes, World War II, bringing the United States to the world superpower. The internet (1969) opened up an entirely new method of learning and communication abilities. The Global Positioning System (GPS) (1957-1973) is amazing and most of us cannot live without it's influence in our daily commuting. Facebook (2004) has an unprecedented amount of power and influence.

Things like *democracy* (traceable to classical Athens 5th or 6th century B.C.E.) as a political system or a system of decision-making is paramount to today's right to vote. The *legal system* originating in Europe, intellectualized within the framework of late Roman law (B.C.), where the core principles are codified into a referable system serves as the primary source of law. What about the drone that started almost as a game? Predator drones of all sizes are now integral to combat operations, primarily providing intelligence, surveillance, and reconnaissance.

These inventions represent tremendous progress for humanity. Yet for all of the wisdom involved, we must agree with the Psalmist who said it is the fear of the Lord that is the beginning of wisdom. Solomon says it is the beginning of knowledge. The dictionary's definition of wisdom is: learning and understanding what is true, right, or lasting. Good judgment, common sense. So then wisdom is the correct use of knowledge, because human knowledge *per se* is a compilation of information held to be factual by majority opinion. It is possible to "know" something and be completely wrong. In contrast, the Bible repeatedly encourages us to seek the ability to see things from God's perspective. That wisdom—gained through the "fear of the Lord"— results in genuine knowledge and enlightenment. We can look at many of these inventions and acknowledge their overwhelming benefits but through the light of the Word of God, we can also see the shortcomings of man's wisdom. For all these inventions, with man's intellect and creativity, can man rescue the soul? Is man able to devise a plan and grant eternal life? This should drive us to pursue the wisdom of God.

Well, what does any of this have to do with the discussion of salvation? In short, these are great inventions that have brought about tremendous progress when it comes to man's condition in his natural surroundings. However, it is God that has given man wisdom. For all of his wisdom and creativity, can he create a plan of salvation? Unfortunately, man has convinced himself that his knowledge is sufficient and only needs to depend upon himself. He prefers to work things out for himself and therefore eliminate the need for God. Once able to perform and produce on his own, he believes he should no longer need God. Only the poor and the weak need God. He believes he is his own God.

Wisdom teaches us better. Man pales in comparison to God. Everything man knows stems from his experiences and external data gathering – in other words, his knowledge is limited; it is finite. Anyone who ever studied the book of Job must admit that Job proclaimed an incredible summation as he eloquently described the magnificent and then accredited it to the Creator. However, God put the right questions to him in Job 38-41. From this, we can safely conclude that as much learning as man labors toward, he can only attain to the extent of his finite knowledge. How well can we speak of the creation? Upon whose authority can we accredit such magnificent work to the sovereign God? Can we judge His works? "Then the Lord answered Job out of the whirlwind, and said, Who is this that darkeneth counsel by words without knowledge? Gird up now thy loins like a man; for I will demand of thee, and answer thou me. Where wast thou when I laid the foundations of the earth? Declare, if thou hast understanding. Who hath laid the measures thereof, if thou knowest? or who hath stretched the line upon it? Whereupon are the foundations thereof fastened? or who laid the corner stone thereof?" (Job 38:1-6).

After all that has been achieved over the years with the wonderful discoveries of science and technology advancements, we can barely answer any of the questions God gives Job. Yet God knows every little detail concerning man physically and spiritually. And why not? He is the Creator. He knows the intricacies of the universe and the plans for the future. If not for God and His Word, man's knowledge and understanding of many aspects of life would be severely lacking. Man's desire to promote his own knowledge and failure to seek God's wisdom has caused him to ignore what is critical to his salvation. God's knowledge far surpasses our own and knows no bounds. It is not limited to the physical realm of this earth.

Man has increased in knowledge and developed beyond measure when it comes to understanding and adapting to the changes in his environment. However, for all of the dedication to his physical condition and natural state, it is rather disappointing that the spirit man has been so neglected. Such devotion to knowledge and higher learning has been exceptional but somehow seems to have surpassed man's capacity for spiritual maturity and ability to respect God's creation. It is as though the more higher knowledge attained, the less spiritual progress.

Human Development

Babies have a built in capacity to know what their bodies need. Babies have an unmatched capacity to communicate with us through their own movement. They understand emotions, grasp what words mean, and make connections. When they cry, the sound and intensity of it can be heard at a sufficient distance with adequate transmission to let someone know what kind of attention is needed and how quickly. Every movement of the baby is made with purpose and as children grow, they purposefully make decisions to expedite their growth. But this does not mean they have the wisdom required to keep them out of trouble. If we prevent their proper development, they will springboard prematurely into young adulthood and miss out on the little things that are foundational to their maturity. This may account for the many disparaging reports concerning young teenagers today. Let's face it. Our children need saving; that is, those that are still in grade school as well as those that are walking around in life-sized adult bodies. We all need saving.

Some years ago my sister and I were in the kitchen trying out a new recipe and doing things that we often did when hanging out together. We were having such a great time when all of a sudden for some odd reason, my hair stood up on the back of my neck. I spun around in the kitchen and called sharply for my two year old daughter. My sister, instantly recognizing my panic stricken tones, moved into motion as I bounded through the doorway and rounded the corner to the front of the house. Almost at that precise moment, we heard the front door slam. I charged out the door without regard for my bare feet. That's when I heard the horrible crunching sound of screeching brakes, blasting of a horn and screaming voices. My daughter, who was just inside the kitchen doorway only moments before, was racing at breakneck speed down the walkway to the street. She was completely oblivious to the warning sounds around her as she laughingly sped down the walkway. To her, it was a wonderful game between her and Mommy. She was laughing merrily. And then she stopped. The car was seconds before hitting her and she had a startled, panicky look on her face. She did not know which way to go – the jaws of death were upon her. My own legs felt like lead iron. My heart pounded furiously as if it would rip right through my chest. I stopped breathing. It was at that moment that I snatched her out of the jaws of death and folded her in my arms as I ran back up the walkway. It all happened within split seconds. She did not understand. I barely calculated the velocity, the direction of the car, the driver's frantic, the screaming neighbors and my daughter's next move. She could not know the danger. In her innocence, she was heading toward the very thing that could have destroyed her life. And mine. Somehow she realized in that instance, that she needed help but there was no time to understand, frame or articulate a cry for help; she just needed to be rescued. Today we remain thankful to God for saving her by His grace. She was just a child, equipped with free will, fast moving legs, and a desire to express her independence. Her wisdom carried her only as far as her maturity permitted. Were it not for the watchful eye and passionate love of a doting mother, the story's ending would be quite different.

We all need saving; we cannot save ourselves. Salvation is a gift from God, poured out freely from His grace. It is available to everyone who accepts Jesus as their Lord and Savior. The Bible tells us that there is only one way to Heaven. Jesus said, "I am the way and the truth and the life. No one comes to the Father except through me." (*John 14:6*)

If I had attempted to reason with my daughter in that horrifying moment, it is highly unlikely that she would be here today. That was not the time to chit chat. Or if someone else had attempted that rescue but without the same kind of determination to save her, the result may have been very different. Our wisdom can only get in the way. When we get too philosophical or dive too deep before we introduce salvation to someone, I think we have missed the mark ourselves. Only the Lord can save us. In other words, there is too much red tape and the enemy is using it to strangle the gospel in today's world. Jesus simply asked the question, "Will thou be made whole?" I believe the word of God is so powerful that it can transform every life. There is power in His word to make what was old become new; to change what does not appear to upon His word, appear. There is executive power and authority in the word that proceeds out of His mouth.

Here is the bottom line. We are made of three vital elements known as spirit, soul, and body (*1 Thessalonians 5:23*). Man has two major aspects that define who he really is. The first one is the spiritual aspect, and the second one is the physical aspect. From a biblical perspective, everyone who comes into this wicked world, comes disconnected from God which can lead to spiritual death. In fact, that is a direct result of the sinful nature that we've inherited. The bottom line is that life is not only limited to the physical one we currently have as many falsely believe. The truth is that there is another one found in Christ alone, which is infinitely better and greater than this one we have today. Despite that many have been exposed to the message of the gospel, they live their lives just as if Christ had never died for them. Sin along with Satan have also implanted within people's minds all types of deceptive and destructive beliefs which appeal to the pride of life.

Rescuing my daughter was a physical aspect of saving her. Now, with this being my daughter, I have to admit, that was a very blessed day never to be forgotten. I would have died to save that child; she would not have been able to comprehend it, but God put His love in my heart so that I was willing. And yet He spared us both. That was a free gift. However, there is something even far greater than the physical salvation of life. This is what where simplifying the state of our condition would be helpful to the average person who does not understand God's plan of salvation.

First, when we explain that every person born on this earth is basically selfish, it may raise a few eyebrows. However, it becomes clear once it is explained that we all hurt others, we disobey, lie, steal, think, say and do bad things. And we know this. It is not some big secret. We have a conscience and know when we do wrong. This is sin. (*Romans 3:23*) As human beings, we miss the mark since we are not perfect like God who is always good. In the Bible, all the wrong things we do are called "sin." *Second*, we have some good news. That is, we do not have to remain that way because God has prepared a solution. He loves us so much, that He sent His Son, Jesus, to die on the cross to pay for all our sins. Even for those who say they never committed any sin, they were nonetheless born in iniquity. There is forgiveness for anyone who asks. Because of Jesus, all the wrong things we've ever done can be forgiven. We simply need to ask for forgiveness. *Third*, when God forgives us, He makes us His child – we're in His special family who believe in Jesus. (*John 1:12*) Once part of God's family, we can talk to Him every day and be close to Him.

Acknowledgments

◆ ◆ ◆

Nothing can compare to the impact of over 30 years of sunrise services, Sunday School, morning worship, Sunday afternoon and evening services, weekly Bible studies, auxiliary programs, prayer meetings, youth services, missionary leader services, and choir rehearsals. What a long list, right? This is where it all began for me. Then there were the 5th Sunday unity meetings, the sick and shut-in visits, Bible Training Institute, district and state conventions and annual general assemblies. Now, as exciting as they all were, none of these can compare with other activities like youth camp, winter retreats, jamborees, 30-day fasts, all night shut-ins, singing competitions, *"twelve tribe"* rallies, fund-raisers, revivals, healing services or the many choir engagements. These events all played a role in my spiritual outlook. On the other hand, I can say with certainty, after these many years of church program "busyness" and activity, that I finally realize what happened to salvation. Collectively, the events maintained a sense of intimacy, community and relationship but they overwhelmed salvation.

With heartfelt gratitude to all of the wonderful educators and pastors who at various times have extended me their wisdom, insight and forthrightness, I honor you. Foremost, however, is my own father who was an extraordinary man of tremendous faith who was determined to keep his children from the clutches of the enemy whatever the cost. As he always proclaimed, "I opened my mouth to the Lord, and I won't take it back." In that same vein, (I chose this idiom in honor of my father), it was my mother who stuck by my dad. Had it not been for her, I do not think we girls would have been able to understand the importance of these activities. They were not the essence of salvation, but were part of the family circle of events that helped us bond and grow together. Even if we split up, we would still have benefit of those years of converging in a secret place for purposes of building up the ministry. I am grateful to both parents for their involvement in the Body of Christ and how they kept us fully baptized. Though it was every night of the week, we grew up and got over it! In exchange, we stayed connected with others of similar convictions. Eventually, our eyes came open to what salvation is all about and we discovered what is most important.

I grew up with the impression that salvation was simply a matter of accepting Jesus Christ as the Son of the living God to be my personal Savior. I knew nothing concerning Calvinism or Arminianism nor that I was probably one of them. It is also interesting that though I was at the tender age of nine years of age when I accepted Christ, God has kept me all these years. Thanks to Dr. Timothy Wood of Calvary Christian College, I entered into a concentrated, in depth study on this topic. Not only was I enlightened to the importance of understanding the fundamentals of Soteriology, I was now better equipped to speak on matters concerning the effect of the different views of salvation and how various church doctrines have come to be so skewed. Without Dr. Wood's wisdom and encouragement, I would probably not have been drawn to such an intense level of study and perhaps would not have undertaken the effort to write this book.

In addition to the aforementioned, I must also recognize that during the making of this book, I had the complete support of my son Justin, who stuck by me through some really challenging times as I tunneled through some of the deeper theological questions and waded through rivers of spiritual waters. He maintains a love for the truth of God and has a degree of passion and loyalty for his family that is almost impossible to find anymore.

I have a tremendous respect for my daughter, Shelli, who must be a speed reader for although she spent countless hours editing and reviewing most of the works that went into the creation of this book, her turnaround time was always well in advance of an agreed upon time. I am grateful for such love and sacrifice. I must mention my dear sister, Jessie McNeely, who remains my personal encourager and supporter. She never turns away my calls no matter how little interest she has in my never ending list of topics. She seems to have a special connection with God and is quite the prayer warrior.

My sister, Geraldine, of the Perry Group, never ceases to amaze me with her flair for words and her love of platform. She has truly blessed me during great moments of discourse and reflection.

For a variety of other forms of help and encouragement, I acknowledge faculty and advisors at both National Bible College & Seminary, in particular Dr. Aaron Jones and Dr. Samuel Odenyo, and the esteemed Dr. William Gray at Calvary Christian College, for their dedication and integrity in working with the students.

Introduction

◆ ◆ ◆

Man, despite all his education, wealth and power, cannot escape the fact that he was born in sin and is incapable of eternal rest apart from his dependence upon God. There is no getting around this fact. In everything and in every way, we need God. He designed us that way. We have an absolute and universal reliance upon our Creator. Not only that, God intended for us to be totally dependent upon Him constantly, recognizing that apart from Him we can do nothing. Without Him, it would be impossible to face the future. For one thing, there would be no point to life and therefore, no reason to exist. Secondly, with no reason to live, man would be hopeless, having only death to look forward to after the grave. Does this not explain the suicide rate? If we are dependent upon Him and would obediently acknowledge Him in all our ways, we would be able to trust Him no matter the circumstance. Albert Camus once said "A man devoid of hope and conscious of being so has ceased to belong to the future."[5]

Yet man, having garnered all of the intelligence of his finite mind, continues to explore the possibility of life without his creator. For all his efforts at trying to get rid of God, German philosopher Friedrich Nietzsche, known for having declared that God is dead and for his written works challenging man to find a replacement, only managed to get a taste of some aspect of his theoretical success in that he proved how devastatingly destructive life would become in the absence of God. How absurd that just when he thought he had finally extinguished God, Nietzsche became the epitome of hopelessness

[5] Albert Camus, *The Myth of Sisyphus*; translated from the French by Justin O'Brien (Harmondsworth: Penguin Books, 1975), p. 11.

and chaos, losing his mind in the process. Section 125 of one of his works, *The Gay Science*, depicts the "Parable of the Madman" who is searching for God. He accuses us all of being the murderers of God. "'Whither is God?' he cried; "I will tell you. *We have killed him*—you and I. All of us are his murderers."[6]

To remove God from man's existence is to remove man from his own existence – where is the logic in that? Ah, but then the wisdom of man is foolishness in God's eyes. By the time Nietzsche finally came to realize his folly, it was too late – he had opened Pandora's box and all manner of evil was introduced and flying around the world. Now a new god would come on the scene to take up residence in the hearts of man. Adolf Hitler, would gladly fill the empty void once filled by God. Nietzsche's dark radical ideas were ironically accepted by diametrically opposing groups and by World War I, his philosophy had become the inspiration for right-wing German militarism. Not that he was in agreement with them, but his words strengthened their cause nonetheless. In fact, so great was the influence, that his reputation suffered a direct hit because of the fascism that evolved. He was left without friends or hope. Perhaps if the relationship with his religious sister had been better, there would have been something to look forward to besides the four walls. Perhaps he might even have attempted to reclaim his words or clear his name, but having served Satan's purpose, Nietzsche was no longer needed, so instead, he went mad. The Holocaust which means "sacrifice by fire," was ignited in 1933 as Hitler came to power in Germany and ended in 1945, but not before an estimated 11 million people were killed (six million of these were Jews and 1.1 million children). Oh, America, watch and pray! Take note of how such evil stemmed from this same man, Nietzsche, who once declared, "All I need is a sheet of paper and something to write with, and then I can turn the world upside down."[7]

---

6 *The Gay Science* aka *Joyous Wisdom* (German: *Die fröhliche Wissenschaft*) poetic book by Friedrich Nietzsche, first published in 1882 after the completion of *Thus Spoke Zarathustra* and *Beyond Good and Evil*, in 1887. This substantial expansion includes a fifth book and an appendix of songs. It was noted by Nietzsche to be „the most personal of all books", and contains the greatest number of poems in any of his published works. http://en.wikipedia.org/wiki/The_Gay_Science
7 Daniel Coenn Friedrich Nietzsche: His Words._KG:Munich 81675: BookRix GmbH & Co., 2014.

It all started with words, faith in the proclaimed word, and an instrument through which to step out and execute. The bottom line is this: If there is no God, then life is not worth living. Both the entire human race and the universe would be doomed; there would be no objective standards of right and wrong and therefore no morality. With no faith, moral accountability, or standards, man would be unimaginably wild and ruthless in his unchecked reign over the weaker ones in society. As long as God exists, there is hope, but without Him – the world is lost. This is the reason the question of God's existence and our salvation is so vital to man. If He does not exist, the only thing left is despair. Without Him, man will seek to secure power for himself. Nietzsche's words, "And when you look into the abyss, the abyss also looks into you" depicts a wildly desperate man, in search of answers and hope; one who wants to be rescued from his own worst enemy – self.[8] Anything can grow out of the abyss. We do not have to look far. We can see this all over the globe in the lives of those who do not know God - suicide, immorality, drugs, violence, murder, perversion, terrorism and disregard for innocent lives.

When God is not allowed to rule and reign in our hearts, then the door is wide open for foul play. Given half the chance, the enemy will befriend and entice you away from your safety zone, take up residence with you, and slyly chip away at your belief foundation until he has sufficient power to destroy your life. Without God, there would be no common means by which to judge right or wrong. Everyone would be left to their own discretion and to decide what is right in their own eyes. The concept of morality loses all meaning in a universe without the Lord. Good and evil do not exist; there is no one to say we are right or wrong. That means there is no love. It is clear that man is being lured in that direction. That is the reason for so much despair in the world today. To "kill" God is to "kill" oneself and to destroy faith in God's judgment and power to reward or punish man. That is the crux of atheism: it removes reason to be humane which then

---

8 146 of Nietzsche's "Beyond Good and Evil," in the section entitled "Epigrams and Interludes." Full quote is "Whoever fights monsters should see to it that in the process he does not become a monster. And when you look into the abyss, the abyss also looks into you."

removes the restraints. Without restraint to hold back the depths of man's wickedness and rage, evil prevails. When evil prevails, there is no comfort. In the absence of comfort, man needs God.[9] Like all biological organisms, man, too, must die but man's life was not intended to end in infinite blackness. With God, he may have eternal life. Without God, there is no hope of immortality, and life leads only to the grave. Can man achieve blessedness or inner peace without the Almighty God? Of course not. He does not have such power. He is totally dependent upon God to enter God's heavenly kingdom.

Although Nietzsche's pride and arrogance never brought him to understanding, the Word of God has saved millions of people's lives, both famous and obscure. History is filled with those who sank to their knees in surrender to Jesus Christ. Testimonies of these changed lives - thieves, murderers, liars - reflect the power of the Word, its effect on them and those around them.

Faith in the Word of God is not a new phenomenon but in certain instances, it is nothing short of a miracle. For David Berkowitz, otherwise known as the Son of Sam, it is a miracle. Berkowitz was convicted and sentenced to life in prison for brutally murdering six people and wounding several others in the late 1970's. He once terrorized and brought New York City to its knees for a full year. In an interview with CBN, Berkowitz admitted to Satan worship and that he once referred to himself as the Duke of Death, after the name of the demon that controlled him.[10] Despite being brought up in a loving home, he had emotional and mental problems. He was constantly in and out of trouble but was also a good manipulator.

Growing up, Berkowitz had violent seizures that required his father to hold him down with great restraint. He recalled loving darkness so much that he would lock himself in a closet or under the bed for hours at a time; his parents were totally unaware that he was in the house. At night, he felt a craving to sneak outside during

9 William Lane Craig, *The Absurdity of Life without God*, http://www.reasonablefaith.org/the-absurdity-of-life-without-god#ixzz2zvfkYjOX
10 Scott Ross, *Son of Sam Becomes Son of Hope*, The 700 Club, http://www.cbn.com/700club/scottross/interviews/sonofsam.aspx

the wee hours. He had no joy or happiness; was mentally confused; and could not be controlled. Even as a small child he would just go berserk in the apartment. Finally he grew up and after a short time in the army, he returned home. He had no friends. Something inside made him vulnerable. He was lonely and longed for acceptance. Gradually, he was introduced to a young group of pagans through whom he experienced and practiced Satanism, complete with rituals, pentagram and the summoning or calling upon demonic "angels." His life became even more bizarre.

Eventually he brutally murdered six people for which he received six consecutive life sentences, equating to three hundred years in prison. He was considered depraved and evil; hopeless and useless. They said he was psychotic. But he said there was another side. Berkowitz wanted to get delivered. Living without hope, he sought to escape and surrendered himself to the devil. However, once arrested, a fellow prisoner turned Christian, eventually gave Berkowitz a little pocket Bible. As David read the book of Psalms, something began to happen. Though hardened against life's disappointments behind prison bars with his knife and reputation of being a troublemaker, his heart began to soften and he started to change. Sometimes, while reading the Scriptures, he would find himself crying. He did not understand what was happening but the Lord began to speak to his heart. Late one day when alone in his cell, close to midnight, he turned on his little lamp, and while reading Psalm 34, where it says, "This poor man cried, and the Lord heard him and saved him out of all his troubles," he stopped there, repeating the words until as he read verse 8, "Oh taste to see the Lord is good. Blessed is the man that trusts in him," something burst open in him. Berkowitz fell on his knees and cried out his heart unto the Lord. Though he did not know what to say or whether God was even listening, the guilt came crushing down on his head. It was a great weight. There he repented for all of the evil he had ever done and the lives he had destroyed. He poured out his heart until finally he realized for the first time in his entire life, he felt different. He did not understand it but he knew something had happened. He felt peace for the first time and slept like a baby all night.

Since that time, he discovered what it meant to be born again and a whole new life opened up to him. Now he understands why, even though his parents gave him a lot of love, he was never happy - at any time in his life. He explained that his parents knew nothing about Jesus nor did they know how to help him. His words were, "They tried their best, but without the Lord, there really is nothing. The Lord is faithful. He has delivered me and brought me through storms. For every person that puts their faith in Jesus Christ, He has great things and a great purpose for their life. Lord has done that for me -- He has given me a hope."[11]

Since receiving Christ, Berkowitz's father became upset that his son believes Jesus is the Messiah, (they are Jewish) and that he is a minister of the gospel. How ironic that he was more concerned about his Jewish heritage than his son's need for salvation! Berkowitz has finally found peace within prison, and has become – an effective man at last. He now shares his redemption story with others in prison behind bars. Despite his earthly father's religious views, he continues to declare Christ as his Lord and Savior. Even if the world is skeptical, this once upon a time serial killer believes in the power of salvation through Jesus Christ. Only Jesus Christ could rescue him from the torment he suffered. There is hope in the Lord. The Lord is the high point of our salvation!

We were all born with a sinful nature that is completely contrary to God (*Psalm 51:5*) but thanks be unto God, we have a high calling that causes us to press in order that we meet the mark (*Philippians 3:14*). Adam also had the high calling from God to obedience. That is the ultimate destiny of those who receive Him!

11 Scott Ross, *Son of Sam Becomes Son of Hope*, The 700 Club. Retrieved November, 2015 from: http://www.cbn.com/700club/scottross/interviews/sonofsam.aspx

What is Soteriology?

◆ ◆ ◆

*"To be "in Christ" is to place one's trust in Him for salvation from sin.
To be "in Christ" is to trust His goodness, not our own; to trust that His
sacrificial death on the cross paid the complete debt of death we owe for
our sin; to trust that His resurrection gives us eternal life instead of
relying upon our own ability to please God."*

Charles R. Swindoll

The simple message of Jesus Christ is sometimes so cluttered with human interpretation and the church's programs, that many people have either no idea or the wrong idea of what the Gospel really is.

The Gospel is the central message of Christianity and every disciple of Jesus Christ is expected to share the message. But with the proliferation of evangelical churches and Christian denominations it seems that there is a misunderstanding of what the message is. The goal of this book is not to showcase theological knowledge but rather to clarify some misconceptions about the Gospel message. Through our discussion on Soteriology we will address that and we will cover what Jesus preached. We must be clear on what is true and what is important for eternal life. In those cases where the lengthy commentary is of little or no value, we will move on. Life is too precious to waste on false conjectures.

Soteriology is the academic study of salvation. In English versions of the Bible the words salvation and save are not technical theological terms, but are intended to denote deliverance in almost any sense. In systematic theology, however, salvation signifies the whole process by which man is delivered from all that would prevent his attaining to the highest good that God has prepared for him.[12] There are two major divisions within this doctrine which will help bring clarity and perspective. They include first, the basis of salvation resting upon the work of Jesus, in His atoning death; and secondly, the application of that work within the salvation of the sinner.[13] Soteriology, then, is divided into two categories: *Objective* (justification, sanctification, and calling) which would be salvation bought and *Subjective* (faith, love, and hope) which has to do with the person's standing in Christ and his position in Christ, his conviction, repentance, conversion, regeneration, union with Christ, justification, and sanctification.[14] The fundamental truth of the "in Christ" central theme from Paul's preaching is that God united our redeemable humanity with Christ's divinity at the incarnation and basically rewrote our history. We no longer have to die an eternal death; we have a new birth and promise of eternal life in Him! He put us in Christ and Christ in us!

Objective soteriology, *(you in Christ), or imputed righteousness,* considers the work of redemption worked out according to the divine plan by God and accomplished without the conscious efforts of the sinner or consent of the distinct group for which it was accomplished. Man had nothing to do with this part of redemption.[15] Objective soteriology, which is the work of Jesus involving salvation bought, consists of the foundation or basis of salvation; the work of Christ in His propitiation for this doctrine; redemption as an eternal decree of God; conceived for all eternity; election and pre-destination; one mediator between God and man; the three-fold office of Christ as prophet, priest, and king; and the atonement.[16]

---

12 Baker's Evangelical Dictionary of Biblical Theology, http://www.biblestudytools.com/dictionary/salvation/
13 E. C. Bragg, Systematic Theology Soteriology, http://trinitycollege.edu/assets/files/ECBragg/SoteriologyR.pdf
14 Fred H. Klooster, Aspects of Soteriology of Karl Barth, Read at the Nyack, N. Y. meeting, Dec. 31, 1958, http://www.etsjets.org/files/JETS-PDFs/2/2-2/BETS_2-2_6-14_Klooster.pdf
15 E. C. Bragg, Systematic Theology Soteriology. Retrieved November 2015 from: http://trinitycollege.edu/assets/files/ECBragg/SoteriologyR.pdf
16 E. C. Bragg, Systematic Theology Soteriology. Retrieved November 2015 from: http://trinitycollege.edu/assets/files/ECBragg/SoteriologyR.pdf

Subjective soteriology, *(Christ in you), or imparted righteousness,* refers to the individual accomplishment in each person of that redemption, and it must occur with the consent of that individual. God worked out His plan after His own sovereign decree and purpose, and no one could stay His hand. When working it out in the individual for his own personal redemption, it must always be, with his consent, and his free moral agency. It is well to remember this when reading the Scripture, which seems contradictory; one speaks of God's role in redemption, another speaks of man's responsibility.[17] Application of the work of redemption accomplished for the sinner now worked out in him consists of: **a)** the nature or application of salvation to the individual sinner; **b)** the out-working of that salvation in the individual case of man's redemption in the sinner; **c)** man's standing and his position in Christ; **d)** man's conviction, his repentance and conversion, regeneration; and **e)** man's union with Christ, justification and sanctification.[18]

1.0 Salvation – What is the Point of It?

One of the most heart-felt statements on salvation can be found in Earl D. Radmacher's *Salvation* work, in which he declares salvation as the most exciting and promising deliverance available to a human being, because it reaches deep into the need and has past, present and future implications expressed through justification, sanctification and glorification. Our past lives are forgiven, present lives saved from power of sin and our future lives will be saved from presence of sin in heaven.[19] Salvation, or the state of being saved, signifies redemption from the power of sin. In practical terms, God's salvation is required in order to attain eternal life.[20] Besides its generic description of being delivered from a dire situation, or as in religion, the saving of the soul from sin, salvation is a rescue operation. It includes the reconciliation or the repairing of relationship with God.[21]

---

17 E. C. Bragg, Systematic Theology Soteriology, http://trinitycollege.edu/assets/files/ECBragg/SoteriologyR.pdf
18 Ibid.
19 Earl D. Radmacher, Salvation, Word Publishing, A Thomas Nelson Publishing Co., P.O. Box 14100, Nashville, TN 37214, 2000 pp.5-6
20 General Editor Cliff Leitch, *Christian Bible Reference Site*. Retrieved November, 2015 from: http://www.christianbiblereference.org/faq_salvation.htm
21 Michael Morrison, *Grace Communion International*. Retrieved November, 2015 from: http://www.gci.org/disc/16-salvation

"For God so loved the world that He gave His only begotten Son..." (*John 3:16*). This is the only perfect measurement of the love of God. Every doctrine of the Word of God is bound up in the one great work of Christ, which gave a complete satisfaction to divine justice and opened the way into God's presence for guilty sinners, giving them perfect exoneration or justification from all sins.[22] In the study of the atonement of Jesus Christ we are witnessing the finishing of the work which the Father gave Him to do in the accomplishment of the eternal plan of God.

All creation is put on the earth and maintained with the expectation of returning a joyful response of obedience to God. This was intended in order to keep the universe balanced in harmony and synchronization as God intended. It is man's iniquity, the condition of spiritual separation from God that is the reason the orchestration of creation is out of balance. It is the driving force behind extreme and perverse behavior that runs us ragged until we finally slam up against a brick wall. It is the crooked, perverse nature of man that once upon a time, caused God to wipe man from the face of the earth. He saw that man's wickedness was great in the earth, and that every imagination of the thoughts of his heart *was* only evil continually. (*Genesis 6:5*). When man sins against God's word, iniquity is birthed; this state of depravity is contrary to God.

God was pleased with His creation when He first made humans. Man was made in His image from dust, yes, but brought to spiritual life by the very breath of God (*Genesis 1-2*). We are in some ways like God himself – the intelligence, creativity and dominion over the earth. We have the ability to have relationships and to make moral choices. Because of sin, we became separated from Him. In order to be reconciled and brought back into fellowship, we must be redeemed. Iniquity then is the condition of man that comes before God after man has missed the mark. This is why the priests in the books of Exodus and Leviticus were required to not bear the iniquity but to seek

---

22 E. C. Bragg, Systematic Theology Soteriology, Retrieved November, 2015 from: http://trinitycollege.edu/assets/files/ECBragg/SoteriologyR.pdf

pardon, cleanse and bring reconciliation. Iniquity is a serious matter before God; it is born and redeemed in the sanctuary. The destruction of Sodom and Gomorrah was not due to their transgressions and sins, but rather due to their iniquity (*Genesis 19:15*). Transgression is serious because it produces iniquity. Look at the after effects of Adam and Eve's transgression. Iniquity is what caused Lucifer to fall from heaven. He was an anointed cherub at one point, perfect in his ways from the day he was created. But his heart became lifted up because of his beauty and he chose to overstep his bounds. He transgressed repeatedly. He thought he could be equal to God.

Ever since Lucifer's fall, his intent has been to destroy us. He will do anything possible to keep us from being in the kingdom of God. Regardless of his devious activity, we know that when man gets into trouble, it is still a subliminal cry for help. Our challenges and troubles are always an opportunity to ask God for help and when we do, God will hear us. He is a rescuing, saving, delivering God! It is only God who can bring a clean thing out of an unclean thing (*Job 14:4*). Who can explain why God even cares enough to clean up this sinful, self-willed, wicked man and give him dominion over the earth? And what is man, who is born of a woman, that he should be made righteous? (*Job 15:14*).

Man's need for God is so obviously undeniable that it is both pathetic and sometimes laughably paradoxical to see someone persistent in struggling against the tide and proudly fighting to stay above water when all one has to do is to reach out and accept God's welcoming lifesaving raft of salvation.

If we look around, we can see many examples of the many cries for help all over the world. Right here in our country within the entertainment industry, we have seen countless situations – it has been happening for years. We have seen it in the lives of famous entertainers. In the case studies below, we will see that their stories have much in common. Satan was after them before they started on their journeys. People underestimate the powerful affect of music that is in the church and how much Satan covets what he believes belongs to God. He will come right into the church, and whisk them right out from under the watchful care of the saints. Where was Adam when Eve was tempted? Eve was at home in the place where God came to meet them early in the morning. We are not sure where Adam was. The eyes of the church must be open and the members of the body of Christ must be good stewards. Satan is bold and he wants to make a mockery of all that is good.

Each of these people started out with some belief in God. They had time for church before their careers took off but as they became more and more in demand, they went to the top of the chart. With that fame and demand on their lives, how could there be time for the slow, quiet, pace required to spend time in God's presence. Their work was very energetic and unique. "You can't do traditional work at a modern pace. Traditional work has traditional rhythms which require you to be calm. You can be busy, but you must remain calm."[23]

In the case of many entertainers, the fast paced life often leads into a dependency on some substitution for peace – pills, drugs, alcohol, sex – something that will fill the emptiness. Often, they are surrounded by an entourage of people that is of no real good service to them. After getting in so deep into the demands of the entertainment world, most want to "get away" from the world which begins to consume them. These artists were no different. They could not rest and constantly wrestled for peace. They wanted an escape. It was an opportunity to come to Christ. All of their stories are publicly known. Sadly, all of the stories seem to start and end the same way. The names are not really important for the purpose intended so we will refer to these as case studies.

Case Study 1. This young man grew up as a Jehovah's Witness. His father pushed the family into show business. But by the time he died

---

23 Bill Bunford, Heat: An Amateur's Adventures as Kitchen Slave, Line Cook, Pasta-Maker, and Apprentice to a Dante-Quoting Butcher in Tuscany

at age 50, the pop star had explored a number of religions. He had converted to Islam within a year of his death. It is reported that he paid someone to put him to sleep every night because he could not sleep on his own. His doctor was indicted for improperly prescribing and illegally administering certain drugs to the entertainer. Several gospel singers, while they did confirm meeting with and having prayer and singing with the pop star only weeks before his untimely death, did not volunteer information or attempt to speculate on the condition of his soul. They certainly did not indicate whether he accepted Christ. To many Christians, this is of utmost interest since this is the ultimate call of God in our lives when it comes to ministry. However, the report is that he wanted understanding concerning the anointing of the Holy Spirit, how to make his music more 'spiritual.' He wanted to know "what makes your hands go up" and "come out of yourself" and what gives a "spirituality" to the music. An engineer recorded the song the singers sang that night and within three weeks, the pop star was dead.[24]

***Case Study* 2.** A young man growing up in a holiness church down south might one day grow up to be a minister of the gospel. This one did not. Instead, he grew up to become a king of rock and roll. However, the beliefs he found in that holiness church did not depart him as an adult. He hungered for an understanding of God that went deeper than simple theology. He was just barely out of school when the enemy came for him and isolated him from his family. He was introduced to mood altering prescription drugs. From his first hit record, he became a product of the world. Eventually, he could not sleep at night because the world had begun to consume him. He was no longer free. He could not rest most nights until someone sang Thomas Dorsey's *Precious Lord, Take my Hand*. There were times, however, when he was alone and with no one to attend him. He had been snatched during his childhood; he needed someone to care for him. Comments to the effect that he never really grew up had an eerie resemblance to the young man in Case Study 1. Similarly, he

24 World Net Daily, *Did Michael Jackson Repent, Accept Christ?* WND-TV, Published: 06/30/2009.
http://www.wnd.com/2009/06/102625/#d6jd40zixojsF1za.99

died under mysterious circumstances. In his case, this 42-year old rock and roll star was all alone in his bathroom when he overdosed. His doctor was indicted on 14 counts of over-supplying drugs to him and other famous patients.[25]

Case Study 3. Young people today are easily swept into the world of pop music and new age culture. Cast Study victim 3 struggled between the world of secularism and religion. He had grown up in a Pentecostal church and began singing at a tender four years of age. As a mistreated middle child, he escaped brutal beatings from his father by dropping out of high school to join the military. He was 19 years old when he was discovered by the trappings of the entertainment industry and his career took off almost instantly. Considered an adult now, this young man was confronted with all kinds of choices and used cocaine to cope with decision-making and pressures of the road. He was offered all kinds of coping mechanisms to relieve the pressure. He suffered depression after his female singing partner died on stage during a live show and then developed paranoia over an alleged attempt on his life. Every worthy mother knows that a son at age 19 is actually a big little boy in a grown man's body. Fathers are not always so understanding; they want their sons to grow up and be men but may not be able to communicate very well and demonstrate the love necessary to fix the situation. This particular young man could not rest in the house with his father and after a series of terrible encounters with his father, he attempted to kill himself by jumping out of a speeding sports car. His sister witnessed the incident and realized her brother really wanted to die because "he could not take it anymore."[26] Then four days later, on the eve of his 45th birthday, this prince of Motown was killed by his own father in his bedroom after an altercation in which this young tried to protect his mother from his father. His emotional brother held him as he lay bleeding profusely to death. His last words, spoken barely speaking above a whisper, were to his brother. He said the end result is what he desired,

---

25 Retrieved November, 2015 from: http://www.dailymail.co.uk/news/article-1243063/They-called-The-Man-Who-Killed-Elvis-Now-stars-doctor-finally-reveals-true-madness-Kings-final-days.html
26 Retrieved November, 2015 from: http://en.wikipedia.org/wiki/Death_of_Marvin_Gaye

that he hadn't been able to do it himself, so he had his father do it. He declared that he had run his race but there was no more left. How sad. The enemy will take the lives of our young people if we do not stop the madness. This young man's father was a Pentecostal church bishop – but his son was stolen, killed and destroyed. According to the mother, the father never wanted nor liked the some reason, he did not love the child, nor did he want the mother to love him. Were it not for his mother, this Prince of Motown's life would likely have ended in suicide when he was a child. He had spoken of it more than once.[27] When his life fell apart, he resorted to drugs as his only comfort.

Case Study 4. This is an exceptional case and bears record with me personally. They say that in her latter days this young lady talked about Jesus all the time and carried a Bible everywhere she went. She had reached that pinnacle of success where the enemy was ready to dash her against the stones. She was even baptized in the River Jordan to escape the horrible circus her life had become. But within less than a few years later, the enemy came for her. Daughter of a famous gospel artist, she grew up in church. It was not long after her first solo, he showed up, right inside the church to claim her for hell. Oh yes, he came right into the church and wooed her. Even under the watchful eye of her mother and all the church folk, he whisked this child right out from under their noses – she was only 14 years old. Satan is not playing games; he is bold. He came right into the church and dangled his carrot in front of the unsuspecting child. We expect that some of the children may fall prey; but we do not expect the parents and certainly not the whole church to fall asleep. Like so many others, she was soon living a miserable life, surrounded by people on the payroll. No longer free. No longer in charge of her life; she was just a product. She, too, had willingly signed a contract for which the return on the investment would be collected one day. When she sang "Yes, Jesus Loves Me," for the last time in public during the eve of her death, she probably knew she was close to the end of her natural life. She may

27 Retrieved November, 2015 from: http://en.wikipedia.org/wiki/Marvin_Gay,_Sr.

have even prayed for the end. She was 48-years old. But it did not stop there. The heroes of ministry were present and on program at the funeral, but did not speak as customary in the house of God. They were not probably not allowed to overstep their contract agreement. We can only speculate. But if there was a time to lift up the name of Jesus, if there was ever an opportunity to witness for the Lord, and if ever there was a time to not be ashamed of the gospel of salvation, this was it. And yet, for all the speaking that was done, it was clear that the enemy was running the "show".[28]

Everywhere we look, someone is in dire need of help; someone needs rescuing. Why have we chosen to look at these four individuals? Certainly, we can find examples much closer to home, on our very streets in our own neighborhoods or communities, on the job and all around us. However, these four have risen above their meager beginnings and somehow represent some aspect of success for all people on the earth. Does God care about the human condition? Of course He does. The people of our case studies started out in ordinary households and have lived out their lives in public display for all to see. Some were born into the music business. Some of them were just "around the corner" or the "guy" next door. They were regular people, all of whom represent someone we are able relate to when it comes to man's condition. All of them were once upon a time impressionable little children in the church family. They had a gift that could move the people and a spirit that connected with the masses but at some point, a decision was required. They slipped out from under the protective covering of the church and family; Satan became their covering. They were all whisked away from the church family when they were practically babes. He took them up high and used them in their youth; he pimped and prostituted them until eventually the pressure was too great. One day, they realized they could no longer continue performing at such extreme levels of insanity and wanted their lives back but it was too late. They had signed on the bottom line; the show must go on according to agreement. They became a liability;

---

28 Retrieved November, 2015 from: http://straightfromthea.com/2012/02/20/whitney-houston-obituary-homegoing-funeral-program-full-official/

they were no longer of any use to Satan. Satan had a secretly devised plan to build them up and then tear them down - we Bible believing Christians have read the story about how he came to kill, still and destroy. He claimed them. He made sure they were lonely, isolated, in trouble with the law; unable to rest and had a drug dependency.

Someone made a deal with the devil; someone was the devil's workshop. They were all seeking a hiding place. They knew they were in trouble but their money could do no good. One moved out of the country for several years. Another ran away for awhile. Somebody tried escaping into a reality show. They all tried different escape routes. They could not buy, bargain or negotiate terms in order to own their final resting place. There is only one way to eternal rest. When we see others in trouble, who are in need of salvation, we need to remember that Jesus says, "If I be lifted up, I will draw all men unto me." (John 12:32) He says He will draw them. Sometimes, we want to save people but we can only speak the Word. Though we are not always able to influence change; we are always able to say the name, Jesus.

1.2 Salvation - A Major Topic of Scripture

It is clear that there is more to salvation than we may presuppose. It is good to put some of the questions on the table and attempt to address them through this book. Why do we need salvation, how do we get that salvation and what is it's evidence? Why is there such a big divide concerning the subject? What, if anything, has changed since the time of Christ and the early church? How do we view salvation today?

In its most basic sense, salvation involves the act of saving someone from harm or death. For example, in Psalm 44:4 (ESV) it is used in reference to saving Israel from their enemies and in Mark 5:28 it is used in reference to healing a person from illness. New Testament Scripture expands the basic definition to include the deliverance from the penalty and power of sin. Thus it is not unexpected that salvation is the most widely used theological term to express the provision of God for saving man from the plight caused by sin.[29] For Israel, any saving act – even a physical deliverance or the release from national bondage has always been considered a spiritual act since God is its author. The most frequently referenced saving event in the Old Testament is the Exodus from Egyptian bondage, an event which demonstrated both God's desire and ability to save His people. When confronted and caught between the Red Sea and Pharaoh's army who was giving violent chase, Moses rallied the people and addressed the crowd with assurance that they were not to be afraid. They would surely see the Lord's salvation. To this day, Israel celebrates this pivotal deliverance from Egyptian bondage event in the annual observance of Passover (*Exodus 12*).

For God, salvation is instantaneous. He says it and it is so. However, for us, God's redemption is not simply a one-time deliverance event. It is an ongoing provision as the change is manifested in our lives through the saving work of Jesus Christ. This is why one may rightly declare, "I have been saved, I am being saved, and I shall be saved." We are a work in progress. Hershel Hobbs argued that failure to recognize this distinction could lead to many errors, "such as believing in salvation by works, believing in falling from grace, and uncertainty as to one's salvation until one appears before the judgment seat of Christ (*Hebrews 9:28*). But when this distinction is preserved, it adds to the meaning of salvation in its larger sense" (*The Baptist Faith and Message [Revised Edition]*, Convention Press, 1996).[30]

Salvation in the Old Testament has both corporate and individual implications. David and some of the prophets connect salvation with the creation of a new heart and a right spirit (*Psalm 51:10*).[31] In the book of Ezekiel chapter 36, the prophet spoke of cleansing from filthiness, the removal of a heart of stone and the replacement with a responsive heart; a heart which would be empowered to observe God's ordinances. This transformation would not only "save" them

---

29 Kenneth S. Hemphill, Sinners ~ In Desperate Need of Salvation, http://www.sbclife.net/Articles/2010/04/sla5, April 2010
30 Ibid.
31 Kenneth S. Hemphill, Sinners ~ In Desperate Need of Salvation, http://www.sbclife.net/Articles/2010/04/sla5, April 2010

from their uncleanness, it would cause them to be fruitful again so that the nations would know that God is Lord (v. 25-38).

In the New Testament, the context around salvation is a distinctive sense of deliverance from sin and the wrath of God.[32] Paul declared in Romans 5:9-10, "...since we have now been declared righteous by His blood, we will be saved through Him from wrath. For if, while we were enemies, we were reconciled to God through the death of His Son, how much more, having been reconciled, will we be saved by His life." Though salvation is sometimes mentioned in context of healing people from disease or used in a distinctive sense of deliverance from harm based on the Old Testament understanding of God's gracious action toward His people, Jesus succinctly stated that the thrust of His ministry was to come to seek and to save the lost (Luke 19:10).[33] The event of salvation, however, always seems to be followed by the ongoing provision for the living out of redemption work of Jesus Christ.

The concept of salvation is so rich that Scripture uses a wealth of images to describe the event. The Bible uses terms such as "new birth," "ransom," "redemption," and "reconciliation." Paul employed the concept of adoption (Romans 8:15; Galatians 4:4-5; and Ephesians 1:5). This may be in order to focus on God's graciousness to allow us to become His son or daughter. The other more impressive thought is that this new birth saves us from belonging to and being like the enemy. The enemy is full of darkness, negativity, arrogance and evil. All of his decisions are motivated out of darkness. In Colossians 1:13-14, Paul spoke of salvation in terms of being rescued from the domain of darkness; being transferred into the kingdom of the Son; redemption; and the forgiveness of sins.[34]

---

32 Kenneth S. Hemphill, Sinners ~ In Desperate Need of Salvation, Retrieved November, 2015 from: http://www.sbclife.net/Articles/2010/04/sla5, April 2010
33 Ibid.
34 Ibid.

Life Application for Personal Reflection

What is Soteriology?

1. If salvation has nothing to do with our own works how would you explain Philippians 2:2 "...work out your own salvation with fear and trembling"?

2. Do you believe that a person must be really good to go to heaven? What is meant by the saying that it is not by our goodness that we get there?

3. What does it mean when one says that they are saved by grace alone?

Suggested Reading

What is Soteriology?

1. MacArthur, John, Jr. *The Gospel According to Jesus,* Grand Rapids, MI: Zondervan Publishing Company, 1988.

2. Murray, John. "Faith and Repentance." *In Redemption Accomplished and Applied.* Grand Rapids, MI: Eerdmans Publishing Company, 1955, pp106-115.

3. Strong, James. LL.D. "Seeking God." *The Strongest Strong's Exhaustive Concordance of the Bible, the only Strong compiled and verified by computer technology with Nave's Topical Bible Reference; most up-to-date Hebrew and Greek dictionaries for precise word studies, corrects all others.* Grand Rapids, MI: Zondervan, 2001, p 1788. – "Salvation." *The Strongest Strong's Exhaustive Concordance of the Bible, The Strongest Strong's Exhaustive Concordance of the Bible,* Grand Rapids, MI 49530, 2001, 1784.

The Blood Will Never Lose Its Power

Lyrics by ANDRAE CROUCH

The blood that Jesus shed for me,
way back on Calvary;
the blood that gives me strength
from day to day,
it will never lose its power.

Chorus:
It reaches to the highest mountain,
and it flows to the lowest valley;
the blood that gives me strength
from day to day,
it will never lose its power.

It soothes my doubts and calms my fears,
and it dries all my tears;
the blood that gives me strength
from day to day,
it will never lose its power

REFLECTIONS

THE SPIRIT OF POWER

A young man growing up in the wrong part of Houston became a bully but later learned to channel it into boxing. He began to make a lot of money. One day, while training for an upcoming bout, he learned that his favorite nephew now lay in a coma in the hospital. Doctors said he would probably die, but that if he came out of the coma he wouldn't have human functions. He shouted, "Momma, tell those doctors to give him the best of everything. Tell them who I am, I'll take care of everything — whatever it costs." His mom spoke to the doctors, but then told him, "Son, you're just going to have to pray." He realized then, how grave the situation was. Then it hit him. All of his money, fame, influence, friends — none of that could solve this problem. It was out of his hands, the doctor's and everyone else's hands. For the first time, totally powerless, George Foreman dropped to his knees and prayed. He wasn't sure God existed, but he knew that when all else failed, people prayed. He asked God, if he really existed, to help his nephew. Then he got back in bed. A few seconds later, he got back on his knees and offered to give up all his wealth if God would heal his nephew. Then he got back in bed again only to get back on his knees a third time in anger at God for letting this happen. He told God to take his life instead; only let the boy live. The next day his nephew woke up. He could move his eyes, but the doctors said he would never walk again. Yet he began moving his toes and the next day he was talking. A week later he went home, "walking, talking, and back to normal with no logical explanation. But George Foreman knew God had just given him a miracle.

Text Illustration shared by Austin Mansfield, Holy Faith Anglican Church. The Spirit Of Power October 2007. Retrieved November 12, 2015 from ttp://www.sermoncentral.com/illustrations/sermon-illustration-austin-mansfield-stories-friend-63731.asp

Salvation – Evidence for the Need

◆ ◆ ◆

"Self-sufficiency is the enemy of salvation. If you are self-sufficient,
you have no need of God. If you have no need of God, you do not seek Him.
If you do not seek Him, you will not find Him."

William Nicholson, Shadowlands

▼

The world does not understand what is taking place today because it does not know about or understand God's master plan but the Christian community knows that for approximately 6000 years, humanity has gone its own way. Since 7000 years were allotted, it is fairly safe to say that these years are almost over. These millenniums of human civilization are nearly over. In the meantime, we should be aware of the signs of the times around us. It is obvious that God is about to intervene in world affairs by sending Jesus Christ. Not until He returns will we have 1000 years of peace.[35] Now would be a good time to spread the good news and tell others about God's saving grace.

The Bible reveals the basic need of man and the kind of salvation he needs. His need is spiritual salvation, an internal change which is only offered through Christ. This need has surfaced because man's spiritual life is in danger.[36] Have we ever seen such a time in which

---

35 Retrieved November, 2015 from: http://www.cogwriter.com/six_thousand_year_plan_6000.htm
36 Retrieved November, 2015 from: http://gracepeace.net/light/salvation4.htm

so many young people are outwardly choosing death over life? Who would have thought we would ever see so many misguided people choose to destroy innocent life rather than save it? Did you ever think you would live to see so much hatred among fellow citizens? Who would dream there would be such hatred of self, that one would try to destroy his own country? Patriotism? Loyalty? Honor? Are they a thing of the past? And how can these things be? Could it be that the foundation upon which our youth was built is crumbling? We are living in a society that has unwittingly "out programmed" itself. It's definition of progress has turned inwardly against itself. Wisdom is being overtaken by philosophical ills; norms by theoretical science nonsense and leadership is being replaced by a mockery. In a world filled with science-based perspectives and secular educators, the scales of faith-based beliefs are so off-balance. However, in Christ's time, the world was desperately seeking peace and security in the midst of uncertainty of life and even the terror of death. In fact, two thousand years ago, Rome ruled the world. One in every four people on earth lived and died under Roman law. The Empire mixed its sophisticated civilization with terror and brutality, tyranny and greed.[37] People did not necessarily realize they had a need for God and yet, their search for a safe haven resulted in the founding of various religions. This is simply a reflection of man's need for salvation. The Bible gives us a complete picture of salvation revealed both in the Old Testament and New Testament.

The human race is a unit. Because of the initial act of rebellion, sin entered the world and through sin, death entered (Roman 5:12). Because the human race is in Adam, everyone is spiritually dead and if this is not corrected, the ultimate result is eternal death. Until a person accepts Christ as Savior, his heart is deceitful, motives impure and his energy stems from self, the world and the god of this world. All of the good works and kindness may be viewed as humane gestures but they do not save one from sin. One must have a divine nature in order to be in fellowship and right standing with God. In short, man

---

37 Public Broadcast Station, The Roman Empire in the First Century, http://www.pbs.org/empires/romans/empire/index.html

needs to be saved.[38] When the Lord saw the wickedness of man and that his thoughts were continually evil, it was not a minor situation. He said he would destroy man (Genesis 6:7). Man's behavior was a major offense.

Man not only needs deliverance. He needs a God who cares despite all of man's improprieties. We cannot make it in our world without common grace because of the destructive behavior of man, the judicial effects of sin, corruption and its morally decaying impact on society, and the deceptive, blinding and debilitating effects of sin.[39]

When a faithful church-going grandmother died at 98 years old, neighbors closest to her said nothing was wrong with her but old age. She had never been to see a doctor, was never sick – other than a little arthritis – and she was as spry as the little ground hogs out back of her house. It was just her time to go home. When the coroner examined the body, he was astounded. She was full of disease: ulcers, cancer, liver disease, collapsed lungs. He said it was a miracle she had lived as long as she did. Often, a patient is unaware of some of the serious sicknesses in the body. Medical experts may notice it because of certain symptoms but only a thorough investigation will reveal the true state of that person's health condition. Similarly we may feel good in the normal sense but a close examination will identify the actual facts of the matter. The Bible not only refers to symptoms of man's spiritual state but it reveals his true condition as well.

Man needs to be saved from his sinful nature. Religion cannot save him from this sin. Organized religion is just a plethora of laws, rules and the sayings of prophets which have no power to save man from sin, for the very reason that no man can ever obey these rules and laws nor cause these rules to make man a good person. "The imagination of a man's heart is evil from his youth (*Genesis 8:21*). Man was born with the nature of sin in him and will only do evil continually. Yet this was not the case when God created man.

---

38 Earl D. Radmacher, Salvation, Word Publishing, A Thomas Nelson Publishing Co., P.O. Box 14100, Nashville, TN 37214, 2000 pp.7-9
39 Earl D. Radmacher Salvation, Word Publishing, A Thomas Nelson Publishing Co., P.O. Box 14100, Nashville, TN 37214, 2000 pp.79-80.

According to the Bible, Adam, the first man, was created in the image of God (*Genesis 1:26*). Since he was created in the image of God, he was imbued with true knowledge, righteousness and holiness (*Genesis 1:31; Ecclesiastes 7:29; Colossians 3:10; Ephesians 4:24*). By nature, Adam was good; he had the spiritual and ethical capacity inside him to obey God. But Adam was told by God not to eat the forbidden fruit and if he did, he will surely die (*Genesis 2:17*). We all know the story. Adam disobeyed God and ate the forbidden fruit. But God loved the people of this world so much that He gave His only son, so that everyone who has faith in Him will have eternal life and never die (*John 3:16*). Jesus said: "I came so that everyone would have life, and have it in its fullest" (*John 10:10*).

Since God put a plan in motion for us to have life more abundantly, then why are so many people hurting? False teachers, operating on behalf of the enemy, is one of the main reasons that so many people are confused and their souls are in danger. The other part of John 10:10 says "The thief comes not but for to steal, and to kill, and to destroy. The real problem is separation from God. Yes, He gave us a will and a freedom of choice but it was in order that could get close to Him and have a joy-filled life. Since the beginning of time, man has chosen to disobey God and go independently about his own willful way. This results in separation from God and ends in misery, and possibly death if the sin is not forgiven.

People have tried many ways to "fix it" but there is only one way to reach God. All have sinned and fall short of the glory of God. (*Romans 3:23*) We cannot go any further until we come to terms with this first step – we are all sinners. No matter how good we think we are, we must see our life as falling short of the perfection required by God. No one is "good enough" to go to Heaven. Only Jesus Christ can bring us back to God. He is the only answer to this problem. He died on the Cross and rose from the grave, paying the penalty for our sin and bridging the gap between God and people (*1 Timothy 2:5*). God has provided the only way -- we must make the choice. Without repentance, man will perish. (*Luke 13:5, Acts 3:19, 2 Peter 3:9*)

There is only one way to be made clean – that process is called Salvation. Salvation is a gift from God, freely given to all who ask – it can never be earned. By grace you have been saved through faith – and this not from yourselves, it is the gift of God – not as a result of works, so that no one can boast. (*Ephesians 2:8-9*) Grace means "unmerited favor". It means we are granted favor when we have done nothing to deserve such favor. We cannot rid our life of sin and all our "goodness" cannot bring us one step closer to Heaven. This can be a difficult step. Many of us are so consumed with pride that it's difficult to ask for help – but God requires us to humbly acknowledge that we cannot get there through our own effort. We must admit that we are lost without help to cleanse us of our sins."[40]

Fortunately, God has a wonderful plan already laid out to move us from an eternal death to an eternal life with Him. God so loved the world that He gave His one and only Son, that whoever believes in Him will not perish, but have eternal life. (*John 3:16*) This verse is probably the most recognized verse in the whole Bible. But the all important phrase, "believes in Him", is not made very clear. Our sin can only be forgiven through a proper sacrifice. Jesus Christ died and rose again in order to be the sacrifice for those who will believe. God presented Him as a sacrifice of atonement, through faith in His blood. (*Romans 3:25*) The death, burial, and resurrection of Jesus Christ, provides us the opportunity to be washed clean – the opportunity to have our sin debt canceled – the opportunity to spend eternity in Heaven. Jesus is the Savior who allows us into Heaven – He's the only way! Jesus said to him, "I am the way, the truth and the life; no one comes to the Father, but through Me." (*John 14:6*)

What do the Christian churches believe now? In recent centuries, the conservative body of Christianity have generally taught that the vast majority of individuals are "unsaved". They are isolated from God, and lost in their sins. Although everyone has eternal life after

---

40 Ontario consultants on the Bible. Retrieved November, 2015 from http://www.religioustolerance.org/sal_over.htm

death, only those who are "saved" eventually go to Heaven, where they receive rewards beyond our imagination. The vast majority of humans end up in hell where they are tortured endlessly without hope of mercy or relief from their pain. The losers would presumably include all Agnostics, Atheists, Buddhists, Hindus, Muslims, and followers of other non-Christian religions. To this list of the "lost" are added many Christians who had not met certain specific criteria for salvation. During the 20th century, there has been considerable softening about the teachings on hell and salvation within many denominations. As with the early Church, today's denominations are currently divided about how one is saved.

Fundamentalist and other Evangelical Christian denominations. This group teaches only a small minority of individuals who trust Jesus as Lord and savior will be saved. They are justified through faith and therefore, a person's actions, works and deeds have no impact on their salvation. However, once saved, they will exhibit their new status through the good deeds that they do, because they have become a "new creation in Christ." Salvation forms a major part of their faith -- it motivates many believers to save as many other people as possible from the horrors of hell. This group believes that Jesus Christ is the only way of salvation.[41]

The Southern Baptist Convention believes the Bible is inerrant and infallible, without error. They believe that there is no salvation apart from personal faith in Jesus Christ as Lord.

Roman Catholicism. This group teaches that infants are justified when they are baptized into the Roman Catholic Church. Later, when they mature to the point where they are accountable for their actions, they lose their justification whenever they commit a mortal sin. Church sacraments can restore their status so that they are once more justified. A person's actions and regular presence during the sacraments are of paramount importance in determining whether they will make it to heaven. They consider the topic of salvation to be

---

41 B.A. Robinson. Ontario Consultants on Religious Tolerance, 2012-DEC-10

relatively unimportant. Those liberals who believe in the existence of heaven generally expect that everyone will eventually go there after death.[42]

Mainline Christian denominations teach beliefs that correspond with those of Evangelical Christianity, or liberal Christianity, or which lie somewhere between these two extremes. Individual members do not necessarily agree with the stated position of their denomination. Informational sources were used in developing this section. The hyperlinks are not necessarily still active today.[43]

What about mystery of salvation? In Acts 16:31 we read: "Believe in the Lord Jesus, and you will be saved—you and your household" (NIV). In Romans 10:9, Paul writes, "If you confess with your mouth that Jesus is Lord and believe in your heart that God raised him from the dead, you will be saved." But what about the people who have never heard the gospel? What about those with geographical disadvantages, who aren't as fortunate as we are to be born in a culture where Christianity is an accepted part of society? Some people reason from a presumption of innocence that it's not only unlucky for some to be born in a Muslim culture or an atheistic family, but it's just not fair that God would deny "good people" salvation simply because they didn't have the right beliefs.[44] It is not their fault they do not believe, so why should they endure an eternity of separation from God? So rather than accepting God at His word—even though we don't understand the true mystery of salvation—too often we begin to rationalize based on what makes us more comfortable. The problem with such rationalization is that, as kind as it seems, it destroys the mission of the church and sacrifices the gospel on the altar of reason.[45] It says that although it is Jesus who ultimately saves, individuals are not required to name Jesus as their Savior to avoid going to hell. Although it's a mystery how and why salvation works the way it does,

---

42 B.A. Robinson. Ontario Consultants on Religious Tolerance, 2012-DEC-10
43 Ibid.
44 Sarah Flashing, Why Are Some People More Fortunate? Retrieved November, 2015 from: http://www.todayschristianwoman.com/articles/2012/marchapril-issue/embracing-mystery-of-salvation.html
45 Sarah Flashing, Why Are Some People More Fortunate? Retrieved November, 2015 from: http://www.todayschristianwoman.com/articles/2012/marchapril-issue/embracing-mystery-of-salvation.html

we must accept it based on scriptural authority—even when we don't fully understand. I have heard many testimonies of people who cried out for help in their times of captivity. Never having heard of the name Jesus, they yet gave witness that a great light came into their prison walls and a man came forth, telling them his name is Jesus. Some of them were from foreign countries.

If we look around, there is plenty evidence for the need of salvation but let us start from the beginning and work our way forward.

Genesis tells us that the first humans did something God had warned them against (*Genesis 3:1-13*). Their disobedience showed that they did not trust God, and it was a violation of his trust in them. By their disobedience and lack of faith, they offended God and missed the mark. They were becoming less like God. Now they would have to suffer pain and death (*vv. 16-19*). Anytime we disobey God, we will end up doing things the hard way. We can have high goals, but still be boorish. We are similar to God, but then wicked and underhanded. It is stunning that despite the fact that we have bungled things, God still considers us to be made in his image. The potential is still there for us to be like Him. (Genesis 9:6) God can give us endless life, free from torment, so we are on great terms with Him and with each other. This is the reason He safeguards us, to spare us, and to restore the relationship he had with us. He wants our intelligence, creativity and power to be used for good. He wants us to be like Him and even better than the first humans. There are three principal problems connected with the fall of man.

First, Adam and Eve were created morally sinless beings so they made a decision from without, to disobey God and chose to obey or accept the deception of the evil one – one whom they did not know and had no relationship or history. The God given desire for beauty, knowledge and food was used by Satan to tempt them into rebellion. This begs the question, how does a holy being of God fall? *Secondly*, God, being a just God, gave humanity the freedom to choose but man chose otherwise. He allowed Adam and Eve to be tempted. Jesus did not fall into temptation. He resisted and if we resist, Satan will flee. Adam and Eve did not resist. By resisting temptation, man's holy nature would have been confirmed in holy character. *Thirdly,* a great penalty was attached to man's disobedience. The severity of the punishment is a reflection of how significant disobedience is. The decision made by Adam and Eve was death over life.[46]

The only answer is salvation. When we think about the many rescue operations that God has been involved in - Lot and his family, Joseph, Daniel, the Three Hebrews boys, Moses, Jesus Christ himself, and the list goes on. It is amazing how Jesus always shows up when there is a need. He did back then and He does today. Follow this for a moment. The Son of God became a human, came into our atmosphere of wickedness, lived a perfect life, loved humanity, made people whole and healed many, and we killed him. So now in order to be saved, we have to ask the Father in the name of the one we killed. How ironic that we should be saved by a victim. The disciples were looking for Jesus to rise up as King and slay the Romans but what really happened was that Jesus, the Lion of Judah showed up on earth as an infant and a gentle loving voice in the land. He became flesh so he could die for us because there is no greater love than this. Love conquers all. In the death and resurrection of Jesus, the death and salvation of humanity is represented and made possible. Jesus Christ died for us, and was raised for us (*Romans 4:25*). Our old self died with him, and a new person is brought back to life with him (*Romans 6:3-4*). In one sacrifice, Jesus atoned "for the sins of the whole world" (*1 John 2:2*). The payment has already been made; all we have to do is participate in the plan through repentance and faith and receive the benefits.[47]

In one sense, salvation is no different than being saved from a burning house, an overturned car, a raging river or any other

46 Lectures in Systematic Theology, Henry C. Thiessen, Revised by Vernon D. Doerksen, William B. Eerdmans Publishing Company, 255 Jefferson S.E., Grand Rapids, MI 49530, 1998, pp 175-177.
47 Baker's Evangelical Dictionary of Biblical Theology, Retrieved November, 2015 from: http://www.biblestudytools.com/dictionary/salvation/

dangerous predicament from which one cannot deliver himself. It means delivered from a fate that, without intervention by another party, would result in injury or death. It means to be *preserved*. Any good dictionary will tell you that being saved, in the religious sense, involves deliverance or preservation—redemption. God says true salvation is being delivered from death, but this is not what is commonly believed. [48] I have attended and played for many funerals. I have heard numerous long, speeches about where the dead have gone—how they have not really died. I have watched preachers represent death as a "friend" met at the end of "life's journey." It is as though the bereaved can take comfort if they can picture the dead as not really dead, but alive somewhere else. However, without salvation, we perish.

Life Application for Personal Reflection

Salvation Evidence for Need

1. Do you recall how your life was before you realized you needed salvation?
2. What evidence do you have of your personal need for salvation?

Suggested Reading

Salvation Evidence for Need

1. Hagin, Kenneth E. *In Him*, RHEMA Bible Church AKA Kenneth Hagin Ministries, Inc., Tulsa, OK, 1980.
2. Hodge, Charles. *Systematic Theology*. 3 vols. Reprint edition: Grand Rapids: Eerdmans, 1970. First published 1871, pp 313, 516-517.
3. Nave, Orville J. *Nave's Topical Bible, A Digest of the Holy Scriptures,* Nashville, TN: Thomas Nelson Publishers, 1979, 1208-1223.
4. Stott , John. *The Beatitudes, Developing Spiritural Character,* IVP Connect, An imprint of InterVarsity Press, P.O. Box 1400 Downers Grove, IL 60515-1426, 1998
5. Strong, James. LL.D. "Seeking God." *The Strongest Strong's Exhaustive Concordance of the Bible, the only Strong compiled and verified by computer technology with Nave's Topical Bible Reference; most up-to-date Hebrew and Greek dictionaries for precise word studies,* corrects all others. Grand Rapids, MI: Zondervan, 2001, p 1788. – *"Salvation." The Strongest Strong's Exhaustive Concordance of the Bible, The Strongest Strong's Exhaustive Concordance of the Bible, Grand Rapids, MI: Zondervan, 2001, 1784*

---

48 David C. Pack, The Restored Church of God. Retrieved November, 2015 from http://rcg.org/books/jwis.html

Promises

By DOTTIE RAMBO

He didn't promise that I would never stumble,
But He did say He'd be there if I fall;
He didn't tell me He'd hear all things I whisper,
Oh, but He did say He'd hear me if I call.

Promises, promises and all of them true,
He's done exactly what He said He would do;
He didn't tell me my heart would not be broken,
Oh, but He did say He'd mend it again.

He didn't promise my cross would not be heavy,
Oh, but he did say that He my load would share;
He didn't tell me He'd grant my hopes and wishes,
Oh, but He did say He'd hear my earnest prayer.

Promises, promises and all of them true,
He's done exactly what He said He would do;
He didn't tell me my heart would not be broken,
Oh, but He did say He'd mend it again.

Promises, promises, and all of them true.

REFLECTIONS

BEHOLD I STAND AT THE DOOR AND KNOCK

A pastor was visiting a family one day. He knocked on the door but no one answered it. He knocked again and again, but still no answer. He thought he heard someone inside but they just wouldn't answer the door. Finally he wrote a note and slipped it under the door. It was Rev.3:20: "Behold I stand at the door and knock. If any man hear my voice and open the door, I will come in." Four days later he received a note in the mail and it was Genesis 3:10: "I heard the sound of thee in the garden and I was afraid because I was naked and I hid myself."

- Bruce Howell
Lighthouse Community Church

Source: A Pastor Was Visiting A Family One Day. Text Illustration shared by Bruce Howell, Lighthouse Community Church, Wesleyan, Pastor/Minister, February 2001. Retrieved October 23, 2015 from http://www.sermoncentral.com/contributors/bruce-howell-sermons-4805.asp

➤ Over the last decade, considerable attention has been focused on theological correction concerning this passage which pertains to the Lord Jesus Christ knocking at the door of the lukewarm church, Laodecia. The importance of this theology has been aimed at clarifying the image of Jesus who is not pleading with the sinner to accept Him. As we know, none can come to the Father except by Jesus (John 14:6) the Father draws them. The clearest verse on God's drawing us to salvation is where Jesus declares that "no one can come to Me unless the Father who sent Me draws him, and I will raise him up at the last day." (John 6:44) However, at the end of the day, who is the church? Where is the need for salvation?

Man's Need for Salvation

◆ ◆ ◆

"[I] know that love is ultimately the only answer to mankind's problems...."
Martin Luther King Jr.

▼

It is only logical to explore man's need for Salvation and how that came about in this world. We can begin with certain Scriptures that explain it biblically. For example, we know we were created by God, for His purposes and that all things everywhere - dominions, or principalities, or powers – were made for him (*Colossians 1:6*). His plan for us existed before we showed up on the earth (*Jeremiah 1:5*). It does not matter what race, creed, gender or culture, every single individual on the earth matters to God. He designed and set us apart because he had a plan with something particular on His mind for us and very clearly – our existence. Clearly, it was all for His glory (*Psalm 139:13-16*). Now, despite the fact that He made man a little lower than the angels and crowned man with glory and honor (*Psalm 8:5*), man simply cannot seem to grasp or appreciate what this means.

There has been much debate concerning whether salvation is both individual and corporate. Does man need both? Let's discuss this. Even though some writers have made assumptions or have drawn conclusions based upon Paul's epistles which were written to churches and not individuals, everything in the work of redemption is personal and individually prepared for each person. People cannot depend on the saving faith of others. It is not Scriptural. An individual passes from death to life - not a corporate entity. Jesus told Nicodemus personally, "You must be born again" (John 3:3). Paul was converted on the road to Damascus. We are not saved collectively.

In the story about how the Good Shepherd will go searching for the one lost lamb we can see the individual aspect of salvation. Notice that the shepherd is so anxious to recover the lost sheep that he leaves the ninety-nine immediately to go after the one who is lost. He doesn't leave it up to the lost one to make his way back to the ninety nine. And neither does the Shepherd look to the ninety nine to bring the lost sheep back. It is personal for him. He goes after the sheep until he finds it. Unlike Christianity, Judaism holds that personal salvation is not needed.[49] In contemporary Judaism, redemption is described as God redeems the children of Israel from exile.

Among the evangelical Christian community, emphasis is on having a personal relationship with Jesus Christ. However, Reformed Christians focus more on fellowship with Christ through the fellowship of the divinely-appointed church body and its administration of the means of grace, the preaching of the Word of God and the administration of the sacraments of baptism and holy communion. Well, Jesus came and taught us to love God and one another as He loved us. Personal sin had impact to others, our neighbors and ourselves. However, God provided for our personal salvation – even if it is intended that we are part of a corporate body. We must always consider both the personal and corporate aspect of any our doctrines in order to get the full view. In the letters to the churches in the book of Revelation, we can see the different characteristics that are outlined. Yet the church is made up of individuals who collectively, are joined together. As we move into further study, we should be able to see the impact of one on the other.

---

49 Redemption (theology), online encyclopedia. https://en.wikipedia.org/wiki/Redemption_(theology) Retrieved November, 2015 from: https://en.wikipedia.org/wiki/Judaism

A nation, culture, race, sect or simply a small family. We are able to compare Martin Luther King, Jr., the great civil rights activist, and leader of one of history's greatest transformations, to Moses in the Old Testament. Like Moses, King became the voice of a nation of people in trouble and who was crying out for deliverance. In his famous *I Have A Dream* speech, King said he was not worried or fearful of any man because his eyes had seen the glory of the Lord. He knew God was sovereign in the situation.[50] Like Moses, he reluctantly accepted the challenge of striving to be what the people needed at the time. He was a living sacrifice. He knew he would be denied entrance into the world of racial harmony and social justice that he had devoted his life to create. Despite being a target for enemies both within and outside, the crowd still demanded civil liberties. He was threatened by racist enemies on all sides, the subject of an unrelenting surveillance by the FBI on the other, accused of being a Communist, questioned about financial improprieties and personal misconduct – and all the while, the wall of the crowds pressed against him for salvation. They nearly suffocated him to death in their search for their own deliverance. This is deliverance from evil of man. Is this a corporate or individual issue? King was just a young man. He said, "Certainly I don't want to die. But if anyone has to die, let it be me."[51] While accepting the Nobel Peace Prize on December 10, 1964, King said, "I believe that unarmed truth and unconditional love will have the final word in reality." While powerful words, no one could put it better than John who says, "Greater love hath no man than this, that a man lay down his life for his friends." *(John 15:13)*

Individuals. For example, when the lady with the issue of blood touched the hem of Jesus' garment, He said, "Who touched me? *(Luke 8:45).* Peter and some of the disciples were having a difficult time understanding how, with such an enormous throng of people, Jesus could even ask such a question. In fact, they were not particularly interested in the individuals. It was far too crowded. They were

50 Martin Luther King, Jr, *I Have a Dream*, delivered 28 August 1963, at the Lincoln Memorial, Washington D.C., Retrieved November, 2015 from: http://www.americanrhetoric.com/speeches/mlkihaveadream.htm
51 Dr. Ts Timely Tips" by Dr. Tony Alessandra, http://www.alessandra.com/timelytips/105.asp#ixzz2zLHniVsl Retrieved November, 2015 from: http://www.alessandra.com/timelytips/105.asp

probably more concerned with making their way through the throng. We have all been in large gatherings and know that huge crowds can turn into a raging mob at any moment. The disciples took exception to Jesus' question. Any number of people could have touched Jesus at the same time. He wanted to see who it was that had such great faith that the virtue departed Him. I have heard some ministers say, "The Lord does not care where you park your car. Quit praying for a parking space." Well, because of personal experience, I know differently. Maybe God does not care where those ministers park, but the Lord cares where my car is parked all the time! Constant fellowship and the consistent entrusting of concerns pertaining to my life, ministry and my family to my Lord's care has proven to be a real safeguard. Either we are serious about wanting divine protection and intervention from the Lord or we are wandering about aimlessly. Satan is not playing. He is out to kill, steal and destroy. Many disastrous situations have been circumvented because the Lord cares for His own.

In the case of the woman with the issue of blood, Jesus said, "The virtue has gone out of me (*Mark 5:30-32*). According to Mosaic Law, women who were ceremonially unclean were not allowed to touch anyone, let alone the Son of God. But desperate people do desperate things. For 12 long years blood had flowed from her body, making her physically sick and socially unacceptable. The physicians of her time were unable to relieve her suffering and despite spending all she had, here she was – broke and still sick. She "spent all she had, yet instead of getting better she grew worse" (*Mark 5:26*). Some of us have been there, dealing with a prolonged illness or stubborn medical condition.

It's frustrating, even embarrassing, to keep going to the doctor, only to return home with an expensive prescription and little hope. Now here this lady was, ceremonially unclean and not allowed to touch anyone. Nonetheless, there she was, touching the Son of God. What made her do that? It was sheer desperation. What else did she have to lose? And not that Jesus was ignorant of who had touched him – He knew. I believe when we receive something from the Lord, that we overcome by our testimony. Then, as a consequence of her declaration, she would be able to hear him confirm that her faith had saved her; and because of it, others might come forward for healing as well. Notice that at the same time, the virtue went out of Him. He is affected by our infirmities. It is amazing that in the middle of all of the miracles that Jesus performed, and with the people increasingly demanding more, He was still acutely aware of this woman's situation. This reflects the genuine loving nature of our Lord. How many conversations have you participated in where you wished the other person was really listening to you? Or how many times have you tried to tell your story but just as you got to the most intimate part of it, somebody put you on hold? Christ is constantly telling us by example, of how to care for each other in the middle of our salvation experience. We may not receive if we are so caught up with the theological correctness of the application of ministry. However, Jesus was controversial in many ways. Let us be reminded that He healed people on the Sabbath Day; He spent time with the outcasts; He loved the sinner. Many pressed in around Him but often it was for selfish miracles - to see miracles, to get the benefits, to receive the blessings for themselves – they could not see past their infirmities to see their human condition. In many ways, it was as though they completely missed the point. They failed to see the bigger picture and the reason that the Messiah had come. And yet, that did not stop Him from seeing or meeting the needs of the people. He showed up wherever there was a need.

Jesus knew the Samaritan woman would be at the well (*John 4*). He strategically planned to be there to speak with her. It was God's plan to further reveal who Jesus was and to bring the Samaritan woman and many in her village to salvation. This is not something that we understand on the outset of the story. Nor do we comprehend the significance of Jesus' journey into that land of prejudicial behavior until later. The Samaritans were a people of mixed Gentile and Jewish blood who lived in the area on the west side of the Jordan River between Judaea and Galilee. The Jews detested them and would not consider traveling through Samaria at the risk of defiling themselves. This too gives us insight into the prideful hearts of the Jews who thought themselves superior to all non-Jews and especially to the Samaritans. Even though they were the chosen people who would reveal God to the rest of the world they knew nothing of God as a God of love. The Messiah was to be the Savior of the world, not just to Israel. God revealed His Abrahamic concerning the blessing upon Israel also to Moses, explaining, that "...thou shalt become an astonishment, a proverb, and a byword, among all nations whither the LORD shall lead thee" (*Deuteronomy 28:37*). God also said, "Let all the nations be gathered together, and let the people be assembled: who among them can declare this, and shew us former things? let them bring forth their witnesses, that they may be justified..." (*Isaiah 43:9-10*) but the Jews because of their sinful and proud hearts never really accepted this truth. Similarly, Jonah did not really want to be a witness and was rather angry when God spared the Ninevites. God used Jonah as a sign to the Ninevites. Sadly, Jonah was a reluctant witness, as were the Jews in Jesus' day (*Luke 11:28-29*).

The people of Samaria were a people of mixed Jewish and Gentile blood. During the period of the divided kingdom, the Assyrian king Shalmanessar IV, attacked and destroyed the northern country of Israel in 721 B.C. He took the ten northern tribes into captivity in Babylon. The Assyrian king then sent various Gentile people from the north to resettle the area Israel has occupied. The population of the area continued to be mostly Jewish, but in time they intermarried with the Gentiles immigrants. The result was that the religion of the Samaritans became a combination of Judaism and pagan beliefs. Later in 586 B.C. Nebuchadnezzar, the Babylonian king, destroyed the southern nation of Judah, which were the two remaining tribes of Israel in the south, and took them into captivity in Babylon. Seventy years later, the Jews were allowed to return to Jerusalem to rebuild the temple. However, because of their false religion and intermarriage with Gentiles, the Jews shunned the Samaritans and would not allow them to take part in rebuilding the Temple in Jerusalem. In turn, the

Samaritans built their own temple on Mount Gerizim, which was later destroyed by the Jews. The Samaritans then built another temple at Shechem. The Jews hated the Samaritans and the rivalry was strong during the time of Jesus. Yet he said it was necessary travel through Samaria. This was not something an ordinary Jewish man would do for any reason.

Jesus, in going to Samaria and offering salvation to the woman at the well, revealed the Messiah. Now they would be able to see that salvation was not just for the Jews but for the Gentiles as well. Jesus talked about this in John 3:16 to Nicodemus. "For God so loved the world that he gave his only begotten Son..." He traveled north into Samaria not far from Sychar where He stopped at Jacob's well. Jesus was sitting alone on the well when the Samaritan woman arrived to draw water. It was somewhat unusual for her to walk this distance in the heat of the day to draw water. However, as John reveals, this woman was of dubious character and probably came at this time to avoid the stares and ridicule of the other women of the nearby village. On the other hand, Jesus, the Saviour of the world, was waiting patiently and He was thirsty. This was clearly not a chance meeting, but an event of divine intervention.

The whole story is interesting. The woman was a little shocked by the fact that a Jew was not only speaking to her, he wanted to drink from her pot. Jews held the Samaritans with such disdain they would not speak, look at, or touch them. If they had to travel through Samaria, they would brush the dust off of their feet when leaving their country. Jesus had a powerful message for this woman and her world of Samaritans. This woman was the first of many Samaritans who would eventually come to believe and receive Jesus as their Messiah and Savior. Phillip went into Samaria and preached the Gospel and many believed (*Acts 8:5-14*). When the Apostles in Jerusalem heard that many there had been saved, they sent Peter and John there to continue preaching. Later, Acts 9:31 speaks of the churches in Judaea, Galilee and in Samaria having a period of rest from persecution after

Saul (Paul) was converted. Acts 15:3, records that Paul and Barnabas also preached in Samaria and the brethren received the news of the conversion of Gentiles with great joy. Here at the well, Jesus offered her "living water." That is, God's promise of the Messiah, the true "living water" which is the message of salvation. She could not understand it at first. She sought to challenge the Lord for whatever suspicions or reasons she had.

Sometimes, we cannot see or hear beyond the spoken words. It reminds me of the year my father went home to heaven. My sister put him on the phone to me. He wanted to talk with me. The instant he told me he was ready to go home, I knew he was telling me he was leaving for heaven. He wanted my acceptance; my agreement. Although I drove home every weekend to see him, he told me he would not be there on the next visit. We said our goodbye's but not before he told me to tell my sister to stop trying to make him eat. He did not want anything more, no food or anything else. He made me promise to explain it to her. She was there with him. I was over 500 miles away. There was no such thing as "explaining" it. What could I possibly know? And she wasn't ready. She fought it; oh she was a strong fighter. But he was stronger in His desire to see Jesus. She called me many times the next day telling me he refused to eat; she gave a blow by blow account, as they say. Then he sent her away to get him a drink of water; it was only a few steps off into the kitchen. By the time she came back with two pieces of ice in his favorite cup, he had slipped away. That was only two days later.

Though the Samaritan woman clearly did not understand what Jesus was truly saying, we know that salvation is a miraculous spring that brings a refreshing, satisfying peace and joy to the soul. It offers new life that never ends and brings spiritual growth or "springs of living water." The world cannot possibly satisfy; it always leaves a void; we are unfulfilled.

The woman responded with earthly understanding, asking Jesus to give her this water so that she would no longer need to come to the well each day and draw water (*John 4:15-16*). She walked approximately two miles every day carrying water and wanted to eliminate this drudgery task. Jesus used the question concerning her husband (she had many men) to reveal the spiritual need in her life. She needed to see her real need that she might subsequently desire to be saved. She needed to be brought face to face with her life of immorality. Not that she was unaware of her sin prior to that – we all know when we have sinned. But it feels different when you see yourself through the eyes of the Lord.

Though a stranger, Jesus knew the Samaritan woman's story. She was with a man that was not her husband and she had previously been with five men always in hopes of finding the right man, hoping to be satisfied. Jesus knew these things, without anyone having to tell Him so she perceived Him to be a prophet, but then became defensive as sinners do when confronted with the truth. She shifted the conversation to a religious question.

Jesus did not fall for the diversion but instead, enlightened her on what was most important. The Samaritans, although claiming to be true worshipers of God and followers of the Pentateuch, rejected God's revelation through the prophets and the rest of the Old Testament. They were a false religious sect or a cult of Judaism. Jesus plainly stated that the Samaritan beliefs were false and declared that it was through the Jews that salvation was come to the world. They worshiped according to the traditions of their rabbis according to the Talmud. They had the right Bible, the word of God, but did not follow its teachings, thus their worship was also unacceptable to the Lord. Their religious leaders twisted God's word to fit their own agendas. They liked the prestige, money, and power that their false teachings gave them over the people. Jesus warned that we must worship in spirit and in truth. The Church Age would soon begin; the present dispensation of the Old Testament would pass away.

Even today, like the Samaritans and the Jews, false prophets teach erroneous doctrines which pervert the word of God. Their worship is not acceptable to God because it lacks truth. True worship recognizes God's instruction as to how He is to be worshiped. Today's worship is polluted, making worship a dead ritual or an irrelevant emotional entertainment. Biblical worship is supposed to be a heartfelt outpouring of praise, thankfulness, and adoration of God. But in our modern times, it has been turned into entertainment. The Devil has always had his "ministers of light" which fool the unwise. God's truth is ignored by these false teachers and in its place, these wolves in sheep's clothing, teach the corrupt wisdom of men. All over the world, church denominations and cults of Christendom zealously proclaim their polluted doctrines and millions are deceived. Little has changed since Jesus' day. Yet, there has always been and will continue to be a remnant who hold to God's truth. As saved spiritually born again believers, they truly worship and serve the Almighty God.

There is something about salvation that is undeniably personal. Even in cases where the corporate body needs rescuing, it is the individual members that feel the brunt of it and the pressure that gets the corporate body spun up into action. If a member of the body suffers pain, the whole body feels the distress. If the body aches, the corporate body hurts also. This applies to other corporate bodies as well as the body of Christ.

When a co-worker reached out to me for an answer some years ago, my only response was "Jesus". No matter what the question, struggle or circumstance, that is the one sure gospel truth. It is always Jesus. For an individual who has no salvation experience with Christ and no way to relate, that answer is impossible to accept without faith. Unless on their deathbed, they will want to talk it out, analyze it step-by-step, or map it out so they can visually see all options for getting to the desired destination point so as to predict at what point certain events would potentially happen on that journey.

In this particular instance, it was maddening because I knew I might very well be the only Jesus she might get to see. She wanted salvation counseling from a Christian – but without Jesus. Charlie had chosen unconventional, freestyle communal living as an affront to her parents' traditional but disastrous marriage. She decided communal living with its lack of rules or regulations where any and everyone regardless of race, gender, creed and culture was welcome, would free her from old fashioned traditions and commitment worries. This way, there were no expectations and no disappointments. It would produce better outcomes. There was no real value system; her communal group shared everything. For her, it was like playing in the sandbox with many playmates.

By avoiding the establishment, she thought she could escape social responsibility, discipline and religion. In essence, she was looking for utopia. Utopian thought, as the basis of communal ideology, idealizes social unity and maintains that humanness exists only in intimate and collective life. Within these small scale communities however, some emphasis is placed on providing a somewhat controlled and manipulated environment in which social life may be structured to create the illusion of a perfect human being. In other words, the belief of happiness in the present, or heaven on earth underlies the establishment of Utopian communities (Kanter).[52]

Of course this idealism does not work for long – for obvious reasons. More importantly, it has the ability to upset or destroy someone's life. And this situation was no different. Blinded by the god of this world, Charlie's independence and determination to find her knight in shining armor led her from one horrific experience to another. In her confused state, she tried everything bad but shunned everything good. She was anxious for a resting place but so desperate that she overlooked it when it appeared. Being forced to look in the mirror of truth was a real turn off. Her vision and hearing were impaired by sin soaked eyes and ears. Fairly analytical, she wanted a quick, man-made solution. When that did not work, she tried a few eastern religions because they were less threatening. Eventually Charlie found herself in deeper trouble – financially ruined, sexually

---

52 Kanter, Rosabeth. *Commitment and Community*: Communes and Utopias in Sociological Perspective. Cambridge: Harvard University Press, 1972, p 32.

traumatized, physically and mentally abused, and even diseased. Distressed and full of guilt, she finally slammed up against a brick wall. At her lowest and weakest points in life, she was finally able to hear the call of God. This time, only the name of Jesus would do and she cried out for deliverance of her soul and mind from the very pit of hell. She held onto the name of Jesus repeating it when she woke up in the morning, before she went to bed at night and on into the wee hours. Oh indeed, the enemy meant to destroy her life, but when she cried out to Jesus, the Lord rescued her. Today, she is a worshiper and follower of Jesus Christ. Since receiving the gift of the Holy Spirit, she has been actively involved in church, singing and writing songs for Christ. She went back and got her daughter who experienced very similar sufferings, and brought her to Christ. Now married to a man of God, they are going forth together to help others to see Jesus.

We know our prayers were answered in this instance and that prayer changes things. However, we cannot boast of our own strength. We cannot take credit for having prayed the prayer that yielded the results. We cannot credit the results to our heritage or the family values instilled in us over the years, for it is only because of God's grace that any of us can receive Him. When we reach forward and accept His mercy, it is by His saving grace. We cannot boast of having never sinned because we were raised in a Christian home. While the intent may be to give praises to the Lord, we need to realize we do not have bragging rights. If we would search back far enough back through the Scriptures, we would see that our ancestors, Adam and Eve, are the root cause of all the sin and separation in the world today. God is the ultimate cause for whatever good we have. Without Him, this good would not be imparted to us. In fact, He is good itself.

This seems to be the whole point of God's creation. We are dependent upon Him for everything. We exist because of Him and whether we admit it, we are nothing without Him. During the course of life, man will continue to experience all kinds of challenges and situations – some good and others not so easy to handle. Many of them will be driven out of fear and disease, sickness and death, sadness and sorrows. These life events will cause us to cry for mercy; for life's circumstances can be extreme and relentless. I suspect that, for those of us who acknowledge the Lord in all of our ways, the events we face is a life giving opportunity to prove Him to others. It is more of a "laboring together" experience. It encourages us as we encourage others. For those who have not come to Christ, it is more of an opportunity for the Lord to show up and introduce Himself as the savior. Either way, man is always faced with a choice – will I choose to accept help or not?

We have seen this repeatedly in the Old Testament. Jacob ran from Esau. Joseph's brothers threw him in a pit. Moses ran from Pharaoh. David fled from Saul. Elijah hid from Jezebel under a juniper tree, praying that he could die. Jonah was swallowed up by a whale.

Central to human dignity is the understanding that every human being is created in the image of God and made savable by Jesus Christ, our Redeemer. It is the pressing against our humanity and the challenges we face in everyday living that make us determined to move into our destiny. It is the enemy who tries to destroy or prevent us from achieving what needs to be accomplished. Whether it is a conscious awareness or not, most people long for salvation. The desire stems from a common longing to be rescued. Every person knows deep within that they need to be saved, but they do not always explore and connect their feelings with the need to be rescued. It is as though man is in a deep sleep entirely regarding the human condition. Similarly, he seems completely unaware of what Jesus had to go through in order to save him.

"Hosanna! Blessed is the one who comes in the name of the Lord!" This was the shout of praise or adoration made in recognition of Jesus as the Messiah on his triumphal entry into Jerusalem. The word hosanna is from Hebrew word hôshia-na' which is short for the Aramaic word meaning "save, rescue" (possibly "savior"). Hosanna refers to a cry expressing an appeal for divine help. In the Hebrew Bible it is used only in verses to convey a need for help or to be saved (*Psalm 118:25*).

Jesus' entry into Jerusalem was very dramatic yes, and for the people, it was triumphal. However, by openly entering the city in the manner that He did during Passover with the enormous swelling crowds waving the palm branches, He was now clearly a marked man. When the crowd shouted, "Blessed is the King of Israel!" they were not simply hailing and acknowledging him as king, they were also sending an 'in your face" challenge to the great King of the city that here was their victorious ruler. It was obvious that they saw Jesus as the answer to their problems; but at the same time, they did not recognize the dilemma they created for Him.

This was the final confrontation. Everyone was so caught up in the swirl of events that not even the disciples really understood the reality (*Acts 1:6*). The disciples and the crowd thought they were honoring Jesus, and they were. But they did not fully comprehend the true meaning of what was happening. They had not really thought about it enough to put into context the events of Jesus' entry into Jerusalem together with the Scripture in Zechariah Chapter 9 which explains that the king is coming, but He would be seated on a donkey's colt. There are several things that we need to understand about crowds. They are lower orders of people. They are anonymous and only definable through a common purpose or set of emotions. Their actions are not necessarily logically driven or correct. The one thing they have is passion stemming from a deep conviction. They feed off each other and it only takes approximately six percent of a crowd to change the entire direction the crowd is traveling. That means they are also fickle.

Due to the potential for enormous swelling, crowds always attract a lot of attention. Therefore, their outcries and demands are likely to be heard and considered. This crowd demanded deliverance by the new king of the Jews from the oppression imposed upon them by the existing establishment. They could not understand that while Jesus would do that very thing, it would not occur through a political liberation platform. They did not realize the jeopardy and toxicity of the situation. In other words, in order for Him to deliver them, He must sacrifice His life. If they had known, would they have been as jubilant about their deliverance?

We sing the several Hosanna songs in church. Occasionally, this is accompanied by an exuberant outward expression of emotion and excitement. However, if we understand the true meaning, the expression becomes more of an inward reflection of Jesus Christ and all He suffered in order to free us from the clutches of hell.

My earliest recollection of that immediately flashes me back to old time religion and the hell fire altar calls that I became accustomed to in the early days when I was just a kid. People who wanted to be saved would run forward in church, kneel at an old fashioned wood altar, and cry their way to God. Some people would shake all over, wave their hands excitedly, writhe about, or snap their heads back, while a few scattered converts would roll around on the floor. Out of most of those experiences, I wanted nothing to do with this salvation. Now, I knew something was happening and that whatever it was, it might be a good thing for advertising Jesus. And it was good entertainment for some of us astonished onlookers! But it was not something I particularly wanted to happen to me. Somehow I didn't quite see myself falling down, writhing about or rolling around on the floor. It was not until it was explained that I was born in sin, shaped in iniquity and that only the Lord Jesus could keep me from a life of destruction, that I knew I wanted to be saved. I was nine years old. Well I made my way down front to the altar, prayed the salvation prayer with the rest of the crowd and waited. Nothing happened. I didn't fall down, writhe about or carry on. But as I waited, I just felt sunshiny inside. Like a great weight had been lifted. Funny how we see things as a kid. Even after accepting Jesus Christ as my Lord and Savior, it was not until seven years later when one of my good friends, and I sat together at a state convention talking excitedly about things that teens talk about, that the question of salvation started to overtake me. I will never forget that day.

We sat about 30 rows back in the middle of the Greenville, South Carolina's Convention Center far away from the watchful eyes of our parents, when all of a sudden, the speaker mentioned something about choosing life or death. Cathy who was talking to me about an old boyfriend stopped mid-sentence, mouth open. She froze. All I saw were teeth and tongue. She had a "locked jaw" look on her face. Then her mouth twisted, her eyes pierced me through to my heart as one lone tear traveled down her left cheek. I do not remember the exact words the minister said but it was something about needing to choose life and it did not matter whether you were young or old – but one day we would all die. We would not know the day or hour, but Jesus was coming soon. With tears in her eyes, she asked me to go with her down front. It was my first time seeing the true effect of the call to redemption. As many times as I had fussed with her about joking so much and tried to get her to accept Christ, I was totally unprepared for what happened. We fell on the floor that night.

This was a complete change. I mean you'd have to know Cathy to understand. She was known for making wisecracks, never showed her true feelings. It did not matter that her stepfather was a respected bishop or that her mother was a fireball of a preacher – Cathy would carry on about almost anything. Much of it was probably for shock value. Most of us would look at her and shake our heads. I used to pray for her to leave me alone because her jokes were too colorful sometimes. But here she was – wanting me to go with her to the altar and lead her to Christ. I did not say a word, just threw my arms around her and walked with her. From that day, Cathy was different. No more off color jokes. Within a few short years, her mother died. I believe God saved Cathy's life. God had saved her life. She married a Church of God preacher and she has been teaching the gospel of Jesus Christ ever since.

What if she had been tricked into believing she did not require salvation? Or what if falling on the floor had been a show stopper? Satan continues trying to deceive man just as he did in the Garden of Eden with the Fall of Man. It was only when man and woman (Adam and Eve) disobeyed God that sin entered the world. They probably did not realize at first that disobeying God would cost them so much. But that does not really matter, because they still disobeyed. Because of sin, man lost paradise. Because of sin, death came; man was alienated from God and from each other. Soon, one of them murdered his own brother; for which he did not repent, possibly due his independence and arrogance, or fear of punishment. After the murder, then came fear, then man's distrust of one another, followed by jealousy, envy, murder, and the list goes on. Eventually man deliberately left God out of his life and the world became increasingly corrupt and violent. This unsavory behavior led to God sending the flood but thankfully, He gave us another chance.

Through that salvation, which brought the next line of people, God visited and made covenant with Abram (whom He later renamed Abraham) that he would become the father of many nations (*Genesis 12*). God promised to make him a source of blessing for all people. Abraham obediently moved from what is known today as Iraq, to Canaan, which later became Israel. God rewarded his faithfulness, making Abraham the father of Israel. Now today, we are heirs to that promise. God looked beyond the faults of man and our need through the cross. Though man may not understand or appreciate the earnestness of hope in us that is wrapped up in this promise of God, we know He uses the foolish things of the world to confound the wise. (*1Corithinians 1:28-29*).

3.1 Saving Salvation

We are living in a culture that at times seems foreign. Things have shifted. I remember going to church when I was young. Everything was easier; we had overflowing love. We sang wonderful songs and talked things through when there was miscommunication. There was almost never controversy about what was right or wrong; there wasn't a lot of rebellion. I don't really know this America anymore. Society has been turned upside down. America is suffering from crime, perversions and all manner of evil. The stage is set; the die is cast. Unless we pray and repent, it is possible that America will lead the world into a particular darkness that none of us wants to discuss – the New World Order. Christians see and recognize the signs of the time (*Matthew 24*). However, all is not lost – we are still a praying nation. The Word of God is still alive and active. We are reminded that if we repent, God will hear us and heal our land. "If my people, which are called by my name, shall humble themselves, and pray, and seek my face, and turn from their wicked ways; then will I hear from heaven, and will forgive their sin, and will heal their land." (*2 Chronicles 7:14*)

SOCIETY. There are forces at work in society that cause confusion and make it difficult for the seed of the gospel to take root and grow. Those forces not only affect gospel outreach and bringing in the lost, but it also affects the family. Imagine what damage Satan can do if he prevents Christians from passing on their faith and knowledge to their children. Satan's attacks are often very subtle and we cannot always pinpoint when or how we began to stray from God's path. In the last decade, however, he has begun pulling out all of the stops and his attacks are very direct. He is unabashed, the subtlety is gone, and he is charging from every direction, using a multi-prong approach with his fiery darts. The intent is that even though we may be able to deflect some of the darts, one or two may get through and disable us long enough for him to close in for the kill. His agenda has not changed but it is becoming more exposed now as he assaults everything America once held dear. In order to destroy God's Church family, Satan does not simply attack people individually. As part of his plan, he is also altering the very fabric of society that has made it possible for the family and church to thrive. These are the areas presently under bold attack through which we can see how he hopes to destroy God's plan of salvation. All societies are founded on principles or rules called mores or norms. Certain activities considered to be outside the boundaries of acceptable behavior are taboo. Norms and taboos are shaped by institutions. Apart from the Family, the major institutions in our culture are Government, Schools, Mass Media, and the Church. Satanism has definitely impacted each. Let's look at some of the results of his attacks within America.

FAMILY. Satan has always hated Family since God ordained it back in the Garden of Eden. Notice that the family in America is in steep decline. Not too long ago the family was generally comprised of a husband, wife, and children with extended members including other relatives by birth or marriage. The husband and wife have always been the core of the family. Despite problems caused by tragedies, and the different family models, the standard and basic structure remained the same. The effort to blur the idea of marriage began in 1960's, with unrestricted sex outside the bonds of marriage. It wasn't long before alternative marriage arrangements, such as communes, mate sharing, and living together were represented as social experimentation. Soon after, we began to see this gradually played out in television programming, generally introduced through comedy. Before long, it became widely acceptable. The New Age Movement has always espoused a communal atmosphere rather than the traditional family. Divorce, separation, domestic abuse, violence, children abuse, pedophilia, abortion and attacks against the masculinity of men are all being used to destroy the family. Even though it has been said that "It Takes A Village (To raise a child)" that is not biblical. Giving your child over to other people with different value systems and religious backgrounds is not wise. Acceptance and promotion of fornication and adultery continue in mockery of God's institution of marriage. The blurring of the lines has continued with the push to accept homosexual relationships as simply another alternative to the marriage of husband and wife. However, this is another ploy by Satan to steal the strength of the nation. It is a veiled attack against manhood, the love and relationship of the family and ultimately it undermines the foundational strength of the Military. The world does not want hear or to obey God (*Isaiah 6:9-10; Isaiah 28:9-13*). Replacing God's love with a counterfeit will only result in a counterfeit army. It may look like and walk like what God put in place, but it will never be the same. The harshness and rebellion that comes from disobedience to God may be blanketed by man's laws, but the natural laws still exist and the results of disobedience will be manifested but the results of disobedience is in plain sight.

MARRIAGE. The state of marriage is now weakened as an institution in the United States, with less people committing to it than ever. A study done by National Marriage Project at Rutgers University indicates the national marriage rate has dropped 43 percent over the past four decades to its lowest point ever and the blame for the declining trend is that more couples are opting for alternatives such as living together outside of marriage or putting off marriage until later in life. The breakdown of the family, has resulted in stronger peer culture, which includes "pop" culture and according to the study, nothing could be more anti-marriage than much of the popular culture.[53] Fundamentalists have been saying this for at least four decades to no avail. Instead, society has become increasingly, harsh, and more in tune with traditional Satanic values. We are now approaching critical mass and the alarm is sounding. Why are sociologists beginning to worry about severely declining marriages in this country? It is because case histories of dozens of cultures throughout the world have been studied and it is a known fact that no country can survive without the core unit of the family. Unless the institution of marriage and family can be reversed, America is facing serious issues.

CHILDREN. Both popular perceptions and epidemiological studies of the prevalence of child behavior problems suggest a steady increase in the number and intensity of school-age children's problem behaviors in recent years (Achenbach & Howell, 1993; Rahim & Cederblad, 1984). A nonclinical sampling of 413 concerning about childrearing difficulties, child behavior problems, and their own needs for support

---

53 David Popenoe. The State of Our Unions: The Social Health of Marriage in America. Rutgers University. Study co-authored by David Popenoe, sociologist from Rutgers University, and defender of Liberalism and Secular Humanism. http://www.cuttingedge.org/news/n1309.cfm

reported that raising young children is difficult. One of the top issues parents of adolescents complain about is teen attitude and backtalk. Disrespect, rudeness and rebellion are types of behavior that parents are schooled to tolerate on a regular basis. This lack of respect and discipline combined with lack of prayer in schools is a recipe for disaster.

Misconduct. A study done by the Rochester Institute of Technology in 2005 on childhood conduct disorder, attention deficit disorder with or without hyperactivity and antisocial personality and how they act as factors in predicting a child's future criminal activity provided us some insight. Children with childhood or adolescence onset of conduct disorder, attention deficit disorder with or without hyperactivity (ADHD), and/or antisocial personality disorder (ASPD) are more predisposed to a life of criminal activity. These disorders are often co-morbid, which means they affect the occurrence of one or the other, and in the instances where a child has more than one disorder, the higher his inclination for adult criminality will be. Males are more influenced by these disorders than females. Females usually learn to channel their behavioral problems or develop psychological problems or disorders. In some cases, this means that these women will become criminals. However, this does not mean that every child who is diagnosed with one or more of the disorders mentioned will be a criminal, but the rate of occurrence is significantly high. Around half or more of these children will commit serious criminal activities and develop arrest records. In short, there are distinct paths from childhood conduct problems to adult criminality.[54] To bring this home and make it clearer, let's take a look at a few statistics.

Crime. As of 2005, there were at least 2,225 child offenders serving life without parole sentences in U.S. prisons for crimes committed before they were age 18, of which 16 percent were between 13 and 15 years old at the time they committed their crimes, according to a joint report by Human Rights Watch and Amnesty International.

---

54 Tiffany L. Panko. Pathways From Childhood Conduct Problems to Adult Criminality, November 2005. Retrieved November, 2015 from: http://www.personalityresearch.org/papers/panko.html

An estimated 59 percent were sentenced to life without parole for their first-ever criminal conviction. Forty-two states currently have laws allowing children to receive life without parole sentences. While child advocacy groups seek new laws, there is evidence that while fewer youth are committing serious crimes such as murder, states are increasingly sentencing them to life without parole for the crimes they are committing.[55] It appears that we need salvation, and we need it while children are young. I have spoken with any number of parents who have said rather than influence their children, they believe it is better to allow their children to decide, when they grow up, if they want salvation. I really do not believe it is necessary to share my reaction in this book but isn't it amazing that we do not give our children a choice when it comes to going to secular school, circumcision, watching television, and the list goes on. How can a child make a "choice" about something they know nothing about or have absolutely no foundation? Many of such parents have made that decision out of rebellion against the way they were raised. Raising a child in the religion of a parent at least provides some fundamental knowledge of what religion is. It is a start. We need to protect and bring a fresh reminder of the meaning and hope of salvation!

GOVERNMENT AND LEADERSHIP. When America was founded in 1776-89, our Forefathers created the Government according to Christian principles. Christianity was so prevalent among the American population that it influenced all of society. Though not personally of the Christian faith, political leaders respected, demonstrated an appreciation for and held to the nation's views. Christian precepts were reflected in the major fundamental documents which created our system of Government from the Declaration of Independence, to the Constitution, and to our Bill of Rights. To hear people declare today that the Forefathers were not Christian or to dispute the obvious intentions concerning our nation, should cause an outcry from the Christian community. American born people in succeeding generations also have been influenced in

55 United States: Thousands of Children Sentenced to Life without Parole, National Study by Amnesty International and Human Rights, October 11, 2015. https://www.hrw.org/news/2005/10/11/united-states-thousands-children-sentenced-life-without-parole

their attitudes and actions by this Christian foundation. All of this has been a safeguard to ensure our nation is secure and protected by God. The last 200 years of freedom is testimony and evidence that our Constitution and our nation having been based upon the Bible, was right and it has served the nation well. Sadly, however, America is systematically rejecting our entire Christian heritage, Since before prayer was removed from the schools, Satan has been whittling away at our Christian foundation. In its place we can see our values are being replaced with a satanic-oriented foundation. Since all attitudes and actions of both the Governments and its people flow from their foundational base, we should not be surprised to see the many negative changes happening in our society. It is no wonder that our legal system is changing. It is no wonder that there is overstepping by the judicial branch in making laws. The world at large is laughing. There is no honor among thieves. We are seeing changes throughout society of individuals that clearly indicate that our Government is making decisions more in alignment with Satanic oriented values. If there is any question in your mind, let's look at them. Such values include self indulgence: selfishness, greed, lust of the eyes, lust of the flesh, and pride of life, anger, gluttony and laziness. This value system is all about who has the most power. Desire for wealth is so great that people will do almost anything to get it. Many people in the entertainment industry have spoken very frankly and openly about selling their souls to the devil. They actually did not realize how real the devil was until after signing their contracts. Similarly, there is an overwhelming desire also for immoral or illicit sex. Violence and murder are all fair gain – all of this is a part of the pop culture's obsession with death. The enemy has blinded the eyes and the minds of the unsuspecting. The principle of fidelity within marriage has been eroded due to infamous sexual escapades that have publicly flaunted and raged about from the highest of offices in the land. Collectively, all of this has damaged the institutions of family and marriage. It has naturally filtered over into government. People have become so confused that it is difficult for them to understand that they need salvation. This is what needs to come across the pulpit in Sunday morning sermons. If we do not save the idea of salvation by preaching, teaching and living it, then many people may never reap its benefits.

THE CHURCH. Satan is an experienced strategist. He knows he must weaken man's foundation in order to become successful so he continues to rage against the churches throughout the land. Why the church? Well the word "church" comes from the Greek word ekklesia which is defined as "an assembly" or "called-out ones." The root meaning of it is people. Most people people identify with their church as a building but Paul refers to the church in Romans 16:5—not as a church building, but a body of believers. He says to "... greet the church that is in their house." The church is the body of Christ. It is made up of believers in Jesus Christ and is comprised of two aspects:

The *universal church* consisting of those who have received salvation through faith and now have a personal relationship with Jesus Christ (*1 Corinthians 12:13 and John 3:16*)

The *local church, a* local body of believers (as described by Paul in Galatians 1:1-2) through which members of the church at large can fully apply the "body" principles of 1 Corinthians chapter 12: encouraging, teaching, and building one another up in the knowledge and grace of the Lord Jesus Christ

If we look at the churches in the book of Revelation Chapters 2 and 3, we can see their weakness and sin. One church lost its first love, another was seduced and fell prey to fornication, one was pagan and idolatrous, another deceived by her riches, one was lukewarm and hypocritical, and one was even dead but was completely unaware. False teaching was rampant and just as Paul warned the first century Christians about the demons that would seek to destroy them, John was forewarning the churches. Since we are the Church, we should take heed individually and corporately, to the warning. Satan's persecution of Smyrna is minor in comparison to what is planned for the post modernism Church.

Someone declared recently that Satan is raping the church, but let's talk about what is happening today. The wheat and tares are growing right alongside each other. In the parable of the wheat and the tares (*Matthew 13:24-30*), the workers realized the enemy had come along and sowed weeds among the good seeds. They asked permission to remove the tares but the farmer explained that it would be easier to tell the difference at harvest time. They would harvest all of it and then once the wheat was inside the barn, they would separate the tares into bundles and burn them. The tare is a poisonous weed which looks a lot like wheat in its early stages. However, if eaten by a person or an animal, nausea would occur, convulsions, and in certain circumstances, even death. Planting the tares is a spiteful act of malice. The enemy wants to destroy the crop and he thinks no one can tell the difference between the good and the bad. This is what is happening. Will everyone who goes to church go to heaven? I would like to think that if the rapture occurred at the next Sunday morning worship service, that the entire sanctuary where I attend would be raptured at that time. Well, according to the Bible, it's not going to happen. Someone will be left behind.

When we see how Satan is charging against the church, it is ugly, vile and even demonic. We see his work and attacks aimed in many areas of the church with specific intent of bringing into question the value and effectiveness of the church. Many of us are aware of some of his attacks in these areas.

Televangelists. Evangelists seen on TV, living lavish lifestyles while preaching a prosperity gospel message that does not conform to the Word of God have been investigated among complaints from people who had given their last dollars to in exchange for a promised return on their faith-inspired giving. The IRS and whistle blowing organizations have been working together to sort through perverted theology, corruption in religious organizations, and the operations of direct mail shops to determine how many damage and to what extent victims are exploited. The unregulated industry of televangelism is estimated to generate more than $1 billion. Watchdog groups, government agencies, the media, and other groups work undercover in order to expose the truth. Some ministries financial practices go against those set forth by the Evangelical Council for Financial Accountability, whose standards include maintaining an independent board of directors with at least five members and allowing the public to view its finances. This organization gained popularity after the televangelist scandals of the 1980s and the intent was to ensure transparency with the donors. While we have heard reports of how one Fort Lauderdale based televangelist, who at the height of success took in over $80 million annually appearing on every U.S. television market daily, put checks or cash in one pile while dumping the accompanying prayer requests into the trash, we know that Satan is both the tempter, deceiver and the accuser of the brethren. This is why saving salvation is needed. We get no joy out of these reports. We must always pray for those that are on the front line. Who can understand the temptation? Who can imagine the seemingly innocent opportunities that come to entrap the men and women of God? As some of them rise to the top, Satan sends someone over to have a conversation with them - just like he did in the Garden of Eden. He can make the offer sound so good. If the offer has anything to do with bringing you fame or fortune, you can be sure, it did not come from the Lord because we already have everything we need in Him. Beware lest we forget and take our eyes off the Lord!

We will only be as pure and holy as our relationship is with God. If we remain in humble submission to God, stay in prayer and permit the Holy Spirit to be our teacher and guide, He will protect us. We can find no fault in Him. There has been countless tax fraud sentencing, investigations into the opulent lifestyles of those that have used donations intended for ministry expansion, and charges against those that are taking advantage of ailing believers seeking miracle cures. This amid entertainment news and reports of unashamed acts of adultery, fornication, violence, divorce, embezzlement, homosexuality, pedophilia and outright heretical teaching has taken a toll on the gospel industry. The greed, outrageous conduct, lack of accountability (financial or spiritual), and general sense that they are untouchable affects the average person's perception and it has disillusioned many people.

Pastors and Leadership. Christianity Today, reported that at least 400 church leaders would be resigning after the list of customers to Ashley Madison was released in August 2015.[56] The exposure of adultery and the site itself are all reprehensible and sinful but a church leader falling into sin brings a reproach upon himself, the Church and the Lord Jesus. This encourages the world to continue in sin and to rebel against God (2 Samuel 12:14). More is expected of those who have accepted Christ as Lord and are upholding the standard of God's Word. More importantly, it falls on those who are leaders to carry and adhere to the standard. Sin is rebellion against God and His Law and leadership is held to a higher standard as well. They are recognized by the community as those who are the mouthpiece of God and they are held in esteem for spiritual guidance and instruction. Without leaders, where are the followers? It is no longer surprising to learn that the porn industry generates $13 billion each year in the United States but it is disheartening to know that 90% of boys and 60% of 10 girls have been exposed to pornography before the age of 18 with the average age of first exposure at approximately 11 years old. The real discouragement is in learning that it is no longer true that only the world is obsessed with sex and pornography. It is no longer limited to people outside the church walls. Statistics show that pastors and lay leaders also struggle with keeping themselves, pure. There are many who consider themselves not of this world – in other words, the church, and the bodies that inhabit the church pews, who are now struggling with this problem. Fifty percent of Christian men and 20% of Christian women say they are addicted to pornography. And the

56 Ed Stetzer. Expert: 400 Church Leaders Will Resign This Sunday Because Names Surfaced in Ashley Madison Hack, August 2015. http://www.relevantmagazine.com/slices/expert-400-church-leaders-will-resign-sunday-because-names-surfaced-ashley-madison-hack

most popular day of the week for viewing porn is Sunday. Fifty-one percent of pastors admit that pornography is a possible temptation. Nearly 20% of the calls received on Focus on the Family's Pastoral Care Line are for help with issues such as pornography and compulsive sexual behavior. Of 1,351 pastors surveyed on porn use at Rick Warren's website, Pastors.com, 54% said they had viewed internet pornography within the last year and 30% of those had visited within the last 30 days. Other surveys reveal that 63% of pastors surveyed confirm that they are struggling with sexual addiction or sexual compulsion including, but not limited to, the use of pornography, compulsive masturbation, or other secret sexual activity.

Music Department and Musicians. Sexual sin and deviant behavior does run deep. Accountability is important and there are great resources available whether online or with a therapist for every aspect of treatment. Amidst the moral decline and harsh poles of declining cultural relativism of the church, we can hear the cry of worship and outreach reform but, these are not greatest concern when it comes to the church. People are not dropping out of church necessarily because of these reasons. Even the scandals are not the driving force behind the decline in church attendance. There is something for more serious lurking beneath the surface and to top it off, the church seems to be totally blind to what is really happening. There are various reasons for people being turned off and away from church but none of these turnoffs are at the root of the problem. For example, people may complain about how often the offering plate is passed, how loud the music is, the unkindness, and some leave because it is too boring. However, it is when the pastor fails to preach the Word with conviction and when the church waters down the gospel to the point of compromising with the world, then it can no longer be effective. When the choir director or the musicians are in flagrant violation of God's laws, when discipleship is ignored, when the truth is not preached, when you cannot distinguish the church from the world, then what is the point? It's actually just the Pharisees all over again. Many are nice people, but they are religious, legalistic people. Many have the titles but not the anointing. If they are not authentic Christians (in the Biblical sense), that singular infirmity will hinder true worship.

If the musician plays the same instrument in the night club and then brings it to church, can the music be anointed? Can they usher people into God's presence? People can spot watered down gospel. They can recognize people who carry the nightclub swagger. They know when the truth has been compromised – they know because they do not feel conviction. Without conviction, there is no reason to change. They feel the disappointment of not being able to get cleansed. Without conviction, they cannot get rid of the guilt. They will walk away feeling frustrated and not truly understand why. They are unable to grieve or be convicted unless they are confronted with the seriousness of their sins. Sit outside any "church" in America and watch the people come out after the service. Is there any evidence that they have been in the presence of a holy God? In the Bible, people were frequently either devastated by God's holiness or horrified by their own sinfulness. Paul cautioned the saints in his day not to trifle concerning things consecrated to God, pointing out that such misbehavior had cost some their lives. Oh we need to keep salvation at the forefront.

Dumbing down or watering down the Word of God to attract the crowds is making a terrible mistake and God will hold us accountable. When a pastor moves away from the Lord's way, then the congregation loses its way. We can see very clearly that many have done that. As the church loses its way, those who should be very active and involved becomes more and more absent. It affects the level of involvement with the community as well. Real Christian service comes from a heartfelt response to God's work in us. Without solid biblical instruction, there will be no conviction or learning of what we are and should do. Preaching needs to be biblically sound, based on its principles and proclaimed with power and conviction.

However, the best remedy known to be tested and proven is salvation. Satan would have man to walk in darkness. It goes back to the days in the Garden of Eden when Eve entertained a conversation with Satan. Oh, how smooth was he? Slick talking, silvery tongued, he was able to trick her into disobeying God by encouraging her eyes to be wayward. God is able to keep those who will accept His Lordship and be obedient. This is a matter of decision.

MASS MEDIA. The media, which includes television, radio, movies, the internet, newspapers or magazines, is a significant force in America's modern culture. I almost hate to talk about it because although there are a lot of positives about the media, it seems the negatives far outweigh them. I once took a few steps back and wondered who could write such filth that we see in the programming. Then it occurred to me that only someone in darkness could offer up some terrible programming. Sociologists refer to the mass media as a mediated culture whereby the media reflects and creates the culture. Communities and individuals are bombarded constantly with messages from a multitude of sources including TV, billboards, and magazines, to name a few. These messages promote not only products, but moods, attitudes, and a sense of what is and is not important. We are witnessing a major cultural revolution that is having an incredible impact on our society. Yet, despite numerous warnings, few seem to understand what is really going on or where this surging wave of social change is taking us. In the last 50 years the electronic media—radio, television, movies, video games and now the Internet—have enveloped the globe and transformed nearly every aspect of our lives. This incredible power has a darker side. Because of its tremendous potential to influence culture, television is the most "effective propaganda vehicle" available today (Redeeming Television, Schultze, p. 49). The average person has no clue about how mass media operates, the personal agendas of scriptwriters and producers, the ultimate consequences to society of what is portrayed on the screen and how watching hours of television affects the developing human brain. Many assume today that when and what we watch is merely a matter of personal taste. Some claim that only "extreme right wing religious fanatics" become upset over the content of films and television and that "mature" individuals prefer the "adult content" of modern media entertainment. However, these assumptions are self-serving myths unsupported by actual evidence. In fact, knowledgeable members of the media and communications fields are increasingly vocal about the extremely detrimental effects of this modern electronic revolution. We need to understand how the media molds the world and the potential consequences of indiscriminate viewing on children, family, the community and our country. There is more at stake than many critics realize!

Electronic media has taken over and it has come about because of greed. The major television networks in America are owned by large corporations that are in business to make money. The goal of film studios is to generate profits through box office receipts. Television studios make money by attracting sizable audiences and selling to advertisers. This is one of the reasons sex and violence play such prominent roles in films and television. Sex and violence sell and this translates into cash. More important is the influences of personal agendas of writers and producers who desire to reshape society along the lines of their preferences. The movers and shakers in the media industry "are generally liberal... inclined toward secularism, left of center... [with a] radical bent for shaking up the status quo" (Redeeming Television, Schultze, pp. 151, 156).

Surveys indicate that 90 percent of Hollywood executives favor abortion, more than half feel that adultery is not wrong and almost 75 percent see nothing wrong with homosexuality (ibid.). Nearly 45 percent of this group claim no religious affiliation, and 93 percent seldom or never attend church. Entertainment created by such individuals is often in direct conflict with Judeo-Christian values that have anchored western societies for centuries. Film critic Michael Medved explains that this small group of liberal-minded social revolutionaries has turned the Hollywood dream factory into a "poison factory" that attacks religion, assaults the legitimacy of the family, promotes sexual perversions and glorifies ugliness (Hollywood vs. America, p.3). When we view entertainment, we enter a world created by people whose values are often at odds with our own—we need to be aware of what is happening.[57] We need to guard our minds and the minds of our children. We are talking about American entertainment media having adopted Satanic values.

The current level of media saturation has not always existed. Availability of all forms of media has catapulted, and programming is increasingly diverse with shows aimed to appeal to all ages, incomes, backgrounds, and attitudes. This widespread availability and exposure makes television the primary focus of most mass-media discussions. More recently, the Internet has increased its role exponentially. Together, the internet and television play a super powerful role in culture, as do other forms of media. Legislatures, media executives, local school officials, and sociologists have all debated the controversial question regarding the role that mass media play? While opinions vary as to the extent and type of influence the mass media wields, all sides agree that mass media is a permanent part of modern culture. American youth live in an environment saturated with media. They enjoy increasing access to television, movies, music, games, websites, and advertising—often on pocket-size devices. Given the prominent and growing role that media plays in the lives of U.S. children and adolescents, parents need to be aware that the more sexual content that kids see on television, the earlier they initiate sexual activity, and more likely they are to have an unplanned teen pregnancy. There is a causal but strong connection between youth exposure to violence in the media and violent or aggressive behavior and thoughts.[58]

It is clear that the war being waged is the same today as the one committed by Satan against the seven churches of Asia. The churches and congregations today are exhibiting the same kinds of problems.

57 Douglas S. Winnail. How the Media Mold the World, 2003 January-February.Television, movies and the Internet are having an effect on mankind that would have been unimaginable even a century ago. The media—print and electronic—shape our lives and our minds in ways that most fail to realize, and with sobering effects. Retrieved November, 2015 from: http://www.tomorrowsworld.org/magazines/2003/january-february/how-the-media-mold-the-world#sthash.A99phEs1.dpuf
58 Ibid.

We see the church embracing all of the lifestyles of the world. Many ministers and their families are living secret lives today and are being held hostage in order to prevent them from preaching the gospel truth. As a result, the different church ministries have forsaken God's commandments. Satan wants to destroy the church. If he can get people to no longer believe in the credibility of the witness of the leaders or members then he believes he can discredit any ministry associated with the church, thereby bringing down God's Church.

Has the Church become culturally irrelevant? We know that we are in a transition. This is evidenced by what is going on in our culture and in our church. Most of the statistics tell us that nearly 50% of Americans have no church home. In the 1980s, membership in the church had dropped almost 10%; then, in the 1990s, it worsened by another 12% drop-some denominations reporting a 40% drop in their membership. And now, over half way through the first decade of the 21st century, the figures continue to drop. What is going on with the Church in America? The United States Census Bureau Records give some startling statistics, backed up by denominational reports. In short, more than 4000 churches close their doors each year while we are seeing just over 1000 new churches. Between 1990 and 2000, approximately 4,500 new churches started. Every year, 2.7 million church members fall into inactivity which translates into the realization that people are leaving the church. The research indicates they are leaving because of disillusionment and hurt. This is a very broad description and some of this is a result of neglect, but what it means is people need salvation. From 1990 to 2000, the combined membership of all Protestant denominations in the USA declined by almost 5 million members (9.5 percent), while the US population increased by 24 million (11 percent) and some of that due to immigration. This in turn, influences our ratios. At the turn of the last century (1900), there was a ratio of 27 churches per 10,000 people, as compared to the close of this century (2000) where we have 11 churches per 10,000 people in America. Now the United States ranks third (3rd) following China and India in the number of people who are not professing Christians; in other words, the U.S. is becoming an ever increasing "un-reached people group." Half of all churches in the US have failed to add new members to their ranks in the last few years. So, apart from dying, why are the people leaving?

My father often preached about the "gates of hell" and I have seen the phrase referenced in Christian books countless times. The second half of Matthew 16:18 has to be one of the top ten favorite Bible promises. I can hear the voices right now: "Think about the picture here. Jesus says the gates of hell will not prevail against the church. Now tell me, how do gates prevail? When have you ever seen gates marching? They do not attack or retreat. They fortify. They are there to hold their ground. That's all. Hell is not on the offensive. The church is on the offensive. The church is marching in this world, but on up to Zion and as the very face of darkness and wickedness in high places appear, the church takes the territory by force, reclaiming what the enemy has stolen. We will prevail. It's time to put the Devil on the run. It's time to save souls and destroy strongholds. It's time to reclaim this world for Christ. "The gates of hell shall not prevail against us." We have the promise of salvation from the Lord and we will not give up; we are saving it by keeping it ever before us and telling others. We are commissioned by Jesus Christ who shed His blood for us, to go into all the world and make disciples.

3.2 The High Point of Our Salvation

For centuries skeptics have argued that if an all-powerful God really does exist but refuses to put an end to evil, then obviously, he could not possibly be good. But God is not responsible for evil nor for the suffering of this world. Man introduced sin into the world through human rebellion (*Romans 5:12*). In the final analysis, we must acknowledge that we simply are not qualified to judge God. Even the patriarch Job had to learn this lesson when, out of his pain, he became very critical, questioning the Lord's wisdom. God gave him an examination to show him the greatness of God and the limitations of man (*Job 38-41*). Job was in no position to subject the works of the Almighty to critical analysis. "O the depth of the riches both of the wisdom and the knowledge of God! How unsearchable are his judgments, and his ways past tracing out! For who hath known the mind of the Lord? or who hath been his counselor?" (*Romans 11:33-34*).

The argument against the goodness of God on the basis of earthly evil is groundless. God's goodness is revealed by His sovereignty and providential activity that he richly provides for His creation through the skillfully designed systems that he ordained for regulation of this planet. For those who have discernment, the manifestation of God's good character is evident in abundance. All that flows out from God including His creation, decrees, prophecies, laws, providences, power can only be considered good. "And God saw everything that He had made, and, behold, it was very good" (Genesis 1:31). Thus, the "goodness" of God is seen, first, in Creation. Then everything He gives is good. "Every good gift and every perfect gift is from above, coming down from the Father of lights, with whom can be no variation, neither shadow that is cast by turning" (James 1:17). In spite of the fact that this planet is cursed with the effects of sin (cf. Romans 8:20-22), there is still ample testimony of Heaven's goodness. The Lord's goodness is evidenced by the revelation of himself to humankind, both abstractly and concretely. He has wonderfully revealed himself in the intricacies of a brilliantly designed Universe. "The heavens declare the glory of God; And the firmament showeth his handiwork" (Psalm 19:1).

"For the invisible things of him since the creation of the world are clearly seen, being perceived through the things that are made, even his everlasting power and divinity; that they may be without excuse" (*Romans 1:20*). God's goodness is also manifest through the revelation of Jesus Christ (*Hebrews 1:1-2*), which, in the context of the book of Hebrews, is the New Testament itself. We can see His goodness in the amazing unity of the Bible, its astounding prophecies, and its precision. The more closely we study humanity, the more apparent is

God's goodness.

There have been countless testimonies of God redeeming lives from destruction, restoring sight to the blind, saving marriages, healing diseases, making a way out of no way, providing answers, renewing relationships, performing miracles – who could possibly believe He is other than good!

The Psalmist said, "I will praise Thee, for I am fearfully and wonderfully made: marvelous are Thy works." (Psalm 139:14). Everything about the human body attests to the goodness of God. Truly, "The earth is full of the goodness of the Lord" (Psalm 33:5). God's benevolence appears in other places – the wonderful variety of flavors in our foods, the vibrant colors in nature, the enjoyment of day to day living and all that He allows us to experience through our senses. We could have made it through life without all of the magnificent wonders of nature, but He sought to please us with beautiful flowers and delightful fragrances. Indeed, "The tender mercies of the Lord are over all His works" (*Psalm 145:9*).

The goodness of God is seen especially in that when man transgressed the law, the wrath of God did not descend at one. Whereas God could have deprived humanity of some many things, He instead, offered man mercy and extended grace along with judgment. Regardless of man's fallen state, God balanced good with everything. With comparatively rare exceptions, men and women experience a far greater number of days of health, than they do of sickness and pain. There is much more goodness and mercy in our lives than the misery of this world.

Despite the tragedy of human sin which is reflected in the insolent attitudes of today's ungrateful world (*Jeremiah 11:10; Acts 7:57*), God has remained faithful and good. Sin is transgression of the law of God (*1 John 3:4*), and missing the mark or failing to do what is right (*James. 4:17*). It is deserving of death and yet, God has proven His love for humanity. The ultimate of God's goodness is perhaps most supremely demonstrated through redemption. He has made provision for sinful man's condition and to redeem him from the very clutches of evil. Scripture declares that "all have sinned, and fall short of the glory of God" (*Romans 3:23*). Sin has left sickness and disease, death, unhappiness, and those who remain it have the promise of eternal death.

God was never under any obligation to redeem humanity from the clutches of sin. The fact that He gave us His only begotten Son speaks volumes of His love for us. Many things could be said and many verses could be brought to bear to show God's goodness. We could spend many hours over many messages covering all of the aspects of God's goodness. We should remind ourselves of this aspect of God's nature and consider what means to us. "For while we were yet weak, in due season Christ died for the ungodly. (*Romans 5*). For scarcely for a righteous man will one die: for peradventure for the good man some one would even dare to die. But God commends his own love toward us, in that, while we were yet sinners, Christ died for us" (6-8). Notice how we are described — weak, ungodly, sinners, and enemies subject to divine wrath (9-10).

We are unable to fathom or to express the amazing goodness of our Creator as expressed in the gift of Christ (*2 Corinthians 9:15*). "The goodness of God endureth continually" (*Psalm 52:1*) The "goodness" of God respects the perfection of His nature: "God is light, and in Him is no darkness at all" (*1 John 1:5*). There is such an absolute perfection in God's nature and nothing is wanting nor defective in it, and nothing can be added to it to make it better. He is originally good, good of Himself, for all creatures are good only by participation and communication from God. He is essentially good; not only good, but goodness itself: the creature's good is a super added quality, in God it is His essence. He is infinitely good; the creature's good is but a drop, but in God there is an infinite ocean or gathering together of good. He is eternally and immutably good, for He cannot be less good than He is; as there can be no addition made to Him, so no subtraction from Him. (Thomas Manton).

Many in the Church today are frequently told we are sinful, terrible human beings. The problem with this thinking is it suggests that all we are is sinners. The Bible begins in a different place. The truth is, the first thing we learn about human beings in the book of Genesis is that we bear the image of the Almighty God. This means we are not only sinners. We may come from the dust of the earth, but we are made in the image of the one who was crushed beneath the indignity of sin. God saw the mess humanity had made of His beautiful creation, but in His deep love for us, He did not abandon us. Rather, in Jesus, He became one of us. Only a sovereign merciful God would make us in His image, forgive us for our sin, sacrifice His own son for us, and still call us His beloved children.

Satan is attacking the people of God, the Lamb and the Word of God today because he wants to destroy the protection – the salvation, that Jesus Christ offers. He is working a multi-channel, daily operational plan in order to convince people that he is in control and there is nothing they can do now. The kingdom of darkness is trying to rule our world today. It is as real as light and darkness. The spiritual blindness instilled into people's hearts is designed to promote fear and to make our world a dark place to live. The darkness is designed to lead us to a point where every thought and inclination of our hearts is evil continually. We must not forget. The enemy did it once already; he wants to do it again (*Genesis 6:5*). However, God extended His love and mercy then, and we can be assured that He will do it again!

In the following verses Paul describes such a world. He says they are darkened in their understanding and separated from the life of God because of the ignorance that is in them due to the hardening of their hearts. Having lost all sensitivity, they have given themselves over to sensuality so as to indulge in every kind of impurity, with a continual lust for more. (*Ephesians 4:18-19*). The enemy continues to promote religious division and distractions in order to discredit Christianity. Many church goers are calling into question whether there really is a God. Others are confused about their identity. Still others are fighting over secondary doctrines or teachings that are not determining factors for entering into heaven.

Competitions among churches and refusing to unite against the enemy is a self-destructive foolish decision. Misuse of the house of God and money that pours into the storehouse is shameful and nothing but temptation from the devil. Who would believe that elders and ushers would steal money right out of the offering plate and feel no shame? The attack on the church is not always aimed from outside; Satan has strategically placed people within the church. He wants people to believe that there is nothing that can be done to stop the decadence of society; he wants to turn the church upside down so as to weaken the church of God. The only reason it could be hopeless is if we refuse the blood of the Lamb and the Word of God. Satan is definitely out to make war against God's saints. However, as He makes war against the children of God, let us remember. We are yet assured of God's protection in the face of spiritual battles. Nothing shall separate us from the love of God! The Lord is the greatest and above all others. His goodness is unmatched for it is the essence of His eternal nature. As God is infinite in power from all eternity, before there was any display of it or any act of omnipotence, so was He eternally good before man was put on the earth. The first manifestation of this Divine perfection was in giving being to all things. "Thou art good, and doest good" (*Psalm 119:68*). God has in Himself an infinite and inexhaustible treasure of all blessedness enough to fill all things.

Jesus warned us and gave us some important clues for discerning the approach of the end times. "Many will come in my name, claiming, 'I am the Christ,' and will deceive many. You will hear of wars and rumors of wars, but see to it that you are not alarmed. Such things must happen, but the end is still to come. Nation will rise against nation, and kingdom against kingdom. There will be famines and earthquakes in various places. All these are the beginning of birth pains." (*Matthew 24:5-8*). An increase in false messiahs, an increase in warfare, and increases in famines, plagues, and natural disasters—

these are signs of the end times. In this passage, though, we are given a warning: we are not to be deceived, because these events are only the beginning of birth pains; the end is still to come.

The goodness of God appeared most illustriously when He sent forth His Son "made of a woman, made under the law, to redeem them that were under the law, that we might received the adoption of sons" (*Galatians 4:4, 5*) Then it was that a multitude of the heavenly host praised their Maker and said, "Glory to God in the highest and on earth peace, good-will toward men" (*Luke 2:14*).

God brings salvation through grace that is available to all me (*Titus 2:11*). Man cannot question God's goodness. O that men would praise the Lord for His goodness, and for His wonderful works to the children of men!" (Psalm 107:8).The goodness of God is our lifeline and because His goodness endureth forever, we should never be discouraged. "The Lord is good, a stronghold in the day of trouble, and He knoweth them that trust in Him" (*Nahum 1:7*).

When others mistreat us, we should be all the more determined to give thanks unto the Lord, because He is good! No matter how strong we are on our own, we all encounter attacks where we may be challenged. Pray for your enemies - that they will come to Jesus. We have prayed many prayers for people who sought to do us harm and asked that they would be spared from God's wrath. It is not the Lord's desire that any should perish but they could into the knowledge of Christ. We should want what God desires for us. He knows, in His infinite wisdom who will heed the call. He knows who desires to live for Him. The most catastrophic blunder man we can make is to try to combat Satan without submitting to God. Many are disarmed by believing the devil is not fierce. We must decide to submit to God. His promise is, "Submit yourselves therefore to God. Resist the devil, and he will flee from you" (*James 4:7*). To resist Satan without submitting to God is only half the strategy.

Even after recognizing the enemy and deciding to seek help, we must still put on the armor. God's arsenal is open to us. The battle array comes in all sizes. "Wherefore take unto you the whole amour of God, that you may be able to withstand in the evil day, and having done all, to stand. Stand therefore, having on the breastplate of righteousness; and your feet shod with the preparation of the gospel of peace; Above all, taking the shield of faith, wherewith you shall be able to quench all the fiery darts of the wicked. And take the helmet of salvation, and the sword of the Spirit, which is the word of God" (*Ephesians 6:13-17*).

There have been countless testimonies of God redeeming lives from destruction, restoring sight to the blind, saving marriages, healing diseases, making a way out of no way, providing answers, renewing relationships, performing miracles – who could possibly believe He is other than good!

Life Application for Personal Reflection

Man's Need for Salvation

1. Since the essence of sin is selfishness and because of it, man fails to conform to God's moral law in behavior, attitude or in his nature, and therefore is destructive to God's plan for our holiness, what are your thoughts pertaining man's need for salvation? Should man have a choice?
2. What temptations have you faced or are you now facing? What can we, as Christians, do to guard against sin?

Suggested Reading

Man's Need for Salvation

1. Booker, Richard. *The Miracle of the Scarlet Thread,* for new believers and seasoned Christians-this practical book helps the Bible come alive with fresh insights, Shippensburg, PA: Destiny Image Publishers, 1981.
2. Hodges, Charles. *Hodge's Systematic Theology Collection* (3 Volumes), Hendrickson Publishers (June 1999).
3. Horton, Michael. *For Calvinism,* Grand Rapids, MI: Zondervan, 2011.
4. Lucado, Max. *Grace: More Than We Deserve, Greater Than We Imagine,* Nashville, TN: Thomas Nelson Publishers, 2012

I Bowed on My Knees and Cried Holy

Lyrics by LARI GOSS

I dreamed of a city called Glory,
So bright and so fair.
When I entered the gates I cried, "Holy"
The angels all met me there:
They carried me from mansion to mansion,
And oh the sights I saw,
But I said, "I want to see Jesus,
The One who died for all."

Chorus

Then I bowed on my knees and cried,
"Holy, Holy, Holy."
I clapped my hands and sang, "Glory,
Glory to the Son of God."
I bowed on my knees and cried,
"Holy, Holy, Holy."
Then I clapped my hands and sang, "Glory,
Glory to the Son of God."

As I entered the gates of that city,
My loved ones all knew me well.
They took me down the streets of Heaven;
Such scenes were too many to tell;
I saw Abraham, Jacob and Isaac
Talked with Mark, and Timothy
But I said, "I want to see Jesus,
'Cause He's the One who died for me."

REFLECTIONS

MAN NEEDS SALVATION

In the 1950s a psychologist, Stanton Samenow, and a psychiatrist, Samuel Yochelson, sharing the conventional wisdom that crime is caused by environment, set out to prove their point. They began a 17-year study involving thousands of hours of clinical testing of 250 inmates in the District of Columbia.

To their astonishment, they discovered that the cause of crime cannot be traced to environment, poverty, or oppression. Instead, crime is the result of individuals making, as they put it, wrong moral choices. In their 1977 work The Criminal Personality, they concluded that the answer to crime is a "conversion of the wrong-doer to a more responsible lifestyle."

In 1987, Harvard professors James Q. Wilson and Richard J. Herrnstein came to similar conclusions in their book Crime and Human Nature. They determined that the cause of crime is a lack of proper moral training among young people during the morally formative years, particularly ages one to six.

- Christianity Today

Source: Stanton Samenow, Text Illustration shared by SermonCentral, December 2005. Christianity Today, August 16, 1993, p. 30. Retrieved November 2015 from http://www.sermoncentral.com/illustrations/sermon-illustration-stories-becomingachristian-23298.asp

We all want someone who will love us forever, through thick and thin, no matter how we look, what we do, or what we become. Human beings are rarely capable of this kind of love because it is almost impossible to prevent self from getting in the way. Unconditional love is the highest form of love and it is not easy. On the other hand, unconditional love is easy for God -- with his infinite patience and boundless capacity to forgive. He is invincible; you cannot hurt Him. But humans are vulnerable. We often have hidden motives and want to know what's in it for us. If we get hurt or betrayed, the disappointment is often enough to destroy our love and faith.

Even unconditional, genuine love does not merely involve passive acceptance and blind forgiveness. In fact, it can be quite the opposite! Unmitigated love can actually be tough and demanding. When our children do bad things, we give them stern messages and punish them because of our love for them. Though unconditional love may be selfless but it is not self-destructive. We can be thankful to God for His love.

– The Author

The History of Calvinism and Controversy

◆ ◆ ◆

"It wasn't a potential atonement actuated by the sinner, it was an
actual atonement initiated by the savior."
John F. MacArthur Jr.

Calvinism has shaken theological minds for centuries. It has spawned movements, sparked controversy and spearheaded political and theological revolutions. Wars have been fought both to defend and destroy it. It has stirred countries such as Switzerland, Germany, France, Spain, England and America.

In modern America those who hold to "free will theology" are uncomfortable at the thought of the Calvinistic perspective. Arminians by-pass the "Calvinistic scriptures" in order to maintain their theology. The main problem arises when one seeks to term this theology Calvinistic instead of Biblical. The Arminian is taught to reject the findings of Calvinistic doctrines because they were brought up that way and took the pastor's word at face value. There has been much debate on the validity of both theological views, that many have put forth their perspectives based on personal opinion, conjecture and their drive to persuade others to join them. The Bible is our authority and if arguments are not predicated on Scripture, they are not valid. God warns that we should neither add to nor take away from His Word.

At the center of Calvinism was a Frenchman named John Calvin, whose father was administrator to a Bishop and wanted Calvin to become a priest. Although Calvin started working in the church at the age of 12 in preparation for priesthood training and an ecclesiastical career, as life would have it, the plague hit the Noyon commune where he lived at the cathedral. He was sent along with the Bishop's children to Paris and before long, he found himself in college. Later he switched to another school of higher learning where the atmosphere was more ecclesiastical and where he was introduced to sound training in dialectics and scholastic philosophy. He studied law, became quite an avid reader; and as a student of philosophy, he was quite successful in rising above his competitors in oral debates.

He was frequently called upon to lecture concerning the law. He was taught Greek and after studying the New Testament scriptures in the original language, he became dissatisfied and changed his mind about becoming a priest. He fell out of favor with the cathedral chapter back at home and eventually left the Catholic Church. Calvin's lectures and writings took on a life of their own. His influence and perspective on Christian life according to the evangelical model became center stage as many sought him for counsel. He became known as the founder of the comprehensive theological system chiefly known as Calvinism today. However, he was actually the champion rather than the founder."[59]

Distinguished by its view of God and His relationship to man, the system of Calvinism bases it doctrine solely upon God's Word and God's sovereignty. It holds that by God's sovereign grace, He can do whatever He desires with His creation. It also holds that God

---

[59] Saint-Clair, Geoggrey, Who's Who in the Reformation, Catholic Education Resource Center, retrieved November 2015 from http://www. catholiceducation.org/en/religion-and-philosophy/apologetics/whos-who-in-the-reformation.html . Calvin possessed political influence well beyond that of a mere pastor or civic leader.

predestines people for salvation, that Jesus died only for those who are predestined and that God regenerates the individual in such a manner by which it becomes possible to make a choice to accept God. It also encourages the belief that it is impossible for those who are redeemed to lose their salvation.

The Calvinistic Reformation was a premier turning point in history. To this day, it continues to be controversial. It has not been limited to the span of Calvin's life. Other great Calvinistic or Reformed theologians, impelled by the Roman Catholic counteract, have greatly influenced England for hundreds of years. The Counter-Reformation, also referred to as the Catholic revival, was a comprehensive effort composed of four major parts: an ecclesiastical or restructuring, religious orders, spiritual movements and political impact. The hope was to try to reconvert areas such as Sweden and England that were at one time Roman Catholic. But Calvinism has persisted.

Though King Henry VIII was exalted for his defense of the seven sacraments and deemed Holy Defender of the faith, Calvin seemed seemed convinced that the King was only familiar with the teachings he had adapted from the Roman Catholic Church. With the succession of Edward IV, Calvin began to exercise a direct influence upon the Anglican Church and the Reformation.[60] It has always been intended that Christianity should permit people to worship in a language they understand. Even though Edward was only nine when he came to the throne, his mother's brother, the duke of Somerset, was appointed Regent. Church services were put in common language instead of Latin.

An Act of Uniformity in 1549 provided for a use of the book of Common Prayer. Its second printing was more Protestant and reflected the Calvinistic points of view in theology and church worship. Then Queen Mary Tudor came to the throne. Unlike her father, King Henry VIII, she wanted to reform the church back to

60 C. Matthew McMahon, A Short History of Calvinism, the Reformation, and England, *An historical sketch of the beginnings of Calvinism.* Retrieved November, 2015 from: http://www.apuritansmind.com/the-reformation/a-short-history-of-calvinism-by-dr-c-matthew-mcmahon

Catholicism. She persecuted the Protestant churches severely and killed three hundred of those who would oppose her; so as a result many fled to Switzerland, including Calvin, to find refuge.[61] During the persecutions of Queen Mary, the Geneva Bible, translated by Theodore Beza and John Calvin, came into existence and was the most popular Bible within the European countries even after the famous version of 1611 was introduced. The Protestant martyrs during the time of Bloody Mary compelled John Foxe to write his book, *"Foxe's Book of Martyrs"* recounting the deaths of over one hundred martyrs.[62] Foxe was convinced that the Roman Catholic Pope of the Counter Reformation which was forced by Queen Mary, was the Antichrist of Revelation and that this was a time of persecution and Satanic attack against the saints.

The reign of Queen Elizabeth was an answer to prayer. Calvin's theological influence reigned supreme and continued throughout the seventeenth century. His work, Institutes of the Christian Religion, was revised six times during her reign and was widely used throughout the established church of England.[63] It was used as a foundation for the next generation. *The 42 Articles*, which had been drawn up shortly before Edward IV's death, were restored as doctrinal affirmation of the Church of England and later revised to Queen Elizabeth's prescribed 39 Articles. As a result of the Reformation under Queen Elizabeth, the English Bible was brought to the people. England became the champion of Protestantism in Europe and helped the Dutch and French Calvinistic Protestants against their Roman Catholic rulers.

Queen Elizabeth did clean up the corruption, somewhat, in the English church, but only with considerable help from the very much

---

61 J. I. Packer has stated in his book on Puritanism that Mary Tudor was afraid one man, John Owen; not because he had militant power, but because he had written a book, The Death of Death in the Death of Christ, that she felt was anointed by God. He was the only man that ever opposed her and lived. (Owen's book has never been disputed by any theological perspective. It is one of the leading Calvinistic works which is exhaustive; it focus on the limited atonement of Christ and completely destroys the Arminian perspective of man's free will in salvation and Universal Redemption.)

62 Edited by William Byron Forbush, One of the great English classics. History of Christian Martyrs. After the Bible itself, no book so profoundly influenced early Protestant sentiment. It is more than a record of persecution. It is an arsenal of controversy and a source of edification." Retrieved November, 2015 from: http://www.ccel.org/ccel/foxe/martyrs/files/martyrs.html

63 Published first in 1536, the Institutes of the Christian Religion is John Calvin's magnum opus. Extremely important for the Protestant Reformation, the Institutes has remained important for Protestant theology for almost five centuries. Written to "aid those who desire to be instructed in the doctrine of salvation," the Institutes, which follows the ordering of the Apostle's Creed, has four parts. The first part examines God the Father; the second part, the Son; the third part, the Holy Spirit; and the fourth part, the Church. Through these four parts, it explores both "knowledge of God" and "knowledge of ourselves" with profound theological insight.

enthusiastic Puritans. Under the leadership of William Ames and William Perkins with their interpretations of Calvinism, the Puritans had their greatest influence at Cambridge which they deemed their headquarters. Eventually, in 1593, Elizabeth passed an act against the Puritans in order to restrain them; they had to attend Anglican Church or become imprisoned by the decree. This worked for some time until other sects emerged from the Puritans and they grew in number.

James I, known as James IV of Scotland, came to the throne after the death of Elizabeth in 1603. The King James Version of the Bible was inaugurated by his decree. He adapted the full extent of Calvinism and wrote four books on that theology. King James, though corrupt himself, sought to prove his Calvinistic loyalty by punishing what he considered to be heresy. The Calvinists disagreed vigorously in the way he went about his Christianity. In short, during the reigns of both Queen Elizabeth and Kings James, many heretics were burned at the stake. Their greatest adversary was Arminianism (the name comes from Professor Jacob Harmensz; Latin for Harmensz is Arminian, thus, Jacob Arminius, and yes, Arminius was executed). The opponents of Arminianism and Calvinism finally debated it out at Dordtrecht. The victor was the orthodox Calvinistic theology. Summing up the council of Dort, the acrostic TULIP was formed stating a basic premise of the theology of Calvin; 1) Total depravity, 2) Unconditional election, 3) Limited atonement, 4) Irresistible grace, and 5) Perseverance of the saints.[64] Thus in orthodox Calvinism the sovereignty of God was reasserted against the free will of man.[65]

Charles I gained the throne after the death of James I. Charles held to Arminianism, not because it was a better theology, but because he was convinced that it would offer a suitable inspiration for a working

---

64 C. Matthew McMahon, The TULIP doctrine of Calvinism is not a comprehensive look at the doctrine. Calvinism is often seen as the five-point doctrine but this is a common misconception. Calvinism is hundreds of points which come together in a unified whole. TULIP is only a very brief, basic, look at Calvinism and an easy way to remember it. Sometimes people will say they are a three point Calvinist or a four point Calvinist, but this cannot be so. Calvinism as a whole cannot be broken down into separate parts just because that person doesn't feel that he\ she cannot cope with a certain perspective. Three and four point Calvinists are simply confused Arminians.

65 The Synod of Dort is not the only council which condemned Arminianism. Throughout the entirety of church history, at each council, synod or diet, one can find that one of the Arminian doctrines, or the whole system of Arminianism has been condemned at one time or another. Only since the birth of the Charismatic movements of Wesley, Pentecostals and Neo-Pentecostals have the Arminian heresy come to life again.

partnership of kings and priests against Puritan troublemakers. To believe a free will as a theological theory meant to accept the King's will in practice. Calvin, being one of the radicals of the faith, had devastated the old order of Catholicism. He challenged traditional roles, authorities, popes, councils, ecclesiastical customs, the role of the clergy over the laity, the hierarchy, the validity of the canon law, dogmas about purgatory, the sacrifice of the mass and all its related Medieval practices. He challenged the whole system of man's contribution to salvation. As a result, the Word of God and Christ became the central focus in the theological interpretation of the Bible with the new emphasis on the promises of God and the benefits of Christ. It is easy to see the impact which the Calvinistic doctrine had on England and its surrounding countries as well. Calvin's theology has not only affected the thoughts of sixteenth century England but also of the modern world. His theology was carried along to this country with the Puritans and Reformers giving doctrinal orthodoxy reign in this country as well.[66]

Many Calvinists believe that Calvinism is the pure gospel of the Christian Church – and it does not matter that the majority of the Christian Church has not been Calvinists. If you are not a Calvinist, then the general consensus is that you are not saved. Not all hold to this but many of them do believe that Calvinism contains the truth of God therefore it should be defended against all enemies because when you attack Calvinism, you are attacking God Himself.

4.1 Three Theological Systems

Since we have nose-dived into this subject with its meaning, some of the controversies, and how it all got started, it seemed worthwhile to identify at a very high level, the three (3) most common theological views first. They are not in any particular order Arminianism, Pelagianism and Calvinism.

---

66 C. Matthew McMahon, A Short History of Calvinism, the Reformation, and England, *An historical sketch of the beginnings of Calvinism*,http://www.apuritansmind.com/the-reformation/a-short-history-of-calvinism-by-dr-c-matthew-mcmahon, Calvin's theology is not a unique theology; Calvin did not create this theology single-handed. It is only a rehashing of the teachings of Augustine of Hippo and the Apostle Paul, not to mention the rest of the Biblical authors. His theology is a systematic approach to the promise, covenant, and providence teachings of the grace of God found throughout the Scriptures.

1. Arminianism, named for Dutch reformed theologian Jacobus Arminius (1560–1609) a student of Beza (successor of Calvin), is based on his theological ideas and those of his historic supporters (Remonstrants). His teachings held to the five Solae of the Reformation, but were distinct in some ways from particular teachings of Martin Luther, Zwingli, John Calvin, and other Protestant Reformers. Arminianism was originally articulated in the Remonstrance (1610), a theological statement signed by 45 ministers and submitted to the States-General of the Netherlands. The Five Articles of Remonstrance asserted the following:

◆ Salvation (and condemnation on the day of judgment) was conditioned by the graciously enabled faith (or unbelief) of man

◆ The Atonement is qualitatively adequate for all men, "yet that no one actually enjoys [experiences] this forgiveness of sins, except the believer..." and thus is limited to only those who trust in Christ

◆ "That man has not saving grace of himself, nor of the energy of his free will," and unaided by the Holy Spirit, no person is able to respond to God's will

◆ The (Christian) grace "of God is the beginning, continuance, and accomplishment of any good", yet man may resist the Holy Spirit

◆ Believers are able to resist sin through grace, and Christ will keep them from falling, but whether they are beyond the possibility of ultimately forsaking God, "must be more particularly determined."

Many Christian denominations have been influenced by Arminian views on the will of man being freed by grace prior to regeneration, notably the Baptists in the 16th century, (See *A History of the Baptists Third Edition* by Robert G. Torbet) and the Methodists in the 18th century and the Seventh-day Adventist. The original beliefs of Jacobus Arminius himself are commonly defined as Arminianism, but more broadly, the term may embrace the teachings of Hugo Grotius, John Wesley, and others as well.

Classical Arminianism, to which Arminius is the main contributor, and Wesleyan Arminianism, to which John Wesley is the main contributor, are the two main schools of thought. Wesleyan Arminianism is often identified with Methodism. Louis Berkhof, in his *Systematic Theology*, takes a few shots at Arminians by noting that Arminians refer to sin as a disease and that Arminians will themselves to salvation. Arminians reject the view of the loss of human freedom. Arminius believed that, apart from the grace and goodness of God, no person could be saved. He taught that salvation is a gracious work of God and not by works (*John 1:12-13; Ephesians 2:8-9; Titus 3:5-7*). In summary, Arminius held that men are slaves to sin as well.

Calvinism and Arminianism share both history and many doctrines, and the history of Christian theology. Arminianism is related to Calvinism historically. However, because of their differences over the doctrines of divine predestination and election, many people view these schools of thought as opposed to each other. In short, the difference can be seen ultimately by whether God allows an individual freedom of choice to supersede or resist God's desire to save all of mankind or if God's grace is irresistible and limited to only some (in Calvinism). Put another way, is God's sovereignty shown, in part, through allowing freedom of choice? Many consider the theological differences to be crucial differences in doctrine, while others find them to be relatively minor.

2. Pelagianism, named after Pelagius (354, 420 or 440), is the belief that original sin did not taint human nature and that man is still capable of choosing good or evil without special Divine aid. Generally associated with the rejection of original sin and the practice of infant baptism. Beliefs include:

◆ Death did not come to Adam from a physical necessity, but through sin.
◆ New-born children must be baptized because of original sin.
◆ Justifying grace is available for forgiveness of past sins and avoidance of future sins.

◆ The grace of Christ will help one to obey God's commandments.

◆ Without God's grace it is absolutely impossible to perform good works.

◆ Believers must confess to sin.

◆ The saints also have humility.

3. Calvinism. A system of theology which holds to all the essentials of the faith, such as the full authority of Scripture and the deity of Christ. Historic Calvinism has been a bulwark against the inroads of Rationalism and Liberalism. All Evangelical theologies agree that salvation is solely by God's grace, but Calvinism alone says that it is sovereignly given to whomever God chooses. To fully understand the words, then, one must understand the Calvinist teaching on the sovereignty of God and what is also referred to as the doctrines of grace." These are usually summed up as the Five Points of Calvinism by the popular acronym TULIP:

◆ Total depravity

◆ Unconditional election

◆ Limited atonement

◆ Irresistible grace, and

◆ Perseverance of the saints

Calvinism stresses the five great doctrines rediscovered in the Protestant Reformation, namely *Scripture alone, Grace alone, Faith alone, Christ alone and to God alone be the glory*. Calvinism is without question the one system that unequivocally denotes that God is sovereign. It is not a compromising faith. Calvinism is an old theology taught in both testaments of the Bible. Many of the early church fathers taught it, especially the great Augustine. Most of the Protestant Reformers were either Calvinists or in basic agreement with its theology, i.e., Martin Luther. The English and American Puritans believed in Calvinism. John Bunyan and Matthew Henry, and the later well known Calvinist preachers and theologians include the likes of Charles Hodge, Charles Haddon Spurgeon, Martin Lloyd-Jones and Jonathan Edwards are all well known for their forthrightness and position. Calvinism has thrived in Britain, Holland and America. Most Protestant denominations that originated in the Reformation are founded on official confessions of faith that are clearly Calvinistic, such as the Westminster Confession (Presbyterian), the Canons of Dort (Reformed), the Thirty-nine Articles (Episcopalian), the Baptist Confession of 1689 (Baptists), the Savoy Declaration (Congregational) and many others. Historic Lutheranism is very close to Calvinism. Our world has changed over the years but Calvinism, which is quite old, has stood the test of time.[67]

4.2 Biblical Defense and a Few Theological Greats

As far back as I can remember, there was some kind of order to my Christian life. There was church and in home Bible studies three or four times during the week. God was consulted on everything. We did not play cards, watch much TV, or go to the movies. The church we attended was founded in 1903 by nine men of which several were Puritans and the others were diverse. The founders also included a diverse group of people which was definitely not allowed in the mountains of Tennessee or North Carolina. However, of all those years in tent meetings, Bible training camps and other assemblies,   there was never a discussion on whether we were Calvinist or Arminian. It was quite startling to hear a Bible student stand up and declare, "I am a Calvinist and proud of it." The rest of the students yawned and glanced away, clearly unimpressed or bored. Clearly, they thought nothing of the declaration. I, on the other hand, immediately began to ponder the question. It never occurred to me to identify myself by a set of theological systems or arguments. I believe in the whole Bible as the word of truth, that it is infallible and without error; and that I am a follower of Christ. However, this study opened up a new world of understanding and as I look back over the history of Calvinism, the church with all the controversies and man's struggles on the earth, I commit with humility, that I remain a child of God in His service.

---

67 Grudem, Wayne. Systematic Theology, An Introduction to Biblical Doctrine. InterVarsity Press 38 De Montfort Street Leicester LE1 7GP Great Britain, Grand Rapids, MI:Zondervan Publishing House, 5300 Patterson Ave., 60515, Chapter 24, pp 497-498

Now we will explore the lives of a few of the theological greats in order to understand more on the subject of Calvinism. First generation Reformers include theologians greats such as Huldrych Zwingli, Martin Bucer, Wolfgang Capito who all came from diverse academic backgrounds. The second generation include theologians like John Calvin, Heinrich Bullinger, and Wolfgang Musculus. Toward the middle of the 16th century, the Reformed began to commit their beliefs to confessions of faith which would share the future and ultimately propel forward to today. The contributions of these men are great and rank high in the Christendom hall of fame. Even today, we do not know who walks among us. In reviewing a list of names pulled from *Baker's Systematic Theology*, it was clear that names like Macarthur (not a full Calvinist), Charles Hodge, Loraine Boettner, Louis Berkhof, and R.C. Sproul should live on forever. Once, while running for his life, Elijah told God that there was no one else; that he was the only remaining prophet. but God's reply revealed that there are and will always be other prophets. Other great preachers and theologians may have started out as Calvinists (i.e., Robert Schuler) but dropped have their Reformed theology later. Reformed seminarians (e.g. Beza, Olevianus, Francis Turretin, Berkhof), are renowned seminary professors in the United States. Some serve as head pastors (Sproul, Riddlebarger and still others are held in great esteem by those of us who require timeless daily devotions or classic commentary on the Bible and the Christian life (such as produced by Bunyan, Edwards, Henry). There were so many wonderful men of God but here we will only review several. Since John Macarthur commands a lot of respect and seems to speak with a more contemporary voice. This is reasonably comfortable place to begin.

◆ **John Macarthur.** Categorized a Calvinist, he prefers the term Biblicist. He grew up in a Baptist kind of "middle ground" environment – not liking Calvinists or the Arminians, where his father was the preacher. Predestination or election was viewed as something for dead Presbyterians. He attended two Methodist colleges one steeped in Arminian theology and the other Wesleyan before going on to a

Presbyterian influenced seminary. Finally after moving from the Arminian side to the Reformed side, he then turned to the Bible to find out what the Bible said. During a question/answer session in 2012 he is said, "Without all the presuppositions cast in stone, I was able to let the Bible speak. Through the years, the Bible, I believe, speaks very clearly about what the truth is. If people could divest themselves of their presuppositions and if they could be willing to eat a little humble pie and say, "It's possible that I might be wrong," and take another hard look at the Word of God, they would come to the right answers. It's a very simple point to make, and it is this: if two people take two opposing views of something, they cannot both be right. Somebody is wrong. As many of us immerse ourselves in this debate, we would do well to immerse ourselves in Scripture and abandon the turbulent sea of subjective emotionalism of taking a side based on studying the behavior of advocates from either side.[68]

◆ **Louis Berkhof.** Well-respected Calvinist theologian and writer, in his Systematic Theology holds to the traditional teaching of original sin as taught by nearly all Calvinist seminaries to this day. In his chapter on "Sin in the Life of the Human Race" Berkhof explains that the term original sin is derived from the original root of the human race, is present in the life of a person from birth and not the result of an imitation, and says it is the inward root of all the actual sins that defile the life of man. Berkhof notes that God created mankind in His image (*Genesis 1:26-27*) but man rebelled willfully and so sin became part of our existence through Adam (*Romans 5:12, 18*). Berkhof embraces the Augustine teaching that all human beings inherit the guilt of Adam. Berkhof notes that there are two basic elements of original sin **a)** *Original Guilt* and **b)** *Original Pollution* which suggests that the makeup of humanity includes two things: the absence of original righteousness (*Genesis 1:31*) and the presence of evil. Sin is not a disease notes Berkhof and he attacks Arminians as teaching as such. On Total Depravity, he taught that the term means that our

68 Cameron Buettel, The Bottom Line, Advocating the One True Biblical Gospel of Jesus Christ, Defending the Authority of Scripture, Contending for the Christian worldview, http://onceuponacross.blogspot.com/2010/04/john-macarthurs-journey-through-calvin.html, Tuesday, July 10, 2012

entire substance has been tainted by sin and there is no spiritual good that we do in relation to God or toward God. We are perverted, fallen creatures before a holy God. He taught total inability meaning that while mankind is able to do natural good, civil good, and externally religious good, humans are still left with a guilty, sinful nature that cannot be changed apart from the grace of God. Our guilt is such that we are incapable of pleasing God. Berkhof's view is the mainline Calvinist view regarding the teaching of original sin, holding that Romans 5:12-21 emphatically teaches the doctrine of original sin. Berkhof is somewhat of a disappointment in that he often takes aim at Arminians in a general way without accrediting Arminius for his actual views.

♦ **Charles Hodge.** A Presbyterian theologian, and deeply rooted in the Scottish philosophy of Common Sense Realism, he argued strongly that the authority of the Bible as the Word of God had to be understood literally. He was considered the greatest defender of historical Calvinism in America during the 19th century and was the premier public intellectual among Christians in America during that time period. No one taught more graduate students and his literary output is difficult to be compared. It makes one wonder if he had other aspects to his life. Raised and catechized as a Presbyterian, the one job he held his entire life (1797 to 1878) was as professor at Princeton Seminary. During his tenure, the institution became a reliable source for biblically based thinking on a wide range of issues. As theologian, exegete, ecumenist, apologist, critic, and philosopher, this devout disciple wrestled with what it means for the church to bear witness faithfully in a rapidly changing world. He was trained in Hebrew by a rabbi and traveled in order to study under the leading experts in the Greek language. Hodge's theology was born from deep and detailed interaction with the Scriptures. Charles Hodge commands a place in this exposition for several reasons. **1)** this man's life has proven to be exemplary of a man with a mission to help God's people stay as close to every letter of God's truth as is possible. **2)** Hodge remained devoted to his calling. **3)** He shows us how powerful an impact one man can make in this world for the good of a nation. He made a lasting contribution in many powerful and positive ways towards productive living. **4)** He was a pioneer, paving the way for some many to develop a hunger and thirst for truth. **5)** He had a vision that he latched onto and did not let go. **6)** He helped to lay a strong foundation in our nation.

Princeton Seminary was founded in response to the demand for church planters and the need for an institution committed to robust evangelical theology. Princeton grew out of the legacy of a home-based academy in Bucks County, Pennsylvania---affectionately known as the Log College---considered by some to be the first institution in America whose sole purpose was to educate and train men for the gospel ministry. It took over from where Harvard and Yale left off – they could no longer be relied upon for a sound theological education and the College of New Jersey's focus had turned to science and politics, making ministers a shrinking minority in graduating classes. The Princeton seminary was launched with an original goal of producing men of great learning and piety. The leaders of Princeton were men who advocated for Calvinism and the Great Awakening. They were Reformed revivalists. Their wanted to produce ministers who were biblically grounded, theologically enlightened, and spiritually awakened. Though governed by Presbyterians, Princeton Seminary welcomed students from diverse backgrounds. It graduated men who became leaders in Presbyterian, Episcopal, and Baptist churches. Among Princeton's first graduates was Charles Hodge, who would become the seminary's leading influence in the 19th century. In the 19th century, Princeton was a leader among conservative evangelicals in America. Through *The Biblical Repertory and Princeton Review*, a prominent voice in 19th-century religious journalism, it apprised Presbyterians of the latest thinking among biblical scholars, engaged in controversies facing the church, and responded to challenges in the surrounding culture. Charles Hodge was front and center.

◆ **Matthew Henry.** Matthew Henry was primarily home-educated by his father, Rev. Philip Henry, and also at the Thomas Doolittle academy from 1680-1682. Henry studied law instead of pursuing a career in law he began to preach in his neighborhood. He was privately ordained in London, and began his regular ministry as non-conformist pastor of a Presbyterian congregation where he remained for 25 years. Henry's reputation rests upon his renowned commentary, *An Exposition of the Old and New Testaments* (1708-10, known also as *Matthew Henry's Commentary on the Whole Bible*). He lived to complete it only as far as to the end of the Acts, but after his death other like-minded authors prepared the remainder from Henry's manuscripts. This work was long celebrated as the best English commentary for devotional purposes and the expanded edition was initially published in 1896.

It is somewhat difficult to find a classic five point Calvinist these days. However, almost every religious denomination has adopted a Calvinistic like theology. Calvin accurately taught the correct concept of man before the fall: "Man, in his state of innocence, had freedom and power to will and to do that which is good and well-pleasing to God; but yet mutably, so that he might fall from it." "God has endued that will of man with that natural liberty and power of acting upon choice, that it is neither forced for, by any necessity of nature, determined to do good or evil."[69] This freewill nature of man did not change when Adam and Eve sinned but is the same today. Even some of the cults have accepted some Calvinistic principles. The Jehovah's Witnesses, for example, believe in the concept of inherited sin.[70]

Charles Spurgeon wrote "The root of every heresy in history is adding something of our own to the work of Christ.[71] There is no such thing as preaching Christ and Him crucified unless we preach what is today called Calvinism.[72] The doctrines of grace which are referred to as Calvinism are actually spinoffs of Calvinism.[73]

69 Calvinism Refuted, Westminster Confession of Faith, Retrieved November, 2015 from: http://www.bible.ca/calvinism.htm
70 Calvinism Refuted, Retrieved November, 2015 from: http://www.bible.ca/calvinism.htm
71 Michael S. Horton, For Calvinism, MI: Grand Rapids, 45930, Zondervan Publishing Co., Year 2011.
72 Ibid.
73 Ibid.

4.3 Calvin and TULIP

Calvinism is a system of biblical interpretation taught by John Calvin who lived in France in the 1500's at the time of Martin Luther who sparked the Reformation. There are two mains camps of theology within Christianity in America today. The system of Calvinism focuses on God's sovereignty, stating that God is able and willing by virtue of his omniscience, omnipresence, and omnipotence, to do whatever He desires with His creation.[74] Arminianism, on the other hand, maintains that God predestined, but not in an absolute sense. Rather, He looked into the future to see who would pick him and then He chose them. Jesus died for all peoples' sins who have ever lived and ever will live, not just the Christians. Each person is the one who decides if he wants to be saved or not. And finally, it is possible to lose your salvation.

There are 5 major points of Calvinism. These 5 points are known by the acronym: T.U.L.I.P. which must be accepted or rejected as a unit. Refute any one element and the whole system falls. This is referred to as the Domino Theology.

Total hereditary depravity. Babies inherit the sin of Adam and are totally depraved and therefore unable to respond to the gospel.

Unconditional election. (Predestination) God had a list of those who will be saved and those who will go to hell (before creation in Genesis 1:1). The list is the unchangeable message of Christ.

Limited atonement. Christ did not die for all men but only those on the "saved list"

Irresistible grace. God sends the Holy Spirit only to those on the saved list which removes their depraved nature inherited from Adam and creates within them a saving faith in Christ. The Holy Spirit guides them to understand and correctly interpret the Bible.

Perseverance of the saints. A child of God once saved, cannot be lost.

---

74   The Five Points of Calvinism, Retrieved November, 2015 from: http://www.calvinistcorner.com/tulip.htm

4.3.1 Unconditional Election

God does not base His election on anything He sees in the individual. He chooses according to the kind intention of His will (*Ephesians 1:4-8; Romans 9:11*) without any consideration of merit within the individual. Nor does God look into the future to see who would pick Him. Also, as some are elected into salvation, others are not (*Romans 9:15, 21*). This election is personal. He chose the elect by name. And since it is not conditional upon anything in us, it is absolutely certain that all the elect will be saved one day. This is how we come to the term unconditional election. The election is irreversible. When one comes to believe in Christ unto salvation, he then has the privilege of knowing that he is one of the elect (*2 Peter 1:10*).

Calvinism teaches us that God did not choose all men. He did not choose Satan or any of the demons, and He did not choose all sinful human beings. Some are elected, the rest were left in their sins (*Romans 9*). This is the doctrine of Reprobation, or non-election. Since they were not chosen to salvation but left in their sins, they were foreordained to receive the due penalty for their sins-eternal wrath (*1 Thessalonians 5:9; 1 Peter 2:8; Proverbs 16:4*). Their names were not written in the Book of Life in eternity past (*Revelation 13:8, 17:8*), nor were they ever known by Christ in the election of grace (*Matthew 7:23*).

In time, God leaves them in their evil nature and even hardens their hearts and further blinds their minds (*John 12:39-40; Romans 9:18, 11:7; Deuteronomy 2:30; Joshua 11:20*). God is fattening them up for the slaughter which they deserve. This sounds unfair but no man can blame God, for Man is sinful Man and God is a holy God. No man deserves to be elected; all deserve to be rejected. The wonder is not that God rejected some sinners; the wonder is that He chose any sinners to be saved.

4.3.2 Limited Atonement

Limited atonement holds that Jesus died only for those who are unconditionally elected, not for all mankind. Though Jesus' sacrifice was sufficient for all, it was not efficacious for all. Jesus only bore the sins of the elect. Support for this position is drawn from such scriptures as Matthew 26:28 where Jesus died for 'many'; John 10:11, 15 which say that Jesus died for the sheep (*not the goats, per Matthew 25:32-33*); John 17:9 where Jesus in prayer interceded for the ones given Him, not those of the entire world; Acts 20:28 and Ephesians 5:25-27 which state that the Church was purchased by Christ, not all people; and Isaiah 53:12 which is a prophecy of Jesus' crucifixion where he would bore the sins of many (not all as has been occasionally misinterpreted). God, then, chose some sinners to save. It only guarantees that they certainly will be saved in the end. Two more things needed to be done: prepare the means for their salvation and apply it to them. First, we read in Scripture that God foreordained that Jesus Christ would become a man and would die on the Cross as the means of salvation (*Acts 2:23; 4:28*). Christ died as a substitute for others (*1 Corinthians 15:3; Romans 5:8*). He suffered the infinite wrath of God for sin, and satisfied that wrath. This is called propitiation (*1 John 2:2, 4:10*). Because Jesus was a perfect man and God in the flesh, His sacrifice had infinite value. He did not pay an exact equivalent for our sins; He paid a super-abundant payment infinitely above what we owed. All that He did would have been necessary had only one sinner been chosen, but He would not have had to do any more had all sinners been chosen.

Historic Calvinists teach that there are two aspects of this one atonement. The first is that there is a sense in which Christ died for all men everywhere (*John 1:29, 3:16*). By His death on the Cross, He removed all legal barriers in case any man believes. His death for all men also purchased the common bounties of life for all men. It also secured a delay of judgment for them, as it were, though not a permanent one. All will one day be judged, but the fact that all men are not already in Hell is due to the atonement of Christ. Moreover, on the basis of this universal aspect of the atonement, salvation is offered freely to all men: "Come and dine, for all is ready!" (cf. *Matthew 22:2-14; Luke 14:16-24*). Also, Christ died for all men in this sense in order to be Lord of all men, whether alive or dead, elect or non-elect (*Romans 14:9; Philippians 2:10-11*).

Most Evangelicals will agree with this analysis so far, but the Calvinist goes further, teaching that the death of Christ is sufficient for all men, but is efficient only for the elect. There is a sense in which Christ died for all, but there is a sense in which He died only for the elect. He died for all, but especially for the elect (*1 Timothy 4:10*). He purchased some blessings for all men, but all blessings for some men.[75] Since the elect are scattered throughout the world and mingled together with the non-elect, Christ purchased the whole world with the special intent of owning the elect (cf. *Matthew 13:44*). This special aspect of the atonement is what is called Limited Atonement. Some call it Particular Redemption. Ephesians 5:25 says, "Christ also loved the Church (referring to the elect) and gave Himself up for her." This is similar to how a man loves all other people, but has a special love for his wife and will do some things for her that he will not do for all others. Calvinist say that this is the same with Christ. He has a general love for all men and did something for all men at the Cross because they were His creatures. But He has a special love for His bride and did something special for her at the Cross.

He died for her in such a way as to guarantee that she would be saved, made perfectly holy and ready for Heaven (vs.26). There are other verses that indicate this special intent of the atonement. John 10:15, 17 and 18 say that Christ the Good Shepherd died for *"the sheep"*. Lest somebody think that this could include all men everywhere, Christ goes on to say that some people are not His sheep (vs. 26) Hence there is a sense in which He died for the sheep (the elect) and not for the goats and wolves (the non-elect). Later in John 15:13-14, Christ

---

75 Grudem, Wayne. Systematic Theology, An Introduction to Biblical Doctrine. InterVarsity Press 38 De Montfort Street Leicester LE1 7GP Great Britain, Grand Rapids, MI:Zondervan Publishing House, 5300 Patterson Ave., 60515, Chapter 24, pp 315-317

said that He would lay down His life for His "friends." But not all men are His friends. Isaiah 53:8 prophesied that Christ would die for God's "people", but not all men are God's people-only the elect. Acts 20:28 says that Christ purchased "the Church" with His blood, but not all men are the Church. Further, Romans 8:32 says that if God gave Christ to die for us, then He will surely give us all other things. Since He does not give all these things of salvation to all men, then it follows that Christ was not given for them at the Cross in this special way.

Christ died so as to make possible the salvation of all men, but He died to make definite the salvation of the elect. It was designed for the elect. Again, there are many objections to this truth, but they can all be answered by pointing out that no man deserved for Christ to die for him. Actually, there is no dispute that Christ did not die for Satan or the demons; the atonement is clearly limited there. But the Calvinist teaching is that non-elect are in the same situation as Satan – none will be saved because none were elected. The thing to keep in mind is that the atonement was designed for the elect.[76]

4.3.3 Irresistible Grace

Irresistible Grace (Law and Works): When God calls his elect into salvation, they cannot resist. God offers to all people the gospel message. This is called the external call. But to the elect, God extends an internal call and it cannot be resisted. This call is by the Holy Spirit who works in the hearts and minds of the elect to bring them to repentance and regeneration whereby they willingly and freely come to God. Some of the verses used in support of this teaching are Romans 9:16 where it says that "it is not of him who wills nor of him who runs, but of God who has mercy"; Philippians 2:12-13 where God is said to be the one working salvation in the individual; John 6:28-29 where faith is declared to be the work of God; Acts 13:48 where God appoints people to believe; and John 1:12-13 where being born again

76 Grudem, Wayne. Systematic Theology, An Introduction to Biblical Doctrine. InterVarsity Press 38 De Montfort Street Leicester LE1 7GP Great Britain, Grand Rapids, MI:Zondervan Publishing House, 5300 Patterson Ave., 60515, Chapter 24, pp 315-317

is not by man's will, but by God's. "All that the Father gives Me shall come to Me, and the one who comes to Me I will certainly not cast out," (*John 6:37*). Since man can do nothing to respond to God's will, God sends the Holy Spirit to act directly and irresistibly on the hearts of the elect to enable them to believe and obey.

God chose the elect and Christ died for them in a special way, but this redemption must be applied to them in order for them to be saved. This leads us to the Fourth Point of Calvinism. First, let us get the general picture and then the precise focus. As we have shown, there is a general sense in which God loves all men as His creatures (*Matthew 5:44-45; Luke 6:35-36; Psalms 33:5,145:9, 14-16*). We call this Common Grace. God gives them the bounties of life on this planet. Moreover, there is a sense in which God wills all men everywhere to be saved (*1 Timothy 2:4*), and so He offers them salvation indiscriminately. We call this the Free Offer of the Gospel, and it is seen in the Great Commission (*Matthew 28:18-20*). God issues a general "call" to all who hear the Gospel (*Matthew 22:14*). All who hear are invited. But because all men are totally depraved and hate God, they resist this call and the work of the Spirit (*Acts 7:51*).

Evangelicals agree so far, but again Calvinists go a step further. God has a special love for the elect and will do more than simply give an external invitation. He does something that guarantees that they will accept this invitation. He overwhelms them with what we call Irresistible Grace. In addition to the general call to all men, God gives them a special call (*Romans 8:28-30; 2 Peter 1:10*), or what Paul describes as a *"holy calling"* (*2 Timothy 1:9*). It is a calling by special grace (*Galatians 1:15*). God thereby draws the elect irresistibly to Himself with special lovingkindness (*Jeremiah 31:3; Hosea 11:4; Song of Solomon 1:4*). He causes the elect to come to Him (*Psalm 65:4*) by turning our wills around (*Proverbs 21:1*). This is irresistible, for God *"draws"* us to Christ (*John 6:44*) and *"compels"* us by divine omnipotence to come (*Luke 14:23*). He actually changes our wills so that we come willingly (*Philippians 2:13; Psalm 110:3*).

Now, exactly how does God do this? There is much mystery in how God works grace in the hearts of the elect, but the Bible tells us some definite things about the process. God sovereignly opens the hearts of the elect (*Acts 16:14*). It is not that they opened their hearts to receive Christ; Christ opened their hearts that He might enter. Only as a result can it be said that they opened the door. So, He opens our hearts, and with the doors of our hearts being opened we can hear His voice (*John 10:16,27*). This is the special call of Christ in Scripture. In the process, God gives the elect the new birth (*John 3:1-8; 5:21; James 1:18*).[77] They did not regenerate themselves; they were regenerated sovereignly by God's free grace (*John 1:13*). No spiritually dead man can make himself alive any more than a corpse can. Matter cannot create itself, and the new birth is a new creation that is given only by God's grace (*2 Corinthians 5:17; Gal 6:15*). It is a spiritual resurrection (*Ephesians 2:1, 5; Colossians 2:13*).

The elect are not born again because they believe; rather, they believe because they have been born again (*1 John 5:1*). The new birth is a sovereign gift, and so is faith (*2 Peter 1:1; Ephesians 2:8-9; Philippians 1:29; John 3:27, 6:65; 1 Corinthians 3:6; 4:7; Romans 12:3*). Repentance is also a free gift that is sovereignly bestowed (*2 Timothy 2:25; Acts 5:31; 11:18*). Because the elect now have faith, God justifies them and they are saved.

The distinctive of Calvinism on this point is that *"Salvation is of the Lord"* (*Jonah 2:9*). If any man is ever to be saved, it is only by God's free grace from first to last. Evangelicals in general will agree that salvation is by grace and not by works (*Ephesians 2:8-9*), but Calvinists go a step further and state that this saving grace is sovereignly given to the elect. It is not merely offered, for it is offered to all. It is irresistibly given to the elect and to them alone. It is not given to the non-elect. Calvinist upholds that we can do nothing toward our salvation, everything is up to God. He unconditionally elects or chooses certain individuals to be saved. This choice has nothing whatever to do with

---

77 Grudem, Wayne. Systematic Theology, An Introduction to Biblical Doctrine. InterVarsity Press 38 De Montfort Street Leicester LE1 7GP Great Britain, Grand Rapids, MI:Zondervan Publishing House, 5300 Patterson Ave., 60515, Chapter 24, pp 315-317

our character, choice, conduct, attitude, or will, either now or in the future. Those whom God does not so elect to save, will be doomed to eternal torment and there is nothing they can do about that. God does this "without any foresight of faith or good works." It is of God's grace alone.

4.3.4 Perseverance of the Saints

The easiest way to explain this and remember this doctrine's meaning is the saying: "Once saved, always saved." The Bible teaches that those who are born again will continue trusting in Christ forever. When we are born again, we receive the promised indwelling presence of the Holy Spirit that is God's guarantee that the Lord is able to complete the good work that He began in us (*Philippians 1:6*). God, by His own power through the indwelling presence of the Holy Spirit, keeps or preserves the believer forever. [78] Believers are sealed with the Holy Spirit of promise, who is the guarantee of our inheritance. (*Ephesians 1:13-14*). In order for us to lose our salvation after receiving the promised Holy Spirit, God would have to break His promise which He cannot do.[79] Therefore, the believer is eternally secure because God is eternally faithful. The understanding of this doctrine really comes from understanding the unique and special love that God has for us. children. The believer must understand the promises and provision made according to Romans 8:28-39 as follows: 1) no one can bring a charge against God's elect; 2) nothing can separate the elect from the love of Christ; 3) God makes everything work together for the good of the elect; and 4) all whom God saves will be glorified. God loves His children so much that nothing can separate them from Him. Of course this same truth is seen in many other passages of Scripture as well. Jesus says, "My sheep hear My voice, and I know them, and they follow Me; and I give eternal life to them, and they will never perish; and no one will be able to snatch them out of My hand (*John 10:27-30*). My Father, gave them to Me, and no one is able to snatch them out of the Father's hand. I and the Father are one."

---

78 Retrieved November, 2015 from: http://www.gotquestions.org/perseverance-saints.html#ixzz3OOE4TEjh
79 Ibid.

Another evidence from Scripture of the eternal security of a believer is found in John 5:24, where Jesus says, "… he who hears My word, and believes Him who sent Me, has eternal life, and does not come into judgment, but has passed out of death into life." Eternal life is not something we get in the future but is something that we have once we believe. By its very nature, eternal life must last forever, or it could not be eternal. This passage says that, if we believe the gospel, we have eternal life and will not come into judgment; therefore, it can be said we are eternally secure. There is really very little scriptural basis that can be used to argue against the eternal security of the believer.

While there are a few verses that, if not considered in their context, might give the impression that one could "fall from grace" or lose his salvation, when these verses are carefully considered in context it is clear that is not the case.[80] Many people know someone who at one time expressed faith in Christ and who might have appeared to be a genuine Christian who later departed from the faith and now wants to have nothing to do with Christ or His church. These people might even deny the very existence of God. For those who do not want to accept what the Bible says about the security of the believer, these types of people are proof that the doctrine of eternal security cannot be right. However, the Bible indicates otherwise, and it teaches that people such as those who profess Christ as Savior at one time only to later walk away and deny Christ were never truly saved in the first place. For example, 1 John 2:19 says, "They went out from us, but they were not of us; for if they had been of us, they would have remained with us; but they went out from us, in order that it might be made manifest that they all are not truly of us."

The Bible is also clear that not everyone who professes to be a Christian truly is. (*Matthew 7:21-22*). Rather than proving we can lose our salvation, those people who profess Christ and fall away simply reinforces the importance of testing our salvation to make sure we are in the faith (*2 Corinthians 13:5*) and making our calling and election

---

80 Grudem, Wayne. Systematic Theology, An Introduction to Biblical Doctrine. InterVarsity Press 38 De Montfort Street Leicester LE1 7GP Great Britain, Grand Rapids, MI:Zondervan Publishing House, 5300 Patterson Ave., 60515, pp 315-317

sure by continually examining our lives to make sure we are growing in godliness (*2 Peter 1:10*).

One of the misconceptions about the doctrine of the perseverance of the saints is that it will lead to "carnal Christians" who believe that since they are eternally secure they can live whatever licentious lifestyle they wish and still be saved. That is a misunderstanding of Bible doctrine. A person who believes he can live any way he wants because he has professed Christ is not demonstrating true saving faith (*1 John 2:3-4*). Our eternal security rests on the biblical teaching that those whom God justifies, He will also glorify (*Romans 8:29-30*). Those who are saved will indeed be conformed to the image of Christ through the process of sanctification (*1 Corinthians 6:11*). When a person is saved, the Holy Spirit breaks the bondage of sin and gives the believer a new heart and a desire to seek holiness. Therefore a true Christian will desire to be obedient to God and will be convicted by the Holy Spirit when he sins.

True Christians will never "live any way they want" because such behavior is impossible for someone who has been given a new nature (*2 Corinthians 5:17*). If someone is truly saved, he has been made alive by the Holy Spirit and has a new heart with new desires. Because of His unique love for His children, God will keep all of His children safe from harm, and Jesus has promised that He will lose none of His sheep. The doctrine of the perseverance of the saints recognizes that true Christians will always persevere and are eternally secure because God keeps them that way. Because the term "perseverance of the saints" can cause people to have the wrong idea about what is meant, some people prefer to use terms like "preservation of the saints," "eternal security," or "held by God." Each of these terms reveals some aspect of what the Bible teaches about the security of the believer. However, like any biblical doctrine, what is important is not the name assigned to the doctrine but how accurately it summarizes what the Bible teaches about that subject. No matter which name you use to refer to this important doctrine, a thorough study of the

Bible will reveal that, when it is properly understood, it is an accurate description of what the Bible teaches.[81]

Life Application for Personal Reflection
History of Calvinism and Controversies
1. Do you worry about whether you are really born again? Do you have any doubt regarding your eternal security? What can you do in order to resolve these concerns? (Study Matthew 11:28-30, John 6:36-37, and 2 Peter 1:5-11).
2. Did you know the Lord does not want His people to be concerned about whether you belong to Him? What can you do to relieve yourself of worry? (1 John 5:13)
3. What is the difference between common grace and irresistible grace?

Suggested Reading
History of Calvinism and Controversies
1. Berkhof, Louis. *Systematic Theology,* New Combined Edition containing the full text of Systematic Theology and the original. Williams B. Eerdmans Publishing Company, 255 Jefferson Ave., S.E., Grand Rapids, MI 49503, 1996, pp 445-449.
2. Grudem, Wayne. "Atonement." *Systematic Theology, An Introduction to Biblical Doctrine.* InterVarsity Press, 38 De Montfort Street Leicester LE1 7GP Great Britain, Grand Rapids, MI: Zondervan Publishing House, pp 657-721.
3. Hodge, Charles. *Systematic Theology.* 3 vols. Reprint edition: Grand Rapids: Eerdmans, 1970. First published 1871, pp 593-648.
4. Thiessen, Henry C. *Lectures in Systematic Theology,* Revised by Vernon D. Doerksen, , Grand Rapids, MI: William B. Eerdmans Publishing Company, 1998.
5. Spurgeon, C.H. *A Defence of Calvinism, The Banner of Truth Trust,* # Murrayfield Road, Edinburgh, EH 124 6EL UK, P.O Box 621, Carlisle, PA 17013, 2008.
6. Steele, David N. and Curtis Thomas. *The Five Points of Calvinism: Defined, Defended, and Documented,* Phillipsburg, NJ: R&R Publishing, 2004.

---

81 Grudem, Wayne. Systematic Theology, An Introduction to Biblical Doctrine. InterVarsity Press 38 De Montfort Street Leicester LE1 7GP Great Britain, Grand Rapids, MI:Zondervan Publishing House, 5300 Patterson Ave., 60515

Amazing Grace

Lyrics by WILLIAM WALKER

Amazing grace, How sweet the sound
That saved a wretch like me.
I once was lost, but now am found,
Was blind, but now I see.

'Twas grace that taught my heart to fear,
And grace my fears relieved.
How precious did that grace appear
The hour I first believed.

Through many dangers, toils and snares
I have already come,
'Tis grace has brought me safe thus far
And grace will lead me home.

When we've been there ten thousand years
Bright shining as the sun,
We've no less days to sing God's praise
Than when we've first begun.

REFLECTIONS

A DIFFERENT KIND OF CONTROVERSY

It had been a hard winter in the Rockies. The snow piled deeper and deeper. The temperature dropped below zero and stayed there. The rivers froze over. People were suffering. The Red Cross used helicopters to fly in supplies. After a long hard day, as they were returning to their base, the rescue team in a helicopter saw a cabin nearly submerged in the snow. A thin wisp, of smoke came from the chimney. The men figured those people in that cabin were probably critically short of food, fuel, and medicine. Because of the trees they had to set down about a mile from the cabin. They put their heavy emergency equipment on their backs, trudged through waist deep snow, and reached the cabin exhausted, panting, and perspiring. They pounded on the door and a thin, gaunt mountain woman finally answered. The lead man panted, "ma'am, we're from the Red Cross."

She was silent for a moment, and then she said, "It's been a hard long winter, sonny. I just don't think we can give anything this year!"

Source: It Had Been A Long Hard Winter In The Rockies. ext Illustration shared by SermonCentral February 2007, Retrieved November 2015 from http://www.sermoncentral.com/illustrations/sermon-illustration-stories-31443.asp

Redemption

◆ ◆ ◆

"I waited patiently for the Lord; and he inclined unto me, and heard my cry. He brought me up also out of an horrible pit, out of the miry clay, and set my feet upon a rock, and established my goings." (Psalm 40:1-2)

King David

What is redemption? It is the act of saving or being saved from sin, error, or evil, occurs by the regaining or gaining possession of something in exchange for payment, or clearing a debt. It includes: **1)** The act of redeeming or the condition of having been redeemed. **2)** Recovery of something pawned or mortgaged. **3)** Payment of an obligation, as a government's payment of the value of its bonds. **4)** Deliverance upon payment of ransom; **5)** Rescue and recovery of something spawned. **6)** Christianity salvation from sin through Jesus' sacrifice.

The basic definition of redemption is "the act of purchasing back something previously sold".[82] The Christian application for this is the act of delivering from sin or saving from evil but it is the deliverance upon payment of ransom to the prison keeper that is the key to the

---

82 Grudem, Wayne. Systematic Theology, An Introduction to Biblical Doctrine. InterVarsity Press 38 De Montfort Street Leicester LE1 7GP Great Britain, Grand Rapids, MI:Zondervan Publishing House, 5300 Patterson Ave., 60515, Chapter 24, pp 315-317

rescue operation. These definitions are similar if you realize that in the beginning mankind did not need to be redeemed. This was because the world was without sin and Adam and Eve were in fellowship with God. The need for redemption started when Adam and Eve ate the forbidden fruit in the Garden of Eden. Even though God loved them, He cursed them for their disobedience and sent them out of the Garden of Eden. At this point mankind needed redemption, a savior, to remove the curse and to reconcile them back to God.

Mankind's savior is Jesus Christ who loves us and whose act on the cross has provided all of us with the opportunity for redemption. See the following doctrinal teachings, scriptures and discourse concerning the Christian redemption definition and the need for mankind's redemption. To understand the redemption definition, we must understand that at one time we were in fellowship with God. We were not separated from God. There was no need for redemption. There was no sin in the world.

It is impossible to explore the rudiments of salvation and redemption without a New Testament discussion. There are too many reference points to ignore. For example, there was John the Baptist a New Testament favorite of most Christians, who was cousin to Jesus and a great preacher. John, who was actually ascetic – no frills or fanfare – enjoyed a steady diet of locusts and wild honey (*Matthew 3:4*). He dressed differently from regular people, wearing camel hair rough clothing and like other Prophets, he was pretty serious and was not much for socializing. According to Jesus: "John came neither eating nor drinking, and they say, He has a demon," (*Matthew 11:18*). John was like an Elijah (*Luke 1:16, Matthew. 11:12-15, John 1:6*).

Now John was the forerunner to Jesus Christ. He was like the "announcer" that always arrived ahead of the king in order to alert the subjects that royalty was coming in order for them to make proper arrangements to suitably and honorably receive the king. We find the declaration of John's coming in the book of Malachi from 400 years before Christ came. The great prophet Isaiah also spoke of John as "the voice of one that crieth," who would "prepare in the wilderness the way of Jehovah," and "make straight in the desert a highway for our God" (*Isaiah 40:3*). This was centuries even before the birth of Jesus. Obviously this would be a fanfare extraordinaire.

Well, John urged the people to get baptized, cleaned up and to prepare themselves for the Messiah. He is a reminder of Elijah's personality and some of the Old Testament Prophets.

This represented one view of John through the rose colored lenses of our eyeglasses. In other words, this man, who hung out in desolate places and was referred to as having a demon (*Mark. 5:2-3*) was sought after by the crowds. He did not pump himself up, instead, they came looking for him. He may have been somewhat reclusive and disheveled in appearance, but his phenomenal message gripped them and many were baptized by him (*John 10:41*). John did not perform a lot of miracles but his message was powerful and recognized by the people as a voice from God.

Why salvation? What did they need to be saved from or for and why? What was it all about and what was the urgency? John's mission was to "bear witness of the light of Christ (*John 1:7-8*). The fact that out of his mission came an astounding change cannot be argued: Jesus Christ and the birth of Christianity came along and the world has not been the same since. John preached concerning Jesus, the kingdom, and the judgment and it was clearly not just for the Jews, but the entire world. He brought attention to "the lamb of God that takes away the sin of the world" (*John 1:29*). John was sensitive to the moral corruption taking place and he knew it was an offense to God. "Repent, for the kingdom of heaven is at hand" (*Matthew 3:2; cf. Mark. 1:4*). This phrase came about in the New Testament. What was going on during this time that John had to come? Why did they both spend time in the wilderness? What was so urgent that caused Jesus to appear on the scene? One word: corruption. It was happening everywhere within society including among those who had made themselves responsible for the law. When Jesus came on the scene,

Judaism was collapsing under the weight of oppression by the Roman empire. They no longer respected God's commandments and their lives were being turned upside down by the invasions because of their failure to love, honor and obey God. They became more concerned about tradition and their hearts turned away from God. Jewish culture was getting swallowed up as the children of Israel began to accept practices and ideals of other people and their idolatrous ways. There was spiritual corruption from the religious leaders who piled on additional laws to Moses' Law. The people were confused and no longer knew the truth because the spiritual leaders had sold out and were making God's law of no effect.

The same moral decay of those times is happening today. There is an open display of boldness and blatant disregard in people today that they refuse to respect the things of God. Salvation is required to change man's condition and reform his personality, to cause him to remember and honor that which is sacred to God. We know that society has reversed the expectation for good and perverted right teaching with relativism. It has brought about the demise of our standards and given license for evil to prevail. Society has attempted to make the kingdom of God a politically correct, world oriented system, but it does not work that way

Our view of salvation today seems so different than the preaching of Jesus and the disciples. As Jesus preached and went about the healing the brokenhearted, opening the eyes of the blind, setting the captives free, the disciples struggled with social and economic freedom questions. Their all encompassing message was about life in the kingdom of God for humanity on the earth and our existence in the now and hereafter. Sometimes we are so focused on being heavenward bound, we have lost our voice and we miss our opportunity to offer a redemptive word for today.

What is the point of salvation if there is no redemption while we are yet living? Paul spoke of transformation. What would be the point in transforming the human personality to be like Christ if it was only for our life in the hereafter? Yes, we should be thankful for eternal life and that Jesus Christ shed His blood that we might have a right to the tree of life but when we miss the entire point of why He gave His life, we are selling His message short.

God gave us life, creating man "in His Image and His likeness" (Genesis 1:26). That is, God intended man to be like Him by grace. The damage suffered by human nature as a result of the "original sin" included the loss of the Kingdom of God which was the most severe consequence of the fall. Adam and Eve had already had a glimpse and a taste in Paradise but after that fall, man himself departed in soul from God and became unreceptive to the grace of God which was opened to him. Man could no longer hear the divine voice of God. He grew further apart from the Lord. It is no different today. When one stays away from God or moves out of His presence, it becomes harder to hear the voice of the Lord. The further away one moves, the greater the distance and the sound waves get distorted with all of the other traffic in between. Salvation is the restoration of the wholeness of God's image in us, of the possibility of our union with God. It is the restoration of our original essence. When we accept Christ, our lives should be transformed so that God gets the glory while we are still living and walking around on the earth. It requires faith and the desire for God in our lives. Otherwise, why not wait to save us until we get us into heaven? Even then, what would be the point of saving us from our sinful selves merely to get us into heaven? However it is awesome to know that we are all beneficiaries of this great transfer, no matter what stage of life. This transfer of guilt for innocence, shame for honor, punishment for freedom, and ultimately, death for life is the most noble expression of love known to mankind. No one other than God's Son could do this. "There is no greater love than to lay down one's life for one's friends." (*John 15:13*)

God knew this when He told Abraham that he would not have to sacrifice his son on the altar after all. "Lay not thine hand upon the lad, neither do thou anything unto him: for now I know that thou fearest God, seeing thou hast not withheld thy son, thine only son from me." (*Genesis 22:13-17*) Instead, for his faithfulness, the Lord pronounced supernatural great blessing and he would be blessed even above his enemies. God always intended to rescue fallen man. He was testing Abraham. He knew that only one sacrifice could make that great transfer possible. God loved us that much that He put a plan together since we could not help ourselves. It is written, "For God loved the world so much that he gave his one and only Son, so that everyone who believes in him will not perish but have eternal life." (John 3:16)

This plan worked even for someone facing the threat of death. When the crowd was given a choice to either let Jesus, the innocent One, go free or to free the worst criminal in that day, they chose Barabbas. They knew he was guilty. He was the first who was full of sin and guilty of wickedness, to have his guilt transferred to Jesus, and the innocence of Jesus transferred to him.

God transferred our sin to Jesus on the cross, and transferred His righteousness to us. As a result, we are declared innocent in God's eyes, as Jesus. This is a sovereign act and we would never have thought of it. We would not dream of asking anyone to take our place in going to a death sentence. How amazing is the Lord!

My suggestion here is that many of us think salvation is only about heaven when really, we should be like Christ. While on the earth, we should radiate the same love, joy, peace, longsuffering, gentleness, goodness, faith, meekness, and temperance of the Holy Spirit. (Galatians 5:22) Salvation is necessary for us in our earthly living as we share our lives with others and minister as God calls us on the earth.

Sin is the root cause of mankind's need for redemption. Something had to be done in order for reconciliation to occur. In the first chapter of Colossians, verses 15-20, Paul draws our attention to the absolute supremacy of Jesus Christ. That supremacy is focused in two areas: His supremacy in relationship to all creation and His supremacy in relationship to the work of reconciliation. The creation needs to be reconciled to God. But in all of this, the overriding emphasis is that Jesus Christ is supreme. Note the last phrase in verse 18: "... so that He Himself will come to have first place in everything." That provides a backdrop to verses 15-20. Paul talks about His relationship to creation and to reconciliation. At the heart of it all is that He might come to be preeminent in everything.

Paul begins by talking about the relationship of Jesus Christ to creation in verses 15-17. He demonstrated that Christ was supreme over all creation because He was before all creation and He is the creator of all creation. You are going to see basically the same arguments repeated when Paul talks about reconciliation. He is before all creation, and He is the creator of all creation. He is God. Verse 15 says, "And He is the image of the invisible God..." When you have seen Jesus Christ, you have seen God. He is God manifest in human form. He is the firstborn of all creation, but He is not part of creation. He precedes creation. As such He is preeminent over creation. [83]

Two ideas are entailed in firstborn - priority in time and preeminence in position. This is demonstrated in verse 16: "For by Him all things were created..." We note three prepositional phrases here - For by Him, then at the end of the verse, through Him and for Him. All creation is centered in Him. As a result of His creative energy, nothing is created outside of Him. It's all done through Him as the mediating agent of the triune God. It is all ultimately for Him; He is supreme. He is before all things, verse 17 said. He precedes everything, and in Him all things hold together. You see the person and work of Jesus Christ constantly emphasized in verses 15-17, and 17. In His person, He is the image of the invisible God. He is before all things. He is God. In His work, He is the creator of everything. Not only is He the creator of everything, but in Him everything holds together.

---

83 Grudem, Wayne. Systematic Theology, An Introduction to Biblical Doctrine. InterVarsity Press 38 De Montfort Street Leicester LE1 7GP Great Britain, Grand Rapids, MI:Zondervan Publishing House, 5300 Patterson Ave., 60515, Chapter 24, pp 315-317

God's Eternal Purpose in Redemption[84] Here we are interested in the fact that redemption was not a system of restoration which took advantage of circumstances as it progressed, until God finally worked out a contrivance to save man; contrariwise, "Known unto God are all His works from the creation" and "declaring the end from the beginning." His attribute of foreknowledge makes Him to know all things past, present, and future in one, intuitional redemption should follow. Being omnipotent and omniscient, nothing could stay His plan. This is what we mean by God's plan of redemption and His eternal purpose in redemption. What He has eternally decreed, He is able to perform.[85]

Life Application for Personal Reflection

Redemption

1. If salvation is by grace alone and not by works then could not a Christian live any old way if grace alone saves?
2. If once saved always saved what are your thoughts about Judas? Was he once saved and lost again?

Suggested Reading

Redemption

1. MacArthur, John, Jr. The Gospel According to Jesus, Grand Rapids, MI: Zondervan Publishing Company, 1988.
2. Murray, John. "Faith and Repentance." In Redemption Accomplished and Applied. Grand Rapids, MI: Eerdmans Publishing Company, 1955.
3. Strong, James. LL.D. "Redemption."The Strongest Strong's Exhaustive Concordance of the Bible, the only Strong compiled and verified by computer technology with Nave's Topical Bible Reference; most up-to-date Hebrew and Greek dictionaries for precise word studies, corrects all others. Grand Rapids, MI 49530, 2001, p 1780.
– "Salvation." The Strongest Strong's Exhaustive Concordance of the Bible, The Strongest Strong's Exhaustive Concordance of the Bible, Grand Rapids, MI, 2001, 1784.

---

84 E. C. Bragg, Systematic Theology Soteriology, Retrieved November, 2015 from: http://trinitycollege.edu/assets/files/ECBragg/SoteriologyR.pdf
85 Ibid.

I'm Just a Sinner Saved by Grace

Lyrics by BILL GAITHER

If you could see what I once was; if you could go with me
Back to where I started from, then I know you would see
A miracle of love that took me in it's sweet embrace
And made me what I am today - just an old sinner saved by grace.

I'm just a sinner saved by grace
When I stood condemned to death He took my place
Now I live and breathe in freedom with each breath of life I take
Loved and forgiven, back with the living
I'm just a sinner saved by grace.

How could I boast of anything I've ever seen or done?
How could I dare to claim as mine the vict'ries God has won?
Where would I be had God not brought me gently to this place?
I'm here to say I'm nothing but a sinner saved by grace.

I'm just a sinner saved by grace
When I stood condemned to death He took my place
Now I live and breathe in freedom with each breath of life I take
Loved and forgiven, back with the living
I'm just a sinner saved by grace.

REFLECTIONS

REDEMPTION AND RESTORATION IN REAL LIFE

A tragic shooting involving several people on Colorado Springs church grounds left three dead and three wounded. The shooter killed himself after being shot by a security guard. Earlier that day, he had entered a church building in suburban Denver, shooting four and killing two. The tragedy struck hard. The church had just started to come out of a painful and very public story about their former pastor's sexual sin. Now they were faced with this terrible tragedy.

Brady Boyd, the Senior Minister, called the shooter's parents and made arrangements for them to come to New Life to see where "their son had passed away." When asked, they agreed to meet with family members who had lost two teenage daughters that morning. They met with the grieving family in Boyd's office. The two families embraced, weeping and lamenting; they prayed together. Later the security guard who had been forced to shoot Murray joined them. The Murrays embraced and hugged her, releasing her from any guilt and remorse. "Please know we're so sorry that you had to do what you did. We're so sorry," the father said.

What can we learn from this? "We can talk philosophically about repentance and redemption and going forward with God, but what I saw in that room in my office was the greatest testimony of forgiveness and redemption that I have ever seen. It was a testimony that God really can restore and redeem."

– Brady Boyd

Redemption and Restoration in Real Life. Text Illustration shared by Jim Kane, First Church Of God, September 2008. Retrieved October 31, 2015 from http://www.sermoncentral.com/illustrations/sermon-illustration-jim-kane-stories-forgivenessforothers-69071.asp

Faith

◆ ◆ ◆

"It was only by faith in Christ that they could secure pardon of sin and receive strength to obey God's law. They must cease to rely upon their own efforts for salvation, they must trust wholly in the merits of the promised Saviour, if they would be accepted of God."

Ellen G. White, Patriarchs And Prophets

▼

What is saving faith? Can people accept Jesus as Savior and not as Lord? God himself (through the human preaching of the Word) issues the gospel call to us and, by the work of the Holy Spirit, regenerates us, imparting new spiritual life within. In this chapter we examine our response to the gospel call. We may define conversion as follows: Conversion is our willing response to the gospel call, in which we sincerely repent of sins and place our trust in Christ for salvation. The word conversion means "turning"—here it represents a spiritual turn, a turning from sin to Christ.

The turning from sin is called repentance, and the turning to Christ is called faith.[86] We may therefore define saving faith in the following way: Saving faith is trust in Jesus Christ as a living person for forgiveness of sins and for eternal life with God. This definition

---

86 Grudem, Wayne. Systematic Theology, An Introduction to Biblical Doctrine. InterVarsity Press 38 De Montfort Street Leicester LE1 7GP Great Britain, Grand Rapids, MI:Zondervan Publishing House, 5300 Patterson Ave., 60515, pp 710-712

emphasizes that saving faith is not just a belief in facts but personal trust in Jesus to save me. As we will explain in the following chapters, much more is involved in salvation than simply forgiveness of sins and eternal life, but someone who initially comes to Christ seldom realizes the extent of the blessings of salvation that will come. The definition emphasizes personal trust in Christ, not just belief in facts about Christ. Because saving faith in Scripture involves this personal trust, the word "trust" is a better word to use in contemporary culture than the word "faith" or "belief." The reason is that we can "believe" something to be true with no personal commitment or 7 times 6 is 42, but have no personal commitment or dependence on anyone when I simply believe those facts.[87]

The word faith, on the other hand, is sometimes used today to refer to an almost irrational commitment to something in spite of strong evidence to the contrary, a sort of irrational decision to believe something that we are quite sure is not true! (If your favorite football team continues to lose games, someone might encourage you to "have faith" even though all the facts point in the opposite direction.) In these two popular senses, the word "belief" and the word "faith" have a meaning contrary to the biblical sense.

The word trust is closer to the biblical idea, since we are familiar with trusting persons in everyday life. The more we come to know a person, and the more we see in that person a pattern of life that warrants trust, the more we find ourselves able to place trust in that person to do what he or she promises, or to act in ways that we can rely on. This fuller sense of personal trust is indicated in several passages of Scripture in which initial saving faith is spoken of in very personal terms, often using analogies drawn from personal relationships. John says, "To all who received him, who believed in his name, he gave power to become children of God" (*John 1:12*). Much as we would receive a guest into our homes, John speaks of receiving Christ. John

---

87 Grudem, Wayne. Systematic Theology, An Introduction to Biblical Doctrine. InterVarsity Press 38 De Montfort Street Leicester LE1 7GP Great Britain, Grand Rapids, MI:Zondervan Publishing House, 5300 Patterson Ave., 60515, pp 711-712

3:16 tells us that "whoever believes in him should not perish but have eternal life." Here John uses a surprising phrase when he does not simply say, "whoever believes him" (that is, believes that what he says is true and able to be trusted), but rather, "whoever believes in him." The Greek phrase pisteud eis auton could also be translated "believe into him" with the sense of trust or confidence that goes into and rests in Jesus as a person.

Jesus speaks of "coming to him" in several places. He says, "All that the Father gives me will come to me; and him who comes to me I will not cast out" (*John 6:37*). He also says, "If any one thirst, let him come to me and drink" (*John 7:37*). In a similar way, he says, "Come to me, all who labor and are heavy laden, and I will give you rest. Take my yoke upon you, and learn from me; for I am gentle and lowly in heart, and you will find rest for your souls. For my yoke is easy, and my burden is light" (*Matthew 11:28-30*). In these passages we have the idea of coming to Christ and asking for acceptance, for living water to drink, and for rest and instruction. All of these give an intensely personal Picture of what is involved in saving faith. The author of Hebrews also asks us to think of Jesus as now alive in heaven, ready to receive us: "He is able for all time to save those who draw near to God through him, since he always lives to make intercession for them" (*Hebrews 7:25*). Jesus is pictured here (as many times in the New Testament) as one who is now alive in heaven, always able to help those who come to him.

Grudem makes some very good points. Saving faith includes knowledge, approval, and personal trust. Knowledge alone and approval are not sufficient. We must depend on Jesus for salvation. Faith Should Increase as Our Knowledge Increases. Faith and Repentance which continue throughout life must come together.[88] When we turn to Christ for salvation from our sins, we are simultaneously turning away from the sins that we are asking Christ to save us from. If

---

88 Grudem, Wayne. Systematic Theology, An Introduction to Biblical Doctrine. InterVarsity Press 38 De Montfort Street Leicester LE1 7GP Great Britain, Grand Rapids, MI:Zondervan Publishing House, 5300 Patterson Ave., 60515

that were not true our turning to Christ for salvation from sin could hardly be a genuine turning to him or trusting in him. Although we have been considering initial faith and repentance as the two aspects of conversion at the beginning of the Christian life, it is important to realize that faith and repentance are not confined to the beginning of the Christian life.[89]   They are rather attitudes of heart that continue throughout our lives as Christians. Jesus tells his disciples to pray daily, "And forgive us our sins as we also have forgiven those who sin against us" (*Matthew 6:12, author's translation*), a prayer that, if genuine, will certainly involve daily sorrow for sin and genuine repentance. And the risen Christ says to the church in Laodicea, "Those whom I love, I reprove and chasten; so be zealous and repent" (*Revelations 3:19; cf. 2 Corinthians 7:10*).

With regard to faith, Paul tells us, "So faith, hope, love abide, these three; but the greatest of these is love" (*1 Corinthians 13:13*). He certainly means that these three abide throughout the course of this life, but he probably also means that they abide for all eternity: if faith is trusting God to provide all our needs, then this attitude will never cease, not even in the age to come. But in any case, the point is clearly made that faith continues throughout this life. Paul also says, "The life I now live in the flesh I live by faith in the Son of God, who loved me and gave himself for me" (*Galatians 2:20*).

With this understanding of true New Testament faith, we may now appreciate that when a person comes to trust in Christ, all three elements must be present.[90] There must be some basic knowledge or understanding of the facts of the gospel. There must also be approval of, or agreement with, these facts. Such agreement includes a conviction that the facts spoken of the gospel are true, especially the fact about being a sinner in need of salvation and that Christ alone has paid the penalty for our sin and He offers salvation to us. It also

89 Grudem, Wayne. Systematic Theology, An Introduction to Biblical Doctrine. InterVarsity Press 38 De Montfort Street Leicester LE1 7GP Great Britain, Grand Rapids, MI:Zondervan Publishing House, 5300 Patterson Ave., 60515.
90 Ibid.

includes an awareness that we need to trust in Christ for salvation as He is the only way to God, and the only means provided for our salvation. There are so many false teachings in the world today; people need know that there is only one way to God. This approval of the facts of the gospel will also involve a desire to be saved through Christ. True saving faith only comes, however, when we make the decision to depend on Jesus Christ as Savior.

Life Application for Personal Reflection
Faith
1. What are your thoughts on faith and your ability to trust completely in God? Do you trust in Him as far as you can see Him at work? Or can you trust Him past the point of your disastrous circumstances?
2. Have you ever experienced a devastating situation and had no choice but to trust God? Did you seek God? How have you grown spiritually since that event?

Suggested Reading
Faith
1. Hodge, Charles. Systematic Theology. 3 vols. Reprint edition: Grand Rapids: Eerdmans, 1970. First published 1871, pp 104-170.
2. Nave, Orville J. Nave's Topical Bible, A Digest of the Holy Scriptures, Nashville, TN: Thomas Nelson Publishers, 1979, 356-573.

Redeemer

Lyrics by NICOLE C. MULLEN LYRICS

"But as for me, I know that my
Redeemer lives, and he will stand upon the earth at last."
Job 19:25

Who taught the sun Where to stand in the morning
And who taught the ocean you can only come this far?
And who showed the moon where to hide till evening -
Whose words alone can catch a falling star?

Chorus:
I know my Redeemer lives
I know my Redeemer lives
All of creation testifies
This life within me cries
I know my Redeemer lives!

The very same God that spins things in orbit
Runs to the weary, the worn and the weak
And the same gentle hands that hold me when I'm broken
They conquer death to bring me victory!

He lives to take away my shame and He lives forever I'll proclaim
That the payment for my sin was the precious life He gave
But now He's alive and there's an empty grave!

REFLECTIONS

NAPOLEON AND THE PRIVATE

It is said of Napoleon that while he was reviewing his army one day, his horse became frightened at something, and the Emperor lost his rein, and the horse went away at full speed, and the Emperor's life was in danger. He could not get hold of the rein, and a private in the ranks saw it, and sprang out of the ranks towards the horse, and was successful in getting hold of the horse's head at the peril of his own life. The Emperor was very much pleased. Touching his hat, he said to him, "I make you Captain of my Guard." The soldier didn't take his gun and walk up there. He threw it away, stepped out of the ranks of the soldiers, and went up to where the body-guard stood. The captain of the body-guard ordered him back into the ranks, but he said "No! I won't go!" "Why not?" "Because I am Captain of the Guard." "You Captain of the Guard?" "Yes," replied the soldier. "Who said it?" and the man, pointing to the Emperor, said, "He said it." That was enough. Nothing more could be said. He took the Emperor at his word. My friends, if God says anything, let us take Him at His word. "He that believeth on the Lord Jesus Christ shall not perish, but have everlasting life." Don't you believe it? Don't you believe you have got everlasting life? It can be the privilege of every child of God to believe and then know that you have got it.

- D.L. Moody
Moody Bible Institute

Source: Dwight Lyman Moody. Anecdotes and Illustrations of D.L. Moody, Dwight Lyman Moody, Christian Classic Books, Retrieved November 14, 2015 from http://www.biblestudytools.com/classics/moody-anecdotes-illustrations/assurance.html

A little pre-school girl was at the doctor's office. When the doctor was listening to the little girl's heart through a stethoscope, he asked her, "Who do I hear in there? Is Donald Duck in there? Is Barney in there?"

The little girl corrected him very seriously: "No! Jesus is in my heart; Barney is on my underwear!"

Even a little child can understand having Jesus come into their hearts. That's what Jesus was talking about when he made this promise: "I will ask the Father, and he will give you another Counselor to be with you forever—the Spirit of truth. The world cannot accept him, because it neither sees him nor knows him. But you know him, for he lives with you ... and will be in you. I will not leave you as orphans; I will come to you." John 14:16-18

– K. Edward Skidmore
Castle Hills Christian Church

Justification

◆ ◆ ◆

"There is not a point that needs to be dwelt upon more earnestly,
repeated more frequently, or established more firmly in the minds of all
than the impossibility of fallen man meriting anything by his own best
good works. Salvation is through faith in Jesus Christ alone."

Ellen G. White

▼

The Bible explains salvation in many ways: ransom, redemption, forgiveness, reconciliation, adoption, justification, etc. That is because people understand their problem in different ways. For those who feel dirty, Christ offers cleansing. For those who feel enslaved, he offers redemption, or purchase. For those who feel guilt, he gives forgiveness. While regeneration is a secret act of God within us in which he imparts new spiritual life to us, justification is a judgment of God with respect to us. As a judge gives a verdict regarding our judicial status, God declares our innocence accordingly. We need to understand the distinction between the act of the one who renews us and the act of a judge.[91] In regeneration God gives us new spiritual life within but in justification God gives us right legal standing before him.

Just what is justification? We may define it as follows: Justification is an instantaneous legal act of God in which he **(1)** thinks of our

91 Grudem, Wayne. Systematic Theology, An Introduction to Biblical Doctrine. InterVarsity Press 38 De Montfort Street Leicester LE1 7GP Great Britain, Grand Rapids, MI:Zondervan Publishing House, 5300 Patterson Ave., 60515, pp 722-723

sins as forgiven and Christ's righteousness as belonging to us, and (2) declares us to be righteous in his sight.[92] After effective calling and the response that it initiates on our part, the next step in the application of redemption is "justification."[93] Here Paul says this is something that God does: "Those whom He called He also justified." Justification then, is that state wherein one is declared a righteous man. For example, if one is judged and condemned by the court to be punished and then granted amnesty (pardon) he has received forgiveness. But if proclaimed as without guilt after being judged by the court, this to him is justification. Salvation is complete in that He not only forgives, He justifies.

Paul quite clearly teaches that this justification comes after our faith and as God's response to our faith. He says that God "justifies him who has faith in Jesus" (*Romans 3:26*), and that "a man is justified by faith apart from works of law" (*Romans 3:28*). He says, "Since we are justified by faith, we have peace with God through our Lord Jesus Christ" (*Romans 5:1*). Moreover, "a man is not justified by works of the law but through faith in Jesus Christ" (*Galatians. 2:16*).

For people who feel alienated and put at a distance, he offers reconciliation and friendship. For those who feel worthless, he gives an assurance of value. For people who don't feel like they belong, he describes salvation as adoption and inheritance. For those who are aimless, he gives purpose and direction. For those who are tired, he offers rest. For the fearful, he gives hope. For the anxious, he offers peace. Salvation is all this, and more. Let's look at justification. The Greek word is often a courtroom term. People who are justified are declared "not guilty." They are exonerated, cleared, acquitted, declared OK. When God justifies us, he says that our sins will not be counted against us. They are removed from the record.[94]

92 Grudem, Wayne. Systematic Theology, An Introduction to Biblical Doctrine. InterVarsity Press 38 De Montfort Street Leicester LE1 7GP Great Britain, Grand Rapids, MI:Zondervan Publishing House, 5300 Patterson Ave., 60515, pp 722-723
93 Ibid.
94 Michael Morrison, Grace Communion International, http://www.gci.org/disc/16-salvation

When we accept that Jesus died for us, when we acknowledge that we need a Savior, when we acknowledge that our sin deserves punishment and that Jesus bore the punishment of our sins for us, then we have faith, and God assures us that we are forgiven. No one can be justified, or declared righteous, by observing the law (*Romans 3:20*), because the law does not save. It is only a standard that we fail to meet, and by that measurement, all of us fall short (*v. 23*). God "justifies those who have faith in Jesus" (*v. 26*). We are "justified by faith apart from observing the law" (*v. 28*).

To illustrate justification by faith, Paul uses the example of Abraham, who "believed God, and it was credited to him as righteousness" (*Romans 4:3, quoting Genesis 15:6*). Because Abraham trusted God, God counted him as righteous. This was long before the law was given, showing that justification is a gift of God, received by faith, not earned by law-keeping.

Justification is more than forgiveness, more than removing our debts. Justification means counting us as righteous, as having done something right. Our righteousness is not from our own works, but from Christ (*1 Corinthians 1:30*). It is through the obedience of Christ, Paul says, that believers are made righteous (*Romans 5:19*).

Paul even says that God "justifies the wicked" (*Romans 4:5*). God will consider a sinner righteous (and therefore accepted on the day of judgment) if the sinner trusts God. A person who trusts God will no longer want to be wicked, but this is a result and not a cause of salvation. People are "not justified by observing the law, but by faith in Jesus Christ" (*Galatians 2:16*).

The gospel call (in which God calls us to trust in Christ for salvation), regeneration (in which God imparts new spiritual life to us), and conversion (in which we respond to the gospel call in repentance for sin and faith in Christ for salvation). But then we have to reckon with the guilt of our sin? The gospel call invited us to trust in Christ for forgiveness of sins. Regeneration made it possible for us to respond to that invitation.[95] In conversion we did respond, trusting in Christ for forgiveness of sins. Now the next step in the process of applying redemption to us is that God must respond to our faith and do what he promised, that is, actually declare our sins to be forgiven. This must be a legal declaration concerning our relationship to God's laws, stating that we are completely forgiven and no longer liable to punishment.[96]

A right understanding of justification is absolutely crucial to the whole Christian faith. Once Martin Luther realized the truth of justification by faith alone, he became a Christian and overflowed with the new-found joy of the gospel. The primary issue in the Protestant Reformation was a dispute with the Roman Catholic Church over justification. If we are to safeguard the truth of the gospel for future generations, we must understand the truth of justification. Even today, a true view of justification is the dividing line between the biblical gospel of salvation by faith alone and all false gospels of salvation based on good works.

Justification includes a legal declaration by God.[97] The verb justify in the New Testament (Gk. dikaiod) has a range of meanings, but a very common sense is "to declare righteous." This sense is particularly evident, for example, in Romans 4:5, "And to one who does not work but trusts him who justifies the ungodly, his faith is reckoned as righteousness." Here Paul cannot mean that God "makes the ungodly to be righteous" (by changing them internally and making them morally perfect), for then they would have merit or works of their own to depend on. Rather, he means that God declares the ungodly to be righteous in his sight, not on the basis of their good works, but in response to their faith.[98] This declaration involves

95 Grudem, Wayne. Systematic Theology, An Introduction to Biblical Doctrine. InterVarsity Press 38 De Montfort Street Leicester LE1 7GP Great Britain, Grand Rapids, MI:Zondervan Publishing House, 5300 Patterson Ave., 60515, Chapter 24, pp 315-317

96 Grudem, Wayne. Systematic Theology, An Introduction to Biblical Doctrine. InterVarsity Press 38 De Montfort Street Leicester LE1 7GP Great Britain, Grand Rapids, MI:Zondervan Publishing House, 5300 Patterson Ave., 60515, pp 722-723

97 Ibid.

98 Grudem, Wayne. Systematic Theology, *An Introduction to Biblical Doctrine*. InterVarsity Press 38 De Montfort Street Leicester LE1 7GP Great Britain, Grand Rapids, MI:Zondervan Publishing House, 5300 Patterson Ave., 60515, pp 722-727

two aspects. First, it means that he declares that we have no penalty to pay for sin, including past, present, and future sins. "There is therefore now no condemnation for those who are in Christ Jesus" (*Romans 8:1*). In this sense those who are justified have no penalty to pay for sin. This means that we are not subject to any charge of guilt or condemnation: "Who shall bring any charge against God's elect? It is God who justifies; who is to condemn?" (*Romans 8:33-34*). The idea of full forgiveness of sins is prominent when Paul discusses justification by faith alone in Romans 4. This came about through the obedience of Christ, for Paul says at the end of this extensive discussion of justification by faith that "by one man's obedience many will be made righteous" (*Romans 5:19*). Secondly, the other aspect of God's declaration in justification, then, is that we have the merits of perfect righteousness before him. But questions arise: How can God declare that we have no penalty to pay for sin, and that we have the merits of perfect righteousness, if we are in fact guilty sinners? How can God declare us to be not guilty but righteous when in fact we are unrighteous? The notes below help us to understand how this is possible.

God imputes Christ's righteousness. This means that God applies Christ's righteousness to us and it is viewed as belonging to us. He "reckons" it to our account. In this way, Christ's righteousness became ours. Paul says that we are those who received "the free gift of righteousness" (*Romans 5:17*). Therefore, it is clearly contrary to the New Testament evidence to speak about the possibility of having true saving faith without having any repentance for sin. It is also contrary to the New Testament to speak about the possibility of someone accepting Christ "as Savior" but not "as Lord," if that means simply depending on him for salvation but not committing oneself to forsake sin and to be obedient to Christ from that point on. Some prominent voices within evangelicalism have differed with this point, arguing that a gospel presentation that requires repentance as well as faith is really preaching salvation by works. They argue that the view advocated in this chapter, that repentance and faith must go together, is a false gospel of "lordship salvation." It is essential to the heart of the gospel to insist that God declares us to be just or righteous not on the basis of our actual condition of righteousness or holiness, but rather on the basis of Christ's perfect righteousness, which he thinks of as belonging to us. This was the heart of the difference between Protestantism and Roman Catholicism at the Reformation.[99]

Protestantism since the time of Martin Luther has insisted that justification does not change us internally and it is not a declaration based in any way on any goodness that we have in ourselves. If justification changed us internally and then declared us to be righteous based on how good we actually were, then **(1)** we could never be declared perfectly righteous in this life, because there is always sin that remains in our lives, and **(2)** there would be no provision for forgiveness of past sins (committed before we were changed internally), and therefore we could never have confidence that we are right before God.[100] We would lose the confidence that Paul has when he says, "Therefore, since we are justified by faith, we have peace with God through our Lord Jesus Christ" (*Romans 5:1*). This gives us the assurance of forgiveness with God, and confidence to draw near to him "with a true heart in full assurance of faith" (*Hebrews 10:22*). Sometimes we hear "just as if I had never sinned." It is a clever play on words but the definition is misleading because it mentions nothing about Christ's righteousness which is reckoned to my account. We would not be able to speak of "the free gift of righteousness" (*Romans 5:17*), or say that "the free gift of God is eternal life in Christ Jesus our Lord" (*Romans 6:23*). The traditional Roman Catholic understanding of justification is very different from this. The Roman Catholic Church understands justification as something that changes us internally and makes us more holy within.[101]

---

99 Grudem, Wayne. Systematic Theology, An Introduction to Biblical Doctrine. InterVarsity Press 38 De Montfort Street Leicester LE1 7GP Great Britain, Grand Rapids, MI:Zondervan Publishing House, 5300 Patterson Ave., 60515, Chapter 24, pp 315-317

100 Grudem, Wayne. Systematic Theology, *An Introduction to Biblical Doctrine*. InterVarsity Press 38 De Montfort Street Leicester LE1 7GP Great Britain, Grand Rapids, MI:Zondervan Publishing House, 5300 Patterson Ave., 60515, pp 723-728

101 Grudem, Wayne. Systematic Theology, *An Introduction to Biblical Doctrine*. InterVarsity Press 38 De Montfort Street Leicester LE1 7GP Great Britain, Grand Rapids, MI:Zondervan Publishing House, 5300 Patterson Ave., 60515, pp 722-734

Justification comes by God's grace alone. According to Paul no one will ever be able to make himself righteous before God (*Romans 1-3*) for all have sinned and fall short of the glory of God and we need God's unmerited favor.[102]

God justifies us through our faith in Christ. Justification comes after saving faith. According to Paul, we have believed in the Lord in order to be justified by faith in Christ, and not by works of the law, because by works of the law shall no one be justified" (*Galatians 2:16*). Here Paul indicates that faith comes first and it is for the purpose of being justified. He also says that Christ is "to be received by faith" and that God "justifies him who has faith in Jesus" (*Romans 3:25,26*). The entire chapter of Romans 4 is a defense of the fact that we are justified by faith, not by works, just as Abraham and David themselves were. Paul says we are justified by faith. (*Romans 5:1*).

The meaning of a word in the Scriptures is not to be determined by the usage of theology, nor merely from the etymological significance of the word, but from its usage in the Word of God. In no secular writing will you find the richness nor accuracy of meaning attached to the word as in the Scriptures. God attaches new meaning to old words in the Bible, so that the etymology is not always accurate; neither are the theological interpretations through the ages always reliable guides to the real meaning of words. Theology, being a man-made science, goes astray many times and loses the meaning rather than expounds it. Unfortunately, there have been errors in the study of the word regeneration, and in the interpretation of the word justification. Many have made the word justification to mean the act of making one righteous, while the true meaning from the Scriptural usage is to "declare or reckon righteous." [103]

---

102 Grudem, Wayne. Systematic Theology, *An Introduction to Biblical Doctrine*. InterVarsity Press 38 De Montfort Street Leicester LE1 7GP Great Britain, Grand Rapids, MI:Zondervan Publishing House, 5300 Patterson Ave., 60515, pp 722-740
103 E. C. Bragg, Systematic Theology Soteriology, http://trinitycollege.edu/assets/files/ECBragg/SoteriologyR.pdf

Justification is not an act upon the sinner, but one done for him, a purely objective act of God in declaring the sinner righteous. For example, we should examine Romans 4:2-8. "For if Abraham was justified by works, he hath whereof to glory; but not before God, for what saith the Scriptures? And Abraham believed God, and it was reckoned unto him for righteousness. Now to him that worketh, the reward is not reckoned as of grace, but as of debt, but to him that worketh not, but believeth on Him that justified the ungodly, his faith is reckoned for righteousness."

The Biblical meaning of the word justification, therefore, is not to make righteous, but to reckon, declare, or show righteousness. To be justified before God then is to be declared righteous by God.[104] The need of justification is apparent. The sinner is a criminal with many charges against him before God the great judge. He has been regenerated, brought into the household as a Son, but what of His record; what of the condemnation of past sins? Forgiveness is not enough. Can one be thus changed and brought into God's family and still be a condemned criminal?[105] There is a need, therefore, of justification, the judicial legal declaration by God freeing man from his condemnation, "There is therefore now no condemnation to them that be in Christ Jesus." He has passed from judgment unto life and his method of release is by justification, and yet justification is more than a mere technical release from penalty or condemnation, or blotting out of the record against us. There is a positive aspect of justification, which is lost by many theologians who would make it negative as only a release.[106] The negative side is the "blotting out of the sins, the handwriting of ordinances which wore against us, taking it away, nailing it to His cross," but the positive side of justification in the resurrection of Christ is "He was raised for our justification." That is the precious part. By our identification with Him in His death the condemnation is removed, and by His resurrection and our continuance of identification with Him in His resurrection, we

104 E. C. Bragg, Systematic Theology Soteriology, Retrieved November, 2015 from: http://trinitycollege.edu/assets/files/ECBragg/SoteriologyR.pdf
105 Ibid.
106 Ibid.

are brought into new relationship, and in Christ we are as holy as Christ is. His obedience, His holiness, His righteousness, is ours, so that we are declared to be righteous, and as perfect as God demands us to be in Christ. As God reckoned Christ to be sin for me, in my stead and place, so He now reckons me to be holy in Christ.

The double reckoning is a blessed reality which is comforting to the redeemed. It is so much more than a mere legal technicality of releasing from the condemnation of the law. It means that all that Christ is before God, so are we. Is He spotless? So are we. Is He holy before God? Then so are we. Is He innocent, guileless, acceptable, loving, pure, and immaculate? Then, as we are in Him, so are we. Justification is God seeing the believer in Christ, as sinless, innocent, harmless, undefiled, and holy as He is. Justification sees us as more than a released sinner from the law's condemnation, but it sees us as though we had never committed a sin. This certainly is the declaration of 2 Corinthians 5:21, "For He made Him to be sin for us who knew no sin that we might be made the righteousness of God in Him." By no other method could the sinner be declared righteousness, the guilty innocent, the condemned free, the vile holy. We are in Christ. The grounds or basis of our justification does not reside in ourselves, in works which we can do, but upon the works of another - the death and resurrection of Christ. These truths will foster a clearer understanding of justification:

1. There is no justification by the works of the law, Romans 3:20; Galatians2:16.
2. Justification is a free gift of God's grace, Romans 3:24
3. Justification is by faith in Christ, Galatians 3:24; Romans 3:26; 4:5; Acts 13:39.
4. Justification is grounded in the Atonement of Christ, 2 Corinthians 5:31; Romans 5:9.
5. The extent of justification, Acts 13:39; Romans 8:1, 33-34.
6. The results of justification include a) peace Romans 5:1
   b) freedom from any charge (*Romans 8:33-34*) c) saved from

wrath, (*Romans 5:9*); and d) No judgment for sin, only works, whom God justifies He will glorify, Romans 8:30

In summary, justification is the reckoning or declaring by God of the sinner as righteous in Christ. It constitutes the releasing from condemnation, the necessity for punishment, and the blotting out of the record of past sins; but more, it declares the sinner as being in Christ as righteous as He, as obedient as He, as pure and innocent as He. Justification has to do with his state, the righteousness declared by God of Him, the Holy Spirit is sanctification works out in Him, the holiness of God which he imputes he wishes to impart.[107]

Life Application for Personal Reflection

Justification

1. Are you living a "guilt free" life or do you believe that you are being punished by God for sins that happened in your past?

2. Have you challenged others concerning whether they are being punished for past sin? How can you apply the doctrine of justification to your life to help persuade you that God has justified you?

3. What can you do to be confident that God does not require us to pay penalty for sins that have been forgiven by Jesus Christ? (Study Romans 8:1)

Suggested Reading

Justification

1. Berkhof, Louis. *Systematic Theology, New Combined Edition containing the full text of Systematic Theology and the original.* Grand Rapids, MI: Williams B. Eerdmans Publishing Company, 1996, pp 510-524.

2. Strong, James. LL.D. "Redemption." *The Strongest Strong's Exhaustive Concordance of the Bible, the only Strong compiled and verified by computer technology with Nave's Topical Bible Reference; most up-to-date Hebrew and Greek dictionaries for precise word studies, corrects all others.* Grand Rapids, MI 49530, 2001, p 1742. – "Justification." The Strongest Strong's Exhaustive Concordance of the Bible, The Strongest Strong's Exhaustive Concordance of the Bible, Grand Rapids, MI, 2001, 1784.

3. John F. Walvoord, *Systematic Theology: Abridged Edition.* 2 vols. Ed. By Donald K. Campbell, and Roy B. Zuck. Wheaton: Victor, 1988.

---

107 E. C. Bragg, Systematic Theology Soteriology, Retrieved November, 2015 from: http://trinitycollege.edu/assets/files/ECBragg/SoteriologyR.pdf

Fill My Cup Lord
By RICHARD EUGENE BLANCHARD Sr.

Like the woman at the well I was seeking
For things that could not satisfy;
And then I heard my Savior speaking:
"Draw from my well that never shall run dry".

Refrain:
Fill my cup Lord, I lift it up, Lord!
Come and quench this thirsting of my soul;
Bread of heaven, Feed me till I want no more
Fill my cup, fill it up and make me whole!

There are millions in this world who are craving
The pleasures earthly things afford;
But none can match the wondrous treasure
That I find in Jesus Christ my Lord.

So, my children, if the things this world gave you
Leave hungers that won't pass away,
My blessed Lord will come and save you,
If you kneel to Him and humbly pray

REFLECTIONS

A LIFE OF FAITH

Like Abraham, we are justified by faith. The supreme test of Abraham's faith came when Isaac had reached his early teens and God him to "Take now your son, your only son, whom thou lovest, Isaac, and go to the land of Moriah; and offer him there as a burnt offering on one of the mountains ..." (Gen. 22:2).

Though Abraham was accustomed to the pagan practices in the land of Ur, this was Isaac, his special son promised son by God. All the promises of God for the future of Abraham depended on Isaac. How could this possibly fit into the plan of God? But Abraham began the journey. He would obey God. He said, "God will provide for Himself the lamb for the burnt offering, my son" (Genesis 22:8).

Just as Abraham took the knife to take the life of his own son, God stayed Abraham's hand, and told him to offer instead a ram caught in a thicket nearby. Hebrews explains it. "By faith Abraham, when God him, offered Isaac as a sacrifice. He who had received the promises was about to sacrifice his one and only son, even though God had said to him, 'Through Isaac shall your promised offspring come'" (Hebrews 11:17-18).

God intervened and saved the life of Isaac. Even so, the day would come when God's own son would be stretched upon a cross, and God would not undertake to save Him because there was no other acceptable sacrifice for sin.

John F. Walvoord. Learning from Abraham about the Life of Faith, www.walvoord.com, January 1st 2008. Retrieved November 2014 from https://bible.org/article/learning-abraham-about-life-faith

Calling

◆ ◆ ◆

"One of the great virtues of Christianity, according to (John)Wesley, is the way it fills up our every waking hour. Both (N.T.) Wright and Wesley write that Christianity is not just about what God does for us but what God does in us."

John Meunier

▼

The word *called* here refers to the effective calling of the gospel, which includes regeneration and brings forth the response of repentance and faith (or conversion) on our part. When Paul says, "Those whom he predestined he also called; and those whom he called he also justified" (*Romans 8:30*), he indicates that the calling is an act of God. In fact, it is specifically an act of God the Father, for he is the one who predestines people "to be conformed to the image of his Son" (*Romans 8:29*). Other verses more thoroughly describe this calling.

There are some very specific trademarks found in action films that are fairly consistent although there is usually a little extra twist in superhero movies to keep the audience on edge. First, there is always a villain and always a hero. Second, if a villain cannot get to the hero, a strategy is put into place to go after the next best thing which would be the hero's Achilles heel. This is a weakness or a tender spot in the heart of the hero so that despite overall strength, this soft spot may be cunningly used by the enemy to potentially lead to the hero's downfall. While the mythological origin refers to a physical vulnerability, other common attributes or qualities can lead to downfall. However, in the superhero movies, we find always an extra twist. For example, in the movie about the comic strip heroes, Avengers, the fictitious, Loki seeks revenge and hates his brother so much that he launches an unprecedented threat against Earth which his brother, Thor protects. The level of warfare is far above regular human strength. "And there came a day, a day unlike any other, when Earth's mightiest heroes and heroines found themselves united against a common threat.[108]

Another example is in the *Raiders of the Lost Ark*, in which renowned archaeologist and expert in the occult, Dr. Indiana Jones, is hired by the Government to find the Ark of the Covenant, Hitler's agents are also after it because they believe, their armies will become invincible if they can acquire it. With it, they will be able to control the entire world. They try to take advantage of Indiana's respect for historical relics and his pure heart which is required to find the Ark of the Covenant. Jones must recover the Ark to prevent the Nazis from obtaining it. While the threat is against the entire earth, the warfare is in the spirit realm.[109]

In *Batman*, it is the same story of good versus evil in which various villains to try to lure the townspeople into compromising situations. As weak vessels, humans fall for the enemy's tricks while the superhero is still called upon to protect the city.

In these superhero films, there is something very common to all. While the battle is raging in the spiritual realm, the humans wander about aimlessly and carefree, and are completely oblivious to

---

108 On that day, the Avengers were born—to fight the foes no single super hero could withstand!" — Prologue from The Avengers used in the 1970s.
109 Raiders of the Lost Ark. American action-adventure film directed by Steven Spielberg, Released on June 12, 1981 (later marketed as Indiana Jones and the Raiders of the Lost Ark) 1981, Became the year's top-grossing film and remains one of the highest-grossing films ever made; ranked among the greatest films of all time in the action-adventure genre and often in general.

the danger that they bring upon themselves. They impose the same danger upon Batman, the very one who is driven to protect them - and who does it, not for reward, but because he believes he must take care of them since obviously, they cannot take care of themselves. The battle is far above their human capabilities and understanding. In all of the scenarios, the heroes miraculously rescue the people and save the world. Victims who were once blind can now see. They become aware of the battle and its significance.

Something we must not overlook is the impact of a saved life. Prior to being saved, we lived a self-centered life based on following our sinful nature. We did not care about the fact that Christ came and laid down His life on behalf of humanity in order to offer forgiveness and salvation. We were blinded and gave little thought to where we were going to spend our eternity. We were deceived and spent little time wondering about our state of sinfulness.

Why is it important to be born again? The Bible says that all people are sinners and that sin brings death (*Romans 3:23 and 6:23*). The Bible says that God has already made it easy for us by allowing Jesus Christ to die for our sins so that we can have eternal salvation. All we have to do is receive this free gift. It is like a situation in which you cannot get something yourself because the price is too high, and then someone pays for it for you. My daughter could not possibly have paid the price to receive the gift. She still would not have gotten the gift if she had decided to avoid my grasp when I tried to save her from being hit by a car. All of this pertains to the physical aspect of her life. We can imagine the ramifications had she not survived that incident. However, think of the spiritual implications of a life that is cut short. In other words, let's flip that around and think of the benefits or the value of a single life that is saved by God's grace.

Jesus came to earth more than 2000 years ago and died on a cross to pay for the sins of mankind. God the Father then raised Him from the dead, by Resurrection, proving He has power over life and death. The

Bible says that whoever believes in Jesus Christ will not perish, but will have everlasting life (*John 3:16*). Likewise, even though Christ has died for us (*Romans 5:8*), we will not have His gift of eternal life until we decide to receive it by being born again and saved. The Bible says to repent (*Luke 13:5*). That means to be sorry for, and to turn away from, sinful habits. The King James Bible says: "If thou shalt confess with thy mouth the Lord Jesus, and shalt believe in thine heart that God hath raised him from the dead, thou shalt be saved" (*Romans 10:9*).

This book is not simply meant to describe some lengthy process involved in salvation. It is meant to provide enlightenment and clear evidence of the need for every person and to understand what the beliefs are concerning salvation. There have been great theological studies on various subjects. Our eternal salvation is important. However, let us be clear and precise on these points. We need to keep the gospel simple when ministering to people. We do not have to offer a full discourse to someone lying on a deathbed; neither do we have to wax eloquent when speaking with an executive in the board room. When someone's soul is at stake, a simple question is all that is needed.

Jesus did not take forever to heal, restore, save, deliver or even resurrect someone from the dead back to life. He asked an impotent man at the pool of Bethesda, "Wilt thou be made whole?" (*John 5:6*). In modern day vernacular Jesus was asking, "Do you want to get well?" It was up to the man to express his desire. Only then did Jesus command him to get up and walk. We have a part in our solutions. Sometimes we are far too analytical, trying to understand exactly what needs to happen at every stage in the process. We overburden ourselves. We want to know the specific words to say, when to take the next step, how we are going to feel, or what God's next move will be but we need to have faith. There is a legitimate order of process but Jesus did not spend a lot of time walking the people through that explanation. One of the criminals hanging on the cross next to Jesus reprimanded the thief on the other side for calling on Jesus. The thief realized His condition and asked the Savior to remember him in the afterlife. Jesus readily promised that he would be with Him in Paradise. Can you imagine spending your last moments with the Savior of the world in clear proximity and not repent? Can you imagine having a full blown discussion on the steps to salvation while you are dying on the cross? I have visited many people on their deathbeds. I have spent the night in the same room and not once has anyone tried held a long discussion about the process of redemption or say, theories of atonement. An unsaved person wants to know "what must I do" to be saved! Jesus made it simple.

Simple questions like, "Do you know where you will spend eternity if you die today?" is a perfectly legitimate question. In every case, Jesus went straight to the point. He recognized and met the person right where he was. Even in the case of death, Jesus could extend His authority beyond the grave and pull someone out of their present, stinking condition, if they will simply answer His call. "Lazarus, come forth!" Man has been running for years from the very thing he needs most. From the Garden of Eden until now, he has managed to talk himself out of the very great blessing God always had for him. We were told by one Church of God minister, "You talk too much!" Imagine! If man could stop talking so much, and instead, listen to the Lord and honor God, he would not have to work so hard. Yet, man is working hard to give himself just a tiny portion of what God had planned for him.

Our responsibility comes heavily into play in serving the Lord. The core foundation of how He operates is laid upon responsibility with respect to His creation who have the ability to do His will. All throughout history, God has always made the first move when getting things done. However, He's expecting us to make the next one obediently and earnestly in response to His initial move.

If we take a careful look at (*Genesis 2:16-17*), we can clearly see the first responsibility men had with respect to God's commandments was to obey. Moreover, obedience is the first law of heaven. All throughout the Word of God obedience is also something that always plays a foremost role in people's lives that are serving God sincerely. Therefore, obedience is an indispensable necessity as far as serving and seeking God are concerned. Obedience is the foundation of our responsibility to God; in other words, our obedience to God is the very thing that maintains and sustains our responsibilities as His children. We're commanded to respond to God's call and purpose for our lives obediently and diligently. Besides, all blessings are predicated upon obedience. Evidently, God has been assigning humanity with various types of responsibilities since its inception from Genesis in the Garden of Eden to Revelation. Among these are responsibility toward God, toward ourselves, toward our family members, and toward our fellow humans. Out of these responsibilities mentioned above, the one that's more important is what we have toward God. If we're willing to carry it out wholeheartedly that will automatically empower us to carry out the other ones. Since there are quite a number of them, we'll just cover a handful of these responsibilities.

Since we're human, we may be struggling in some areas in our lives with respect to assuming certain responsibilities. We have to invite God to take care of that situation, so that we can do what God has commanded us to do. Our failure to do so or our excuses will not make God change His mind about what He wants us to do.

Ultimately we all need saving and cannot save ourselves. Good works can't possibly make up for the damage that sin has done to our relationship with God. Only He can save us. Salvation is a gift from God, poured out freely from His grace. It is available to everyone who accepts Jesus as their Lord and Savior.

The Bible tells us that there is only one way to Heaven. Jesus said, "I am the way and the truth and the life. No one comes to the Father except through me." (*John 14:6*) When we examine the world in the light of God's Word, what we see makes sense. The approach for studying God's Word, understanding the world, and living our lives for the Lord rests upon a very important question: "Should we use man's or God's wisdom?" The desire for man's wisdom as opposed to God's wisdom within the scientific community has resulted in the tendency to look to man in matters of science and disregard God's wisdom. This broad disregard for God's wisdom has resulted in a struggle to help our brothers and sisters in Christ, as well as helping the unbelieving world understand that it was in wisdom that God has made all things (*Psalm 104:24*).

The Bible touches every aspect of our lives, and it is by the Spirit's leading that we are able to discern the difference. We are then able share that Word with others.

As we study the Bible, it is interesting to discover that the Apostle Paul also considered the issue of whose wisdom we use to be very important for the first-century believers. Similar to today, the first-century church had a problem discerning the differences between man's wisdom and God's wisdom.

The Bible reveals that the people at Corinth held man's wisdom in higher esteem than God's wisdom. In 1 Corinthians 2:1–16, Paul shows that the Greek community of the first century struggled to understand that his message was brought to them by the wisdom of God. The reason being, in the Greek culture, the ability to speak well and the effective use of language (rhetoric) were the most prized abilities. In those days, men would stand at the street corners speaking and people would gather around just to hear well-orated speeches. The listeners would give money to the person who gave the best talk. This culture was all about the exchange of ideas and concepts centered upon man's wisdom in philosophy. The contrast between men's wisdom versus God's wisdom is what Paul addressed in 1 Corinthians 2:1–16, which states the following:

"And I, brethren, when I came to you, did not come with excellence of speech or of wisdom declaring to you the testimony of

God. For I determined not to know anything among you except Jesus Christ and Him crucified. I was with you in weakness, in fear, and in much trembling. And my speech and my preaching were not with persuasive words of human wisdom, but in demonstration of the Spirit and of power, that your faith should not be in the wisdom of men but in the power of God. However, we speak wisdom among those who are mature, yet not the wisdom of this age, nor of the rulers of this age, who are coming to nothing. But we speak the wisdom of God in a mystery, the hidden wisdom which God ordained before the ages for our glory, which none of the rulers of this age knew; for had they known, they would not have crucified the Lord of glory. But as it is written: "Eye has not seen, nor ear heard, Nor have entered into the heart of man The things which God has prepared for those who love Him." But God has revealed them to us through His Spirit. For the Spirit searches all things, yes, the deep things of God. For what man knows the things of a man except the spirit of the man which is in him? Even so no one knows the things of God except the Spirit of God. Now we have received, not the spirit of the world, but the Spirit who is from God, that we might know the things that have been freely given to us by God. These things we also speak, not in words which man's wisdom teaches but which the Holy Spirit teaches, comparing spiritual things with spiritual. But the natural man does not receive the things of the Spirit of God, for they are foolishness to him; nor can he know them, because they are spiritually discerned. But he who is spiritual judges all things, yet he himself is rightly judged by no one. For "who has known the mind of the LORD that he may instruct Him?" But we have the mind of Christ."

Paul was clear. He did not come with a superior way of speaking or with the wisdom of man when he brought the Word of God to the Corinthians. He brought the teaching of Jesus Christ in meekness, fear, and trembling—and by the demonstration of the Spirit in the power of God, not by enticing words. Furthermore, Paul wrote that we who are in Christ have " . . . received, not the spirit of the world, but the Spirit who is from God, that we might know the things that have been freely given to us by God" (*1 Corinthians 2:12*). The Spirit of God helps us to know and understand the things of God.

When looking at the world around us, we base our thinking about it on the Bible since it is our ultimate authority and the infallible source of God's revealed wisdom. Paul stated, "But the natural man does not receive the things of the Spirit of God, for they are foolishness to him; nor can he know them, because they are spiritually discerned" (*1 Corinthians 2:14*). By studying the natural world, we can see God's handiwork, and if we look carefully enough, we can actually see His engineering design at work.

It is easy for us to think we are better than we really are. The Jews, to whom God had given the Law, along with the promise of being a great nation and the source of great blessing to others, thought they were better than the Gentiles. The Gentiles who then came to faith began to look down on the Jews who rejected salvation by faith in Jesus Christ. Paul's words in Romans 11 are intended to bring the Gentiles back down to reality. Paul's purpose is to teach them the truth, which should turn them from arrogance to humility and from self-congratulation to heart-felt worship.

The Jews rejected Jesus as their Messiah and, as a nation, they were in a state of unbelief. They experienced the judgment of God in the form of hardened hearts, and would suffer a great calamity to the detriment of Jerusalem. A number of Gentiles, on the other hand, were coming to faith in Jesus. There came a time when things began to change; there was a shifting in the atmosphere. The complexion of the churches was changing from an almost exclusively Jewish constituency to a predominantly Gentile membership. In chapters 9-11 of Romans, Paul explains what is taking place. Those Jews who had not believed were not chosen (*Romans 9*). Furthermore, those Jews under divine judgment had rejected the gospel, (*Romans 10*).

Nevertheless because God's promises are a matter of sovereign grace and not of human works (*11:5-6*), Israel's hope was still secure and we can be grateful today, that God has always maintained a faithful remnant, preserving the line that He will someday restore and bless. God's purpose of bringing the good news of the gospel to the Gentiles, was so that men from every nation might be saved, and it has been accomplished through Israel's unbelief. If such blessings can come from Israel's disobedience, imagine what blessings will flow from Israel's restoration (*11:12, 15*).

The Gentiles should learn from the mistakes of God's chosen people, Israel, and they should be humbled for Israel's history is no mere academic exercise. If God has not overlooked the transgressions of His chosen people, surely He will not take the sin of Gentiles lightly either. Faith alone is the basis for abiding in God's promised blessings, and unbelief leads to divine judgment. When the Gentiles begin to be proud, they reveal the very same symptoms which led to Israel's demise.

Salvation takes place the very moment that you accept or embrace Jesus Christ as your Lord and Savior, totally trusting in the complete and finished work of Jesus, receiving His Life, Death, Burial and Glorious Resurrection as full payment for your past, present, and future sins. Romans 10:9-10. Someone said we do not have to accept Him as Lord; He can just save us. This is not true; we do have to follow Him. This book on Soteriology walks us through those very questions. Being saved means:

- ◆ To be forgiven of your sins
- ◆ To be justified by God through faith in Jesus (declared righteous, not guilty)
- ◆ To receive the free gift of eternal life through Jesus Christ
- ◆ To experience the new birth (ye must be born again)
- ◆ To have a personal, intimate relationship with the Lord Jesus
- ◆ To be delivered from penalty of sin (which is death, eternal separation from God)

- ◆ To receive the finished work of Jesus
- ◆ To be taken out the kingdom of darkness and put into the kingdom of His light
- ◆ To have a hope that goes beyond the grave, (because He lives, I too will live with Him for all eternity)
- ◆ There are so many precious promises and benefits that comes with being saved, being delivered, being a child of God! To God be the glory for the great and marvelous things He has done!

On another note, I thought about the question and I felt compelled to jot down the following list of short statements of what being saved means to me. The list is a bit long because the more I think and pray about being saved, the more I think of how broad and deep the blessings of the Lord are in salvation. Therefore, don't think this list is exhaustive, it's only what the Lord put on my heart up to this time. I imagine that in eternity the list of blessings of what being saved means to us will be endless and for that we can only praise the Lord for eternity. Perhaps you should make a list too, of what it means to be saved, to you.

Preeminently Important – Being saved is of preeminent importance; it's the most important decision of human existence and determines your eternal destiny. Being saved determines whether or not you will know Jesus and spend eternity with Him or that you will spend eternity in darkness, suffering painfully separate from God's glory. The Bible tells us we must be saved (*Acts 2:40; 4:12*). Being saved is the most important thing in a person's life (*Matthew 16:26; John 3:3-7,36*). God desires that all people be saved (*1 Timothy 2:4*).

Price – Being saved is offered by God freely as a gift of His grace, but it does not come cheaply. Jesus gave His life and shed His precious blood to save us (*1 Peter 1:18-19*). Therefore the first thing I think about when I consider being saved is the price Jesus paid to save me. When I think of the price Jesus paid it results in His empowering me.

Paid in Full – Being saved means the debt I owe God because of my sin has been paid in full by Jesus on the cross. Jesus came to pay a debt He did not owe, for those who owed a debt they could not pay. This is redemption (*Luke 1:68; Galatians 3:13; 1 Peter 1:18-19*). We are the righteousness of God in Him (*2 Corinthians 5:21; Revelation 5:9*). We cannot add or subtract from our state of being saved because the work done to save us was completed by Jesus. We know that because on the cross Jesus said, "It is finished!" (*John 19:30*). Jesus paid the debt for our sin by the once for all substitutionary sacrifice on the cross (*Romans 6:10; Hebrews 7:27; 9:12,27; 10:10*).

Pray for Forgiveness – Being saved means praying to God for forgiveness by His grace through faith in Jesus His Son who died on the cross paying the debt of sin we could not pay. In Jesus we can be forgiven our sins (*Ephesians 1:7; Colossians 1:13-14*). Being saved is only a pray away (*Acts 13:38-39; 26:18*).

Promises – Being saved means that in Christ the floodgates of God's promises are opened to us (*Ephesians 1:3-14*). God's Divine power has given us promises which will get us through life (*2 Peter 1:2-4*). With God's promises in sight, nothing can stop us (*Philippians 4:13*).

Peace – Being saved means I now have peace with God (*Romans 5:1*). Before I was saved I was a child of wrath and at odds with God (*Ephesians 2:1-4*), but He has saved me from all the chaos in my life in exchange for His peace that surpasses all understanding (*Philippians 4:6-9*).

Punishment – Being saved means I no longer face eternal punishment but am saved from the wrath of God (*Romans 5:9; 1 Thessalonians 1:10; 5:9*).

Power – When I think about the price Jesus paid and the love He showed for me on the cross I am grateful and compelled by His love (*2 Corinthians 5:14-15*). That love of God is poured out into my heart by the Holy Spirit (*Romans 5:5*). It is the Holy Spirit that empowers me with love to serve Jesus and others when by faith I trust him to empower me (*John 7:37-39; Acts 1:4-5,8*). Being saved means being given the power over my flesh (*Romans 6-8; Galatians 2:20; 5:16,24-25*).

Personal Presence – Being saved results in reconciliation with God in Christ and having a personal relationship with God in Christ by the Spirit. Being saved brings me into the presence of Jesus by the indwelling of the Holy Spirit (*Romans 8:9,11; 1 Corinthians 3:16*). The indwelling Holy Spirit enables me to know whom I believe in and have an assurance of being saved (*2 Timothy 1:12; 1 John 3:24*).

Prayer – Being saved means I can now come into the presence of Jesus to talk, commune, find direction and help (*Hebrews 4:14-16*). Being saved means praying without ceasing, living and breathing prayers to Jesus in the Spirit (*Romans 8:26-27; 1 Thessalonians 5:17; 1 Timothy 2:8; James 5:13-16*). Being saved means the sin that once separated me form God (*Psalm 66:18; Isaiah 59:2*) has been removed and I can communicate with the Father in Christ by the Spirit.

Purpose – Being saved means finally understanding the purpose of life. We are created to fulfill the purposes of God, not our own purposes (*Revelation 4:11 KJV*). We will only find purpose that fulfills in life when we live for Jesus (*John 10:10; Philippians 1:21*).

Perseverance – Being saved means God's grace is sufficient to guide me and sustain me through this life to my eternal home in heaven with Jesus (*1 Corinthians 15:10; 2 Corinthians 12:9-10*).

Purity – Being saved means the Holy Spirit is in me conforming me to the likeness of Jesus purifying my heart from indwelling sin (*Psalm 51; Romans 8:29; 2 Corinthians 7:10; 1 Peter 1:22*).

Providence – Being saved means God's providence for me will be fulfilled; it means God is in control. Nothing can separate me from the love of God. God is for me and wants His best for me. That truth will get me through anything (*Romans 8:28-39*).

Planted – Being saved means being born again by God's word (*1 Peter 1:23-25*). And being saved means being planted by the refreshing river of God's word (*Psalm 1; Ephesians 5:26*). The word of God is God's love letter and manual for life (*Psalm 119; 2 Timothy 3:16-17*).

Protection – Being saved means that in Christ we have protection from the attacks of the enemy Satan. God has provided spiritual armor for the battle and promised to crush Stan under our feet (*Ephesians 6:10-18; Romans 16:20*). The Bible tells us that He who is in us is greater than he who is in the world (*1 John 4:4*). If we submit to God and resist the devil, the Bible tells us he will flee from us (*James 4:7*). The Bible tells us to be alert and not presumptuous about the schemes of the devil. We should not take him or his schemes lightly, but we should confidently rely on the power of the Spirit in the name of Jesus to bring victory in the skirmishes and outright battles we have with the enemy (*1 Peter 5:8-11*).

Positive Prophetic Prospects – Being saved means now we live with God's providential prophetic picture in view (*2 Peter 1:19-21*). The future is not dark; it is bright with the prospect of God fulfilling faithfully His prophetic plan (*1 Thessalonians 4:16-18; Titus 2:13; Revelation*). This gives us hope in all situations, which anchors our souls throughout life (*Romans 15:4,13; Hebrews 6:19*).

People – Being saved and experiencing the blessings of God, the price Jesus paid, His purpose, presence, providence, promises, and being planted in His word, all cause me to want to share Him with other people (*Matthew 28:18-20*).

Perfect – Being saved makes me complete, ("perfect" means "complete," mature"). I am complete in Jesus (*Colossians 1:27-28; 2:10*). What God gives me in being saved fills me to overflowing (*John 7:37-39; 2 Peter 1:3-4*).

Prize – Lastly, being saved means we have crowns waiting for us in heaven. A crown of righteousness to the faithful (*2 Timothy 4:6-8*), a crown of glory for good shepherds (*1 Peter 5:1-4*), a crown of gold for the redeemed (Revelation 4:4), a crown of rejoicing for those who have led others to Christ to be saved (*1 Thessalonians 2:19*), and an incorruptible crown for those living with self control in the Spirit (*1 Corinthians 9:25*). These crowns will be ours to cast at the feet of Jesus to show our loving appreciation for Him once we arrive in heaven with Him (*Revelation 4:9-11*).

Praise – In light of all that being saved means to us and brings to us, we should live a life of praise to God for sending His only Son Jesus to the cross for us and raising Him from the dead. We should praise Jesus for going to the cross and raising from the dead for us. We should praise the Holy Spirit for revealing this gospel good news to us, for opening up and illuminating God's word to us and for bringing the presence of Jesus into our hearts and lives eternally (*Romans 15:11; Ephesians 1:11-14; Philippians 1:9-11; Hebrews 13:15; Revelation 19:5*).

That's what being saved means to me. This is a serious call by God but it has been toyed with by many who feel they would like to go into ministry and others who are looking for a career in ministry. No matter what area of ministry, if God did not call you, you need to be very careful about saying that He did. I was privileged to meet one of the 9 Tuskegee Airmen several years before his death. He was only too happy to share with me his experiences as a pilot in the U.S. Air Forces. However, he explained that the reason he believes he survived the many ordeals shared by these original Tuskegee Nine is that he was once fully intended to become a Baptist minister. He could not find a decent paying job and had no woman in his life. After contacting one of his Christian friends, he entered a special program of study over the course of a number of months studied diligently. He passed all of the preliminary tests. He was required to prepare for another more rigorous oral examination of more than 150 questions. He passed the exam. In the meantime, he began to think about the possibilities. He knew that they had assigned him a church and that he was expected to pastor. He began to focus on his personal desires and like clergy who chose the pastorate for personal gain, he expected to drive the best cars and have plenty money. But he did not have a relationship with God.

Mr. Val had drafted the letter of acceptance for his appointment and on the very day he was to deliver the letter, he was standing in front of hallway mirror, admiring his stature, his only suit of clothes and his one pair of shiny shoes. As he looked out over the horizon, a very, very, still small voice spoke to him quietly. It was quiet it was almost audible in his ears. According to Mr. Val, his heart was immediately convicted. He did not know God, had never received Christ in his life, and he was not religious. Yet here he was, getting ready to take a position as a pastor. They had accepted his application and his credentials, and all he needed to do was take the job. But this voice in his inner ear stopped him. "What are you doing?" were the words. Mr. Val described the immediate conviction that came over him. He dropped to his knees, opened up his heart to the Lord and when he came up, he had made a commitment that he would not go forward with the assignment. Instead, he joined the military and once there, he carried a little Bible with him wherever he went. After the honorable discharge of the Tuskegee Nine Airmen, he and his comrades eventually received commendations and acknowledgment for their service to the United States Army. He was honored for life by every sitting President until his death. However, Mr. Val honored God. He knew that the only reason he did not died in the military with all of the hatred and mistreatment from people in his own unit was because God forgave him for his treachery and spared his life. This is what Salvation will do for us.

When God calls people in this powerful way, he calls them "out of darkness into his marvelous light" (*1 Peter 2:9*); he calls them "into the fellowship of his Son" (*1 Corinthians 1:9; cf. Acts 2:39*) and "into his own kingdom and glory" (*1 Thessalonians 2:12; cf. 1 Peter 5:10; 2 Peter 1:3*). People who have been called by God "belong to Jesus

Christ" (*Romans 1:6*). They are called to "be saints" (*Romans 1:7; 1 Corinthians 1:2*), and have come into a realm of peace (*1 Corinthians 7:15; Colossians 3:15*), freedom (*Galatians 5:13*), hope (*Ephesians 1:18; 4:4*), holiness (*1 Thessalonians 4:7*), patient endurance of suffering (*1 Peter 2:20-21; 3:9*), and eternal life (*1 Timothy 6:12*).[110] These verses provide insight into this call. This is not merely the powerless call of a human being. This calling is rather a kind of "summons" from the King of the universe and it has such power that it brings about the response that it asks for in people's hearts. It is an act of God that guarantees a response, because Paul specifies in Romans 8:30 that all who were "called" were also "justified." This calling has the capacity to draw us out of the kingdom of darkness and bring us into God's kingdom so we can join in full fellowship with him: "God is faithful, by whom you were called into the fellowship of his Son, Jesus Christ our Lord" (*1 Corinthians 1:9*). This powerful act of God is often referred to as effective calling, to distinguish it from the general gospel invitation that goes to all people and which some people reject. This is not to say that human gospel proclamation is not involved. In fact, God's effective calling comes through the human preaching of the gospel, because Paul says, "To this he called you through our gospel, so that you may obtain the glory of our Lord Jesus Christ" (*2 Thessalonians 2:14*). Of course, there are many who hear the general call of the gospel message and do not respond. But in some cases the gospel call is made so effective by the working of the Holy Spirit in people's hearts that they do respond; we can say that they have received "effective calling."

We may define effective calling as follows: Effective calling is an act of God the Father, speaking through the human proclamation of the gospel, in which he summons people to himself in such a way that they respond in saving faith.

Although it is true that effective calling awakens and brings forth a response from us, we must always insist that this response still has

---

110 Grudem, Wayne. Systematic Theology, *An Introduction to Biblical Doctrine.* InterVarsity Press 38 De Montfort Street Leicester LE1 7GP Great Britain, Grand Rapids, MI:Zondervan Publishing House, 5300 Patterson Ave., 60515, pp 693-694

to be a voluntary, willing response in which the individual person puts his or her trust in Christ. This is why prayer is so important to effective evangelism. Unless God works in peoples' hearts to make the proclamation of the gospel effective, there will be no genuine saving response. [111] Jesus said, "No one can come to me unless the Father who sent me draws him" (*John 6:44*). An example of the gospel call working effectively is seen in Paul's first visit to Philippi. When Lydia heard the gospel message, "The Lord opened her heart to give heed to what was said by Paul" (*Acts 16:14*). In distinction from effective calling, which is entirely an act of God, we may talk about the gospel call in general which comes through human speech. This gospel call is offered to all people, even those who do not accept it. Sometimes this gospel call is referred to as external calling or general calling. By contrast, the effective calling of God that actually brings about a willing response from the person who hears it is sometimes called internal calling. The gospel call is general and external and often rejected, while the effective call is particular, internal, and always effective. However, this is not to diminish the importance of the gospel call—it is the means God has appointed through which effective calling will come. Without the gospel call, no one could respond and be saved! "How are they to believe in him of whom they have never heard?" (*Romans 10:14*). Therefore it is important to understand exactly what the gospel call is.[112] In human preaching of the gospel, three important elements of the gospel call must be included.

1. Understanding Salvation. God has a master plan of salvation in which man can be saved and brought into right relationship. This wider and more general calling is described by Paul in 1 Corinthians 7:20 in which he gives instructions to such followers concerning their condition in which they were called. He also explains that God saved and called us with a holy calling, not according to our own works but according to God's purpose and grace of the Lord Jesus (2

111 Grudem, Wayne. Systematic Theology, *An Introduction to Biblical Doctrine*. InterVarsity Press 38 De Montfort Street Leicester LE1 7GP Great Britain, Grand Rapids, MI:Zondervan Publishing House, 5300 Patterson Ave., 60515, pp 695
112 Grudem, Wayne. Systematic Theology, *An Introduction to Biblical Doctrine*. InterVarsity Press 38 De Montfort Street Leicester LE1 7GP Great Britain, Grand Rapids, MI:Zondervan Publishing House, 5300 Patterson Ave., 60515, pp 695

Timothy 1:9). God's divine call is a holy call. The Bible lets us know that there is a call by God to His service *(Acts 13:2).* For example, Paul was called to be an apostle *(Romans 1:1; 1 Corinthians 1:1).* We know that God has called sinners to be reconciled to Him but that only those who respond to Him on His conditions receive justification. The call to salvation is serious. The Bible says many are called but few are chosen. Romans 11:29 warns that "...the gifts and calling of God are without repentance." Anyone who comes to Christ for salvation understanding of who Christ is and how he meets our needs for salvation. Although many people have received Christ without assistance from others, it is always good to know minimally, who needs salvation and why, the price that is paid for our sins, and how the price was paid. For example, **a)** all people have sinned *(Romans 3:23),* **b)** the penalty for our sin is death *(Romans 6:23),* **c)** Jesus Christ died to pay the penalty for our sins *(Romans 5:8).* However, understanding those facts and even agreeing that they are true is not all that is required. A person must be genuinely sorry for their sins and personally respond or repent of their sins. Some people believe that if they simply utter the prayer, that everything is fine. This is the reason some popular showbiz entertainers think they do not have to make a change in their lives. They have no idea of the depth of sin nor the price that Jesus paid. A number of testimonies from those who felt compelled to leave the business show remarkable understanding and appreciation for the Savior. There was a genuine repentance and turning away from sin.

2. Personal Repentance and Faith. "Come to me, all you who are weary and burdened, and I will give you rest. Take my yoke upon you and learn from me, for I am gentle and humble in heart, and you will find rest for your souls. For my yoke is easy and my burden is light *(Matthew 11:28-30 NIV)*", This powerful invitation to those who are burdened with the cares of this world and the sin that is separating them from God. When overwrought with sin, one cannot be what God wants. That means their life is not blessed. genuine personal invitation requires a personal response from each one who hears it. If either the need to repent of sins or the need to trust in Christ for forgiveness is neglected, there is not a full and true proclamation of the gospel.[113] But what is promised for those who come to Christ? This is the third element of the gospel call.

3. A Promise of Eternal Life. The Bible speaks of the promises to those who come to him in repentance and faith. The gospel message is the promise of forgiveness of sins and eternal life with God. "For God so loved the world that he gave his only Son, that whoever believes in him should not perish but have eternal life" (*John 3:16*). And in Peter's preaching of the gospel he says, "Repent therefore, and turn again, that your sins may be blotted out" (*Acts 3:19; cf. 2:38*). Coupled with the promise of forgiveness and eternal life should be an assurance that Christ will accept all who come to him in sincere repentance and faith seeking salvation: "Him who comes to me I will not cast out" (*John 6:37*).[114]

The doctrine of the gospel call is important, because if there were no gospel call we could not be saved. Many sermons have ended with no gospel call. Some messages are given as the minister's motivational speech of the week. Others are designed for purposeful entertainment. Some are manipulative – perhaps to increase offerings, entice people to participate in different programs, get commitments for pledges. When we change the message to focus of benefits to the ministry instead of to the kingdom of God, we have missed the mark. It is understandable that some ministries want to find ways to attract the people into the church. However, Jesus commissioned us to "go" preach the gospel. We are to set the captives frees, and make disciples. If we do not preach Jesus, then "How are they to believe in him of whom they have never heard?" (*Romans 10:14*).The gospel call is important also because through it God addresses us in the fullness of

---

113 Grudem, Wayne. Systematic Theology, *An Introduction to Biblical Doctrine*. InterVarsity Press 38 De Montfort Street Leicester LE1 7GP Great Britain, Grand Rapids, MI:Zondervan Publishing House, 5300 Patterson Ave., 60515, pp 695-699

114 Grudem, Wayne. Systematic Theology, *An Introduction to Biblical Doctrine*. InterVarsity Press 38 De Montfort Street Leicester LE1 7GP Great Britain, Grand Rapids, MI:Zondervan Publishing House, 5300 Patterson Ave., 60515, pp 695-699

our humanity. He does not save us "automatically" without seeking for a response from us as whole persons. Rather, he addresses the gospel call to our intellects, our emotions, and our wills. He speaks to our intellects by explaining the facts of salvation in his Word. He speaks to our emotions by issuing a heartfelt personal invitation to respond. He speaks to our wills by asking us to hear his invitation and respond willingly in repentance and faith—to decide to turn from our sins and receive Christ as Savior and rest our hearts in him for salvation.

Life Application for Personal Reflection
Calling

1. Could we be saved without the gospel call? (Romans 10:14). What caused you to accept the call? Do you remember where you were and how you felt? How many times did you hear the call before you accepted?
2. What is meant by "For all have sinned, and come short of the glory of God." (Romans 3:23)
3. If Jesus Christ died to pay the penalty for our sins (Romans 5:8) then what is the significance of "The wages of sin is death" (Romans 6:23) and why do people need to understand.

Suggested Reading
Calling

1. Berkhof, Louis. Systematic Theology, New Combined Edition containing the full text of Systematic Theology and the original. Grand Rapids, MI: Williams B. Eerdmans Publishing Company, 1996, pp 454-458.
2. Grudem, Wayne. "Gospel Call." Systematic Theology, An Introduction to Biblical Doctrine. InterVarsity Press, 38 De Montfort Street Leicester LE1 7GP Great Britain, Grand Rapids, MI: Zondervan Publishing House, p 694.
3. Strong, James. LL.D. "Calling, The Christian."The Strongest Strong's Exhaustive Concordance of the Bible, the only Strong compiled and verified by computer technology with Nave's Topical Bible Reference; most up-to-date Hebrew and Greek dictionaries for precise word studies, corrects all others. Grand Rapids, MI, 2001, p 1679.

I Believe in a Hill Called Mt Calvary

GAITHER VOCAL BAND LYRICS

I believe in a hill called Mt Calvary
I believe whatever the cost
And when time has surrendered
And earth is no more
I'll still cling to the old rugged cross.

I believe that this life with its great mysteries
Surely someday will come to an end
But faith will conquer the darkness and death
And will lead at last to my friend.

I believe that the Christ
Who was slain on the cross
Has the power to change lives today
For He changed me completely
A new life is mine
And that is why by the cross
I will stay.

I believe in a hill called Mount Calvary
I believe whatever the cost
And when time has surrendered
And earth is no more
I'll still cling to the old rugged cross.

REFLECTIONS

UNDERSTANDING OUR CALLING

The story is told of a terrible traffic accident. Police officers were called to the scene and when they arrived they found a husband, wife, and two children lying unconscious in the car. They pulled them from the car, and as they waited for the paramedics to arrive they noticed a monkey in the car. Seeing that the monkey was the only witness to the accident who was conscious, the officers decided to question him about the accident. Turning to the monkey they asked, "What was the dad doing at the time of the accident?" The monkey motioned, indicating that the dad had been drinking. The officers next asked what the mother had been doing at the time of the accident. The monkey took his finger and shook it angrily at the unconscious man. The officers then asked what the children had been doing. The monkey this time indicated by hand gestures that the children had been fighting in the back seat. The officers said, "Well, no wonder there was an accident with all of that going on in the car." As they turned to leave, almost as a parting thought they asked, "By the way, what were you doing at the time of the accident?" To which the monkey signed that he had been the one driving.

My friends, I am afraid that there are many churches today headed for trouble. There are many churches heading for an accident because they do not understand God's design for the church. They do not understand God's call for leadership, and as a result they have allowed the noisiest monkeys in the group to run the church. My friends, noise does not equal leadership.

- Gene Gregory
River of Life Church

Source: The Story Is Told Of A Terrible Traffic Accident. Text Illustration shared by Gene Gregory, River Of Life Church, July 2007. Retrieved November 14, 2015 from http://www.sermoncentral.com/illustrations/sermon-illustration-gene-gregory-humor-excuses-62541.asp

"When John F. Kennedy was President of the United States, Life magazine published photos of his children, John Jr. and Caroline, playing with their toys on the floor of the Oval Office. Those images captured the hearts of the American people like nothing before or since. Why? I think it's because it bridged a gap between two thoughts: Kennedy was the President of the United States, but he was also a father. He held ultimate political power in the Free World, but playing at his feet were two little kids who called him Daddy. I don't think your kids would have been allowed to do that. Nor mine. But his kids were. Why? He was their father. He was not only President of the United States; he was also their dad.

In the same way, God is both our Father and the Lord of glory. We can approach Him confidently in prayer because we are His dearly beloved children, but we must never forget that He is also the Sovereign of the universe."

– David Jeremiah
Prayer, the Great Adventure, pp. 89-90.

Election

◆ ◆ ◆

"Faith is the condition under which God primordially wills the reception of salvation by all. "He chooses us, not because we believe, but that we may believe; lest we should say that we first chose Him"
(Augustine).

Thomas C. Oden, The Transforming Power of Grace

▼

God offers to all people the gospel message. This is called the external general call. But to the elect, God extends an internal call and it cannot be resisted.[115] Paul says, "He destined us in love to be his sons through Jesus Christ, according to the purpose of his will, to the praise of his glorious grace" (*Ephesians 1:5-6*). In another passage, he says, "We who first hoped in Christ have been destined and appointed to live for the praise of his glory" (*Ephesians 1:12*). Paul tells the Christians at Thessalonica, "We give thanks to God always for you all.... For we know...that He has chosen you" (*1 Thessalonians 1:2, 4*).

If that does not thrill us, then it is difficult to say what will. Believers are precious to God. We are his bride! And he loves us so much that he will not allow us to get too much ahead of ourselves and become our own God.

---

115 Matthew J. Slick, Calvinist Corner, Retrieved November, 2015 from: http://www.calvinistcorner.com/tulip.htm, 2012

Look at how awesome His love is and His willingness to do whatever it would take (including dying on the cross) in order that we can marvel at him and not have to suffer eternal death? He set up a process -- redemption, propitiation, forgiveness, justification, reconciliation — out of love. He has chosen us. This call is by the Holy Spirit who works in the hearts and minds of the elect to bring them to repentance and regeneration whereby they willingly and freely come to God. Some of the verses used in support of this teaching are Romans 9:16 where it says that "it is not of him who wills nor of him who runs, but of God who has mercy"; Philippians 2:12-13 where God is said to be the one working salvation in the individual; John 6:28-29 where faith is declared to be the work of God; Acts 13:48 where God appoints people to believe; and John 1:12-13 where being born again is not by man's will, but by God's. "All that the Father gives Me shall come to Me, and the one who comes to Me I will certainly not cast out," (*John 6:37*). To understand the basis or precedence for election, we would have to study the Old Testament in Genesis 12:1-3 where the Lord said to Abram, "Get thee out of thy country, and from thy kindred, and from thy father's house, unto a land that I will shew thee: And I will make of thee a great nation, and I will bless thee, and make thy name great; and thou shalt be a blessing: And I will bless them that bless thee, and curse him that curseth thee: and in thee shall all families of the earth be blessed." This Abrahamic Covenant forms the basis for the doctrine of the election of Israel. Widely regarded as God's chosen people, we see that this declaration is appropriate when it comes to Israel, but is also fundamental to the providential plan of God to restore the world into a righteous relationship with God. When God cut this covenant with Abraham, it was intended to be a permanent agreement. The purpose of the Divine election of Israel was stated in the first three verses of Genesis. It was intended that Israel would be blessed so all of the nations on the earth would be blessed as they blessed Israel. God's purpose in the election of Israel was to also bring salvation to the Gentiles. It was not intended that the God of Israel would only be God for the Jews alone.

1) The word denotes the act of selection, or separation of one object from surrounding objects. That is the simple real meaning of the word, selection and separation. We use it every day in voting called "elections" or selections of one object over another. Such is the meaning of the verse, "The Lord hath set apart him that is godly for Himself." Here is the word election meant without using the word itself, "a setting apart" of a certain class of folks for Himself. In Scriptures it means the right to select or choose or separate some.

2) The radical difference between the purpose of election and the actual act of election. You cannot fail to notice the important difference between the purpose to select and the act or process of selection. The purpose of selection exists as a reality as soon as you have made up your mind, but the actual process has no real existence until the time when you actually carry out your purpose of selection. Until that is carried out, there is in reality no election. How important this distinction is: to say that God has purposed the election of every saved person from eternity is one thing; but to say that He decreed their election from eternity so that, in fact, before they are born they had a real election is another thing and runs contrary to some plain Scriptures. We note an illustration from the election of Aaron to the high priestly office, that God purposed from eternity to make Aaron priest is right; but to say that, in fact, the election was carried out from eternity is wrong, as can be seen from the story of its carrying out, Numbers 17:5, "And it shall come to pass that the man's rod whom I shall choose shall blossom;" not that God did not purpose before, but, actually not until Aaron was anointed, did election take place. This is the proper meaning of election. It is the actual deed of separation, "Set apart him that is godly for Himself," but not until he is godly, and only the godly; the sinner is nowhere in God's Book called elect. Only the saved bear that name. Whenever the Scripture speaks of election as from eternity, it means and can mean nothing else than the election in the purpose of God.

There are a number of elections in the Word of God: *angelical election* -"elect angels;' *national election* - Israelites were divinely chosen from all other nations as His peculiar treasure and were an elect nation; *sacerdotal election* - as the case of Aaron and the Levitical priesthood; *regal election* - the choosing of Saul and, after his rejection, the choosing of the house of David to rule Israel; *mediatorial* election - for Jesus the Son of God was styled, "Mine elect in whom my soul delighteth;" then lastly, there is the evangelical election (the one which has troubled folks) - which consists in the separation of those who do believe upon Christ from all the world around them into membership in the Church of Christ, but in all of these there is the same principle. God's purpose in election is one thing and the actual election to the office of elect is another, See Ephesians 3:11. Here the eternal calling of the Church to display the "manifold wisdom of God" is given as existing in the eternal purpose, which He purposed in Christ. The very name Church is "the called-out ones," and the words of Christ, "I have chosen you out of the world." *Note:* Elections from eternity in the mind of God in purpose, and we shall note at the close of this discourse that His fore-knowledge is the basis from which He purposes His election, but the actual election is when the sinner is saved, separated from the rest of the sinners who are non-elect. That act of separation and making one godly is His election. God is the sole source of this election; He is the sole agent. To Him belongs all the credit and glory. No sinner would ever find God without God's influence and drawing him, and God does the separating or electing. God does the choosing or selecting; but as we shall see later, He does it by His foreknowledge. (Here we arrive at mystery again).

3) *The purpose of election, or the ultimate end, which God had in view in election.* There is, of course, only one grand end in all that God has ever done or ever will do - it is the glory of God. There could be no other end than this, spoken of in the Bible as "for My own Name's sake," 1 Corinthians 10:31.

194

While this is the overall grand end and purpose in election, there are two subordinate ends; one has to do with the state of the subjects of election and the other with their character, in their state, to separate them from the world under the protection and daily cleansing and sprinkling of the blood of Christ, 1 Peter 1:2, "Elect unto the sprinkling of the blood of Christ," and 2 Thessalonians 2:13, "God hath from the beginning chosen you unto salvation." That is His purpose from the beginning. In their character, they are elected unto obedience, I Peter 1:2; or Paul in Ephesians 1:4, chosen that they "should be holy and without blame before Him in love;" called or elected unto salvation and perfect standing before God as to their state; and holiness of character as to their daily character; all that He might be glorified by the display of His unmerited grace upon unworthy, hell-bound creatures.

4) *The nature of election.* That there is a point of similarity between all of the elections spoken of in Scripture is assured; but that they are all one and the same in nature, no one would venture to say. Therefore, to alight upon the reference by Paul of God's election of Israel in Rom. 8-9 for a perfect outline of His election of the Church is folly. Some of God's elections are unconditional, as the election of Israel as a nation unto Himself. Nationally, it was unconditional, but individually, conditional, "for they are not all Israel which are of Israel," and His election of David to kingship over Israel. This line of thought can be further traced, and we may have occasion to refer to it again at the close. What then are the distinguishing features of the election of grace now? These conditions were not a part of the other elections. To understand the nature of this election of grace, it is necessary to understand the two hindrances to election, and how election removes these two hindrances out of the way.

What hindrance is there to the daily enjoyment of a sinner to the sprinkling of the cleansing blood of Christ? It is the state of condemnation in which the sinner rests because of unbelief in the saving work of Christ. The second hindrance keeping him from believing in Christ's atoning work for him is his unregenerated nature, which is at enmity with God and voluntarily rejects God's testimony. Here is the two-fold hindrance to election, his state of condemnation and his evil nature, which keeps him there. God's election would remove those two hindrances, and, in its nature, it does just that. To remove the condemnation alone wouldn't be enough; that is justification. To remove the evil heart of unbelief would not be enough; that is regeneration. Both of these two are acts of God alone. Election, however, is both of these two: by that act of election he is removed from under the condemnation of his sin and the enmity from his soul by the implanting of a new, godly nature! This is true and proper evangelical election. Here it is different from all other divine elections. The elect angels never even fell, but are elect only because they never fell.

How different their election is from ours! Aaron's election consisted merely in God choosing him from among all others to fulfill the priestly office, requiring no greater change in his nature to do it. God's choosing of David to be king above all others was such an election, based upon God's foreknowledge that he would be a man after God's own heart. Jesus needed no work of grace in His own heart to be elected by God to be the only mediator between God and man. The election of grace, however, goes far beyond God's election of other men to their positions. The elect Church is justified and sanctified. Summed up, the election of grace is the removal of the evil heart of unbelief and the condemnation of guilt from the sinner, by the means of justification and regeneration, both accomplished only by God; hence, in truth, "It is not of him that willeth nor of him that runneth, but of God who showeth mercy." This truth of election may further be illustrated by the fact that it is not declared as being something finished In the transaction from eternity, but as being accomplished by the use of means.

In 2 Thessalonians 2:13, Paul very distinctly says that we are "chosen to salvation through sanctification of the Spirit and belief of the truth." It is not chosen to sanctification of the Spirit, but chosen to salvation through sanctification of the Spirit. It is not chosen to the truth, but to salvation through the belief in the truth of the fact that, what God does in time, He purposed from all eternity to do. The actual election, according to this verse, is only by the means of the work of the Holy Spirit when the truth is believed; yet, that truth cannot have been believed by the sinner from eternity, nor can the sinner be said to have been sanctified by the Spirit from eternity.

Here is the imperative of the gospels appeal to sinners. God has provided the means for man's election entirely apart from man, without any aid from him. The sacrifice of Christ was accomplished; the Holy Spirit was given; and the good news, or the "Truth of the Gospel," to be believed had been sounded out to the sinner. All things are ready for the immediate election of the sinner, but inasmuch as the sinner is a free agent and is graciously furnished by the Holy Spirit with everything that is necessary for the unbelief of the truth," it is at this point that he is called upon to do his part, to accept "the truth of the testimony of the Spirit" about Christ. The sinner cannot be elected when he refuses the one conditional means to election, "belief of the truth." The only damning sin in the world is unbelief (apart from the unpardonable sin, which is, after all, a form of unbelief). Christ said so, John 3:18; 16: 8-9. As long as the sinner refuses to believe the truth, he cannot be elected unto Christ, separated from the world of sinners. There is no election out of Christ; Paul says, "Elect in Christ."

As long as he remains out of Christ, he is not one of the elect, nor can he be. When the apostle speaks of "chosen in Christ before the foundation of the world," he is referring to the election of purpose, God's purpose to elect from all eternity; hence, the plan of salvation is an eternal plan. This purpose to elect was based on the infallible foreknowledge of God as to how man should choose, Peter calls it "elect according to the foreknowledge of God," See Romans 8:28-30 (interesting - all in the past tense.) Remember that His foreknowledge does not decree anything.

Life Application for Personal Reflection
Election
1. How does the doctrine of election make you feel as one of God's elect? Do you feel that it unfair to others that may not be?
2. Do you think everyone should be among the elect? Why do you feel some people never heed the call? Do you know some people who refuse to accept gospel call? If some are given over to a reprobate mind based on a sovereign decision made by God before creation, it is possible to trust God despite possibly knowing some of these people personally?

Suggested Reading
Election
1. Berkhof, Louis. Systematic Theology, New Combined Edition containing the full text of Systematic Theology and the original. Williams B. Eerdmans Publishing Company, 255 Jefferson Ave., S.E., Grand Rapids, MI 49503, 1996, pp 114-115.
2. Hodge, Charles. Systematic Theology. 3 vols. Reprint edition: Grand Rapids: Eerdmans, 1970. First published 1871, pp 333-349.
3. Klein, William W. The New Chosen People: A Corporate View of Election. Grand Rapids, MI: ZOndervan Publishing, 1990.

There Is A Name

Lyrics by BYRON CAGE

Neither is there salvation in any other: for there is none other name [Jesus] under heaven given among men, whereby we must be saved. (Acts 4:12)

There is a name, (4X)
Precious name
Bless that name
O Jesus there is a name, O Jesus there is a name.

There is a healing in the name
Healing in the name (3X)
Precious name
Bless that name
O Jesus there is a name, O Jesus there is a name.

Does anybody love the name(4x)
Precious name
Bless that name
O Jesus there is name, O Jesus there is a name.

Glory to that name, Glory to that name
Name ---, Bless that name,
O Jesus there is a name
O Jesus there is a name

I'll forever praise that name
Jesus Jesus Jesus Jesus

REFLECTIONS

GOD'S FAVORITES

Conrad Hyers in his book, And God Created Laughter tells of an 8 year old girl who wrote to Abraham Lincoln, who was then running for President suggesting that he grow a beard. In to hide the homeliness of his face. Lincoln could have been offended, but instead he answered her letter personally and thanked her for her suggestion, furthering adding that he'd like to visit with her when his campaign came to her area.

On the day the campaign train was scheduled to pass through, practically the whole town was assembled at the station well, all except the little girl. After all, her father reasoned, Lincoln would be interested only in politicians and voters - not the attention of a little girl. However, that as the train approached, it was forced to stop for repairs. Lincoln, not wanting to sit in the warm train, set off across the field afoot in search of the little girl's home.

When Lincoln introduced himself at the door, the maid was speechless. But the little girl and her playmate, the maid's daughter, welcomed him in as if they were expecting him. They invited him to join them in a little pretend party with tea cups. After a while, Lincoln thanked them for the party, and asked them how they liked his new beard. Then he walked to the waiting train.

When Lincoln boarded the train, it started on its way and went right through the town without stopping. Right past all the waiting dignitaries, politicians, band and the towns people in their Sunday best! Lincoln hadn't come to visit people who were putting on a show for his benefit. He came visit and say thanks to a little girl who just wanted to spend time with him.

Conrad Hyers. And God Created. Text Illustration shared by Jeff Strite, Church Of Christ At Logansport, January 2001. Retrieving November 2015 from http://www.sermoncentral.com/illustrations/sermon-illustra-tion-jeff-strite-stories-promisesofgod-godslove-kingdomofgod-503.asp

Predestination and Foreknowledge

◆ ◆ ◆

"On such sunny, sad mornings I always feel in my bones that there is a chance yet of my not being excluded from Heaven, and that salvation may be granted to me despite the frozen mud and horror in my heart."
Vladimir Nabokov, Pale Fire

▼

This idea of election is consistent with the whole Gospel, which is for every man. It throws the blame for man's impenitence where it belongs, on man and not God. It shows that God is not willing that any should perish but that all should come to acknowledge of repentance, and that Christ died for all men. Here are some important points to seal our understanding:

Election - Not Based on God's Foreknowledge of Our Faith: People readily agree sometimes that God predestines some to be saved, but they will say that he does this by looking into the future and seeing who will believe in Christ and who will not. If he sees that a person is going to come to saving faith, then he will predestine that person to be saved, based on foreknowledge of that person's faith. If he sees that a person will not come to saving faith, then he does not predestine that person to be saved. In this way, it is thought, the ultimate reason why some are saved and some are not lies within the people themselves, not within God. All that God does in his predestining work is to give confirmation to the decision he knows people will make on their own. The verse commonly used to support this view is Romans 8:29: "For those whom he foreknew he also predestined to be conformed to the image of his Son."

Foreknowledge of Persons, Not Facts: But this verse can hardly be used to demonstrate that God based his predestination on foreknowledge of the fact that a person would believe. The passage speaks rather of the fact that God knew persons ("those whom he foreknew"), not that he knew some fact about them, such as the fact that they would believe. It is a personal, relational knowledge that is spoken of here: God, looking into the future, thought of certain people in saving relationship to him, and in that sense he "knew them" long ago. This is the sense in which Paul can talk about God's "knowing" someone, for example, in 1 Corinthians 8:3: "But if one loves God, one is known by him. Similarly, he says, "but now that you have come to know God, or rather to be known by God..." (*Galatians 4:9*). When people know God in Scripture, or when God knows them, it is personal knowledge that involves a saving relationship.

Faith – Not the Reason God Chose Us: In addition, when we look beyond these specific passages that speak of foreknowledge and look at verses that talk about the reason God chose us, we find that Scripture never speaks of our faith or the fact that we would come to believe in Christ as the reason God chose us.

Election Based on our Faith would suggest salvation comes by merit which is not true. Yet another kind of objection can be brought against the idea that God chose us because he foreknew that we would come to faith. If the ultimate determining factor in whether we will be saved or not is our own decision to accept Christ, then we shall be more inclined to think that we deserve some credit for the fact that we were saved: in distinction from other people who continue to reject

Christ, we were wise enough in our judgment or good enough in our moral tendencies or perceptive enough in our spiritual capacities to decide to believe in Christ. But once we begin to think this way then we seriously diminish the glory that is to be given to God for our salvation. We become uncomfortable speaking like Paul who says that God "destined us... according to the purpose of his will, to the praise of his glorious grace" (*Ephesians 1:5-6*), and we begin to think that God "destined us... according to the fact that he knew that we would have enough tendencies toward goodness and faith within us that we would believe." When we think like this we begin to sound very much unlike the New Testament when it talks about election or predestination. By contrast, if election is solely based on God's own good pleasure and his sovereign decision to love us in spite of our lack of goodness or merit, then certainly we have a profound sense of appreciation to him for a salvation that is totally undeserved, and we will forever praise His "glorious grace."

The difference between two views of election can be seen in the way they answer a very simple question. Given the fact that in the final analysis some people will choose to accept Christ and some people will not, the question is, "What makes people differ?" That is, what ultimately makes the difference between those who believe and those who do not? If our answer is that it is ultimately based on something God does (namely, his sovereign election of those who would be saved), then we see that salvation at its most foundational level is based on grace alone. On the other hand, if we answer that the ultimate difference between those who are saved and those who are not is because of something in man (that is, a tendency or disposition to believe or not believe), then salvation ultimately depends on a combination of grace plus human ability.

Predestination Based on Foreknowledge: This does not give people free choice. The idea that God's predestination is based on foreknowledge of their faith encounters still another problem: upon reflection, this system turns out to give no real freedom to man either. For if God can look into the future and see that one person will come to faith in Christ, and that the other person will not come to faith in Christ, then those facts are already fixed, they are already determined. If we assume that God's knowledge of the future is true (which it must be), then it is absolutely certain that the first person will believe and the second person will not. There is no way that their lives could turn out any differently than this. Therefore it is fair to say that their destinies are still determined, for they could not be otherwise. If their destines are determined by God himself, then we no longer have election based ultimately on foreknowledge of faith, but rather on God's sovereign will. However, if these destinies are not determined by God, then who or what determines them? All Christians generally accept that there is no powerful being other than God controlling people's destinies. There really would chaos in the universe. Therefore it seems that the only other possible solution would be to say they are determined by some impersonal force, some kind of fate, operative in the universe, making things turn out as they do. But what kind of benefit is this? We would have then sacrificed election in love by a personal God for a kind of determinism by an impersonal force and God is no longer to be given the ultimate credit for our salvation. This makes no sense.

In conclusion, we must concede that election is unconditional. For the previous the reasons above, it is best to reject the idea that election is based on God's foreknowledge of our faith. We conclude instead that the reason for election is simply God's sovereign choice. (*Ephesians 1:5*). God chose us simply because he decided to bestow his love upon us. It was not because of any foreseen faith or foreseen merit in us. This understanding of election has traditionally been called "unconditional election." It is "unconditional" because it is not conditioned upon anything that God sees in us that makes us worthy of his choosing us. Sometimes people regard the doctrine of election as unfair, since it teaches that God chooses some to be saved and passes over others, deciding not to save them. How can this be fair?

First of all, while some object to the doctrine of election as being unfair, it is nevertheless based upon God's will and His pleasure. He makes the choice for His own reasons. Secondly, God's choice is not capricious or arbitrary; it is not random or made irrationally. God does not elect one because of worthiness but because of His sovereign, mysterious will. Everything God does is good and perfect. Thirdly, unconditional election does not preclude nor stifle evangelism. It actually empowers and confirms it. Preaching the gospel is part of God's plan to call others forth into His will. By understanding election, we can share the gospel one of them could be Christ's sheep. Fourth, our role is not to determine who is among the elect. We are to pray, share the good news and make disciples. If we speak the Word, God will use draw all men unto Himself.

I heard someone complain how monstrous it is that some people will end up in hell because they were of the elect. Nothing could be further from the truth. Unconditional election does not mean that there will be people in heaven who do not want to be there; nor will there be people in hell who wanted to be in heaven or missed the pearly gates because they were not of the elect. God intervenes in the lives of the elect and works in their lives through the Holy Spirit so that they willingly respond in faith to Him. His sheep will hear his voice and follow him" (John 10:1-30). Such is not the case of the non-elect. They refuse to be grateful or acknowledge Him as God. Consequently, they receive the rightful punishment due them. While the elect receive God's perfect grace, the non-elect receive God's perfect justice. There are many arguments against unconditional election but the answer lies in respectively understanding God's passive will in contrast to His decreed will. The passive will of God includes the things He might desire in a sense but does not foreordain or bring to pass. There are things God might desire but does not decree to happen. While He does not desire men to sin or take pleasure in the destruction of the wicked, we know that He allows them free will. His pre-determined plan allows for the fact that some will disobey Him and go to hell. God's sovereign choice is to save people despite their depravity which He accomplishes by predestinating them to be adopted into the kingdom of His dear Son, Jesus Christ. The question we really should ask is not why God chooses only some to salvation, but why He would choose any at all.

This objection of unfairness takes a slightly different form when people say that it is unfair of God to save some people and not to save all. We recognize in human affairs that it is right to treat equal people in an equal way. Therefore it seems intuitively appropriate to us to say that if God is going to save some sinners he ought to save all sinners. But in answer to this objection it must be said that we really have no right to impose on God our intuitive sense of what is appropriate among human beings. God's sovereignty as Creator gives Him a right to do with his creation as he wills (see Rom. 9:19-20, quoted above). If God ultimately decided to create some creatures to be saved and others not to be saved, we have no moral or scriptural basis for complaining.

Life Application for Personal Reflection
Predestination

1. What are your thoughts on God making a sovereign decision to save certain people, not based on their merits, and yet choose to leave certain others behind?
2. Have you ever met a hardened person? Did you offer them the gospel? Did you attempt more than once to persuade them of the love of Christ? Recount the situation and compare it to the Bible (Ephesians 1:1-6, 12 and Rom 8:28-30, Acts 13:8)

Suggested Reading
Predestination

1. Basinger, David, and Randall Basinger, eds. Predestination and Free Will. Downers Grove, IL.: Inter-Varsity Press, 1985.
2. Berkhof, Louis. Systematic Theology, New Combined Edition containing the full text of Systematic Theology and the original. Grand Rapids, MI: Williams B. Eerdmans Publishing Company, 1996, pp 109-118.
3. Grudem, Wayne. "Atonement." Systematic Theology, An Introduction to Biblical Doctrine. InterVarsity Press, 38 De Montfort Street Leicester LE1 7GP Great Britain, Grand Rapids, MI: Zondervan Publishing House, pp 670.
4. Strong, James. LL.D. "Calling, The Christian." The Strongest Strong's Exhaustive Concordance of the Bible, the only Strong compiled and verified by computer technology with Nave's Topical Bible Reference; most up-to-date Hebrew and Greek dictionaries for precise word studies, corrects all others. Grand Rapids, MI, 2001, p 1773-1774.

Great Is Thy Faithfulness!

By THOMAS OBEDIAH CHISHOLM

Great is Thy faithfulness," O God my Father,
There is no shadow of turning with Thee;
Thou changest not, Thy compassions, they fail not
As Thou hast been Thou forever wilt be.

Great is Thy faithfulness!" "Great is Thy faithfulness!"
   Morning by morning new mercies I see;
All I have needed Thy hand hath provided—
   "Great is Thy faithfulness," Lord, unto me!

Summer and winter, and springtime and harvest,
Sun, moon and stars in their courses above,
Join with all nature in manifold witness
To Thy great faithfulness, mercy and love.

Pardon for sin and a peace that endureth,
Thine own dear presence to cheer and to guide;
Strength for today and bright hope for tomorrow,
Blessings all mine, with ten thousand beside!

REFLECTIONS

A SALVATION MYSTERY

A lady once said to me, "I'd like to try Jesus, if I could just get past religion." This story exemplifies her complaint.

Once a bishop traveled by ship to visit a church across the ocean. Once there, he came upon three fishermen on the beach.

Curious about his ecclesiastical robes, they asked him some questions. When they found out he was a Christian leader, they got excited. "We Christians!" they said, proudly pointing to one another. No, they had never heard of the Lord's Prayer.

"What do you say, then, when you pray?"

"We pray, 'We are three, you are three, have mercy on us.' "

The bishop was appalled at the primitive nature of the prayer. "That will not do." So he taught them the Lord's Prayer. The fishermen were poor but willing learners. the next day, they could recite the prayer with no mistakes. The bishop was proud.

On the return trip the bishop's ship drew near the island again and just as he was thinking about the three men a light appeared on the horizon near the island. It seemed to be getting nearer. As the bishop gazed in wonder he realized the three fishermen were walking toward him on the water. When within range, the fisherman cried out, "Bishop, we come hurry to meet you."

"What is it you want?" asked the stunned bishop.

"We are so sorry. We forget lovely prayer. We say, 'Our Father, who art in heaven, hallowed be your name …' and then we forget. Please tell us prayer again."

The bishop was humbled. "Go home, my friends, and when you pray say, 'We are three, you are three, have mercy on us.' "

Source: Max Lucado: Angels Were Silent Text Illustration shared by Daniel Devilder, Monroe Christian Church, December 2006. Retrieved October, 2015 from http://www.sermoncentral.com/illustrations/sermon-illustration-daniel-devilder-stories-30036.asp

There's an old story of the boy who stood on a sidewalk, waiting on a bus. A man walking by spotted the boy, and gave him some gentle instruction. "Son," he said, "if you're waiting on the bus, you need to move to the street corner. That's where the bus stops for passengers."

"It's OK," said the boy. "I'll just wait right here, and the bus will stop for me."

The man repeated his argument, but the boy never moved. Just then, the bus appeared. Amazingly, the bus pulled over to where the boy stood, and the child hopped on. The man on the sidewalk stood speechless. The boy turned around in the doorway and said, "Mister, I knew the bus would stop here, because the bus driver is my dad!"

When you've got a family relationship with the bus driver, you don't need a bus stop. If your mother is a US Senator, you won't need an appointment to slip into her office. If you've given your heart to the King of Kings, you're in a royal family of unspeakable proportions.

– Sermon Central Staff
Outreach Inc.

Adoption

◆ ◆ ◆

"The road that leads to heaven is risky, lonely,
and costly in this world, and few are willing to pay the price.
Following Jesus involves losing your life-and finding new life in him."
David Platt

▼

In regeneration God gives us new spiritual life within. In justification God gives us right legal standing before him. But in adoption God makes us members of his family. Therefore, the biblical teaching on adoption focuses much more on the personal relationships that salvation gives us with God and with his people.[116] We may define adoption as follows: Adoption is an act of God whereby he makes us members of his family. John mentions adoption at the beginning of his gospel, where he says, "But to all who received him, who believed in his name, he gave power to become children of God" (*John 1:12*).[117] By contrast, those who do not believe in Christ are not children of God or adopted into his family, but are "children of wrath" and "sons of disobedience" (*Ephesians 2:2; 5:6*). Although those Jews who rejected Christ tried to claim that God was their father (*John 8:41*), Jesus told

---

116 Grudem, Wayne.Systematic Theology, *An Introduction to Biblical Doctrine*. InterVarsity Press 38 De Montfort Street Leicester LE1 7GP Great Britain, Grand Rapids, MI:Zondervan Publishing House, 5300 Patterson Ave., 60515, pp 733-738 GOOD
117 Grudem, Wayne.Systematic Theology, *An Introduction to Biblical Doctrine*. InterVarsity Press 38 De Montfort Street Leicester LE1 7GP Great Britain, Grand Rapids, MI:Zondervan Publishing House, 5300 Patterson Ave., 60515, pp 733-738 GOOD

them, "If God were your Father, you would love me.... You are of your father the devil, and your will is to do your father's desires" (*John 8:42-44*). The New Testament epistles bear repeated testimony to the fact that we are now God's children in a special sense, members of his family. Paul says: For all who are led by the Spirit of God are sons of God. For you did not receive the spirit of slavery to fall back into fear, but you have received the spirit of son-ship. When we cry, "Abba! Father!" it is the Spirit himself bearing witness with our spirit that we are children of God, and if children, then heirs, heirs of God and fellow heirs with Christ, provided we suffer with him in order that we may also be glorified with him. (*Romans 8:14-17*) [118]

As God's children, we are then related to one another as family members? This adoption into God's family makes us partakers together in one family with Abraham: "Not all are children of Abraham because they are his descendants; but 'Through Isaac shall your descendants be named.' This means that it is not the children of the flesh who are the children of God, but the children of the promise are reckoned as descendants" (*Romans 9:7-8*). He further explains in Galatians, "Now we, brethren, like Isaac, are children of promise... we are not children of the slave but of the free woman" (*Galatians 4:28,31; cf. 1 Peter 3:6*), where Peter sees believing women as daughters of Sarah in the new covenant). Paul explains that this status of adoption as God's children was not fully realized in the old covenant. He says that "before faith came, we were confined under the law... the law was our custodian until Christ came, that we might be justified by faith. But now that faith has come, we are no longer under a custodian; for in Christ Jesus you are all sons of God, through faith". (*Galatians 3:23-26*)[119]

The Holy Spirit bears witness in our hearts that we are God's children: "But when the time had fully come, God sent forth his Son, born of woman, born under the law, to redeem those who were under

118 Grudem, Wayne.Systematic Theology, *An Introduction to Biblical Doctrine*. InterVarsity Press 38 De Montfort Street Leicester LE1 7GP Great Britain, Grand Rapids, MI:Zondervan Publishing House, 5300 Patterson Ave., 60515, pp 733-738
119 Grudem, Wayne.Systematic Theology, *An Introduction to Biblical Doctrine*. InterVarsity Press 38 De Montfort Street Leicester LE1 7GP Great Britain, Grand Rapids, MI:Zondervan Publishing House, 5300 Patterson Ave., 60515, pp 733-738

the law, so that we might receive adoption as sons. And because you are sons, God has sent the Spirit of his Son into our hearts, crying, Abba! Father!' So through God you are no longer a slave hut a son, and if a son then an heir" (*Galatians 4:4-7*). John's first epistle places much emphasis on our status as children of God: "See what love the Father has given us, that we should be called children of God; and so we are.... Beloved, we are God's children now" (*1 John 3:1-2*); John frequently calls his readers "children" or "little children"). Although Jesus does call us his "brothers" (*Hebrews 2:12 NIV*) and he is therefore in one sense our older brother in God's family, he is nevertheless careful to make a clear distinction between the way in which God is our heavenly Father and the way in which he relates God the Father. He says, "I am ascending to my Father and your Father, to my God and your God" (*John 20:17*), thus making that clear distinction.[120]

Life Application for Personal Reflection
Adoption
1. How does the privilege of adoption by God the Father affect the way you interact with people in the world? With the church family? At home with your family?
2. Since having been adopted into the kingdom of God, do you feel accepted or like an outsider? Identify the list of things that have caused any doubt concerning your position in the family of God.

Suggested Reading
Adoption
1. Berkhof, Louis. Systematic Theology, New Combined Edition containing the full text of Systematic Theology and the original. Williams B. Eerdmans Publishing Company, 255 Jefferson Ave., S.E., Grand Rapids, MI 49503, 1996, pp 114-115.
2. Grudem, Wayne. "Adoption." Systematic Theology, An Introduction to Biblical Doctrine. InterVarsity Press, 38 De Montfort Street Leicester LE1 7GP Great Britain, Grand Rapids, MI: Zondervan Publishing House, pp 736-745.
3. Nave, Orville J. Nave's Topical Bible, A Digest of the Holy Scriptures, Nashville, TN: Thomas Nelson Publishers, 1979, 1208-1223.
4. Hodge, Charles. Systematic Theology. 3 vols. Reprint edition: Grand Rapids: Eerdmans, 1970. First published 1871, pp 333-349.

---

120 Grudem, Wayne. Systematic Theology, *An Introduction to Biblical Doctrine*. InterVarsity Press 38 De Montfort Street Leicester LE1 7GP Great Britain, Grand Rapids, MI:Zondervan Publishing House, 5300 Patterson Ave., 60515, pp 733-738

Give Me A Clean Heart

Lyrics by MARGARET PLEASANT DOUROUX

Refrain
Give me a clean heart so I may serve Thee.
Lord, fix my heart so that I may be used by Thee,
For I'm not worthy of all Your blessings.
Give me a clean heart, and I'll follow Thee.

Verse I
I'm not asking for the riches of this land,
And I'm not asking for men in high places to know my name.
Please-- give me, Lord, a clean heart that I may follow Thee.

Verse II
Sometimes I'm up and sometimes I'm down.
Sometimes I'm almost level to the ground.
Please—give me, Lord, a clean heart that I may follow Thee

Repeat Refrain
Give me a clean heart so I may serve Thee.
Lord, fix my heart so that I may be used by Thee,
For I'm not worthy of all Your blessings.
Give me a clean heart, and I'll follow Thee.

REFLECTIONS

REVELATIONS OF DIVINE LOVE

And in this he showed me a little thing, the quantity of a hazel nut, lying in the palm of my hand, as it seemed. And it was as round as any ball. I looked upon it with the eye of my understanding, and thought, 'What may this be?' And it was answered generally thus, 'It is all that is made.' I marveled how it might last, for I thought it might suddenly have fallen to nothing for littleness. And I was answered in my understanding: It lasts and ever shall, for God loves it. And so have all things their beginning by the love of God.

Source: Herbermann, Charles George (1840-1916)Julian of Norwich. Revelations of Divine Love. Christian Classics Ethereal Library. Catholic Encyclopedia, Volume 8: Infamy-Lapparent, 1393. Retrieved November 13, 2015 from http://www.ccel.org/j/julian/revelations/

A couple of years ago on America's Funniest Home Videos, a young boy was shown on Christmas morning. He came down to see a large present beside the tree and ran over to tear it open to see what was inside. The paper went flying and suddenly he broke into a dance and jumped around the room saying, "Wow Just what I wanted I really love it. Wow " After awhile he went over to look at it again and said with a puzzled look on his face, "What is it?"

On that first Christmas the angels announced the birth of a new child. The heavens were opened and all the company of heaven broke into praise. Shepherds went racing to Bethlehem to see what it was all about. And for two thousand years we have been jumping up and down saying, "Just what I wanted Exactly what I needed " But in the next breath we look again inside the stable and ask, "What is it?" We are puzzled by God's gift.

– Rodney Buchanan
United Methodist Pastor, Ret.

Regeneration

◆ ◆ ◆

*"Salvation is the most important thing that a person has and
the devil knows very well what its value is."*

Sunday Adelaja

▼

The online theopedia defines regeneration as the spiritual transformation within a person, brought about by the Holy Spirit, that converts the spiritually dead person to spiritually alive human being. It refers to the new birth or second birth also known as being born again. Regeneration is an intimate act of God in which he imparts new spiritual life to us. This does not happen by the will of man (*John 1:13*) by it is a work of God; we are passive in this instance, and do not play an active role in making this happen. Similar to our passive role in childbirth in which we wait until the mother does all the work before we show up, the spiritual rebirth finds us in a listless position as God does all the work. We did not choose to be made physically alive and we did not choose to be born—it is something that happened to us. If you had to do the work of the rebirth, it would never happen. It is too painful; that is why we need a qualified someone who is willing and able to do the job. Have you ever tried to stop a doctor from fixing you right in the middle of surgery? It is almost impossible when you have already undergone anesthesia, to stop a medical procedure from proceeding. It is like sitting in the dentist chair when you go for a deep cleaning. After the dentist anesthetizes you and perhaps administers nitrous or laughing gas, you lie back and await your regeneration. Then while you lie there in your semi euphoric laissez faire la-la land completely at his disposal, he pulls out his tools and begins to work on you. He pulls and tugs, cleans and scrapes, lifts and shifts so that when it all said and done, you know that you have been renewed. Gone is the build up from years of improper maintenance and the evidence of bacteria and pollution that mirrored your conduct. Gone are the signs of destruction and all those foreign particles that have come to invade your health. You are aware that something is happening to you, but you have no say so. You already signed your consent, granting Him permission to do the work. He does not stop until he has completed the work. Then when he raises you up, you are a new person. You go from an unproductive being to one who is full of life (*cf. James 1:18; 1 Peter 1:3; John 3:3-8*).

These analogies in Scripture suggest that we are entirely passive in regeneration. This sovereign work of God in regeneration was also predicted in the prophecy of Ezekiel. "A new heart also will I give you, and a new spirit will I put within you: and I will take away the stony heart out of your flesh, and I will give you an heart of flesh. And I will put my spirit within you, and cause you to walk in my statutes, and ye shall keep my judgments, and do them." (*Ezekiel 36:26-27*) In biology, regeneration is the process of renewal, restoration, and growth that makes cells or organisms spring back into shape after natural fluctuations or events cause disturbance or damage.

When Jesus speaks of being "born of the Spirit" (*John 3:8*), he indicates that it is especially God the Holy Spirit who produces regeneration. Other verses also indicate the involvement of God the Father in regeneration: Paul specifies that it is God who "made us alive together with Christ" (*Ephesians 2:5; cf. Colossians 2:13*). And James says that it is the "Father of lights" who gave us new birth: "Of his own will he brought us forth by the word of truth that we should be a kind of first fruits of his creatures." We can conclude that both God the Father and God the Holy Spirit bring about regeneration. Peter says, "You have been born anew, not of perishable seed but of imperishable, through the living and abiding word of God. That word is the good news which was preached to you" (*1 Peter 1:23, 25*). And James says, "He chose to give us birth through the word of truth" (*James 1:18 NIV*). As the gospel comes to us, God speaks through it to summon us to himself (effective calling) and to give us new spiritual life (regeneration) so that we are enabled to respond in faith.[121]

The word "regeneration" has been used in theology to mean almost everything the Spirit does for the individual. It has been mistakenly substituted for the workings of repentance, conviction, and saving faith. To many it is merely the influence of the Holy Spirit in conversion. It is the renewal or spiritual quickening wrought within by the Holy Spirit.[122] In Titus 3:5, the Scripture says "He saves us by the washing of regeneration and the renewing of the Holy Spirit." Here the washing, which is regeneration," is the same in meaning as John 3:3, born of the Spirit and the water. Evidently the water is the Word of God, without which no conversion is possible. The sinner is born of the Word of God by the Spirit of God.[123] This is evident in I Peter 1:23 where it says, "Being "born again" not of corruptible seed (human) but of incorruptible (divine), by the Word of God which liveth and abideth forever." That the water of regeneration is the Word of God is further shown in Ephesians 5:26, "That He might sanctify and cleanse it (the Church) with the washing of water by the Word." As the literal meaning of the word "regeneration," it means regenerated or re-born; hence the term "born again," (*1 Peter 1:23*), its mystery; for its necessity, one only needs to study John 3:1-9. There is the full meaning set in parallel position with natural birth. It is comparable in its realm to the natural birth, hence a re-birth, new birth, born again, born from a new seed. In summary, regeneration is the action of the

121 Grudem, Wayne.Systematic Theology, An Introduction to Biblical Doctrine. InterVarsity Press 38 De Montfort Street Leicester LE1 7GP Great Britain, Grand Rapids, MI:Zondervan Publishing House, 5300 Patterson Ave., 60515. Chapter 33, pp. 692-94, on effective calling.
122 E. C. Bragg, Systematic Theology Soteriology, http://trinitycollege.edu/assets/files/ECBragg/SoteriologyR.pdf
123 E. C. Bragg, Systematic Theology Soteriology, http://trinitycollege.edu/assets/files/ECBragg/SoteriologyR.pdf

Spirit of God in the soul of the sinner, breeding by supernatural birth the very nature and life of God into his soul, literally making him a child of God, imparting unto him a new nature created in God's own likeness in righteousness and true holiness. This new nature, being the nature of God, and the residence of the Spirit of God in the soul, being the very life of God Himself, John says it cannot sin. He means not that the Christian cannot sin, but the seed of God in the soul cannot sin, I John 3:9, "Whosoever is born of God doth not commit sin, for His seed remaineth in him and he cannot sin, because he is born of God." It is God's seed which remaineth in him and cannot sin. The new nature cannot; but the flesh, or old man, can and does sin unless he is kept crucified with Christ. [124] This new nature is truly holy and patterned after the image of God, for it is the very life and nature of God; so, "Beloved, now are we the Sons of God."

Christ settles forever the question of the necessity of regeneration, He says the very emphatic 'must' to being born again without a doubt, "Verily, verily, I say unto you, except a man be born again he cannot see the kingdom of God." The reasons are simple; he lacks the fundamental nature of God with all its faculties to perceive the kingdom of God. When man fell, he lost the image of God, with the spiritual faculties. He states the impossibility of entrance or perception of the Kingdom of God without this new birth. Jesus showed Nicodemus that the process is a mystery explicable to the Spirit alone. How could He say in plainer words the meaning of the word, "born again" or regeneration than when He said, "That which is born of the flesh is flesh, and that which is born of the Spirit is spirit." There is a likeness in the births, the difference being in the realms in which the person is born, born of corruptible seed, human, nothing but corrupt human; but born of incorruptible seed, the Divine, born of the Spirit, then Spirit, belonging then to the realm of heaven. You can worship God "in Spirit and in truth," and not until then, can you understand the things of God or "see" the kingdom of God, for they

---

124 E. C. Bragg, Systematic Theology Soteriology, Retrieved November, 2015 from: http://trinitycollege.edu/assets/files/ECBragg/SoteriologyR.pdf

are spiritually discerned. The regenerated person belongs to the realm of the kingdom of God or the spiritual kingdom. To be born again, then, is to partake of the divine nature of God, to take the Spirit of God's nature, even as when born of human parents I partook of their human natures. That this is the truth concerning regeneration may be abundantly proven from the Scriptures.[125]

Life Application for Personal Reflection

Regeneration

1. Have you ever know anyone to accept forgiveness without repenting of their sin? Do you believe it is possible? How many people do you know who want to be forgiven but do not sincerely repent? Is this a trait that we find in children? How does this speak to grownup Christians?

2. Since regeneration is totally a work of God, what evidence of your new birth do you have?

Suggested Reading

Regeneration

1. Berkhof, Louis. Systematic Theology, New Combined Edition containing the full text of Systematic Theology and the original. Grand Rapids, MI: Williams B. Eerdmans Publishing Company, 1996, pp 465-477.

2. Nave, Orville J. Nave's Topical Bible, A Digest of the Holy Scriptures, Nashville, TN: Thomas Nelson Publishers, 1979, pp 1119-1126.

---

125 E. C. Bragg, Systematic Theology Soteriology, Retrieved November, 2015 from: http://trinitycollege.edu/assets/files/ECBragg/SoteriologyR.pdf

At Calvary

Lyrics by WILLIAM R. NEWELL, pub. 1895

Years I spent in vanity and pride,
Caring not my Lord was crucified,
Knowing not it was for me He died
On Calvary.

Refrain:
Mercy there was great, and grace was free;
Pardon there was multiplied to me;
There my burdened soul found liberty
At Calvary.

By God's Word at last my sin I learned;
Then I trembled at the law I'd spurned,
Till my guilty soul imploring turned
To Calvary.

Now I've giv'n to Jesus everything,
Now I gladly own Him as my King,
Now my raptured soul can only sing
Of Calvary!

Oh, the love that drew salvation's plan!
Oh, the grace that brought it down to man!
Oh, the mighty gulf that God did span
At Calvary!

REFLECTIONS

THE DIVINE PHYSICIAN

This figure upon the Cross is not a MVD agent or a Gestapo inquisitor, but a Divine Physician, Who only asks that we bring our wounds to Him in order that He may heal them. If our sins be as scarlet, they shall be washed white as snow, and if they be as red as crimson, they shall be made white as wool. Was it not He Who told us, "I say to you, that even so there shall be more joy in Heaven upon one sinner that doth penance than upon ninety-nine just who need not penance" (Luke 15:7)? In the story of the prodigal, did He not describe the Father as saying, "Let us eat and make merry: because this my son was dead and is come to life again; was lost and is found" (Luke 15:23, 24)? Why is there more joy in Heaven for the repentant sinner than for the righteous? Because God's attitude is not judgment but love. In judgment, one is not as joyful after doing wrong as before; but in love, there is joy because the danger and worry of losing that soul is past. He who is sick is loved more than he who is well, because he needs it more. Some will feign sickness to solicit love and pretend wounds that the beloved may bind them.

- Fulton J. Sheen
Bishop of the Catholic Church

Source: Peace of Soul: Timeless Wisdom on Finding Serenity and Joy by the Century's Most Acclaimed Catholic Bishop. Retrieved on November 12, 2014 from https://www.goodreads.com/work/quotes/1532889-peace-of-soul Asian Trading Corporation

A grandfather found his grandson, jumping up and down in his playpen, crying at the top of his voice. When Johnnie saw his grandfather, he reached up his little chubby hands and said, "Out, Gramp, out."

It was only natural for Grandfather to reach down to lift the little fellow out of his predicament; but as he did, the mother of the child stepped up and said, "No, Johnnie, you are being punished, so you must stay in."

The grandfather was at a loss to know what to do. The child's tears and chubby hands reached deep into his heart, but the mother's firmness in correcting her son for misbehavior must not be lightly taken. Here was a problem of love versus law, but love found a way. The grandfather could not take the youngster out of the playpen, so he crawled in with him.

God did not spare Paul and Silas the suffering and imprisonment, but He did come down into the prison with them. God did not keep the three Hebrew children out of the fiery furnace, but He went into the furnace with them. God will not always deliver us from trouble and heartache, but He has promised grace for every situation of life.

– By Fred W. Parsons
These Times, March 1969.

Propitiation

♦ ♦ ♦

"The oppressed must be saved, not with a revolutionary salvation,
in mere human fashion, but with the holy revolution of the Son of Man,
who dies on the cross to cleanse God's image, which is soiled in today's
humanity, a humanity so enslaved, so selfish, so sinful."

Oscar A. Romero, The Violence of Love

▼

The idea behind the word "propitiation" is the appeasement or satisfaction, that is intended specifically toward God. It is a two-part act that involves appeasing the wrath of an offended person and being reconciled to him. Propitiation means the turning away of wrath by an offering. In relation to soteriology, propitiation means placating or satisfying the wrath of God by the atoning sacrifice of Christ.[126] To be more specific, propitiation is the process whereby someone's wrath is either 'averted' or 'satisfied', resulting in 'mercy' being received, 'to make expiation'. In short, this is the way back into a relationship with God and the removal of any judgment incurred. To say that Jesus 'made' or 'achieved' propitiation is one thing (in Hebrews 2:17 above we read that He's the High Priest who offered the necessary sacrifice), the statement implying that He caused it to happen

---

126 Charles C. Ryrie (1999-01-11). Basic Theology: A Popular Systematic Guide to Understanding Biblical Truth (Kindle Locations 5503-5504). Moody Publishers. Kindle Edition.

without indicating just how it was done. But to say that Jesus is the propitiation for our sins tells us that God's anger (and, therefore, judgment) was poured out upon Him. Jesus is not just the High Priest who offers the sacrifice but is the propitiatory sacrifice itself. 'By His blood' points us to only one possible place - the cross. It's the cross, then, that's the place where we see both God's anger toward and God's judgment on sin fully satisfied. Propitiation is that process "by which it becomes consistent with His character and government or sovereignty to pardon and bless the sinner. The propitiation does not purchase His love or make him loving; it only renders it consistent for him to exercise his love towards sinners.

Expiation and propitiation are two words that often come up together and spark all kinds of arguments about which one should be used to translate a particular Greek word. Depending on the versions of the Bible used, one of these words will be used. The difference between propitiation and expiation is subtle and since these are not very common words in our day-to-day vocabulary and not entirely sure with exactness what the full intent in Scripture.

In expiate, the prefix ex means "out of" or "from," so expiation has to do with removing something or taking something away. We know that in biblical terms, it has to do with taking away guilt through the payment of a penalty or the offering of an atonement. By contrast, propitiation has to do with being the object of the expiation. The prefix pro means "for," so propitiation brings about a change in God's attitude, so that He moves from being at enmity with us to being for us. Through the process of propitiation, we are restored into fellowship and favor with Him. Further, propitiation literally means to make favorable and specifically includes the idea of dealing with God's wrath against sinners. Expiation literally means to make pious and implies either the removal or cleansing of sin.

The idea of propitiation includes that of expiation as its means; but the word "expiation" has no reference to quenching God's righteous anger. The difference is that the object of expiation is sin, not God.

One propitiates a person, and one expiates a problem. Christ's death was therefore both an expiation and a propitiation. By expiating (removing the problem of) sin God was made propitious (favorable) to us.

In that certain sense, propitiation has everything to do with God's being appeased. One of my favorite examples is when a husband has done something and the needs to appease the wife, he has to pay the price. But perhaps that is not such a good example because the word appeasement functions in military and political conflicts or in situations where one power has a greater power over the other. Philosophically, when dealing with another country or world ruler, then politically, you may have to offer up a sacrifice of some kind - give up another country or decide to remove an ambassador to keep the world power from wiping your country off the face of the map. To appease and cause the rage to die down, you have to give up something to calm the wrath or the raging beast within. Once this anger is satisfied, then favor is restored. Until then, the radar, antennae, satellite and all forms of detections need to be prepared to read incoming advances.

Jesus' blood 'propitiated' or satisfied God's wrath (1:18), so that his holiness was not compromised in forgiving sinners. Again, as it has been argued by some scholars that the word propitiation should be translated expiation (simply wiping away of sin), the word cannot be restricted to the wiping away of sins as it also refers to the satisfaction or appeasement of God's wrath, turning it to favor (cf. note on John 18:11).

This may seem redundant but it is important to understand God's righteous anger needed to be appeased before sin could be forgiven, and God in his love sent his Son (who offered himself willingly) to satisfy God's holy anger against sin. In this way God demonstrated his righteousness, which here refers particularly to his holiness and justice. God's justice was called into question because in his patience he had overlooked former sins. In other words, how could God as the

Holy One tolerate human sin without inflicting full punishment on human beings immediately? Paul's answer is that God looked forward to the cross of Christ where the full payment for the guilt of sin would be made, where Christ would die in the place of sinners. In the Old Testament, propitiation (or the complete satisfaction of the wrath of God) is symbolically foreshadowed in several incidents: e.g., Exodus 32:11–14; Numbers 25:8, 11; Joshua 7:25–26.

With so many interpretations and translations of Scripture, it it particularly notable that it is by God's grace that this has been made possible. We should be careful to not trivialize such mercies and benevolent contributions of such a generous and powerful Almighty God. Propitiation is that priestly work of Christ wherein He removed God's anger and wrath by the covering over of our sins through the substitutionary sacrifice of Himself to God, thus securing our acceptance before God. . . . Christ accomplished His work of propitiation when He was consumed by God's wrath and anger as He was lifted up on the cross as the substitutionary sacrifice for the people of God. The apostle Paul viewed the propitiatory character of Christ's death as being necessitated by the justice and righteousness of God: "Whom God hath set forth to be a propitiation through faith in His blood, to declare His righteousness for the remission of sins that are past, through the forbearance of God; to declare, I say, at this time His righteousness: that He might be just, and the justifier of him which believeth in Jesus." [127] (*Romans 3:25-26*)

When people reach out to clergy or come to church, they are looking for truth and understanding. During the week, they hear conjecture, speculation editorials, and all manner of opinions through the media. The one place they expect to hear the truth is at church. The worst thing Bible scholars or ministers can do is to fabricate or sugarcoat the truth. Generally speaking, anyone who gets up early on a weekend after a full week of working wants to know what God has to say. Paul's ministry was clear in 1 Corinthians 2:1–5. He had spent

---

127 Crossway Bibles (2009-04-09). ESV Study Bible (Kindle Locations 277848-277859). Good News Publishers/Crossway Books. Kindle Edition.

more than a year in Corinth on his first visit there and in his first letter he warned believers against basing their faith on the wisdom of men instead of God's power. He warned that our faith should be in the power of God. He was given the grace of apostleship to bring about the obedience of faith for the sake of the Lord's name among all the nations." (*Romans 1:5*). Speaking the truth helps build faith. Paul was clear that it made a great difference what we offer as the basis of faith. Does it really matter what your faith is based on as long as Christ is the object of your faith? Chapter 1 explains that if you try to base saving faith on the wisdom of men, it ceases to be saving faith. The genuineness of faith, and with it eternal life, is at stake. It is possible to offer a basis for faith which ruins faith. If faith rests in the wisdom of men, then it is a mirage and is impossible to be real faith. It would destruct.

In verses 1 and 2 there is a contrast between trying to deliver a testimony of God with superior words of wisdom on the one hand and preaching Jesus Christ as crucified on the other. What is it about the wisdom of men that makes it so destructive when we try to make it a basis for faith? Verse 18: "The word of the cross is folly (or foolishness) to those who are perishing, but to us who are being saved it is the power of God. Where is the wise man of this age? Has not God made foolish the wisdom of the world (the wisdom of men) in v. 2.5? It should be astounding to us all how it is possible that the lion of Judah is actually the Lamb of God. Is it not amazing that the plan of salvation is offensive to the wisdom of the world? Even the disciples were looking for the Jesus to rise up as King of the Jews and destroy the Romans but look at how salvation comes through the execution of a lowly carpenter's son from a little town called Nazareth and became a teacher who went about healing all that were oppressed of the devil! The cross is foolishness to the wisdom of this world. That's why the wisdom of men is destructive to faith and that is why we should be careful not to turn to the wisdom of men as the basis of faith.

What is there about human wisdom which causes it to regard Christ crucified as foolishness? God chose what is foolish in the world to confound the wise so that no human being might boast in the presence of God. This foolishness referenced by Paul is pride. The death of Christ on the cross is such a radical indictment of the hideousness of our sinfulness that human wisdom has to do everything possible to diminish the significance of what Christ did. We can either regard the death of Christ for our sin as foolishness and therefore maintain our own self-sufficiency and pride, or we can regard it as wisdom of God and accept the work of Christ on the cross. There is only one way that leads to eternal life. Since the wisdom of men is devoted to maintaining independence, it will always reject Christ crucified and attempt to defuse His power by calling him foolish.

This is evidenced by the trend toward relativism – your truth is just as valid as mu truth. We have everything in us to do and be whatever we desire. That we no longer have need of a Savior. This wisdom of man is teaching that people who need God of need a Savior are pathetic; that they "made Him up" because they are too lazy to provide for themselves. This is why it is destructive to faith if we try to base it on merely human wisdom. In other words, the wisdom of the world regards the word of the cross as foolishness and ultimately so leads men away from the cross. Human wisdom is the use of the mind to achieve and maintain pride, but faith in the crucified Christ is death to pride and the giving up of all grounds for boasting, except one: Let him who boasts, boast in the Lord!

The power of God in which our faith should rest is the divine power unleashed by the death of Christ to save sinners, to justify the ungodly. When Jesus was at his weakest in the agony of the cross, God's power was at its strongest, lifting the infinite weight of sin and condemnation off the backs of all who would believe on him. Because Jesus died and bore the punishment of our sin, all the power of God, who created the universe, was loosed for the benefit of God's elect. The power in which saving faith rests is the power of divine grace sustaining the humble, loving heart and which lives through weakness. That is the power that we see in Christ who meekly, humbly, lovingly went to the cross for our sin.

The Apostle Paul realized that, if he was to be an agent of the crucified Christ to win people to faith in him, then he had to follow the way of Calvary. That is, he had to draw people's attention not to his own power or wisdom but to the power of God made perfect in weakness. As intelligent as many scholars may be, it is crucial that the witness proclaims the power of God which is made manifest in the weakness and death of Christ that kindles and sustains saving faith (as 2:5 says).

Paul described the power of his own ministry in 2 Corinthians 4:7–11. He said, "We have this treasure (of the gospel) in earthen vessels (our weak bodies) to show that the transcendent power belongs to God and not to us." We are afflicted in every way, but not crushed, perplexed but not driven to despair, persecuted but not forsaken; struck down but not destroyed, always carrying in the body the death of Jesus, so that the life of Jesus may also be manifested in our bodies. For while we live we are always being given up to death for Jesus' sake so that the life of Jesus may be manifested in our mortal flesh.

Life Application for Personal Reflection
Propitiation
1. Have you ever wondered why Jesus even bothered, knowing that in the future to come, the world would not show appreciation despite all that He did? What was your reaction? How did it make you feel toward Christ?
2. Do you know any other religion apart from Christianity where the sacrifice was not made by the people or the subjects?

Suggested Reading
Propitiation
Grudem, Wayne. "Adoption." Systematic Theology, An Introduction to Biblical Doctrine. InterVarsity Press, 38 De Montfort Street Leicester LE1 7GP Great Britain, Grand Rapids, MI: Zondervan Publishing House, pp 510,575,580.

At The Cross
By ISAAC WATTS

Alas! and did my Savior bleed
And did my Sov'reign die?
Would He devote that sacred head
For such a worm as I?

Refrain:
At the cross, at the cross where I first saw the light,
And the burden of my heart rolled away,
It was there by faith I received my sight,
And now I am happy all the day!

Was it for crimes that I had done
He groaned upon the tree?
Amazing pity! grace unknown!
And love beyond degree!

Well might the sun in darkness hide
And shut his glories in,
When Christ, the mighty Maker died,
For man the creature's sin.

But drops of grief can ne'er repay
The debt of love I owe:
Here, Lord, I give myself away,
'Tis all that I can do.

REFLECTIONS

PARABLE OF CHRIST'S SACRIFICE

The mother of a nine-year-old boy named Mark received a phone call his teacher. "Mrs. Smith, your son did something unusual today. Nothing like this has happened in all my years of teaching and it surprised me so much that I thought you should know about it. The mother began to grow worried.

The teacher continued, "This morning I told the story of the ant and grasshopper for a creative writing exercise: "The ant works hard all summer and stores up plenty of food. But the grasshopper plays all summer and does no work. "Then winter comes. The grasshopper begins to starve because he has no food. So he begins to beg, 'Please Mr. Ant, you have much food. Please let me eat, too.'" Then I said, "Boys and girls, your job is to write the ending to the story."

"As in all the years past, most students ended the story with 'the ant shared his food through the winter, and both the ant and the grasshopper lived.' " Others chided Mr. Grasshopper and admonished him for not working during the summer. So the ant lived and the grasshopper died.

"But your son ended the story in a way different from any other child, ever. He wrote, 'So the ant gave all of his food to the grasshopper; the grasshopper lived through the winter. But the ant died.' At the bottom of the page, Mark had drawn three crosses." 1 John 4:11, Beloved, if God so loved us, we ought also to love one another.

-Brad Walden,
Tates Creek Christian Church, Lexington, KY

Brad Walden, senior minister with the Tates Creek Christian Church, Lexington, KY; true story told by Mark's grandfather at Westwood Cheviot Church of Christ, Cincinnati, OH

Herbert Washington, whom co-workers say was unduly concerned with the rapture and the second coming of Christ, suffered a serious heart attack when co-workers pretended they'd been caught away without him.

"We didn't mean to scare him to death," said one woman. "He's just always talking about it, so today we decided to turn the tables on him."

Washington underwent bypass surgery and is recovering well and "digging into the Bible like never before," says his wife.

– Davon Huss
Pleasant Ridge Church of Christ

Glorification

◆ ◆ ◆

*"God made salvation the most precious gift for humanity which is why only
a few are chosen for God's Paradise in heaven. Matthew 22:11-14"*

Felix Wantang, God's Blueprint of the Holy Bible

▼

Glorification is the exalted state of the believer in his future new body, whether by way of resurrection or transformation, as in I Corinthians 15:50-51, "We shall all be changed," "mortal (living) put on immortality, corruptible (dead) put on incorruption." This is the meaning of "glorify" as used in New Testament. Note: it is used of Jesus in John 7:39, "Jesus was not yet glorified," also John 12:16, He wasn't yet resurrected with His immortal, glorified body. Peter says in Acts 3:13, "God hath glorified His Son Jesus." Glorification for Jesus could bring a change in Him primarily in His body, hence we call it a "glorified body." For us, glorification must include a glorified change in spirit, soul, and body. The church shall be presented someday unto Christ a glorious or glorified church, not having spot or wrinkle, but it should be holy and without blemish, Ephesians 5:27, thus shall Christ be glorified in His saints in that day of glorification, II Thessalonians 1:10, when they "awake with His likeness. [128]

---

128 E. C. Bragg, Systematic Theology Soteriology, Retrieved November, 2015 from: http://trinitycollege.edu/assets/files/ECBragg/SoteriologyR.pdf

When Christ redeemed us he did not just redeem our spirits (or souls)–he redeemed us as whole persons, and this includes the redemption of our bodies. Therefore the application of Christ's work of redemption to us will not be complete until our bodies are entirely set free from the effects of the fall and brought to that state of perfection for which God created them. In fact, the redemption of our bodies will only occur when Christ returns and raises our bodies from the dead. But at this present time, Paul says that we wait for "the redemption of our bodies," and then adds, "for in this hope we were saved" (*Romans 8:23-24*). The stage in the application of redemption when we receive resurrection bodies is called glorification. Referring to that future day Paul says that we will be "glorified with him" (Rom. 8:17). Moreover, when Paul traces the steps in the application of redemption, the last one he names is glorification: "And those whom he predestined he also called; and those whom he called he also justified; and those whom he justified he also glorified" (*Romans 8:30*).

In the context of a discussion of the resurrection of our bodies when Christ returns, Paul says, "Then shall come to pass the saying that is written: 'Death is swallowed up in victory.' 'O death, where is your victory? O death, where is your sting? (*1 Corinthians 15:54-55*). When our bodies are raised from the dead we will experience victory over the death that came as a result of the fall of Adam and Eve. Then redemption will be complete. Glorification is the final step in the process of redemption. It will happen when Christ returns and raises from the dead the Of all believers for all time who have died, and reunites them with their souls, and the bodies of all believers who remain alive, thereby giving all believers at the same perfect resurrection bodies like his own.[129]

Christ will raise our bodies from the dead when he returns (*1 Corinthians 15:20, 23, 49; Philippians 3:21*). What will have a resurrection bodies be like? What is sown is perishable, what is raised

129 Grudem, Wayne.Systematic Theology, An Introduction to Biblical Doctrine. InterVarsity Press 38 De Montfort Street Leicester LE1 7GP Great Britain, Grand Rapids, MI:Zondervan Publishing House, 5300 Patterson Ave., 60515. Chapter 33, pp. 831-832, on effective calling.

is imperishable. It is sown in dishonor, it is raised in glory. It is sown in weakness, it is raised in power. It is sown a physical body, it is raised a spiritual body.... Just as we have borne the image of the man of dust, we shall also bear the image of the man of heaven. (*1 Corinthians 15:42-44,49*) The fact that our new bodies will be "imperishable" means that they will not wear out or grow old or ever be subject to any kind of sickness or disease. They will be completely healthy and strong forever. Also, since the gradual process of aging is part of the process by which our bodies now are subject to "corruption," it is appropriate to think that our resurrection bodies will have no sign of aging, but will have the characteristics of youthful but mature manhood or womanhood forever. There will be no evidence of disease or injury, for all will be made perfect.[130]

Our resurrection bodies will show the fulfillment of God's perfect wisdom in creating us as human beings who are the pinnacle of his creation and the appropriate bearers of his likeness and image. In these resurrection bodies we will clearly see humanity as God intended it to be. Paul also says our bodies will be raised "in glory." When this term is contrasted with "dishonor," as it is here, there is a suggestion of the beauty or the attractiveness of appearance that our bodies will have. They will no longer be "dishonorable" or unattractive, but will look "glorious" in their beauty. Moreover, because the word "glory" is so frequently used in Scripture of the bright shining radiance that surrounds the presence of God himself, this term suggests that there will also be a kind of brightness or radiance surrounding our bodies that will be an appropriate outward evidence of the position of exaltation and rule over all creation that God has given to us. In Matthew 13:43, Jesus says, "Then the righteous will shine like the sun in the kingdom of their Father." Similarly, we read in Daniel's vision, "And those who are wise shall shine like the brightness of the firmament; and those who turn many to righteousness, like the

---

130 That the scars of Jesus' nail prints remained on his hands is a special case to remind us of the price he paid for our redemption, and it should not be taken as an indication that any of our scars from physical injuries will remain: see chapter 28, pp. 616. Grudem, Wayne. Systematic Theology, An Introduction to Biblical Doctrine. InterVarsity Press 38 De Montfort Street Leicester LE1 7GP Great Britain, Grand Rapids, MI:Zondervan Publishing House, 5300 Patterson Ave., 60515. Chapter 33, pp. 692-94, on effective calling.

stars forever and ever" (Daniel 12:3, in a passage talking about the final resurrection). Now both of these statements might possibly be understood metaphorically, and in that case they would not indicate that an actual brightness or radiance will surround our resurrection bodies. But there is no reason in the context of either of them that would cause us to see them as metaphorical, and other pieces of evidence argue against doing so.

The hints of the age to come that were seen in the shining of the glory of God from the face of Moses (*Exodus 34:35*), and, in a much greater way, the bright light that shone from Jesus at the transfiguration (*Matthew 17:2*), together with the fact that we will bear the image of Christ and be like him (*1 Corinthians 15:49*), combine to suggest that there will actually be a visible brightness or radiance that surrounds us when we are in our resurrection bodies.

Our bodies will also be raised "in power" (*1 Corinthians 15:43*). This is in contrast to the "weakness" which we see in our bodies now. Our resurrection bodies will not only be free from disease and aging, they will also be given fullness of strength and power — not infinite power like God, of course, and probably not what we would think of as "superhuman" power in the sense possessed by the "superheroes" in modern fictional children's writing, for example, but nonetheless full and complete human power and strength, the strength that God intended human beings to have in their bodies when he created them. It will therefore be strength that is sufficient to do all that we desire to do in conformity with the will of God.

Several passages indicate that Paul expected a considerable measure of continuity between our present earthly bodies and our future resurrection bodies. Paul said, "He who raised Christ Jesus from the dead will give life to your mortal bodies also through his Spirit which dwells in you" (*Romans 8:11*). When Paul spoke about the nature of the resurrection body he gave an example of a seed sown in the ground: "What you sow is not the body which is to be, but a bare kernel, perhaps of wheat or of some other grain. But God gives it a body as he has chosen, and to each kind of seed its own body" (*1 Corinthians 15:37-38*).

Life Application for Personal Reflection
Glorification
1. Do you sense the Holy Spirit bears witness with your spirit that you are a child of God?

Suggested Reading
Glorification
Grudem, Wayne. "Adoption." Systematic Theology, An Introduction to Biblical Doctrine. InterVarsity Press, 38 De Montfort Street Leicester LE1 7GP Great Britain, Grand Rapids, MI: Zondervan Publishing House, pp 828-839.

Because of Who You Are

Lyrics by VICKI YOHE

Because of who You are, I give You glory
Because of who You are, I give You praise
Because of who You are, I will lift my voice and say
Lord I worship You, because of who You are
Lord I worship You, because of who You are.

Because of who You are, I give You glory
Because of who You are, I give You praise
Because of who You are, I will lift my voice and say
Lord I worship You, because of who You are
Lord I worship You, because of who You are.

Jehovah Jireh, my Provider
Jehovah Nissi, Lord You reign in victory
Jehovah Shalom, my Prince of Peace
And I worship You, because of who You Are.

REFLECTIONS

GLORIOUS SALVATION

While I was in England I visited St. Paul's Cathedral. I stood there in that great place, surrounded by exquisite art and architecture, and said to my friend: "This building makes me believe in God." I think he was somewhat taken back by my statement that a physical, man-made building could make me believe in God. "What else could inspire such a sense of transcendence and create a feeling of otherworldliness — a world of unspeakable beauty and holy purpose?" These glorious monuments to God are all over England and Europe — countries strongly influenced by the Christian faith. "Name me one monument to the devil which has been built in his honor," I said to my friend.

Actually, I have seen a monument to the devil. It exists in a country I visited a few years before, whose national religion is Voodoo, or devil worship — the country of Haiti. It is the center for Voodoo worship — a large mud hole where chickens are strangled and their blood poured into the pool. Rumors are that there are even secret rites where human sacrifices are offered to the devil, and their blood becomes a part of the mud as well. Worshipers come to bathe themselves with the mud of that cursed place. What a difference. All dedicated to Jesus Christ was exquisite transcendent, causing noble and holy thoughts. The monument to the devil was a mud hole, vile and ugly, arousing perverse thoughts and evil acts. One was elevating and the other degrading.

- Rodney Buchanan

Source: For Me, My Belief In God Was Reaffirmed Recently. Text Illustration shared by Rodney Buchanan, Retired April 2002. Retrieved November 2015 from http://www.sermoncentral.com/illustrations/sermon-illustration-rodney-buchanan-stories-theodicy-accuse-godsholiness-7333.asp

Like A Baby

Babies need the basics of life - like food, shelter, warmth and clothing. They also need to feel loved and secure. By giving children all the things they need, we can help them feel safe. This will make them strong and thrive. Secure early bonding is the difference between the baby that grows into a secure, emotionally capable adult, and a baby that will become an anxious child, who finds it difficult to cope with life's ups and downs. Babies and children need to know there is someone who loves them and that their needs will be met as soon as possible – all the time. They must be fed when hungry, clothed when naked, and bundled when cold or in danger. They must be constantly looked after so that they know they can trust you to look after them. Picking them up, holding them, and showering them with hugs and kisses helps them to feel safe. When left to fend for themselves, they do not feel loved. Everybody wants to have that same sense of security. From home alarms to seat belts, from helmets to life jackets -- we all want to feel secure in the things we are doing. Christ also wants to give his people a feeling of security. The sure promises of God to Abraham addressed food, clothing, shelter, companionship, love, and salvation thru Jesus Christ all culminate into that security.

– The Author

Preservation: Eternal Security

◆ ◆ ◆

*"The Law of God was never a ladder for unsaved people to climb up
to heaven. It was always a pattern of life for God's people who had been
saved from judgment by the blood of the Lamb."*

Colin S. Smith, Unlocking the Bible Story: Old Testament 2

▼

No event that happens in creation falls outside of providence. In Wayne Grudem's Systematic Theology we learn that by accepting the doctrine of divine providence, then we should be able to accept preservation as an element of that teaching. Preservation means that God keeps all created things existing and maintaining with the properties that God originally created.[131] Grudem makes basic certain points to help our understanding and points us to those references. For example, Jesus is continually upholding all things by the word of His power (*Hebrews 1:3*) and by Jesus, all things created in the universe consist (*Colossians 1:17*). Ezra says "The Lord of hosts has made all things and is able to preserve them all." (*Nehemiah 9:6*) and Peter tells us that God keeps heaven and earth until the day of judgment (*2 Peter 3:7*).

---

131 Grudem, Wayne. Systematic Theology, An Introduction to Biblical Doctrine. InterVarsity Press 38 De Montfort Street Leicester LE1 7GP Great Britain, Grand Rapids, MI:Zondervan Publishing House, 5300 Patterson Ave., 60515, Chapter 24, pp 315-317

The perseverance of the saints means that all those who are truly born again will be kept by God's power and will persevere as Christians until the end of their lives, and that only those who persevere until the end have been truly born again.[132] This two-part definition includes **1)** that there is assurance for those who are truly born again, that God's power will keep them as Christians until they die, and they will have eternal life and **2)** that continuing in the Christian life is one of the evidences that a person is truly born again. This doctrine has suffered severe disagreement for years because of the potential for false assurance given to people who were never really believers in the first place. Evangelical Christians have and continue to disagree. The Wesleyan/Arminian tradition has taught that it is possible for someone who is born again to lose his or her salvation, while Reformed Christians have held that that is not possible for someone who is truly born again. Most Baptists have followed the Reformed tradition; however, they have frequently used the term "eternal security" or the eternal security of the believer" rather than the term "perseverance of the saints."

Well, what of it? Is this doctrine true or false and how can we be sure? Can true Christians lose their salvation? On the subject of perseverance of the Saints and from a Calvinistic view, you cannot lose your salvation.[133] It holds that since the Father elected us, the Son redeemed and the Holy Spirit applied salvation, those who are saved are eternally secure in Christ. This is substantiated several places. Jesus said His sheep will never perish (*John 10:27-28*). Salvation is described as everlasting life in John 6:47. Romans 8:1 says we have passed out of judgment and in 1 Corinthians 10:13, God promises to never let us be tempted beyond what we can handle; and Philippians 1:6 says God is faithful to perfect us until Jesus returns.

Born again believers will persevere to the end. Jesus says that everyone who believes in him will have eternal life and that He will raise that person up at the last day which, in this context of believing

---

132 This doctrine is one of the five points of Calvinism represented by the "P" in the associated TULIP acronym which summarizes the five points.
133 Matthew J. Slick, Calvinist Corner, Retrieved November, 2015 from: http://www.calvinistcorner.com/tulip.htm,2012

in the Son and having eternal life, clearly means that Jesus will raise that person up to eternal life with him. Does this mean that everyone who truly believes in Christ will remain a Christian up to the day of final resurrection into the blessings of life in the presence of God? Is this what Jesus meant? He is not man that He should lie. Jesus does the will of the Father, which is that he should lose nothing of all that God gave Him (*John 6:39*). It is clear that those given to the Son by the Father will not be lost. There are many passages that teach that those who are truly born again, who are genuinely Christians, will continue in the Christian life until death and will then go to be with Christ in heaven. Jesus says that it is the will of the Father, that He should lose nothing of all that God gave Him, but raise it up at the last day. For this is the will of my Father, that everyone who sees the Son and believes in him should have eternal life; and I will raise him up at the last day (*John 6:38-40*). He also explains the situation of Judas being lost in John 17:12 saying, "While I was with them in the world, I kept them in thy name: those that thou gavest me I have kept, and none of them is lost, but the son of perdition; that the scripture might be fulfilled." Another passage emphasizing this truth is John 10:27-29, in which Jesus says: My sheep hear my voice, and I know them, and they follow me; and I give them eternal life, and they shall never perish, and no one shall snatch them out of my hand. My Father, who has given them to me, is greater than all, and no one is able to snatch them out of the Father's hand. Jesus promises that His sheep, those who follow him, are given eternal life. How comforting to know that we will have eternal life.

It appears that biggest reason for the years of disagreement with this passage is directly related to the tendency for man to judge others. For example, years ago as a teenager, I witnessed the public renunciation of a fallen bishop in a large gathering of church members. It was devastating to many because such confidence had been placed in this man for the many souls won to Christ and the churches founded under his ministry. Now he had committed adultery. It was embarrassing not only for him but for his wife and children. I recall very explicitly how saddened and disappointed I was for the whole situation and the family. I knew the children. Yet my mind flashed back to comments and insinuations made by some of the young ladies in the church and one of my own sisters who went to great lengths to avoid this older man, but it was not a deterrent because of his prowess.

Because it was such a rarity for things of this nature to be raised and put before the general congregation, it stayed with us. From that day on, people were crushed; this was one of our own. He continued for awhile but he was perceived differently. The weight of it tore apart his family. He tried but it did not work. Eventually, he stopped coming; there were rumors that his new life was plagued with infidelity. Small groups of us prayed for him because he was part of us and the Lord loves the backslider. Then within a few more years, it happened in the church leadership again and at the same level. However, this time, it was a bishop that seemed to have all of the gifts of the Spirit. There were miracles, healings, prophecy, and word of knowledge – all operating in every service. He was like a walking miracle himself. Yet, there it was again. Adultery. This time, it was the offending bishop that came before the large assembly to confess. He opened up his heart and told his story. At first, there was stunned silence. What was this? This was our leadership. He was the best. How could he? What was going on and where does that leave the rest of us? But then a still small voice whispered, admonishing me, in my inner spiritual ear in a strange but meaningful context. "There, but by the grace of God, goes I," the Spirit whispered to me. The bishop wept and prayed for forgiveness. The leaders wept. The congregation wept. There was not a dry eye in the house. We wrapped our arms around him in love for when one of our own hurts, we hurt. This bishop second remained within this particular ministry and remains until this day. The New Testament is taken up with instructing believers in various churches on how they should grow in likeness to Christ. Paul says that throughout the

Christian life we all... are being changed into his likeness from one degree of glory to another" (*2 Corinthians 3:18*) and becoming more like Christ as we continue in Him. We must forget the past and press forward (*Philippians 3:13-14*). We are not perfect but if we give up, we will be able to achieve the purposes for which Christ has saved us. Paul told the Colossians to not lie to one another, since they have put on the new nature of the Lord (*Colossians 3:10*), thus proving out our internal sanctification. We have to lay aside every weight that tries to beset us and strive for holiness. (*Hebrews 12:1-14*). We must be holy in all our conduct" (*1 Peter 1:15*). For those whom he predestined he also called; and those whom he called he also justified; and those whom he justified he also glorified. Paul sees the future event of glorification as a certainty in God's settled purpose. This is true of all those who are called and justified—that is, all those who truly become Christians.[134]

We are safe for eternity because we are sealed by the protection of the Holy Spirit. He is the guarantor of our inheritance until we acquire possession of it." (*Ephesians 1:14*). All who are truly born again, who have the Holy Spirit within them, can rest assured of God's unchanging promise and guarantee that the inheritance of eternal life in heaven will certainly be theirs. He who began a good work in us will bring it to completion at the day of Jesus Christ" (*Philippians 1:6*) and God is preserving believers and protecting them from external attacks. According to 1 Peter 1:5, God is guarding us by His power through faith. The Greek word guarded ("phroureo") can mean both "kept from escaping" and "protected from attack." Peter use of it here gives the sense we are continually being guarded. Yet we know that God's power does not work apart from the individual personal faith of those being guarded, but through their faith. The word for faith "pistis" is regularly a personal activity of individual believers in Peter's epistles. Refer to 1 Peter 1:7-21. This guarding is not for a temporary goal but for a salvation ready to be revealed in the last time. This reference to salvation concerns the future with the full possession of all the blessings of our

---

134 Grudem, Wayne. Systematic Theology, An Introduction to Biblical Doctrine. InterVarsity Press 38 De Montfort Street Leicester LE1 7GP Great Britain, Grand Rapids, MI:Zondervan Publishing House, 5300 Patterson Ave., 60515, Chapter 24, pp 793-798

redemption. Though already prepared it will not be revealed by God to mankind generally until the time of final judgment (*cf. Romans 13:11; 1 Peter 2:2*). This makes impossible to see any end to God's guarding activity but it is safe to conclude that God will accomplish that purpose and that believers will attain that final salvation.[135]

All of this depends on God's power. Nevertheless, God's power continually works through their faith. In the example of the two bishops who committed adultery, we cannot make assumptions about either or those individuals. However, we are to pray for one another. Do they wish to know whether God is guarding them? If they continue to trust God through Christ, then God is working and guarding them. Jesus said to those who believed Him, "If you abide in My word, you are My disciples indeed. And you shall know the truth, and the truth shall make you free. (*John 8:31-32*). John clearly states that when people fall away from fellowship with the church and from belief in Christ, they thereby show that their faith was not real in the first place and that they were never part of the true body of Christ. Speaking of people who have left the fellowship of believers, John says, "They went out from us, but they were not of us; for if they had been of us, they would have continued with us; but they went out, that it might be plain that they all are not of us" (*1 John 2:19*). John says that those who have departed showed by their actions that they "were not of us"—that they were not truly born again.

Those who persevere to the end have been truly born again. God guards us but not apart from our faith. Instead, it is through our faith that he enables us to continue to believe in him. In this way, those who continue to trust in Christ gain assurance that God is working in them and guarding them. Jesus warned that one evidence of genuine faith is continuing in His word and believing and living a life of obedience to His commands. He who endures to the end will be saved" (*Matthew 10:22*) is a means of warning people not to fall away in times of persecution.

135 Grudem, Wayne. Systematic Theology, An Introduction to Biblical Doctrine. InterVarsity Press 38 De Montfort Street Leicester LE1 7GP Great Britain, Grand Rapids, MI:Zondervan Publishing House, 5300 Patterson Ave., 60515, Chapter 24, pp 793-798.

Paul preached that Christ reconciled them to God in order to present them holy, blameless and irreproachable before him, but it was with the condition of continuing in the faith and not shifting from the hope of the gospel of Jesus Christ. (*Colossians 1:22-23*).

Paul and other New Testament writers were addressing followers of Christ, without being able to know the actual state of every person's heart. It happened back then and it is happening today. People join in the fellowship of the church, professing faith in Christ and participating in every aspect of the ministry but when the chips are down, it is clear that they never had true saving faith. Is it possible to distinguish such people from true believers? Those whose faith is not real will eventually fall completely away from participation in the fellowship of the church. The only way to avoid giving false assurance is to follow Paul's example.[136] It was important in that time and today as well, to explain that ultimate salvation rests upon whether the individual continues in the faith. (*Colossians 1:23*). Those who continue show thereby that they are genuine believers. But those who do not continue in the faith show that there was no genuine faith in their hearts in the first place. Just as the Scripture emphasizes that those who are truly born again will persevere to the end and have eternal life in heaven with God, there are other passages that speak of the necessity of continuing in faith throughout life. This is why we must hold fast to our confession of faith. We are partakers of and joined to Christ in genuine faith if we continue in faith until the end of our lives.

According to John, when people fall away from fellowship with the church and from belief in Christ they thereby show that their faith was not real in the first place and that they were never part of the true body of Christ. Speaking of people who have left the fellowship of believers, John says, "They went out from us, but they were not of us; for if they had been of us, they would have continued with us; but they went out, that it might be plain that they all are not of us" (*1 John 2:19*). John says

---

136 Grudem, Wayne. Systematic Theology, An Introduction to Biblical Doctrine. InterVarsity Press 38 De Montfort Street Leicester LE1 7GP Great Britain, Grand Rapids, MI:Zondervan Publishing House, 5300 Patterson Ave., 60515, Chapter 24, pp 793-798.

that those who have departed showed by their actions that they "were not of us"—that they were not truly born again. Think of the fragrance of the – it was very sacred for it symbolized the presence of God on a person life. Or the power of God on a person's occupation.[137] People in their coronation, in their commissioning, would receive a measure of the substance by the clergy.

Those who fall away later may appear to have conformed. It is not always clear which people in the church have genuine saving faith. Scripture mentions in several places that unbelievers in fellowship with the visible church can give some external signs or indications that make them look or sound like genuine. For example, Judas, who betrayed Christ, was so convincing in his conformity with similar behavior patterns to the others, that he not only fooled the disciples for three years, he fooled himself. Jesus, however, knew from the beginning that there was no genuine faith in Judas' heart. At one point, he exclaimed, "Did I not choose you, the twelve, and one of you is a devil?" (*John 6:70*). Paul referred to "false brethren secretly brought in" on several occasions (*Galatians 2:4*), admitting that he had been "in danger from false brethren" (*2 Corinthians 11:26*) who "disguised themselves as servants of righteousness" (*2 Corinthians 11:15*). This does not mean that this is true of all unbelievers in the church who pretend to be converted. Some are simply lacking in knowledge, wisdom and truth. They are not all seeking to undermine the work of the church. Some lack genuine faith because they have not really heard the full gospel or come under genuine conviction of the Holy Spirit yet. However some unbelievers in the church will be false brothers and sisters and they are deliberately come to disrupt the fellowship.[138] Others will eventually come to genuine saving faith. In both cases, however, they give several external signs that make them look like genuine believers.[139] If the disciples were as close to Judas for three years and failed to detect his inconsistencies, is that possible for us?

137 Foster, Joan, Classroom Lecture. "Unction to Function Interaction Paper", Calvary Christian College, Waldorf, MD. April 22, 2010.
138 Grudem, Wayne. Systematic Theology, An Introduction to Biblical Doctrine. InterVarsity Press 38 De Montfort Street Leicester LE1 7GP Great Britain, Grand Rapids, MI:Zondervan Publishing House, 5300 Patterson Ave., 60515, Chapter 24, pp 793-803
139 Grudem, Wayne. Systematic Theology, An Introduction to Biblical Doctrine. InterVarsity Press 38 De Montfort Street Leicester LE1 7GP Great Britain, Grand Rapids, MI:Zondervan Publishing House, 5300 Patterson Ave., 60515, Chapter 24, pp 793-794

The points raised in this doctrine will be forever kept with lessons learned and filed in my studies on the Holy Spirit. Having grown up in a household that taught on the spiritual gifts and the need to be able to spiritually discern between spirits – good and evil, right and wrong – it was impossible not to get things wrong even when right. For fear of giving the appearance of judging or falling into wrongful application or even possibly getting into the habit of making judgment calls because of personal instincts and losing friends, it was much easier to push away or silence the warning bells. When you spend a lot of time in His presence, studying His Word, getting to know His character – what He likes and dislikes, it is impossible to not see the world through His eyes. On any number of occasions, after the truth came to light, the Holy Spirit would remind me to trust Him. It requires spiritual maturity to be able to know that when you have spiritually discerned something, you do not ignore it or blow it off as if it is just your instincts. At the same time, you must be able to strike a balance between when to speak and trust God for wisdom for what to say – if you say anything at all. Often, the Holy Spirit will show us in the spirit realm but because the facts have not caught up with the truth, we are deceived into silence or into being of no effect in that matter. By the time the truth is revealed, we have neglected to act or do as God intended. But there are times when it is very difficult to know because the unbelieving pretender has convinced others. The wheat and tares are all growing together. How can you know except by the Spirit?

This is also addressed when Jesus comments on the last judgment: "Not everyone who cries, 'Lord, Lord', shall enter the kingdom of heaven, but he who does the will of my Father who is in heaven. On that day many will say to me, 'Lord, Lord, did we not prophesy in your name, and cast out demons in your name, and do many mighty works in your name'?" Jesus said, "And then will I declare to them, 'I never knew you; depart from me, you evildoers'." (*Matthew 7:21-23*) These people even went so far as to prophesy and cast out demons and did mighty works in Jesus' name, but clearly the ability to do such works did not guarantee that they were followers of Christ. Jesus says, "I never knew you." He does not say, "I knew you at one time but I no longer know you," nor "I knew you at one time but you strayed away from me," but rather, "I never knew you." They never were genuine believers.

A similar teaching is found in the parable of the sower in Mark 4 in the parable of the sower where seed sown upon rocky ground represents people who "when they hear the word, immediately receive it with joy; and they have no root in themselves, but endure for a while; then, when tribulation or persecution arises on account of the word, immediately they fall away" (*Mark 4:16-17*). The fact that they "have no root in themselves" indicates that there is no source of life within these plants; similarly, the people represented by them have no genuine life of their own within. They have an appearance of conversion and joy, but when difficulty comes, they are nowhere to be found—their apparent conversion was not genuine and there was no real saving faith in their hearts. [140]

Finally, there are two passages in Hebrews that also affirm that those who finally fall away may give many external signs of conversion and may look in many ways like Christians. The first of these, Hebrews 6:4-6, has frequently been used by Arminians as proof that believers can lose their salvation. But on closer inspection such an interpretation is not convincing. The author writes, For it is impossible to restore again to repentance those who have once been enlightened, who have tasted the heavenly gift, and have become partakers of the Holy Spirit, and have tasted the goodness of the word of God and the powers of the age to come, if they then commit apostasy, since they crucify the Son of God on their own account and hold him up to contempt. (*Hebrew 6:4-6*)

Hebrews 6:4-6 speaks of people who have been associated with the Holy Spirit, and thereby had their lives influenced by him, but it need not imply that they had a redeeming work of the Holy Spirit in their lives,

---

140 Grudem, Wayne. Systematic Theology, An Introduction to Biblical Doctrine. InterVarsity Press 38 De Montfort Street Leicester LE1 7GP Great Britain, Grand Rapids, MI:Zondervan Publishing House, 5300 Patterson Ave., 60515, Chapter 24, pp 793-803

or that they were regenerated. We have known in our own churches people who have long been affiliated with the fellowship of the church but are not themselves born-again Christians.[141] They have thought about the gospel for years and have continued to resist the wooing of the Holy Spirit in their lives, perhaps through an unwillingness to give up lordship of their lives to Jesus and preferring to cling to it themselves.

Hebrews explains that if these people willfully turn away from all of these temporary blessings, then it will be impossible to restore them again to any kind of repentance or sorrow for sin. Their hearts will be hardened and their consciences calloused. What more could be done to bring them to salvation? If we tell them Scripture is true they will say that they know it but they have decided to reject it. If we tell them God answers prayer and changes lives they will respond that they know that as well, but they want nothing of it. If we tell them that the Holy Spirit is powerful to work in people's lives and the gift of eternal life is good beyond description, they will say that they understand that, but they want nothing of it. Their repeated familiarity with the things of God and their experience of many influences of the Holy Spirit has simply served to harden them against conversion.[142] There is also the group that is in danger of falling away in just this way. They have participated in the fellowship of the church and experienced a number of God's blessings in their lives, yet if they fall away after all that, there is no salvation for them. This does not imply that he thinks that true Christians could fall away. In fact Hebrews 3:14 implies the very opposite. However, like everyone else, they can only obtain assurance of salvation through their continuing in faith, and thereby implies that if they fall away it would show that they never were Christ's people in the first place (see Hebrews 3:6).

We know that temporary blessings and experiences are not enough. People who fall away never had any genuine fruit in their lives. As much as we may not like it, there will be people that we have shared fellowship

---

141 Grudem, Wayne. Systematic Theology, An Introduction to Biblical Doctrine. InterVarsity Press 38 De Montfort Street Leicester LE1 7GP Great Britain, Grand Rapids, MI:Zondervan Publishing House, 5300 Patterson Ave., 60515, Chapter 24, pp 793-803
142 Ibid.

with that will fall away. Oddly enough, we will miss them and desire their return even beyond their desire. If we could, we would probably run a marathon to put everyone we love in heaven – even if they have no desire for it. A few years ago, an old member of the church was overcome with grief that a young man from her church was found to be on his deathbed. He was finally succumbing to the effects of AIDS after so many years battling the many different trips to the hospital. She was in turmoil because no one was there for him. She did not know his story; no one at the church did. He just showed up and started attending. His own family had given up on him a long time ago; few people at the church knew him. She felt for him; she was an intercessor and never wanted anyone to be alone or without help. Yet while she was at his bedside praying for him and seeking some way to get him into heaven, he looked at her and said, "Stop, don't pray for me, Mother Massey. If I had it to do all over again, I would live my life the same way. I enjoyed everything I did and have no shame concerning who I did it with and I am not going to lie about it so you do not need to cry for me. I did not accept Christ before and I do not see the point of accepting him now. If that means I have to go to hell, then so be it but what would it look like if I came crying to God now? I refuse to pretend."

He became quite graphic in his description of the sin and perversion that he claim to have enjoyed to the point that she finally gave up and called me to pray for his soul. That was the first time that I could recall Mother Massey being in such a state of despair. It was a teaching moment, yes, for her but also for me. Such love she had! She hated to see him lost – even if he refused the love of Jesus Christ. The young man died several days later.

On the other hand, there was Robert. He was 26 years old, could not drive or plays sports or do anything that the average guy could. Why, he could barely walk! But he had the sharpest mathematical genius of a mind. My sister formed a protective bond with him the instant she met him, and after several years, they became chums. She would pick him up and take him to church week nights and on the weekends, they did the church books together. Robert had a very slow smile and he always reserved one just for Jessie. He was a model Christian. His face, arms and legs were covered with medium to large growths. Everyone seemed to understand that he was sick, except Jessie. She was the only one who did not feel sorry for him. If he made a mistake, we knew it had something to do with his medicine and he couldn't think straight. So everyone else would make excuses for him. But not Jessie. If he made an error, she lit into him. When he would try to explain, she would challenge him to the point that we all thought Robert would raise up out of his wheel chair already. But no matter what she did, Robert always looked at her and with that slow grin of his, he would come right back at her with kindness.

On that particular Easter Sunday morning, Jessie had gotten up a little later than usual. When somebody reminded her that Robert had asked her to pick him up, she groaned. Oh, why did she always have to be the one? But several hours later as she was racing to get to church, she drove right past the turn off the main highway that she needed to make to get to Robert's house and was well down the road before she realized she had missed the turn. Her mind was bogged down with the order of service and how late she was; she would have to switch the order of some things. She did not really want to turn around to pick up Robert; besides it would take a long time to get back to him. Besides, he was very slow and having to deal with the wheel chair would make her even later. So she conveniently forgot to pick up Robert. Later, she confessed that something kept nagging at her to turn around and go get Robert but she did not. He loved coming to church. Even as she pulled up to the church, something felt wrong. She thought maybe someone else would bring him. Well, Robert did not show up at that service or any other service at church again. He did not call for Jessie to pick him up ever again because he died on that Monday. Jessie struggled with that whole situation. She cried for days because she really loved Robert. We all did. He was the kindest, most gentle human being to walk among us. He never complained, even when he was hurting. We never quite understood how he could live through the pain of that cancer – there was no chemo or radiation treatment for him back then. And yet, with no radical treatment, no real understanding of the illness or treatment options, and no ordinary hope of recovery, he never let us feel the brunt of his bad days. When we asked how he was doing, Robert would always answer in as strong a voice as possible, that he was very well and glad to see another day. Rarely did we see Robert without a smile on his face. He was one of those kind of people that everyone should model. Our comfort to Jessie was the reminder that although he loved us, it was Jessie that kept him going and made him feel like a man. He was true believer and one day, we will see him again in heaven. Today, we can chuckle about it because Robert is in heaven!

Though the author has been speaking very harshly about the possibility of falling away, in Hebrews 6:4-8 he then returns to speak to the situation of the great majority of the hearers, whom he thinks to be genuine Christians. He says, "Though we speak thus, yet in your case, beloved, we feel sure of better things that belong to salvation" (*Hebrews 6:9*). But the question is "better things" than what? The plural "better things" forms an appropriate contrast to the "good things" that have been mentioned in verses 4-6: the author is convinced that most of his readers have experienced better things than simply the partial and temporary influences of the Holy Spirit and the church talked about in verses 4-6.

A believer can have assurance that if we continue in the faith and stand firm until the end, we will be saved. We should edify others in our conversation, prayer, and work of the ministry. There should be evidence of the work of the Holy Spirit in our lives showing that we are continuing to believe and accept the sound teaching of the church. Those who begin to deny major doctrines of the faith give serious negative indications concerning their salvation. [143] No one who denies

---

143 Grudem, Wayne. Systematic Theology, An Introduction to Biblical Doctrine. InterVarsity Press 38 De Montfort Street Leicester LE1 7GP Great Britain, Grand Rapids, MI:Zondervan Publishing House, 5300 Patterson Ave., 60515, Chapter 24, pp 793-803.

the Son has the Father.... If what you heard from the beginning abides in you, then you will abide in the Son and in the Father" (*1 John 2:23-24*). Whoever knows God will continue to read and to delight in God's Word, and will continue to believe it fully. Those who do not believe and delight in God's Word give evidence that they are not of God.[144] Another evidence of genuine salvation is a continuing present relationship with Jesus.

Life Application for Personal Reflection
Glorification
1. Knowing that God preserves all things and how He created them in all aspects of our lives, how does this doctrine comfort you when going through difficult situations?
2. Do you think anything is by chance regarding your personal life? Name circumstances that have recently occurred or issues that have come up in your life and how you are dealing with them?

Suggested Reading
Glorification
Grudem, Wayne. "Adoption." Systematic Theology, An Introduction to Biblical Doctrine. InterVarsity Press, 38 De Montfort Street Leicester LE1 7GP Great Britain, Grand Rapids, MI: Zondervan Publishing House, pp 316-317.

---

144 Grudem, Wayne. Systematic Theology, An Introduction to Biblical Doctrine. InterVarsity Press 38 De Montfort Street Leicester LE1 7GP Great Britain, Grand Rapids, MI:Zondervan Publishing House, 5300 Patterson Ave., 60515, Chapter 24, pp 793-803.

It Is Well with My Soul

Lyrics by HORATIO G. SPAFFORD

When peace, like a river, attendeth my way,
When sorrows like sea billows roll;
Whatever my lot, Thou hast taught me to say,
It is well, it is well with my soul.

Refrain:
It is well with my soul,
It is well, it is well with my soul.
Though Satan should buffet, though trials should come,
Let this blest assurance control,

That Christ hath regarded my helpless estate,
And hath shed His own blood for my soul.
My sin—oh, the bliss of this glorious thought!—
My sin, not in part but the whole,
Is nailed to the cross, and I bear it no more,
Praise the Lord, praise the Lord, O my soul!

REFLECTIONS

THE PRESERVATION OF MAN

The horse and mule live 30 years
And nothing know of wines and beers
The goat and sheep at 20 die
With never a taste of scotch or rye
The cow drinks water by the ton
And at 18 is mostly done
The dog at 16 cashes in
Without the aid of rum or gin.
The cat in milk and water soaks
And then in 12 short years it croaks
The modest, sober bone dry hen
Lays eggs for nogs then dies at ten
All animals are strictly dry –
They sinless live and swiftly die
But sinful, ginful, rumsoaked men
Survive for three score years and ten
And some of us thought mighty few
Stay pickled till we're 92.

~Anonymous~

Source: https://wordpress.com/themes/retro-fitted/. The Retro-Fitted Theme: 365 Days of Poetry, Praise and Quotations, July 23, 2013. Retrieved on November 14, 2015 from https://ppq365.wordpress.com/2013/07/23/the-preservation-of-man/

As a Little Child

Jesus said that we must receive the Kingdom of God as a little child, which means humbling self enough to obey the voice of the Lord. To those who refuse to humble themselves as a little child to be saved, the Bible warns of everlasting punishment and destruction from the presence of the Lord, and from the glory of his power. (Revelation 20:11-15). The fastest way to eternal damnation is to act like an adult who must figure out every little detail and have proof of everything before taking a step forward. Any child can see and marvel that there is a God, a divine Creator. If we'll all be honest in our hearts, then we'll have to agree that there is a God, and He's a good God who's provided wonderfully for the needs of mankind. Only an idiot could study the Bible and the manner in which it came into existence and still not believe that it is God's inspired Word. A child doesn't have to figure everything out to believe it. Children are very honest and humble. Children don't require God to prove anything to them to believe. Adults on the other hand, because of pride, love of sin and a rebellious attitude, continually place God on trial.

– Inspired by Sermon Central Staff
Outreach Inc.

Sanctification

◆ ◆ ◆

"Every time someone reaches out to you, even if it's to point out your
sin and they seem to be judging you, it is a token of God's mercy."
J.E.B. Spredemann, A Secret of the Heart

▼

Through the years, there has been much confusion surrounding
the word sanctification particularly regarding the terms. Some have
referred to it as a baptism of love, a clean heart, a victorious walk
or life, while others have called it holiness, baptism with the Holy
Spirit and still others simply say it is the second blessing or work
of the Holy Spirit. While speaking of the same experience the terms
have varied, and many have denied that anyone else had the same
experience because there was no common usage of terms.

What is sanctification? Let's put the definitions on the table.
The New Testament abounds in a great variety of expressions for the
same Spirit's workings, and under a number of figures it depicts the
various sides to the same truth, such as entire dedication, or a state
of being yielded or crucified, death to the old man, putting off the old
man and putting on the new man, being filled with the Holy Spirit,
or the infilling of the Spirit, sanctification, or holiness of life. Some

theologians make sanctification a sovereign activity of God wrought out independent of our cooperation or wills suggesting that our sanctification is substitutionary and apart from any holiness of living, or heart purity. There are others who would make it synonymous with sinless perfection, as making the one who is sanctified perfect and sinless.

Let's start with the first part of the definition. It is commonly understood that sanctification is God at work renewing the whole of what we are.[145] We have come to designate all the works of the Holy Spirit in the believer's life by the one term sanctification, and have, more or less, made the word to mean a deeper experience of the child of God. This is how the term second work of grace, as differentiating it from the salvation of the sinner as the first work of grace, came into existence and known as the second blessing. It has been the experience as well as the conviction of the average believer that there is a higher plane of Christian experience than current manifested.

The second part of the definition is the continued transformation of moral and spiritual character so that the life of the believer actually comes to mirror that understanding in God's sight.[146] This is the application of redemption that is a progressive work that continues throughout our earthly lives.[147] It is also a work in which God and man cooperate, each playing distinct roles. It is the progressive work of God and man that makes us more like Christ in our actual lives and less inclined toward sin. This is the part described as holy and in this case, means bearing an actual likeness to God. This process by which one's moral condition is brought into conformity with one's legal status before God, continues throughout our Christian life. By applying the work done by Jesus Christ, it is a furtherance of what began in regeneration when newness of life was instilled within

145 Millard J. Erickson, edited by L. Arnold Hustad, Introducing Christian Doctrine, Baker Academic, A Division of Baker House Co., P.O. Box 6287, Grand Rapids, MI, 49516-6287, 2011, p.184.
146 Millard J. Erickson, edited by L. Arnold Hustad, Introducing Christian Doctrine, Baker Academic, A Division of Baker House Co., P.O. Box 6287, Grand Rapids, MI, 49516-6287, 2011, p. 280.
147 Grudem, Wayne. Systematic Theology, An Introduction to Biblical Doctrine. InterVarsity Press 38 De Montfort Street Leicester LE1 7GP Great Britain, Grand Rapids, MI:Zondervan Publishing House, 5300 Patterson Ave., 60515, Chpt. 24.

the believer. The ordinary course of a Christian's life will involve continual growth in sanctification, and it is something that the New Testament encourages us to give effort and attention to. Without this, the believer cannot feel complete victory. The promise that "Sin shall not have dominion over you," requires more than a one-time victory experience. It calls for the blessing of the deeper life, the wholehearted yielding to the infilling sanctifying Holy Spirit. The conviction then of a deeper experience, a victorious life, a fullness of joy, and deeper richer communion with God must abound.

Sanctification is the state of being separate, set apart from the ordinary or mundane, being dedicated to a particular purpose with formal characteristics – whether a person, place or thing. For example, the Holy of Holies, the garments of Aaron the high priest, or the Sabbath Day were all set apart and it identified as belonging to God. This is the third and wonderful part of the definition. It does not stop there. The last part of our understanding has to do with the part that calls for action of the believer. Sanctification is the moral goodness or spiritual worth in which the believer is not only set apart but is called upon to conduct themselves accordingly. There are aspects of a believer's life that must be dealt with through the process.[148] They include the internal condition, the setting apart, and the continuous Christian living and cooperation. There are three stages of sanctification. They include the following:

Sanctification - Definite beginning at regeneration. A definite moral change occurs in our lives at the point of regeneration, for Paul talks about the "washing of regeneration and renewal in the Holy Spirit" (*Titus* 3:5). Once we have been born again we cannot continue to sin as a habit or a pattern of life (*1 John* 3:9), because the power of new spiritual life within us keeps us from yielding to a life of sin. This initial moral change is the first stage in sanctification. In this sense, there is some overlap between regeneration and sanctification,

---

148 Millard J. Erickson, edited by L. Arnold Hustad, Introducing Christian Doctrine, Baker Academic, A Division of Baker House Co., P.O. Box 6287, Grand Rapids, MI, 49516-6287, 2011, pp. 324-325.

for this moral change is actually a part of regeneration when we view it from the standpoint of moral change within us, we can also see it as the first stage in sanctification. This initial step in sanctification involves a definite break from the ruling power and love of sin, so that the believer is no longer ruled or dominated by sin and no longer loves to sin. Paul says we must consider ourselves dead to sin and alive to God in Christ Jesus, that sin will have no dominion over us; we have been set free (*Romans 6:11,14,18*). In this context, to be dead to sin or to be set free from sin involves the power to overcome acts or patterns of sinful behavior in one's life.

Sanctification - Increases throughout life. Even though the New Testament speaks about a definite beginning to sanctification, it also sees it as a process that continues throughout our Christian lives. This is the primary sense in which sanctification is used in systematic theology and in Christian conversation generally today. Sin will no longer be our master. In practical terms, this means on one hand that because our sanctification is a continuous living process, we are continuously working out our salvation. However, on the other hand, we should never give up and say things like, "Oh, that is just my personality" when we do things that are not Christ like. To say this is to allow sin to reign in our bodies and to admit defeat. It is also contrary to Scripture. We were formerly slaves to sin we are enslaved no longer. "You who were once slaves of sin have become obedient from the heart to the standard of teaching to which you were committed, and, having been set free from sin, have become slaves of righteousness" (*Romans 6:17-18*). As Christians, our task is to grow more and more in sanctification, just as we previously grew more and more in sin. "Just as you once yielded your members to impurity and to greater and greater iniquity, so now yield your members to righteousness for sanctification." (*Romans 6:19*)

Sanctification - Completed at death and when the Lord returns. Our sanctification will never be completed in this life. But once we die and go to be with the Lord, then our sanctification is completed in one sense, for our soul is set free from indwelling sin and made perfect. The author of Hebrews says that when we come into the presence of God to worship we come "to the spirits of just men made perfect" (*Hebrews 12:23*). This is only appropriate because it is in anticipation of the fact that "nothing unclean shall enter" into the presence of God, the heavenly city (*Revelation 21:27*).

Sanctification - Never completed in this life. There have always been some in the history of the church who have taken commands such as Matthew 5:48 ("You, therefore, must be perfect, as your heavenly Father is perfect") or 2 Corinthians 7:1 ("let us cleanse ourselves from every defilement of body and spirit, and make holiness perfect in the fear of God") and reasoned that since God gives us these commands, he must also give us the ability to obey them perfectly. Therefore, they have concluded, it is possible for us to attain a state of sinless perfection in this life. They have also inferred that Paul's prayer for the Thessalonians, "May the God of peace Himself sanctify you wholly" (*1 Thessalonians 5:23*), may well have been fulfilled for some of the Thessalonians. John says, "No one who abides in him sins" (*1 John 3:6*). John's statement that "No one who abides in him sins" (*1 John 3:6*) does not teach that some of us attain perfection, because the present tense Greek verbs are better translated as indicating continual or habitual activity: "No one who lives in him keeps on sinning."

"No one who continues to sin has either seen him or known him" (*1 John 3:6 NIV*). This is similar to John's statement a few verses later, "No one who is born of God will continue to sin, because God's seed remains in him; he cannot go on sinning, because he has been born of God" (*1 John 3:9 NIV*). If these verses were taken to prove sinless perfection, they would have to prove it for all Christians, because they talk about what is true of everyone born of God, and everyone who has seen Christ and known him. Therefore, there do not seem to be any convincing verses in Scripture that teach that it is possible for anyone to be completely free of sin in this life. On the other hand, there are passages in both the Old and New Testaments that clearly teach that we cannot be morally perfect in this life. In Solomon's prayer at the dedication of the temple, he says, If they sin against you—for there is no man who does not sin" (1 Kings 8:46). Similarly, we read a rhetorical question with an implied negative answer in Proverbs 20:9: "Who can say, 'I have made my heart clean; I am pure from my sin'?" And we read the explicit statement in Ecclesiastes 7:20, "Surely there is not a righteous man on earth who does good and never sins." In the New Testament, we find Jesus commanding his disciples to pray, "Give us this day our daily bread; and forgive us our sins, as we also have forgiven those who sin against us (Matthew 6:11 -12, author's translation). Just as the prayer for daily bread provides a model for a prayer that should be repeated each day, so the prayer for the forgiveness of sins is included in the type of prayer that should be made each day in a believer's life.

John Murray notes that when Isaiah the prophet came into the presence of God he could only cry out, "Woe is me! For I am lost; for I am a man of unclean lips, and I dwell in the midst of a people of unclean lips; for my eyes have seen the King, the lord of hosts!" (Isaiah 6:5). And when Job, whose righteousness was earlier commended in the story about his life, came into the presence of almighty God, he could only say, "I had heard of you by the hearing of the ear, but now my eye sees you; therefore I despise myself."

Indeed, the more sanctified the person is, the more conformed he is to the image of his Savior, the more he must recoil against every lack of conformity to the holiness of God. The deeper his apprehension of the majesty of God, the greater the intensity of his love to God, the more persistent his yearning for the attainment of the prize of the high calling of God in Christ Jesus, the more conscious will he be of the gravity of the sin that remains and the more poignant will be his detestation of it. Was this not the effect on all the people of God as they came into closer proximity to the revelation of God's holiness?

God and Man Cooperate in Sanctification Some (object to saying that God and man "cooperate" in sanctification, because they want to insist that God's work is primary and our work in sanctification is only a secondary one (*see Philippians 2:12-13*). God works in our sanctification and we work as well, and we work for the same purpose. We are not saying that we have equal roles in sanctification nor that we both work in the same way, but simply that we cooperate with God in ways that are appropriate to our status as God's creatures. The Scripture emphasizes the role that we play in sanctification (with all the moral commands of the New Testament).

Sanctification - God's Role. Since sanctification is primarily a work of God, it is appropriate that Paul prays, "May the God of peace himself sanctify you wholly" (*1 Thessalonians 5:23*). One specific role of God the Father in this sanctification is his process of disciplining us as his children (*Hebrews 12:5-11*). Paul tells the Philippians, "God is at work in you, both to will and to work for his good pleasure" (*Philippians 2:13*), thus indicating something of the way in which God sanctifies them—both by causing them to want his will and by giving them power to do it. The author of Hebrews speaks of the role of the Father and the role of the Son in a familiar benediction: "Now may the God of peace ... equip you with everything good that you may do his will, working in you that which is pleasing in his sight, through Jesus Christ; to whom be glory for ever and ever" (*Hebrews 13:20-21*). The role of God the Son, Jesus Christ, in sanctification is, first, that he earned our sanctification for us. Therefore Paul could say that God made Christ to be "our wisdom our righteousness and sanctification and redemption" (*1 Corinthians 1:30*). Moreover, in the process of sanctification, Jesus is also our example, for we are to run the race of life "looking to Jesus the pioneer and perfecter of our faith" (*Hebrews 12:2*). Peter tells his readers "Christ also suffered for you, leaving you an example, that you should follow in his steps (*1 Peter 2:21*). And John says, "He who says he abides in him ought to walk in the same way in which he walked" (*1 John 2:6*). But it is specifically God the Holy Spirit who works within us to change us and sanctify us, giving us greater holiness of life. Peter speaks of the "sanctification of the Spirit" (*1 Peter 1:2, author's translation*), and Paul speaks of "sanctification by the Spirit" (*2 Thessalonians 2:13*). It is the Holy Spirit who produces in us the "fruit of the Spirit" (*Galatians 5:22-23*), those character traits that are part of our progressive sanctification. If we grow in sanctification we "walk by the Spirit" and are "led by the Spirit" (*Galatians 5:16-18; cf. Romans 8:14*), that is, we are more and more responsive to the desires and promptings of the Holy Spirit in our life and character. The Holy Spirit is the spirit of holiness, and he produces holiness within us.

Our Role in Sanctification. There are two aspects to our role – active and passive. The role that we play in sanctification is passive in that we depend on God to sanctify us. We trust God or pray and ask that he sanctify us. Paul tells his readers, "Yield yourselves to God as men who have been brought from death to life" (*Romans 6:13; cf. v. 19*), and he tells the Roman Christians, "Present your bodies as a living sacrifice, holy and acceptable to God" (*Romans 12:1*). Paul realizes that we are dependent on the Holy Spirit's work to grow in sanctification, because he says, "If by the Spirit you put to death the deeds of the body you will live" (*Romans 8:13*).

Unfortunately today, this "passive" role in sanctification, this idea of yielding to God and trusting him to work in us "to will and to work for his good pleasure" (*Philippians 2:13*), is sometimes so strongly emphasized that it is the only thing people are told about the path of sanctification. Sometimes the popular phrase "let go and let God" is given as a summary of how to live the Christian life. But this is a tragic distortion of the doctrine of sanctification, for it only speaks of one half of the part we must play, and, by itself, will lead Christians to become lazy and to neglect the active role that Scripture commands them to play in their own sanctification.

Our role is active in the sense that we actively strive to obey God and take steps that increase our sanctification. Since sanctification is usually a corporate process and directly impacts the community, we should consider the scripture in Hebrews 10:24-25 which firmly encourages us to "Stir up one another to love and good works, not neglecting to meet together, as is the habit of some, but encouraging one another…". Together Christians are the body of Christ. We are to be a holy priesthood, holy nation" (*1 Peter 2:9*); encouraging another and build one another up" (*1 Thessalonians 5:11*). The body of Christ is intended to function as a unified whole, with each part "working properly, to fulfill God's purpose.

Sanctification Affects the Whole Person. Christians are to be "transformed by the renewing of our mind" (*Romans 12:2*). Although our knowledge of God is more than intellectual, there is certainly an intellectual component to it, and Paul says that this knowledge of God should keep increasing throughout our lives: a life "worthy of the Lord, fully pleasing to him" is one that is continually "increasing in the knowledge of God" (*Colossians 1:10*). Jesus grew in wisdom. The sanctification of our intellects will involve growth in wisdom and knowledge as we increasingly "take every thought captive to obey Christ" (*2 Corinthians 10:5*) and find that our thoughts are more and more the thoughts that God himself imparts to us in his Word. Moreover, growth in sanctification will affect our emotions. We will see increasingly in our lives emotions such as "love, joy, peace, patience" (*Galatians 5:22*). We will be able increasingly to obey Peter's command "to abstain from the passions of the flesh that wage war against your soul" (*1 Peter 2:11*). We will find it increasingly true that we do not "love the world or things in the world" (*1 John 2:15*). Our priorities change. Like our Savior, we delight to do the Father's will. We become obedient from the heart (*Romans 6:17*), and we will "put away" the negative emotions involved in "bitterness and wrath and anger and clamor and slander" (*Ephesians 4:31*).

The more we grow in likeness to Christ, the more we will personally experience the "joy" and "peace" that are part of the fruit of the Holy Spirit (*Galatians 5:22*), and the more we will draw near to the kind of life that we will have in heaven. Paul says that as we become more and more obedient to God, "the return you get is sanctification and its end, eternal life" (*Romans 6:22*). He realizes that this is the source of our true joy. "For the kingdom of God is not food and drink but righteousness and peace and joy in the Holy Spirit" (*Romans 14:17*). As we grow in holiness we grow in conformity to the image of Christ, and more and more of the beauty of his character is seen in our own lives. This is the goal of perfect sanctification which we hope and long for, and which will be ours when Christ returns. "And every one who thus hopes in him purifies himself as he is pure" (*1 John 3:3*).

Just before the conclusion of his booklet *What Do You Mean... Salvation?*, Herbert Armstrong wrote: "But it does not yet appear what you shall be. This scripture does not say 'where you shall go'—or 'where you shall be.' It is talking about a condition, not a place: 'what we shall be'! Salvation is a matter of what you become—not where you shall go! God's purpose is to change you—from your vile character to His glorious character—not to change the place where you are. "But—you are now already a begotten son of God—you may now call Him Father as long as you are led by His Spirit. (*Hebrews 10:26-27*).[149] "There are still some 'ifs.' You must grow spiritually (*2 Peter 3:18*). It is 'To him that overcometh' that Christ will grant to sit with Him on His throne, when He returns to earth (*Revelation 3:21*). If you overcome your own carnal nature, the world and the devil and keep Christ's works (not your own works, but Christ's—by His spirit in you) then you shall reign and rule all nations with Him, in the happy world tomorrow. "The real Christian life is, truly, a life of overcoming, spiritual growing—but it is the only happy life—the abundant life—here and now. Yet we must endure and remain steadfast—for it is he who endures to the end that shall be saved.

---

149 Herbert Armstrong, *What Do You Mean – Salvation?* An Ambassador College Publication, 1973.

Once you have been converted—changed in mind, concept, attitude, direction of way of life—you are begotten as a child of God—you have now eternal life abiding in you—as long as you are led by God's Spirit in God's way—as long as you continue in contact and fellowship with God (*1 John 1*:3)—all by God's grace as His gift, and not anything you have earned by your works; and now if you continue overcoming, growing spiritually—and all this actually through God's power—you shall inherit the Kingdom of God, and be made immortal to live forever in happiness and joy!"

Life Application for Personal Reflection

Sanctification

1. What would people say and how would they react if they were asked whether you are sanctified?
2. Do you remember when you first realized that your life has changed as a result of sanctification? What is the most significant change in your pattern of behavior?

Suggested Reading

Sanctification

1. Grudem, Wayne. "Adoption." Systematic Theology, An Introduction to Biblical Doctrine. InterVarsity Press, 38 De Montfort Street Leicester LE1 7GP Great Britain, Grand Rapids, MI: Zondervan Publishing House, pp 746-762.
2. Hodge, Charles. Systematic Theology. 3 vols. Reprint edition: Grand Rapids: Eerdmans, 1970. First published 1871, pp 213-254.

I Heard the Joyful Sound, Jesus Saves

Urban Lyrics by MARVIN WINANS & THE PERFECTED PRAISE

[Verse 1:]
I heard joyful sound, Jesus saves, Jesus saves.
Spread the tiding, spread them all around,
Jesus saves, Jesus saves. (repeat Verse)

[Chorus 1:]
To the utmost Jesus saves.
To the utmost Jesus saves.
He will pick you up and turn you around,
Hallelujah, hallelujah, Jesus saves.
Hallelujah, hallelujah, Jesus saves.

[Verse 2:]
Now if you're a liar or a cheater,
Don't leave, Jesus saves, Jesus saves.
Maybe you need to go and get a friend,
Go and grab a neighbor,
Tell them that He saves, Jesus saves.
If you're a liar maybe been a cheater,
Jesus saves, Jesus saves.
Go out and get a friend, pick up a neighbor,
The word out on the street is that He saves, Jesus saves.
[Chorus 1]

REFLECTIONS

THE WILD DUCK OF DENMARK

A wild duck was flying northward with his mates across Europe during the springtime. En route, he happened to land in a barnyard in Denmark, where he quickly made friends with the tame ducks that lived there. The wild duck enjoyed the corn and fresh water. He decided to stay for an hour, then for a day, then for a week , and finally, for a month. At the end of that time, he contemplated flying to join his friends in the vast North land, but he had begun to enjoy the safety of the barnyard, and the tame ducks had made him feel so welcome. So he stayed for the summer. One autumn day, when his wild mates were flying south, he heard their quacking. It stirred him with delight, and he enthusiastically flapped his wings and rose into the air to join them. Much to his dismay, he found that he could rise no higher than the eaves of the barn. As he waddled back to the safety of the barnyard, he muttered to himself, "I'm satisfied here, I have plenty of food, and the area is good. Why should I leave.?" So, he spent the winter on the farm. In the spring, when the wild ducks flew overhead again, he felt a strange stirring within his breast, but he did not even try to fly up to meet them. When they returned in the fall, they again invited him to rejoin them, but this time, the duck did not even notice them. There was no stirring within his breast. He simply kept on eating corn which made him fat.

- Soren Kierkegaard
Danish theologian & philosopher

Source: The Wild Duck of Denmark. Text Illustration shared by Steve Malone, Maple Grove Christian Church, March 2004. Retrieved on October 4, 2015 from http://www.sermoncentral.com/illustrations/sermon-illustration-steve-malone-stories-christiandisciplines-character-headship-16116.asp

Besides constant eating, sleeping, and crying, newly born babies maintain the fetal position they had in the womb: clenched fists; bent elbows, hips, and knees; arms and legs close to the front of the body. Newborns have a sucking flex and automatically turn in the direction of food. When startled, they throw out their arms and legs, flailing about. Babies are immature physically and mentally, but we expect them to develop. People understand the concept of growth in the physical development of humans, and we know why it is important.

As much as we love holding and smelling babies, if they do not grow, there is a problem. Spiritual growth is a similar concept but it is far more important. Development is an outward sign of improvement toward "maturity" or reaching perfection. Being a baby is not the goal of life. Though we are born babies, we grow up and are expected to become productive and to lead a useful life. Likewise, we are born again, in order to become mature Christians, actively serving the Lord.

– The Author

Spiritual Maturity and Disciplines

♦ ♦ ♦

"As long as a believer is worrying about whether or not they are truly saved, they will never grow up in spiritual maturity. It basically guarantees that a Christian will remain stuck in spiritual infancy. It cheapens the gift of salvation – the gift of grace – and make God look like a finicky human."

Will Davis Jr., 10 Things Jesus Never Said: And Why You Should Stop Believing Them

▼

From the moment we place our trust in Christ as our Savior and Lord, every Christian begins the process of spiritual growth, with the intent to become more like Jesus Christ. That is how spiritual maturity is achieved. According to the Apostle Paul, who explains in Philippians 3:12-14, that he has not already obtained all that is required nor made perfect, we must press on toward the mark of the prize for which God has called us. We must continually pursue a deeper knowledge of God in Christ and realize that it is an ongoing process that will never end in this life.[150] Christian maturity requires a radical reordering of one's priorities, converting from pleasing self to learning to please and obey God. The key to maturity is consistency and perseverance in doing those things that will bring us closer to the

---

150 Wood, Dr. Timothy, Professor. Classroom Lecture. "Epistles of John", Calvary Christian College, Waldorf, MD. March 4, 2010.

Lord. God is a God of order. As we mature in discipleship He takes us from salvation through sanctification to glorification. Through that life cycle of that process, we become transformed through the training and disciplined living in the Word.

Our heavenly father expects us to mature. Not only does He expect it, but He demands it. He is grieved when we don't grow. We should examine ourselves to see that we are growing. Are we maturing? Or are we like a baby who, although expected to grow, at do nothing but lie around in bed waiting to be fed. They do not even have to walk to a bathroom. Everything comes to them. However, if they do not grow, parents will seek professional help to question why are we not growing. There is an expectation of growth and it grieves a parent if the child does not grow. We want the child to grow mentally and physically. We want that child to mature. We were young once and perhaps immature for a long time. What does it mean if we are born again, but do not grow? Spiritual growth does not determine spiritual standing with Christ. However, if we do not grow, we cannot appropriate His provision and fulfill His purpose for our lives.[151] This is a tragedy. God does not love babes or older ones because of their stage of spiritual growth. We not grow in justification. Sins are either forgiven or not; we are either walking in righteousness or living under condemnation.

There are three categories of Spiritual growth: **1)** newborns; newly born children to the spirit of God, **2)** youth who are developed, productive, strong and skilled, **3)** older men and women, full of depth, stability, with ripeness of Spirit.[152] The newly born understand the basics of what it means to be a Christian and have an awareness of what it means to feel guilty and have an aching conscience. They know what it means to cleansed by the water and the spirit. The key characteristics of this phase include the joy and confidence of having their sins forgiven with condemnation and judgment gone; knowing or possessing the name of Christ but not necessary how to use the

---

151 Wood, Dr. Timothy, Professor. Classroom Lecture. "Epistles of John", Calvary Christian College, Waldorf, MD. March 4, 2010.
152 Ibid.

name of Jesus; and they know the Father – very much the way and a child learns to say it as a first word. It is natural and easy to know God. This is a privilege for the believer.

The youthful are developed in the Lord, productive, full of strength and skill. Acts 2:17 tells us that while old men will dream dreams, that young men will catch vision of wrongs, cause harvest world churches to be built; and foes to be routed in battle. Proverbs 20:29 says the Glory of young men is strength. They are not discouraged, that have the energy, power, skill, and ability to fight, achieve and construct. We need to aspire to this level. This is the group that have overcome the wicked one. They are strong and able to do the work. They are confidence that the Word abides in them; they defend and declare sound doctrine without hesitation. This group quickly detects subtle lies and recognize false doctrine. They are not ruled by emotions and they are skilled enough to handle the word of God and willingly witness for Christ. These strong young believers are not ashamed of their position in the Word of God and have clarity, because they know the promises of God. Demonic attacks will not throw them off their course; they can stand the test of virtue and faith; and they can live above reproach because the Word abides in them. They can fight and build; yet they are spiritually mature; and are not victims. They are victorious. At the highest level are the seasoned ones. These are those believers who are deep in the Word. They are settled, having a satisfying intimate knowledge of God. They know the source of truth. This is where orthodoxy turns into doxology and theology becomes the anthem of praise.

God wants us to grow spiritually. For example, babies may be cute but they can also be selfish, rude and lazy, almost never apologizing voluntarily. They can also be inconsiderate, waking up their parents in middle of the night, and the parents must get involved and set limits. If not, children cannot feel safe and they can self destruct or cause train wrecks wherever they are. Setting limits is what promotes positive behavior change. Knowing the limits is what helps keep the child feel safe and baby Christians are not much different. Spiritual birth cannot wait forever. The longer a person stays away or puts it off, the more twisted or dead they become.[153] The trained ones are under parental instructions but they cannot grow without spiritual activity. The newborns must come under training in order to do things that will help them to grow.

Children are like Israel in that their focus is always on the works of God so they need training that includes: a) nourishment (1 Peter) – They must be fed undiluted milk of the word. Sometimes, they are given a pacifier which is essentially fake food, which tricks the baby into thinking that something's happening but eventually the baby realizes it was just entertainment and they began to demand the real thing. A baby will not grow up on a pacifier – there is nothing of value there. b) spiritual environment – They must be planted in house of God. (Psalm 92:12-15) and c) flourishing in the house of God. This is how they grow. Some people are limited because their vision or their theology is too small. The young men are like Moses. They are on a different, deep spiritual level.

The Father is like the meaning behind the miracles or the face behind the hand. Children, the newborn, newly born to the spirit of God, simply know the Father. The youthful, young men and women, those who are developed, productive, full of strength and skill, are mature and love the Lord. They delight in their experiences and accomplishments, and they constantly kick the devil. The Father, who has depth, stability, ripeness of Spirit, knows the Father, experiences a deep communion with Him, and enjoys openness in Grace. They do not learn a subject and leave it; instead they learn new topics, they study the Word and meditate on it daily, going deeper in the things of God. God is faithful through every journey and experience. As we grow we do not lose strength. We must continue exercising in the Word because through this, we grow more in knowledge. We must accelerate according to our involvement in activities of God.

---

153 Foster, Joan, Classroom Lecture. *"Unction to Function Interaction Paper"*, Calvary Christian College, Waldorf, MD. April 22, 2010.

D.L. Moody grew so fast it was embarrassing. He was asking all kinds of questions at a young age and put so many to shame. He had the power, anointing of God upon his life. His growing rebuked the stagnation of everyone else in church. Many did not like him. The power of growing that takes place in our lives is a reflection of our involvement in God's word.

The anointing was very sacred for it symbolized the presence of God on a person life (or the power of God on a person's occupation). There were only three people in their commissioning, who would receive such a measure of the substance by the clergy: prophet, priest, and king. The unction means to smear; to cover. The three types of anointing and their blessings described in the Old Testament are:

◆ **Protective:** The anointed are people God protects, and that He defends. Psalms says "touch not my anointed and do my prophets no harm".

◆ **Practical:** Jesus read Isaiah 61:1 "The spirit of the Lord is upon me because He anointed me to preach the gospel" in Luke 4 to let the people know that He was fulfilling the messianic predictions. Christ the High Priest, stood there, the anointing was all over Him for it was given to Him without measure. The breaking of the yoke occurs by way of the anointing (*Acts 10:38*) as proven when Jesus went about doing good healing all that were oppressed of the devil. He gives us power to minister to hurting people and to set them free. The anointing gives the edge so that we are greater than the power of darkness.

◆ **Precious:** Though he was a serious man, Jesus had more joy than anyone else in the crowd. He was anointed with the oil of gladness above His fellow peers (*Psalm 45*).

Every believer has and is covered with the anointing. How the anointing is expressed depends on the gifting that God has in your life. John tells the Church at large that we have an unction from the Holy One in order to do the job for which we were called. The prophet, witness, Priest and access to God and His glory, the King in you rules over the power of darkness that comes against you. There is a permanent effect and we can know that He establishes us and seals us with that anointing. (*2 Corinthians 1:21*) Scripture says the anointing which we have received, abideth within you forever. (*1 John 2:27*)

To bring about the transformation in our lives, we must practice spiritual disciplines. Establishing a regular routine of reading/studying the Word of God, prayer, fasting, giving, fellowship, praise/worship, service, and stewardship is the first step in committing to growth after salvation.

No matter how hard we work on those things, however, none of this is possible without the enabling of the Holy Spirit within us. We are to walk by the Spirit (*Galatians 5:16*). The Greek word used here for "walk" actually means to "walk with a purpose in view." Further down in the same chapter, Paul tells us again to "walk by the Spirit" and this time "walk" translated means step by step or one step at a time under the instruction of the Holy Spirit. Since believers are filled with the Spirit, we should also walk under His control. As we submit more to the Spirit's control, we will also see an increase in the fruit of the Spirit in our lives (*Galatians 5:22-23*). This is characteristic of spiritual maturity. Having the fruit of the Spirit that is – love, joy, peace, longsuffering, gentleness, goodness, faith, meekness, and temperance – in operation, makes it that much sweeter when we put the personal functional gifts to work in the Body of Christ.

Given by the Spirit to different ones, the gifts are be used according to God's divine plan. Such gifts include the word of wisdom; word of knowledge; faith; gifts of healing; the working of miracles; prophecy; discerning of spirits; divers kinds of tongues; and interpretation of tongues (*1 Corinthians 12:8-10*). Yet we are to covet the best gifts (power gifts, revelation gifts, utterance gifts (*1 Corinthians 12:31*). In maturing we must remember the significance of and seize opportunity to be a part of serving, discipling, teaching, exhortation, interceding, giving, leading and being full of compassion and mercy. James Wilhoit, Professor of Christian Foundation and Ministry at Wheaton University for twenty years, holds that true Christian spirituality is marked by a widely shared pattern of spiritual growth stemming from nine commonly shared distinctions:

1) a response to the call of the Holy Spirit

2) a commitment to Jesus and a transformational approach to life

3) a nurturing by the means of grace

4) a deep knowing of Jesus and, through Him, the Father and the Spirit

5) a deep knowing of oneself

6) the realization of the unique self that God ordained us to be

7) suffering

8) sharing God's love with others and care for his creation

9) celebration in the Christian community.[154]

Some churches are marked by a presence of a clearly identified culture of formation while others are marked by their many programs and pumped-up activity. While jazzed up programs may attract the crowds, it does not necessarily produce transforming results for the kingdom of God. There is growing anxiety within the Christian community concerning the danger of abandoning healthy nurturing patterns ordinarily associated with spiritual maturity. Some of the practices at risk in today's Christian church are the very disciplines that support a deep foundation and fellowship with Jesus such as:

a) systematic Bible teaching

b) memorization and reading

c) Sunday evening services with an emphasis on testimonies

d) missions and global Christianity

e) Sabbath respect

f) shared church-wide meals

---

154 Wilhoit, James C. Spiritual Formation *as if the* Church Mattered, *Growing in Christ through Community*. 2008. Baker Academic. Grand Rapids, MI 49516. pg. 10-15

g) practiced hospitality

h) bible camps

i) pastoral visitation and

j) significant intergenerational socializing. Similar to taking prayer out of public schools, these changes represent a host of changes in the development of our structures and their effects may take generations to fully manifest themselves.

Spiritual growth takes place in the everyday, mainstream events of life and Jesus' teaching was meant to be worked out in everyday living. His charge to us in commissioning us to go make disciples (*Matthew 28:20*), included outreach, discipleship, and education formation. His instructions are at the heart of spiritual formation through the enabling power of His grace. Even Jesus grew through the disciplines (i.e., solitude, fasting, and meditation) which foster positive spiritual change and give us the desire to obey. For example, the first to partake of a sermon is the preacher. His ministry is marked by acts of devotion which bring spiritual power, love, and insight. As we follow and exemplify Him, we experience the same. Through our relationship and obedience in Him, we are transformed and enabled. Our reverence – acts of humility and devotion to the Lord stem from our intimacy with Him. As we love and obey God we are able to love each another. We are instructed to obey these commands: **(1)** be stewards of the gospel, **(2)** spread the good news, **(3)** have discernment, **(4)** live a life of integrity, **(5)** be good stewards, **(6)** detach from the world, **(7)** extend His compassion, and **(8)** be true worshipers, (totally dependent upon God) and **(9)** cultivate a thriving environment for community formation (receiving, remembering, responding and relating).

Christ-likeness, the primary motivating factor for deep spiritual transformation, is a longing for God Himself. We cannot survive the spiritual journey by our willpower. We are not of this world. Our homesickness — longing for a land and faraway life we never experienced, but know it does or should exist — confirms that we are citizens of heaven. We are living in what is referred to as a permanent, lifelong culture shock. As a result of sin in the Garden of Eden, we have been exiled until Jesus returns. We want a perfect place to live—one that is free of disease and consists of a perfect face-to-face relationship with God. Brokenness and desire for help is what drives us and helps us recognize our need for God. Every story in the Bible with its familiar conflicts and heroes amount to the same bottom-line longings. Broken people, overwhelmed by troubles, turn to God for help. He rescues them, they change, get restored, forget and get in trouble again. Then it starts all over again. Jesus' ministry was predicated on the poor and brokenhearted. Every Christian must be broken, powerless, and in need of help in order to enter the kingdom of God and receive peace. God opposes the proud, but gives grace to the humble. (*1 Peter 5:5*). He wants us to abide in an intimate, close relationship with Him. Spiritual disciplines do not replace Christ in our lives. Rather, we must continually return to the truths of sin, redemption, grace, and holiness, continually receiving and God's grace. Receiving the Lord's love, correction, forgiveness and new life in Him is all part of the process.[155]

Christian spiritual maturity requires openness and discernment of His voice in His call and everyday life. If we do not, we will walk in disobedience which is an act of rebellion that keeps us away from God. Refusal or inability to hear Him is a most stinging indictment given by God (*Jeremiah 6:16-17*), for it is pride and bitterness that blocks intimacy with God. Without that intimacy, transformation cannot come.[156] We must have an open and teachable spirit. A bond of trust between teacher and student causes a student to be receptive but it is that receptivity that calls forth the teacher's best efforts. Such openness is necessary in order to hear God's Word so that we can be persuaded into growth. We must also have transforming vision which provides hope and builds a road map of empowerment to make

---

155 Wilhoit, James C. Spiritual Formation *as if the* Church Mattered, *Growing in Christ through Community.* 2008. Baker Academic. Grand Rapids, MI 49516. pg. 30-33
156 Wilhoit, James C. Spiritual Formation *as if the* Church Mattered, *Growing in Christ through Community.* 2008. Baker Academic. Grand Rapids, MI 49516. pg. 32-39

the change a real possibility. This is what convinces people to realize that they can live differently. The vision is formed as we worship God; it brings a powerful confession which leads to repentance. Although discipleship emphasizes our growth as well as brokenness, the church must cultivate and maintain the right atmosphere for repeatedly receiving those who are broken. A one-time application is insufficient. Prayer promotes direct interaction with God and offers opportunity to receive His care and grace. Wilhoit cited a number of prayer stances that encourage receiving including prayer meetings, ministries, retreats, special seasons of prayer, prayer chains and emails, and immersions.[157]

Remembering what God has done for us is one of the key disciplines. One of the primary goals of Hebrew education, was to make sure the people never forgot the Lord's mighty acts and would therefore, always fear God and obey His commandments. Clearly then, one of the chief problems of man is forgetfulness. People have a tendency to forget God's goodness and often need reminding of how He rescued us. In this information age of microwave, instant recording devices, we do not have to remember anything because we have memory recall electronic gadgets at our disposal. The down side is that we no longer need to exercise that part of our brain as frequently as we once did. Since the church has embraced modern techniques, styles and approaches to ministry, there is seldom time for testimony, reflection, and remembrance. God warns us in Deuteronomy 6 that when our houses are full of good things and our bellies are full we must beware lest we forget the Lord which brought us forth out of our trouble.

We need to hear others testify concerning His work. It will remind us of God's work in our lives, also. When we hear stories of God's faithfulness to His people throughout the centuries; we learn of His wisdom. He tells us that as often as we break bread, that we should do this in remembrance of Him. Engaging in spiritual practices keeps

157 Wilhoit, James C. Spiritual Formation *as if the* Church Mattered, *Growing in Christ through Community*. 2008. Baker Academic. Grand Rapids, MI 49516. pg. 10-15

our minds focused on God; this causes us to remember. When we cease from these practices, we forget whose we are and how we came to this place. We are not our own, we are bought with a price by the blood of Jesus. Solitude moments with God help us to remember Him. The Bible says, "After that generation died, another generation grew up who did not acknowledge the Lord or remember the mighty things he had done for Israel" (*Judges 2:10*). Robert Wicks says, "Spiritual remembering involves gratefully recalling the past moments of epiphany or dramatic awakening in life so that we can muster the courage and perspective to continue seeking God and God's will."[158] I say simply, remembering is a commandment of God for every believer. Remembering is also critical because it is mindful of the grace we received from God. We use that grace as the driving force in our desire to grow and be like Christ.

Too often we nurture in one area but forget the unseen, hidden challenges, failing to work on the root cause or systemic nature of the injury. To encourage community memory, we use stories of **a)** historic church figures **b)** contemporary martyrs **c)** missions and ministries and **d)** the local church history. Other disciplines typically used consist of **1)** small groups of people committed to learning and growing together and **2)** anointed teaching which means the Holy Spirit comes upon the teacher and gives insight, power, and the enabling causing the teaching to go beyond human effort. The very fabric of an anointed message makes it clear to the hearer that the message is a divine message from God.

Actually, receiving, remembering, responding, and relating are a complete package. Responding is the work within the individual heart where one remembers and internalizes the blessings or goodness received from God. Relating is the outer demonstration or the working out of those responses. While grace is the major driver or impetus in responding and relating in a Christ-like manner, all

---

158 Wilhoit, James C. Spiritual Formation *as if the* Church Mattered, *Growing in Christ through Community*. 2008. Baker Academic. Grand Rapids, MI 49516. pg. 105

four dimensions work together to build and reinforce each other. Sharing our lives and effort with each other in community provides the connection, challenge, compassion, and celebration. This sharing breaks the model of individualism and is built on the premise that we serve each other as priests, standing in the gap and being available to one another. This is how we are to respond to God's gospel of love and forgiveness with love and service to God and to those around us. Our responding is an outflow of a changed heart that has been influenced by the gospel. God continues to change us as we live our lives well and reach out in love and service to others. So even as we go in response and out of an outflow of the priesthood to do as Jesus commanded – to make disciples of all the nations, teaching them to obey all His commands – we are still learning. Our responding is to and through grace in which resides God's sustaining and transforming power.

Without relationship, there is no such thing as survival. The key element in spiritual communities is relationship. Each of us has a deep yearning for wholeness which is only found in holiness. Christ alone is holy and it grows as we avail ourselves to the work of God in Christ Jesus which is all about love and relationship. Many churches have lost sight of the true meaning of holiness and as a result, the idea of holiness has been replaced by the mechanics of sin management. It is holiness that allows us to be responsive, to love one another and obey the Lord. It is this holiness that caused Christ to lay down His life for us. It is this same holiness that elicits a compassionate response out of the new life that Jesus models and puts in us a warm heart for God. "For out of the overflow of the heart the mouth speaks" (*Matthew 12:34b*).

God designed us to have a relationship with Him first and then others. We are to give of ourselves as Christ did, seeking out others. According to our text we can measure or relationship with God by the character and quality of all other relationships.[159] Surely we must examine ourselves daily as Paul tells us this in Galatians 6 and 2 Corinthians 13. The relational aspect of Christianity does not simply happen. True spiritual formation must cultivate not just knowledge but service to God through responsible action. Christianity touches all areas of a person's life including thinking, feeling, and doing – enough to impact another person's life. To acknowledge Jesus as Lord means to acknowledge oneself as a servant of Jesus and of others. It means we must be active witnesses of the kingdom of God. Attributes of the forming community are very clear and demonstrable and do not appear in isolation. They function in harmony, reinforcing each other. A church in which God reigns and the kingdom of God is manifest, will demonstrate **1)** meaningful worship, **2)** compassionate service, **3)** public witness, and **4)** disciple making.

When we become Christians, we are given all we need for spiritual maturity and that includes getting the rest that our bodies require. "Come unto me, all ye that labour and are heavy laden, and I will give you rest" (*Matthew 11:28*) makes it very plain. We need rest – and we need it often. Sometimes we need physical rest. Many of us work very hard and forget to break from our activities. Sometimes our bodies will be sick and we are exhausted because we have been fighting disease. Sometimes we need emotional rest. When our minds are in a state of unrest, we can become agitated. Sometimes we cannot sleep because we are emotionally stressed. Sometimes we need spiritual rest. We can have no peace until we are spiritually at rest. Sin is always at the root of failing to get spiritual rest.

Being effective and fruitful in the knowledge of the Lord Jesus is the essence of spiritual maturity. A true sign of spiritual maturity is represented by the following simple statements.

◆ Only one who is under the dominion of the Lordship of Jesus

Christ, instead of the dominance of the flesh, can rest.

159 Wilhoit, James C., John H. Westerhoff reference), III Spiritual Formation *as if the* Church Mattered, *Growing in Christ through Community*. 2008. Baker Academic. Grand Rapids, MI 49516. pg. 105

◆ Without any focus on growth in those areas of our life that are spiritual, then the physical, and emotional areas are going to take over – like weeds take over a garden that is not tended to!

◆ Jesus said "Come unto me, all ye that labor and are heavy laden, and I will give you rest" (*Matthew 11:28*).

This passage of Scripture is probably more familiar to me than most people. First, these words can also be found on page 44 in the Blue Banner Hymnal in the Pentecostal Church where I grew up many years ago. Secondly, I memorized and sang these words for years at almost every single prayer service during the altar call. The tune got old but the lyrics were great and they brought great results. There was a stanza for the children as well as the adults; one for the saved and unsaved. We sang the song – we felt better. We felt better; we sang the song! Even today, that little four-letter word, "rest" brings comfort. It is simple and inviting; comforting and full of promise. All we have to do is obey Jesus' call to come to Him and He will give us rest. Many of us know that we are saved by grace – we testify and speak of it all the time. We share the gospel with others so they can receive the promise. We know that we are commanded to come and rest in Him. So then, if we are no longer sinners under the law but now under His grace; and if there is nothing we can ever do to earn salvation, then why are we, as Christians, working so hard?[160] To be sure, we need plenty of rest – especially in these last days. Yet many Christians have a performance based relationship with God in which they work hard to earn God's love or negotiate terms with Him rather than simply accept the truth that He already loves us. Have we missed the message? What was Jesus was saying to believers in Matthew 11:28?

Perhaps we should explore rest further? A study of the transliteration for the original Greek word ""anapauó", to give rest, give intermission from labor, (by implication refresh), tells us it means to cause or permit one to cease from any movement or labor in

---

160 Wilson, Dr. Michael A., Professor. Classroom Lecture. "Spiritual Formation and Renewal", Calvary Christian College, Waldorf, MD. June 4, 2011.

order to recover and collect strength. It means to keep quiet, be calm in patient expectation and by implication – to refresh oneself. When we take a closer look into that invitation of rest, several observations comes to mind. For example, we need to understand the context of His invitation. Just prior to His intriguing call to the weary, Jesus proclaimed Himself to be the only true revelation of God and the exclusive path to Him (v. 25). He was not speaking merely as a wise teacher, but as the Messiah (v. 23). The rest offered by Him, although of sapient delivery, presumably also had Messianic connotations. In keeping with God's plan of salvation, then, His offer of rest was to the heavily laden. Throughout the gospels, the recurring theme of rest is presented as His gift to us and yet it is a foreshadowing of perfect rest to come. The Old Testament supports the notion that Messianic rest stemmed from an expectation or concept associated with an idealized Sabbath rest in which God would find this resting place among His people while the people would one day be at rest from enemies of this world.[161] Matthew portrays Jesus' offer of Messianic rest through his yoke to those burdened with the Pharisaic interpretation of the law. He is asking the heavily laden, to respond to the revelation of His dominion and knowledge as fulfillment of the law.

Who are the heavily laden and those who labor without rest? What is their labor, and what is the weight that causes them to be burdened? The issue in Matthew 11 was one of Messianic salvation—finding true rest in Christ rather than following meticulous religious rules decreed by the Scribes and Pharisees. There were over 900 laws that had to be followed—of which the three most prominent ones were the food laws, Sabbath, and circumcision. The Law was a heavily imposed yoke. It was a burden to remember and practice. When Jesus used the term yoke in the sense of the requirement of law keeping, He was offering anyone who would come to Him, spiritual rest from works of the law. So Jesus' yoke is in stark contrast to the yoke that the religious leaders put on the people. He is offering salvation to all who

---

161 Bacchiocchi, Samuele, Professor. Matthew 11:28-30: *Jesus' Rest And The Sabbath*, Andrews University Seminary Studies, Autumn 1984, Vol 22, No.3, 289-16.

come to Him by faith. 1 Peter 1:5 says to lay aside every weight (of sin) that so easily besets us. Jesus was speaking of burdens or cares of this world that challenge you – these struggles, doubts, anxiety, stress and anything spiritually distressing that would separate us from His love, joy and peace. These things will manifest physically in your life if not handed over to Christ.

We are not called to overwork ourselves but Christians often go overboard, taking on other people's burdens, working to prove ourselves to others, and seeking reward. It is almost impossible not to be legalistic in today's society because of man's law which similar to the Pharisaical law, was initially intended to protect us. However, either God's Word determines both how we come to God and how we grow in grace, or humans determine these things by pragmatic means. We must resist the tricks of the enemy. Paul warned against works of the flesh. "Are you so foolish? Having begun by the Spirit, are you now being perfected by the flesh?" (*Galatians 3:3*). Paul rejected the idea that we are saved by grace and then perfected by works. We are saved by grace and we grow by grace. Ironically, this is a prevailing problem in the church today: people continue trying to earn God's love. When you love somebody you want to do for them but we should not confuse this selfless act of love with the overworked clergy, leadership, and church workers that suffer burnout. We get over into sin when we work ourselves to the point of extreme exhaustion and then demand reward for something that God has neither blessed nor ordained. Oftentimes, the crowds pressed in on Him but even Jesus went off alone whether up into the mountain or into the wilderness to pray (*Luke 5:16*).

As result of God's love, we are his workmanship created in Christ Jesus unto good works (*Ephesians 2:6-10*). Christians therefore produce Spirit-led good works. Make no mistake about it -- these are impossible for non-Christians to produce. With realization that we are saved by grace and with our spiritual identification, we are thankful for God's abundance of grace and His mercy as His love begins to produce His works in us. He gives us wonderful non–performance based gifts that are offered within the body of Christ. Such personal function gifts of the Spirit–prophecy, service, teaching, exhortation, giving, leadership and mercy (*Romans 12:6-8*) which require us to walk in the Spirit are given out of love. As we are transformed inside (*Romans 12:2*) – it is manifested on the outside. We know our spiritual identification and as we are discipled or trained to follow Christ, we grow in our relationship with God and His work because of His love. We are transformed by the renewing of our mind by **1)** meditating, studying, and applying the Word of God; **2)** fasting and praying; **3)** giving; **4)** praising and worshiping Him and **5)** by serving. The dynamics of spiritual formation teaches us that we are to remain in the growth and development process, experiencing the communal, intra/interpersonal, devotional and divine presence and we become more like Him. (*2 Corinthians 3:17-18*).

As our relationship in Christ matures, our journey with Him should be one of peace and rest in Him. The fact is, however, that many Christians struggle and work so hard that they suffer despair and then they burnout. It is not only a problem among the congregants and the workers, it is also within the clergy. We examined this question in class and determined that some of the reasons Christians struggle sometimes because of unbelief, worldly influences, laziness, not enough Word and lack of knowledge and wanting to "do their own thing." Some have accepted Jesus as Savior but perhaps not as Lord. They desire to be rescued from the perils of life but do not want to follow or obey God Word because of their pride. Sadly, it is only after repeatedly getting into trouble that some Christians willingly seek God for a better way.

In our physical and emotional growth we move through infancy, adolescent, adulthood, middle age, and old age. Spiritually, our growth produces an increasingly intimate relationship with Christ that is meant to continue until we see Him face to face (*1 John 3:2*). Our spiritual journey consists of a redemptive level journey and a mission-oriented service. The Bible provides wonderful examples and models of lives of those we may explore as our individual circumstances change. Each has its own particular pursuits throughout their experiences which fall in one of the three major patterns: intellectual (focus on knowing the truth); contemplative (being present to God with the heart); or social justice (doing love-filled works). Old Testament characters such as Abraham, David and Moses were used by Bruce Demarest, in Soul Guide, to exemplify Biblical characters with whom we should be able to relate.[162] All of the characters went through various stages of knowing, being, and doing.[163] The more contemporary journey model consists of six stages: converted life, discipled life, productive, inward journey, outward journey, and the journey of love. It is the productive or "doing" stage where Christians tend to crash and burn because of the desire to serve beyond their capacity. Many view ministry as performance and often will fall into the trap of serving in the flesh by over extending themselves or seeking praise. Once they are in heavy demand or commitment, their world shifts. They become angry and bitter, often suffering in silence to the point of burnout.

Some Pastors drive their people to give everything they have to the Church. For years I did not know how to respond to the Leadership call. Though there was truly a special anointing on my life and the Music Ministry, I suffered guilt and was torn concerning my family for many years. My desire was to please the Lord but on many occasions, when I would have appropriately prioritized my family first, I was pressured into putting my family last. Most of the support and encouragement from Leadership was directly aimed at the Church's success. Even though other accomplished organists and pianists became available and committed themselves to the Ministry, the outcry or complaints from the people was the music was not anointed. The Pastor would not proceed until I was in the building and at post. Though I understood and desired to be there, I eventually

---

162 Demarest, Bruce, Soul Guide, Following Jesus As A Spiritual Director. 2003 NAVPRESS, Bringing Truth to Life, Colorado Springs, CO 80935. pp 32-38
163 Demarest, pg. 37

removed myself because of the conflict. Our gifts are meant to be given out of love but not out of balance. The love was there – I could play all day and all through the night but the difficult was in the balancing. We cannot continue if we are out of step with what God is speaking in our lives. Jesus ministered to Martha who was overburdened and stressed out by all of the work that was required. She was too overwrought and pressured about doing good service, until she could not enjoy His presence. Our text provided many examples of people who were so busy that they had little time for God. It is almost like buying a new house that is so costly you have to work several jobs to keep it – therefore you are never at home to enjoy it. It reminds me of working to pay a nanny to live in the home and care for the children. Where is the relationship? Jesus corrected Martha in the areas of priorities and excessive busyness. He showed her how to rest in Him and simplify her life. The demon of busyness is a pressure that leaves us emotionally a wreck. Busyness has also invaded the church. Why do we drive ourselves so relentlessly? Why do we work ourselves to the point of exhaustion? Why do we yearn to impress and out-best others? Once upon a time, I felt guilty because of missing a program or not being able to serve in certain capacities when others seemed to work very hard at every function. However, it is impossible to attend everything without some compromise especially when God has a particular call on your life.

When I joined the choir, I enjoyed attending both morning worship services out of a spirited hunger for the Word. At this point, I joined primarily due to pressure from well meaning people. At the time, the choir only rendered selections during the second service which was held at 10:30 am, while special music was provided at the 8:00 am service. Before long, however, it was announced that an additional rehearsal would now occur on Sunday during the 8:00 am service. This would interfere with my being able to hear the first sermon. The routine associated with this change would also interfere with my early morning quiet time with God. Then the services also went live streaming video and the choir became encumbered about with the many rules and media etiquette. All of this caused me to miss the full effects of the message because of audio limitations and visual aesthetic requirements. So now, in a way, I was missing both sermons. Then along came special concerts requiring rehearsals weekly and anyone in lead roles had to come earlier than usual. While others accepted these changes gracefully, the hyper-activeness, mad rushes and noise associated with all of the sound checks and testing of headsets needed for special music made it impossible for me to get into the spirit of worship. I opted out, choosing instead to sit at Jesus' feet. What does all this hustle bustling cost us? Demarest quotes Chuck Swindoll in stating, "Busyness rapes relationship. It substitutes shallow frenzy for deep friendship. It feeds the ego but stresses the inner being. It fills a calendar but fractures a family." The busyness syndrome is a prescription for spiritual burnout.[164]

We need to shed the yoke of busyness in order to get rest. We need to realize that God created us as human beings not human doings. We should seek God in establishing priorities and evaluating our commitments. In doing this, we should intentionally set the margins – for example, the first one should be to rest from six days of work and spend that time resting in God. Only when we create intentional space and time, will God show up for the meeting. We need to slow down and cultivate our relationship with God. This is the only way we can hear His still small voice and behold His face. Most importantly, we must remember to balance our lives. When we love and honor God, first – above all else – it is then that we are able to be in His will. Once we follow these guidelines, the busyness will subside. We will then be able to receive nurture from family and friends. Even Jesus grew mentally emotionally, socially and spiritually as much as He did in the physical. He established relationships with others and He had many followers. People loved to be around Him. Jesus is our perfect model. He was never in a hurry; He was always calm and peaceful;

---

164 Demarest, p 94

ready to minister. He had time for people. He cultivated a prayerful spirit, exhibited a loving concern for others, had a peaceful heart, was discerning, suffered, and yet He developed a sense of wonder.

The world has managed to construct all kinds of fun getaways but the truth is, what the world offers is not enough. Real rest is the ability to relax, and stay at peace even though surrounded by or even buried in trouble. We may never be completely free of legalism but since the garden of Eden, God has been all about grace. Despite that, we have tried (under Satan's pressure) to re-write the truth of the gospel to include merit and performance. As humans, we are addicted to rules but through Jesus Christ, we can be free (*Galatians 5:1*).

The key for those in leadership is to realize the Pastor and Leadership must make disciples and their responsibility is to shepherd people to Jesus and help them transfer their trust to Jesus. Challenges or pressures come primarily from self and others. Such pressures arise from the desire to control things and others. We must remember that God will not be a source of pressure. Granted, it is His glory that we are striving to reveal and explain, but He has made that easy by the immense amount of revelation He already provided in Christ Jesus, the Scripture, and through the creative works of His hands. Jesus said His yoke is easy and His burden is light" (*Matthew 11:28-30*).

At the core of spiritual maturity is intimacy with God through the presence of the Holy Spirit who works in us and among us to do His will.

Man continues to forge ahead with his eyes of a new society in which he lifts up himself and replaces God. He promotes his agenda at every hand and unwisely believes in his own greatness over and beyond God. He has been tricked into believing that man is able to bring about world peace and prosperity without God. Yet the world remains chaotic and in despair. This is a problem that only God can solve. This is called salvation and is the greatest plan known to mankind – now and forever. It embraces all of time as well as eternity past and future. It was designed for all of mankind. It works successfully on individuals, corporate bodies, all kinds of cultures, races, creed and colors. It covers the entire globe. There has never been anything like it since the creation of the universe nor will there be anything remotely resembling the high point of our salvation until the end comes. When a man lies in self pity and depression, Jesus Christ our Lord is the answer. When a community is hit by disaster and there is no man-made system that can save, Jesus Christ our Lord is the answer. When the nation lies in ruin, Jesus Christ is the answer. When our soul lies awake at night, Jesus Christ is the answer. Jesus is the high point of our Salvation!

Life Application for Personal Reflection
Spiritual Maturity
1. Is it possible for someone to be sanctified for years with no evidence of change in their lives? What kinds of situations or circumstances may cause a person to be stunted in their Christian growth after rebirth? Is this a factor of the church, amount of time spent in Bible study or reading the Bible or some other factor?
2. As you have matured in the things of God, are you aware of sin that remains in your life?
3. What (if any) kinds of sinful behavior have you exhibited lately that you are strongly aware of the need to repent? What do you think would happen if you do not repent?

Suggested Reading
Spiritual Maturity
1. Wilhoit, James C., John H. Westerhoff reference), III Spiritual Formation as if the Church Mattered, Growing in Christ through Community. Grand Rapids, MI: Baker Academic, 2008.
2. Carole Lewis. Growing in the Fruit of the Spirit, First Place 4 Health, discover a new way to healthy living, Ventura, CA: Gospel Light Publications, 2009.
3. Bacchiocchi, Samuele, Ph.D., Matthew 11:28-30: Jesus' Rest And The Sabbath. Andrews University Seminary Studies, Autumn 1984, Vol. 22, No.3, 289-16.
4. DeWaay, Bob. A Review of The Spirit of Disciplines by Willard, Dallas. St. Louis Park, MN: Twin City Fellowship, Critical Issues Commentary, 2010.
5. MacArthur, John. Galatians, The MacArthur New Testament Commentary, Chicago, IL: Moody Publishers, 1987.

In Times Like These

Lyrics by RUTH CAYE JONES

In times like these, we need a Savior
In times like these, we need an anchor
Be very sure, be very sure
Your anchor holds and grips the Solid Rock.

Refrain:
This Rock is Jesus, Yes, He's the one
This Rock is Jesus, The only One
Be very sure, be very sure
Your anchor holds and grips the Solid Rock.

In times like these oh be not idle
In times like these we need the bible
Be very sure, be very sure
Your anchor holds and grips the Solid Rock.

In times like these, I have a Savior
In times like these, I have an anchor
I'm very sure, I'm very sure
My anchor holds and grips the Solid Rock.

REFLECTIONS

GO FISH

Now, my dad once told me the story about a peculiar fisherman from Minnesota.

You see, this fisherman was very well prepared. He knew how to fish. He had everything you need to be a good fisherman. He had poles, nets, bait, and even a really nice boat, but this fisherman had a problem.

You see, for all his preparation he never caught anything. Not one fish. Not one, not ever. And you know why he never caught a fish? What do you think? The answers easy: He never went fishing.

He had all the knowledge and all the equipment, but he never got into the boat, he never left the dock.

- Soren Kierkegaard
Danish theologian & philosopher

Source: Now, My Dad Once Told Me The Story About A eText Illustration shared by Andrew Schroer, Divine Savior Lutheran Church, March 2001. Retrieved November 2015, from http://www.sermoncentral.com/illustrations/sermon-illustration-andrew-schroer-humor-sharingyourfaith-evangelismfearof-greatcommission-1749.asp

Appendix

◆ ◆ ◆

ASPECTS OF SALVATION

YOU IN CHRIST	CHRIST IN YOU
Objective Salvation Imputed Righteousness	**Subjective Salvation** Imparted Righteousness
FULL AND COMPLETE Perfect in Christ 1 Corinthians 6:11 Ephesians 1:3-6; Colossians 2:10	ONGOING PROCESS Growing up in Christ Philippians 3:12-14 Colossians 1:27; 2:6
UNIVERSAL Includes all Mankind Romans 5:18 2 Corinthians 5:19 Titus 2:11	PARTICULAR Applies only to Believers John 3:16 Romans 8:9,10; 1 Timothy 4:10
UNCONDITIONAL By Grace Alone Romans 3:21, 28 1 Corinthians 1:30, 31 Philippians. 3:9	CONDITIONAL By Faith Alone Luke 9:23 Galatians 2:20 Philippians 2:12,13
MERITORIOUS Justifies, Qualifies us for Heaven Acts 15:5-11 Ephesians 2:8, 9 Titus 3:5	DEMONSTRATIVE Sanctifies, Witnesses our Justification John 14:12 Ephesians 2:10 Titus 3:8; James 2:17, 20-26

SALVATION – EVIDENCE FOR NEED

Dead in trespasses and sins; fulfilling fleshly desires	Eph 2:3, Col 2: 13
Carnal mind is hostile, enmity against God	Rom: 8:7
Cannot submit to God's Law	Rom 8:7
Cannot please God,	Rom 8:8
Cannot understand the things of God	1 Cor 2:14, Rom 3: 11
Cannot accept the Holy Spirit	John 14:17
Cannot see the Kingdom of God	John 3:3
Cannot hear the Words of Christ	John 8:43
Cannot see the Light of the Gospel (Blinded minds)	2 Cor 4:4
Thinks the Gospel foolishness	1 Cor 1:18
Does not seek for God	Rom 3:11
Does not fear God	Rom 3:1,8
Heart is deceitful and desperately wicked	Jer 17:9

ARMINIANISM vs CALVINISM

Arminianism	Calvinism (TULIP)
Free Will	Total Depravity
Conditional Election	Unconditional Election
Universal Atonement	Limited Atonement
Resistible Grace	Irresistible Grace
Perseverance of some Saints	Perseverance of the Saints

THREE PHASES OF SALVATION

PHASE	THEOLOGICAL TERM	TIME IN BELIEVER'S LIFE	EFFECT ON HUMAN CONDITION	RESULTS
Initial	Justification*	Past	Spirit	Born again
Progressive	Sanctification** Transformation Renewal	Present	Soul (Mind)	Renewed mind
Final	Glorification***	Future	Body (Flesh)	Ressurrected body

*JUSTIFICATION. Deliverance from the PENALTY of sin. Romans 5:1 that we have been justified through faith and because of this, we have peace with God through our Lord Jesus Christ. The word "justification" is a legal term, and means to declare not guilty which in turn pronounces the individual innocent of the crime.

**SANCTIFICATION. Deliverance from the POWER of sin. Philippians 2:12-13 reads "…work out your own salvation with fear and trembling; for it is God who works in you both to will and to do for His good pleasure." It means that having received salvation through faith we are now able and expected to work it out despite the fact that the present is still here and we live in a world full of temptations and sin. The sin of the past has been removed and we have been justified.

***GLORIFICATION. Deliverance from the PRESENCE of sin. This final phase of the believer's salvation experience occurs when the believer leaves this world, either by death or by rapture, and enters into the presence of God in heaven (Rom. 8:17-18). The Christian never achieves sinless perfection until glorified in heaven, at which time the sin nature is removed and the believer is given a perfect body (Phil. 3:20-21). "For our citizenship is in heaven, from which we also eagerly wait for the Savior, the Lord Jesus Christ, who will transform our lowly body that it may be conformed to His glorious body, according to the working by which He is able even to subdue all things to Himself. " Jesus died on the cross to save our souls from eternal death and granting us eternal life. He is coming back to complete our salvation by changing our bodies into immortal glorified bodies to live with Him forever.

ARMINIANISM POINTS	CALVINISM THE "FIVE POINTS"
Free Will or Human Ability	**Total Inability or Total Depravity**
• Human nature seriously affected by the fall	• Human nature seriously affected by the fall
• Free will to choose good over evil	• Unable to choose good over evil
• Individual's will not enslaved to sinful nature	• Individual's will in bondage to his evil nature
• Faith is sinner's gift to God	• Faith is God's gift to sinner
Conditional Election	**Unconditional Election**
• God selected those would freely believe.	• Sovereignly chosen ones drawn to Christ by Holy Spirit
• Sinner's choice is the ultimate cause of salvation.	• Salvation caused by God's choice of sinner
Universal Redemption or General Atonement	**Particular Redemption or Limited Atonement**
• Only those who believe on Him are saved	• Faith secured and salvation guaranteed
• Redemption effective only if man accepts	• Christ's redeeming work saves only the elect
The Holy Spirit Can Be Effectually Resisted	**The Efficacious Call of the Spirit or Irresistible Grace**
• Man able to resist the Spirit's call	• Sinners irresistibly drawn to Christ by Spirit
• Free will may limit the Christ's saving work	• Man's cooperation not required
• The Holy Spirit can only draw those who allow Him to have His way with them	• The Spirit never fails to result in the salvation of those to whom it is extended
Falling From Grace*	**Perseverance of the Saints**
• It is possible for those who are saved to lose salvation	• Those who are chosen, redeemed, and of faith are eternally saved and persevere to the end
*Opinions are divided among Arminians (some hold that believers are eternally secure in Christ once a sinner is regenerated).	
Summary – Arminianism	**Summary – Calvinism**
• Salvation accomplished through the combined efforts of God and man	• Salvation accomplished by the almighty power of the Triune God
• Man's response is the determining factor	• Election, redemption, regeneration is the work of God and by grace alone
• God's provision is effective only for those who accept His gift	• God determines the recipients of salvation

Arminianism View

Election — God foresaw man's fall and elected those He that would repent.

Fall — Man fell into sin but retained free will.

Calling — God calls all who hears the gospel and repents, but they can accept or reject the call; (the Spirit draws them).

Faith — Man yields to the Holy Spirit.

Regeneration — The Spirit performs the work.

Repentance — Man chooses to repent and accept Christ.

Justification — Man is justified before God.

Calvinism View

Total Depravity Man it utterly depraved as a baby and is incapable of responding to the gospel call to choose redemption.

Unconditional Election God already decided and elected those who will be saved; it is not reversible.

Limited Atonement Christ died only for those whom God elected to save (He did not die for all men).

Irresistible Grace The Holy Spirit only draws those whom God already decided would be saved and He creates a saving faith within them.

Perseverance of the Saints Once saved, always saved.

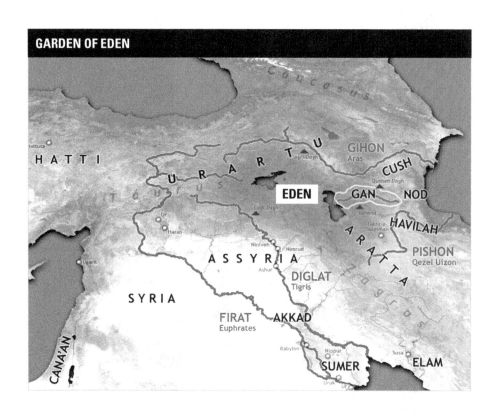

GARDEN OF EDEN

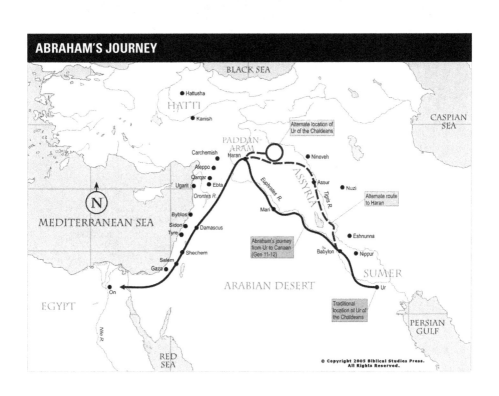

ABRAHAM'S JOURNEY

BLACK SEA

Hattusha

HATTI

Kanish

CASPIAN
SEA

Carchemish

PADDAN-
ARAM

Alternate location of
Ur of the Chaldeans

Aleppo

Haran

Nineveh

Qarqar

Ugarit

Ebla

ASSYRIA

Assur

Nuzi

Orontes R.

Euphrates R.

Tigris R.

Alternate route
to Haran

N

MEDITERRANEAN SEA

Byblos

Sidon

Tyre

Damascus

Mari

Abraham's journey
from Ur to Canaan
(Gen 11-12)

Eshnunna

Shechem

Babylon

Nippur

Salem

Gaza

SUMER

ARABIAN DESERT

Ur

On

EGYPT

Traditional
location of Ur of
the Chaldeans

PERSIAN
GULF

Nile R.

RED
SEA

© Copyright 2005 Biblical Studies Press.
All Rights Reserved.

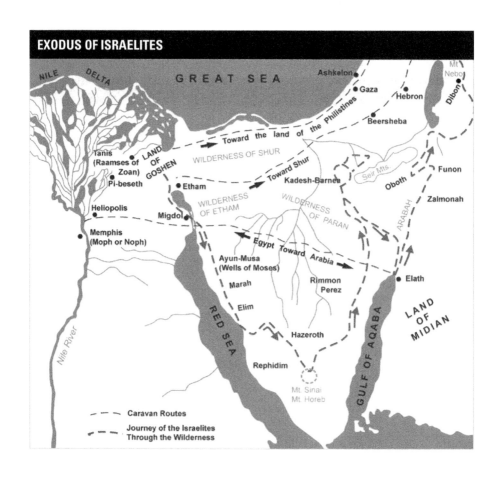

EXODUS OF ISRAELITES

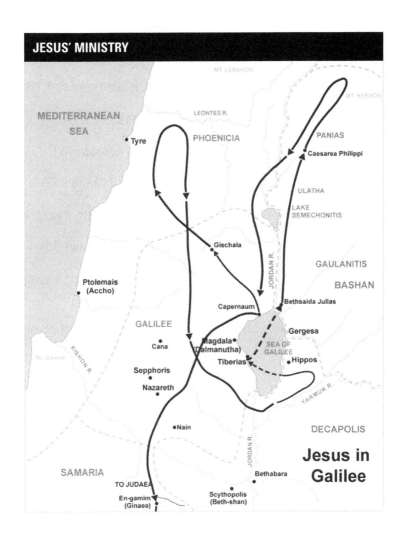

OLD TESTMANT vs NEW TESTAMENT

Old Testament	New Testament
Inferior Covenant	A Better Covenant (Hebrews 8:6)
Inferior Testament	A Better Testament (Hebrews 7:22)
Inferior Promises	Better Promises (Hebrews 8:6)
Inferior Hope	A Better Hope (Hebrews 7:19)
Inferior Sacrifices	Better Sacrifices (Hebrews 9:23)
Inferior Ministers	A More Excellent Ministry (Hebrews 8:6)
Inferior Tabernacle	A True Tabernacle (Hebrews 8:2)
An Imperfect Tabernacle	A Greater and More Perfect Tabernacle (Hebrews 9:11)
Inferior (Man pitched Sanctuary)	Sanctuary, Pitched by God (Hebrews 8:6)

PROGRESSION OF GOD'S COVENANT WITH MAN

Salvation History	Phases
God's Salvation of Israel (History of God as part of Salvation history)	In the Garden Ark of Covenant Tabernacle Temple New Covenant (Jesus) Holy Spirit
Jesus Incarnate (God's master plan of Salvation)	New Testament
Apostolic Work (History of mission of the early church)	Acts of the Apostles
Early Church Fathers (Christian Fathers and their missions)	Beginning of the Church Age
Constantine	Christianity / State Religion Roman Catholic & Orthodox Christianity
Reformation	Martin Luther (Protestant Reformation)
Indigenous Religions	Parachurch missions
Post Reformation Religions	Pentecostals and Charismatics Catholic, Protestants, Lutheran, Episcopalian, Presbyterian
	Cults: Jehovah's Witness, Scientology, Mormonism, Christian Science, New Age Movement, Unification Church, The Masons, Eastern Religions

CHURCH AGE – REVELATION CHAPTERS 2-3

69 WEEKS	Ephesus APOSTOLIC CHURCH 2:1-7 A.D. 33-100	Smyrna PERSECUTED CHURCH 2:8-11 A.D. 100-312	Pergamum INDULGED CHURCH 2:12-17 A.D. 312-606	Thyatira PAGAN CHURCH 2:18-29 A.D. 606-Tribulation	Sardis DEAD CHURCH 3:1-6 A.D. 1520-Tribulation	Philadelphia RAPTURE CHURCH 3:7-13 A.D. 1750-Rapture	Laodicea LUKEWARM CHURCH 3:14-22 A.D. 1900-Tribulation
Period	The early church, to AD 100	The church under pagan persecution, to 313	Paganism enters the church, to 500s	Papal supremacy of Dark Ages, to mid 1500s	Protestant reformation and fossilization, to late 1700s	Awakening, Bible printed and studied, to mid 1800s	End-time church, content but sinful, to the End.
Christ	Holds 7 stars, walks among 7 Lampstands	First and Last, Died and came to life	The One with two-edged sword	Eyes of fire, feet like brass; searches minds	Holds 7 spirits and stars	Holy, true, holds keys, opens and shuts	Amen, true witness, Beginning of creation
Commended	Works, labor patience, Persevered Tested false prophets	Spiritually rich in spite of poverty; Works, trials, poverty; blasphemy of false Jews	Works, Held to My name & faith even in time of martyr	More works, love, service, faith, patience	Works, a name you live Have a few names undefiled	Works, Missions Have Kept My Name Persevered	
Condemned Rebuke	Left first love	(Not one word)	Balaam followers Nicolaitans doctrine False teachers Living at Satan's throne	Jezebel Immorality permitted	Works imperfect		Lukewarm, wretched, blind,poor, naked, Neither cold nor hot
Counseled	Remember from where you are fallen; Repent, do first works	Do not fear suffering	Repent	Hold fast until I come	Watch, strengthen remainder	Hold fast, preserve crown	Buy gold, clothes, eye ointment
Warned	Lampstand will be removed	Be faithful Tribulation coming	Will fight with sword of mouth	Jezebel into sickbed, children killed	I will come as thief if you do not watch		I will spit you out; rebuke and punishment
What you have				Do not have false doctrine, not Satanic depths	A name as alive, but dead (and see above)	A little strength, Kept My word and name	Not what you think you have
Overcomers Reward	Eat from tree of life	Not hurt by second death	Hidden manna, white stone	Millennial Power over nations; morning star	Clothed in white, name in book, confessed	Pillar with God's name My new name	Sit on my throne
Other promises		Eternal life to ones faithful to death		Rest are given no other burden	Undefiled ones will walk in white	Submission of false Jews; Kept from hour of trial	Eat with those who open door

Glossary

◆ ◆ ◆

A

Absolute authority: Highest authority in one's life; an authority that cannot be disproved by appeal to any higher authority.

Absolution: In Catholicism, the act of releasing someone from their sin by God, through the means of a priest.

Active obedience: Referring to Christ's perfect obedience to God during his earthly life that earned the righteousness that God credits to those who place their faith in Christ.

Ad Hominem: From the Latin meaning "to the man." In a theological debate or discussion, it is the act of attacking the person or opponent rather than debating the issues.

Ad Nauseum: The appeal 'to repetition,' using the fallacy of familiarity. It is any argument which asserts or implies that something is more likely to be true, the more often it is repeated.

Adamic Covenant: The Adamic Covenant is also sometimes called the covenant of works. This is the covenant or oath God made with Adam promising him life or death according to his abiding by God's law of the garden of Eden. Jesus Christ, the second Adam, satisfied this covenant or through His human obedience and propitiation.

Adoption: An act of God whereby he makes us members of his family. For example, doctrines which are neither explicitly condemned by scripture, nor explicitly stipulated. Often used in connection with religious tolerance of what is sometimes called, 'the non-essentials.'

Adoptionism: False teaching that Jesus lived as an ordinary man until his baptism, at which time God "adopted" him as his "Son" and conferred on him supernatural powers; this teaching thus denies Jesus' preexistence and divine nature. Adoptionism is an error concerning Christ that first appeared in the second century. Those who held it denied His deity. Adoptionists taught that Jesus was tested by God and after passing this test and upon His baptism, He was granted supernatural powers by God and adopted as the Son. As a reward for His great accomplishments and perfect character He was raised from the dead and adopted into the Godhead.

Advent: From the Latin, "coming." The coming of or the arrival of something very important as in the advent of Christ's return. Advent is also an Christian time of preparation preceding Christmas.

Age of accountability: Term used by some theologians to indicate a point in a person's life before which (according to their view) he is not held responsible for sin and is not counted guilty before God.

Aggiornamento: The process of renewing the church, which was particularly associated with Pope John XXIII and the Second Vatican Council (1962–5). The Italian word can be translated as "a bringing up to date" or "renewal," and refers to the process of theological, spiritual, and institutional renewal.

Agnostic: Derives from the negation of the Greek word [gnosis], which means esoteric knowledge of higher things. Thus, a'gnostic means No-knowledge or not knowing. Agnostics generally believe that no one can not know whether or not God exists. Some take a more liberal approach, saying "they" do not know, but that existence of a Deity might be possible.

Agnosticism: The belief that it is not possible to know if there is or is not a God. (Compare Atheism, Deism, and Theism.)

Albigenses: A heresy during the middle ages that developed in the town Albi in Southern France. This error taught that there were two gods: the good god of light usually referred to as Jesus in the New Testament and the god of darkness and evil usually associated with Satan and the "God of the Old Testament." Anything material was considered evil including the body which was created by Satan. The soul, created by the good god, was imprisoned in the evil flesh and salvation was possible only through holy living and doing good works.

Alexander the Great: The king of Macedonia from 336 - 323 who went on to conquer all of Greece, the Persian Empire and Egypt. He marched all the way to India before his troops forced him to turn back. He died from drinking too much on the way back.

Alexandrian School: A patristic school of thought, especially associated with the city of Alexandria in Egypt, noted for its Christology (which placed emphasis upon the divinity of Christ) and its method of biblical interpretation (which employed allegorical methods of exegesis). A rival approach in both areas was associated with Antioch.

allegory: A mode of speech, generally narrative in form and understanding of how biblical texts are to be interpreted which sees certain biblical images as possessing deeper, spiritual meanings, which can be uncovered by their interpreters, where persons, places, objects, and events have symbolic meanings. John Bunyan's book, Pilgrim's Progress is an allegory of the Christian life. During the middle ages it was common to think that the Bible was allegory, and that objects had symbolic meanings. The allegorical interpretation of scripture has generally been rejected since the time of the Reformation.

Amillennialism: From the Latin [mille], meaning thousand, and [annum], meaning years. The article "a" in Greek (yes Greek) negates the word following it, thus a-millennium literally means no millennium. In Theological terms Amillennialism is the doctrine of no "earthly" millennial reign, or no "earthly" 1000 year reign. The view or teaching that there is no literal 1000 year bodily reign of Christ on earth prior to the final judgment and the eternal state as referenced in Revelation 20. It sees the 1000 year period spoken of in Revelation 20 as figurative. Instead, it teaches that we are in the millennium now, and that at the return of Christ (1 Thess. 4:16 - 5:2) there will be the final judgment and the heavens and the earth will then be destroyed and remade (2 Peter. 3:10). The Amillennial view is as old as the Premillennial view. (Also compare to Postmillennialism). On this view, scriptural references to the millennium in Revelation 20 actually describe the present church age.

Anabaptism: The Greek [ana] meaning again, and [baptismos] meaning baptism. i.e., to re-baptize. Term derived from the Greek word for "rebaptizer," and used to refer to the radical wing of the sixteenth-century Reformation, based on thinkers such as

Menno Simons or Balthasar Hubmaier.

Anabaptists: Any of a group of sects of the early Reformation period of the 16th century that believed in rebaptism of people as adults. Infant baptism was not recognized as valid and the Catholic Mass was rejected. Anabaptist means "one who baptizes again." They believed in non-violence and opposed state run churches.

Analogy of being (Analogia Entis): The theory, especially associated with Thomas Aquinas, that there exists a correspondence or analogy between the created order and God, as a result of the divine creatorship. The idea gives theoretical justification to the practice of drawing conclusions from the known objects and relationships of the natural order concerning God.

Analogy of faith (analogia fidei): The theory, especially associated with Karl Barth, which holds that any correspondence between the created order and God is only established on the basis of the self-revelation of God.

Angel: Messenger. A created, spiritual being with moral judgment and high intelligence, but without a physical body (Psalm 148:2,5; Col. 1:16). Non-human, spirit beings (Heb. 1:14); immortal (Luke 20:36), innumerable (Heb. 12:22), invisible (Num. 22:22-31), sexless (Matt. 22:30), and do the will of God (Psalm 103:20). They guide (Gen. 24:7, 40), protect (Psalm 34:7), and comfort (Acts 27:2, 24). There are good angels (Gen. 28:12; Psalm 91:11) and bad angels (2 Pet. 2:4; Jude 6). The only angels mentioned by name are Gabriel (Dan. 8:16; 9:21), Michael (Dan. 10:13,21; 112:1), and Lucifer (Luke 10:18). Michael is always mentioned in the context of battle (Dan. 10:13) and Gabriel as a messenger (Luke 1:26). Of course, Lucifer, who became Satan, is the one who opposes God. Angels were originally created for the purpose of serving and carrying out the will of God. The fallen angels rebelled and became evil angels. Satan is such an angel (Isaiah 14:12-16; Ezekiel 28:12-15).

Angel of the Lord: A form that God took on at various times in Scripture in order to appear to human beings. The precise identity of the "angel of the Lord" is not given in the Bible. However, there are many important "clues" to his identity. There are Old and New Testament references to "angels of the Lord," "an angel of the Lord," and "the angel of the Lord." It seems when the definite article "the" is used, it is specifying a unique being, separate from the other angels. The angel of the Lord speaks as God, identifies Himself with God, and exercises the responsibilities of God (i.e., Genesis 16:7-12; 21:17-18; 22:11-18; Exodus 3:2). In several of these appearances, those who saw the angel of the Lord feared for their lives because they had "seen the Lord." It is clear that in at least some instances, the angel of the Lord is a theophany, an appearance of God in physical form.

Angelology: The study of angels. There are many unbiblical views of angels today. Some believe angels are human beings who have died. Others believe that angels are impersonal sources of power. Still others deny the existence of angels entirely. A biblical understanding of angelology will correct these false beliefs. Angelology tells us what the Bible says about angels. It is a study of how the angels relate to humanity and serve God's purposes; In the Old Testament it is the Hebrew word [malak] and in the new testament it is the Greek word [aggelos], from where we get the actual word Angel. In both the Hebrew and Greek (Old and New Testament) the words mean, a messenger. It can either refer to a human, or a divine messenger, depending upon the content and context of the passage. The study of angels usually centers upon the divine messengers, rather than the human ones.

Animism: The belief that everything in the universe contains a living soul. The belief that every object is indwelt by a spirit.

Annihilationism: The teaching that when a person dies, he is annihilated, most often this doctrine is applied to the wicked, thereby negating eternal hell fire. This is contradicted by the Bible in Matt. 25:46 which says "And these will go away into eternal punishment, but the righteous into eternal life." Also, degrees of punishment will be given on the day of judgment (Rev. 20:11-15). If all, or only the wicked are annihilated, then degrees of punishment would be pointless.

Antediluvian: From two Latin words. [ante] which means 'before' and [diluvium] which means 'deluge' or massive influx of water. In theological terms, the period before the deluge or flood of Genesis chapter 7 is spoken of as the antediluvian period.

Anthropic Principle: Relating to human beings or their existence. The Anthropic Principle is the Law of Human Existence (Principle means "law)". The idea that the universe exhibits elements of design specifically for the purpose of containing intelligent beings; namely, humans. Much debate surrounds this issue. Is the universe necessarily arranged by God so as to make life possible or is it simply that the universe is godless and that life came into existence due to a chance state that we now find it in?

anthropomorphic language: Manifesting in human form. It is from the Greek "anthropos" meaning "man" and "morphe" meaning "form." In biblical theology, God is described in anthropomorphic terms; that is, in human terms with human attributes. For example, God has hands and feet in Exodus 24:9-11 and is loving (1 John 4:8).

anthropomorphic language: Language that speaks of God in human terms.

anthropomorphism: The Greek [anthropos] meaning human, and [morphe] which means form. It is the doctrine of ascribing human form or human attributes to a deity. In Christianity it is when people ascribe human features like hands, legs, feet, or other such human characteristics, to God. The tendency to ascribe human features (such as hands or arms) or other human characteristics to a being or thing that is not human, usually God.

Antichrist: A figure against Christ, denying the Father and the Son (1 John 2:22), does not acknowledge Jesus (1 John 4:3), and denies that Jesus came in the flesh (2 John 1:7). There have been many "antichrists," as 1 John 2:18 states. But there is also coming the Antichrist. Most Bible prophecy/eschatology experts believe the Antichrist will be the ultimate embodiment of what it means to be against Christ. In the end times/last hour, a man will arise to oppose Christ and His followers more than anyone else in history. Likely claiming to be the true Messiah, the Antichrist will seek world domination and will attempt to destroy all followers of Jesus Christ and the nation of Israel. A spirit of rebellion against God, (1 John 4:3) and of a specific future person identified as the man of lawlessness (2 Thess. 2:3). He actively opposes Christ (2 Thess. 2:4) and when he arrives, he will be able to perform miracles (2 Thess. 2:9). Some believe he will be an incarnation of Satan and as such will be able to deceive many. His number is 666 (Rev. 13:18). A further possible description of him might be found in Zech. 11:15-17). Man of lawlessness who will appear prior to the second coming of Christ and will cause great suffering and persecution, only to be destroyed by Jesus. Term used to describe other figures who embody such an opposition to Christ and are precursors of the final antichrist.

Antinomianism: The word comes from the Greek anti, against, and nomos, law. It is the unbiblical practice of living without regard to the righteousness of God, using God's grace as a license to sin, and trusting grace to cleanse of sin. In other words, since grace is infinite and we are saved by grace, then we can sin all we want and still

be saved. It is wrong because even though as Christians we are not under the Law (Rom. 6:14), we still fulfill the Law in the Law of love (Rom. 13:8,10; Gal. 5:14; 6:2). We are to love God with all our heart, soul, strength, and mind, and our neighbor as ourselves (Luke 10:27) and, thereby, avoid the offense of sin which cost God His only begotten Son. Paul speaks against the concept of antinomianism in Rom. 6:1-2: "Are we to continue in sin that grace may abound? May it never be! How shall we who died to sin still live in it?". We are not to use the grace of God as a means of sin. Instead, we are to be controlled by the love of God and in that way bear the fruit of the Holy Spirit (Gal. 5:22-25). Theologians generally hold that there are two types of Antinomians.
1) "Explicit" Antinomians are obvious reprobates who disregard the laws of God
2) "Implicit" Antinomians are professed Christians who falsely construe that they have New Testament "liberty" from the law of God.
That is to say, because they believe they are saved by Grace and not works, they surmise that it doesn't matter how they live in transgression of laws.

Anti-Pelagian writings: The writings of Augustine relating to the Pelagian controversy, in which he defended his views on grace and justification. See "Pelagianism."

Antithesis: Greek term taken from the words [anti] meaning to be opposed to, or against, and [thesis] meaning to set or lay down. By implication thesis refers to a dissertation, viewpoint, or proposition which is being set down or argued. In theological terms, antithesis refers to a direct opposite, or a figure or type in which thoughts or words are balanced in contrast. The concept in antithesis means that a belief or thesis is 'opposed' to another belief or thesis. It is often used to illustrate that God's people are to be distinct and in contrast to (the antithesis of) the people of the world, or God's law in contrast to man's disobedience.

Apocalyptic: A type of writing or religious outlook in general which focuses on the last things and the end of the world, often taking the form of visions with complex symbolism. The second half of the book of Daniel (Old Testament) and Revelation (New Testament) are examples of this type of writing.

Apocrypha: The collection of seven additional books considered inspires that have been accepted by and included in the canon of Scripture by the Roman Catholic Church but not included in the canon by Protestants (from the Greek word apocrypha, "things that are hidden"). The word apocrypha means hidden. It is used in a general sense to describe a list of books written by Jews between 300 - 100 B.C.

Apollinarianism: The fourth-century heresy which held that Christ had a human body but not a human mind or spirit, and that the mind and spirit of Christ were from the divine nature of the Son of God. Apollinarianism was the heresy taught by Apollinaris the Younger, bishop of Laodicea in Syria about 361. He taught that the Logos of God, which became the divine nature of Christ, took the place of the rational human soul of Jesus and that the body of Christ was a glorified form of human nature. In other words, though Jesus was a man, He did not have a human mind but that the mind of Christ was solely divine.

Anthropocentrism: From the Greek [anthropos] meaning human, and the Latin [centralis] which pertains to the center. It is simply the doctrine that man is the center of all things, and the central fact of all existence, therefore he has no cause for God. It is the view that man is autonomous, and therefore everything must be understood in terms of how it relates to him.

Anthropology: From two Greek words [anthropos] which means human or man, and [logos] which means word or discourse. Anthropology is therefore the study of man or human beings. In theological terms, anthropology is the discourse or study of human existence, origin, behavior, and the nature of his creation in the image of God. It often centers on the revelation of the special position in creation God has placed him in, and his divergence from animals.

Apologetics: The intellectual defense of the Christian faith. The area of Christian theology which focuses on the defense of the Christian faith, particularly through the rational justification of Christian belief and doctrines. The discipline that seeks to provide a defense of the truthfulness of the Christian faith for the purpose of convincing unbelievers.

Apologetics: The practice of defending a belief through a logical speech or explanation. The word "apologetics" is derived from the Greek word "apologia," which means to make a defense. It has come to mean defense of the faith. Apologetics covers many areas: who Jesus is, the reliability of the Bible, refuting cults, biblical evidences in the history and archeology, answering objections, etc. In short, it deals with giving reasons for Christianity being the true religion. We are called by God to give an apologia, a defense: "but sanctify Christ as Lord in your hearts, always being ready to make a defense to everyone who asks you to give an account for the hope that is in you, yet with gentleness and reverence" (1 Pet. 3:15).

apophatic: A term used to refer to a particular style of theology, which stressed that God cannot be known in terms of human categories. "Apophatic" (which derives from the Greek apophasis, "negation" or "denial") approaches to theology are especially associated with the monastic tradition of the Eastern Orthodox church.

Apophthegmata: The term used to refer to the collections of monastic writings often known as the "Sayings of the Desert Fathers." The writings often take the form of brief and pointed sayings, reflecting the concise and practical guidance typical of these writers.

Apostasy: From the Greek [apostasia], which means a departing or separating (2nd Thessalonians 2:3). In Christianity it is a forsaking or departing from the faith, principles, or truth, to which the Church previously held (1st Timothy 4:1, Hebrews 3:12). This abandonment or falling away from the faith is an opposite of the protestant reformation, which was the returning to the faith, principles, and truths which the Church formerly held. It is a revolt against the truth of God's word by a believer. It can also describe a group or church organization that has "fallen away" from the truths of Christianity as revealed in the Bible.

aposteriori: A statement that can be known to be true or false only on the basis of evidence obtained from experience and observation, as in an empirical statement, such as "I have a head" or "the moon has craters."

Apostle: A recognized office of the early church. Apostles are in several ways the New Testament counterpart to the Old Testament prophet and as such had the authority to write words of Scripture. Someone sent with a special message or commission. Jesus is called the apostle and high Priest of our confession in Hebrews 3:1. The twelve apostles of Jesus were Simon Peter, Andrew, James the son of Zebedee, John, Philip, Bartholomew, Thomas, Matthew, James the son of Alphaeus, Thaddaeus, Simon the Zealot, and Judas Iscariot. Paul became an apostle after Jesus' resurrection (2 Cor. 1:1), along with Barnabas (Acts 14:14), and others. Apostles established churches (Rom. 15:17-20), exposed error (Gal. 1:6-9), and defended the truth of the gospel (Phil. 1:7,17). Some were empowered by the Holy Spirit to perform Miracles (Matt. 10:1,8) and they were to preach the gospel (Matt. 28:19,20).

Apostles' Creed: Early statement of Christian belief – a creed or "symbol"; widely used by a number of Christian denominations for both liturgical and catechetical purposes, most visibly by liturgical Churches of Western tradition, including the Roman Catholic Church, Lutheranism and Anglicanism. It is also used by Presbyterians, Methodists and Congregationalists. It is based on Christian theological understanding of the Canonical gospels, the letters of the New Testament and to a lesser extent the Old Testament. Its basis appears to be the old Roman Creed aka Old Roman Symbol. It does not address some Christological issues defined in the Nicene and other Christian Creeds. Therefore it says nothing explicitly about the divinity of either Jesus or of the Holy Spirit. This makes it acceptable to many Arians and Unitarians. Nor does it address many other theological questions that became objects of dispute centuries later.

Apostolic era: The period of the Christian church, regarded as definitive by many, bounded by the resurrection of Jesus Christ (c.AD 35) and the death of the last apostle (c.AD 90?). The ideas and practices of this period were widely regarded as normative, at least in some sense or to some degree, in many church circles.

Apostolic succession: The belief that the 12 apostles passed on their authority to successors, who then passed the apostolic authority on to their successors, continuing throughout the centuries, even unto today. The Roman Catholic Church sees Peter as the leader of the apostles, with the greatest authority, and therefore his successors carry on the greatest authority. The Roman Catholic Church combines this belief with the concept that Peter later became the first bishop of Rome, and that the Roman bishops that followed Peter were accepted by the early church as the central authority among all of the churches. Apostolic succession, combined with Peter's supremacy among the apostles, results in the Roman bishop being the supreme authority of the Catholic Church – the Pope. Nowhere in Scripture did Jesus, the apostles, or any other New Testament writer set forth this idea. Even though Peter had a prominent role, but he was "supreme" over the others. The apostle Paul rebuked Peter in Galatians 2:11-14 for incorrect teaching. Also, Acts records the apostle Paul and Jesus' brother James as having prominent leadership roles as well.

Appropriation: A term relating to the doctrine of the Trinity, which affirms that while all three persons are active in all the outward actions of the Trinity, it is appropriate to think of those actions as being the particular work of one of the persons. Thus it is appropriate to think of creation as the work of the Father, or redemption as the work of the Son, despite the fact that all three persons are present and active in both these works.

Apriori: A statement whose truth or falsity may be known prior to any appeal to experience. An a priori statement might be "I exist."

Aquinas: Saint Thomas Aquinas (1225? - 1274) was an Italian theologian and philosopher known for his allegorical interpretations of scripture and his reconciliation of Aristotle and Christianity. He argued that reason is able to operate within faith yet according to its own laws, so he saw some division between faith and reason.

Aramaic: A northwest Semitic language closely related to Hebrew spoken throughout the Ancient Near East and used for parts of Daniel and Ezra. Its dialects have been in use since the ninth century BC. The Assyrians made Aramaic the common language of the Near East. Some parts of the Old Testament are written in Aramaic (Ezra 4:8-6:18; 7:12-26; Dan 2:4-7:28 and perhaps a few other verses). Hebrew in old (Phoenician), Qumran (Aramaic) and modern scripts. In exile and under the empire Aramaic letters replaced the old (Phoenician) script for writing Hebrew, first in everyday life and then for copying the Bible. The presence of some Aramaic words in the NT (e.g.: "talitha cumi", "maranatha" and "golgotha") suggests that Jesus spoke a dialect of Aramaic.

Archangel: An angel with authority over other angels.

Argumentum ad hominem: An irrelevant attack upon a person to deflect the argument from the facts and reasons.

Argumentum ad judicium: An argument where appeal is made to common sense and the judgment of people as validating a point.

Argumentum ad populum: An argument where appeal is made to emotions: loyalties, patriotism, prejudices, etc.

Argumentum ad verecundiam: An argument using respect for great men, customs, institutions, and authority in an attempt to strengthen one's argument and provide an illusion of proof.

Arianism: The heretical or erroneous doctrine that denies the full deity of the Jesus Christ and the Holy Spirit. This early Christological heresy treated Jesus Christ as the supreme of God's creatures, and denied His divine status. The Arian controversy was of major importance in the development of Christology during the fourth century. It taught that God could not appear on the earth, that Jesus was not eternal and could not be God. Additionally, it taught that there was only one person in the Godhead: the Father. Jesus, then, was a creation. It was condemned by the Council of Nicea in 325. The Jehovah's Witness cult is an equivalent, though not exactly, of this ancient error.

Arius: Libyan presbyter in Alexandria, had declared that although the Son was divine, he was a created being and therefore not co-essential with the Father, and "there was when he was not." This made Jesus less than the Father, which posed soteriological challenges for the nascent doctrine of the Trinity. Arius's teaching provoked a serious crisis.

Arminianism: A theological tradition that seeks to preserve the free choices of human beings and denies God's providential control over the details of all events. There are five main tenets of Arminianism: 1) God elects or reproves on the basis of foreseen faith or unbelief, 2) Christ died for all men and for every man, although only believers are saved, 3) Man is so depraved that divine grace is necessary unto faith or any good deed, 4) This grace may be resisted, 5) Whether all who are truly regenerate will certainly persevere in the faith is a point which needs further investigation.1 (Compare with Calvinism)

Ascension: The rising of Jesus from the earth into heaven forty days after his resurrection.

Asceticism: A term used to refer to the wide variety of forms of self-discipline used by Christians to deepen their knowledge of and commitment to God. The term derives from the Greek term askesis ("discipline"). Approach to living that renounces the comforts of the material world.

aseity: Another name for the attribute of God's independence or self-existence.

Assumption: In Catholicism, the taking of the body and soul of Mary, by God, into glory. Catholic doctrine, apparently, does not state whether or not Mary died, but tradition holds that she died and was immediately afterward assumed into heaven both body and soul.

Assurance: Theologically, assurance is the state of being confident in a condition or outcome. Usually it is applied to one's assurance of salvation. Texts often used to support assurance of salvation are John 10:28 "and I give eternal life to them, and they shall never perish; and no one shall snatch them out of My hand," and 1 John 5:13, "These things I have written to you who believe in the name of the Son of God, in order that you may know that you have eternal life." This assurance is given by the Holy Spirit.

assurance of salvation: The internal sense we may have based upon certain evidences in our lives that we are truly "born again" and will persevere as Christians until the end of our lives.

Atheism: This word comes from two Greek words, a the negator, and theos, God. Atheism teaches that there is no God of any kind, anywhere, anytime. Some atheists claim to "Excercise no belief in a god" the same way they would exercise no belief in pink unicorns. Logically, an atheist would be an evolutionist. The Bible teaches that all men know there is a God (Rom. 2:14-15). Therefore, they will be without excuse (Rom. 1:20) on the day of judgment. Instead, atheists willingly suppress the knowledge of God by their unrighteousness (Rom. 1:18-19).

Atonement: An English term originally coined in 1526 by William Tyndale to translate the Latin term reconciliation. It was how he translationed the latin word [reconciliatio], which means to bring together again, conciliate, or restore to union. It's where we get the word reconcile. In Theological terms it has more commonly come to mean, 'the work of Christ on the cross' in making amends for the enmity and the crimes committed by man, against the laws of God. It has since come to have the developed meaning of "the work of Christ" or "the benefits of Christ gained for believers by his death and resurrection." The work Christ did in his life and death to earn our salvation. To atone means to make amends, to repair a wrong done. Biblically, it means to remove sin. The Old Testament atonements offered by the high priest were temporary and a foreshadow of the real and final atonement made by Jesus. Jesus atoned for the sins of the world (1 John 2:2). This atonement is received by faith (Rom. 5:1; Eph. 2:8-9). Man is a sinner (Rom. 5:8) and cannot atone for himself. Therefore, it was the love of the Father that sent Jesus (1 John 4:10) to die in our place (1 Pet. 3:18) for our sins (1 Pet. 2:24). Because of the atonement, our fellowship with God is restored (Rom. 5:10). (See Reconciliation.)

attributes of being: Aspects of God's character that describe his essential mode of existence.

attributes of purpose: Aspects of God's character that pertain to making and carrying out decisions.

Augustine: One of the Latin Church Fathers, (354-430) generally recognized as the greatest thinker of Christian antiquity. He fused the Bible and Platonic philosophy. The City of God is his most famous work.

authority of Scripture: The idea that all the words in Scripture are God's in such a way that to disbelieve or disobey any word of Scripture is to disbelieve or disobey God.

Autograph: An original writing of a biblical document. The original manuscript written. The autographs would be the actual, original written document from which copies are made.

Autonomy: Freedom from all external constraints. Independence consisting of self-determination.

Axiology: from the Greek [axios], meaning worthy, and [logy], meaning discourse. Axiology is thus the discourse or study of the philosophy or system of value judgments or worthiness. In Christianity, Axiology is the branch of Theology dealing with the nature and types of value, such as law, ethics, conduct, order, and morality.

axiom: A proposition assumed without proof for the sake of studying its consequences. See Presupposition.

#

Babel, Tower of: The tower built the builders at Babel constructed which became a symbol of their defiance against God (Gen. 11:1-6). It was probably modeled after a ziggurat which is a mound of sun-dried bricks and was probably constructed before 4,000 BC.

Bacon: (1561-1626) Francis Bacon was an English philosopher and essayist. Author of Novum Organum (1620), he argued that faith and reason are absolutely separate.

Baptism: An immersion or sprinkling of water that signifies one's identification with a belief or cause. In Christianity it is the believer's identification with Christ in His death, burial, and resurrection (Rom. 6:4-54). It is done in the name and authority (Acts 4:7) of Christ with the baptismal formula of Father, Son, and Holy Spirit (Matt. 28:19). It does not save us (1 Pet. 3:21). However, it is our obligation, as believers, to receive it.

baptism by the Holy Spirit: A rendering of a phrase also translated "baptism in/with the Holy Spirit." The translation of the Greek preposition en with the word "by" can seem to indicate that the Holy Spirit is the agent doing the baptizing, but the phrase more accurately refers to the Spirit as the element "in" which (or "with" which) believers are "baptized" at conversion.

baptism in/with the Holy Spirit: A phrase the New Testament authors use to speak of coming into the new covenant power of the Holy Spirit. This would include the impartation of new spiritual life (in regeneration), cleansing from sin, a break with the power and love of sin, and empowering for ministry.

Baptismal Regeneration: The belief that baptism is essential to salvation, that it is the means where forgiveness of sins is made real to the believer. This is incorrect. Paul said that he came to preach the gospel, not to baptize (1 Cor. 1:14-17). If baptism were essential to salvation, then Paul would have included it in his standard practice and preaching of the salvation message of Jesus, but he did not. (See also Col. 2:10-11.)

Barthian: An adjective used to describe the theological outlook of the Swiss theologian Karl Barth (1886–1968), and noted chiefly for its emphasis upon the priority of revelation and its focus upon Jesus Christ. The terms "neo-Orthodoxy" and "dialectical theology" are also used in this connection.

beatific vision: A term used, especially in Roman Catholic theology, to refer to the full vision of God, which is allowed only to the elect after death. However, some writers, including Thomas Aquinas, taught that certain favored individuals – such as Moses and Paul – were allowed this vision in the present life. The true and real, though not exhaustive, seeing of God that will occur in heaven (lit., "the vision that makes blessed or happy").

Beatitudes: A term used to describe the eight promises of blessing found in the opening section of the Sermon on the Mount (Matthew 5: 3–11). Examples include "Blessed are the pure in heart, for they shall see God" and "Blessed are the peacemakers, for they shall be called children of God."

beauty: That attribute of God whereby he is the sum of all desirable qualities.

belief: In contemporary culture this term usually refers to the acceptance of the truth of some thing, such as facts about Christ, with no necessary element of personal term often involves this sense of commitment (cf. John 3:16; see also "faith").

believers' baptism: The view that baptism is appropriately administered only to those who give a believable profession of faith in Jesus Christ.

biblical theology: The study of the teaching of the individual authors and sections of the Bible and of the place of each teaching in the historical development of the Bible.

Bibliology: The systematic theological study of the Bible

Big Bang hypothesis: A theory of the origin of the universe, widely accepted, which states that between 10 and 20 billion years ago a very dense primeval aggregate of matter (a singularity) exploded into the expanding universe which evolved over the years into the galaxies, which are still receding from each other.

binding and loosing: Words of Jesus that refer to the actions of placing under and releasing from church discipline (Matt. 18:17-18; 16:19).

bishop: Translation of the Greek episkopos, a term used interchangeably with "pastor," "overseer," and "elder" to refer to the main governing office of a local church in the New Testament. The term also refers to a priest who has authority over a group of churches in an episcopalian form of church government.

blameless: Morally perfect in God's sight, a characteristic of those who follow God's word completely (Ps. 119:1).

Blasphemy: The unusually malicious, willful rejection and slander against the Holy Spirit's work attesting to Christ, and attributing that work to Satan (also see "unpardonable sin"). Speaking evil of God or denying Him some good which we should attribute to Him. Blasphemy of the Holy Spirit is stating that Jesus did his miracles by the power of the devil (Matt. 12:22-32) and is an unforgivable sin (Mark 3:28-30). Blasphemy arises out of pride (Psalm 73:9,11), hatred (Psalm 74:18), injustice (Isaiah 52:5), etc. Christ was mistakenly accused of blasphemy (John 10:30-33).

blessedness: The doctrine that God delights fully in himself and in all that reflects his character.

blood of Christ: A phrase referring to Christ's death in its saving aspects, since the blood he shed on the cross was the clear outward evidence that his life blood was poured out when he died a sacrificial death to pay for our redemption.

body of Christ: A scriptural metaphor for the church. This metaphor is used in two different ways, one to stress the interdependence of the members of the body, and one to stress Christ's headship of the church.

Born Again: A scriptural term (John 3:3-8) referring to God's work of regeneration by which he imparts new spiritual life to us. The new birth enjoyed by a Christian upon his conversion and regeneration. It is a work of the Holy Spirit within a believer. It is related to faith in Christ and Him crucified (John 3:3-5). It means that the person is no longer dead in sins (Eph. 2:1), no longer spiritually blind (1 Cor. 2:14), and is now a new creation in Christ Jesus (2 Cor. 5:17).

born of the Spirit: Another term for "regeneration" that indicates the special role played by the Holy Spirit in imparting new spiritual life to us.

born of water: A phrase used by Jesus in John 3:5 that refers to the spiritual cleansing from sin that accompanies God's work of regeneration (cf. Ezek. 36:25-26).

C

Calvinism: Theological tradition named after the sixteenth-century French reformer John Calvin (1509 - 64) that emphasizes the sovereignty of God in all things, man's inability to do spiritual good before God, and the glory of God as the highest end of all that occurs. Ambiguous term, used with two quite distinct meanings referring a) to religious ideas of religious bodies (such as the Reformed church) and individuals (such as Theodore Beza) influenced by John Calvin, or by his writings b) religious ideas of John Calvin himself. System of Christian interpretation emphasizes predestination and salvation. The five points of Calvinism were developed in response to the Arminian position (See Arminianism). Calvinism teaches:

1) **Total depravity:** that man is touched by sin in all parts of his being: body, soul, mind, and emotions,

2) **Unconditional Election:** that God's favor to Man is completely by God's free choice and has nothing to do with Man. It is completely undeserved by Man and is not based on anything God sees in man (Eph. 1:1-11)

3) **Limited atonement:** that Christ did not bear the sins of every individual who ever lived, but instead only bore the sins of those who were elected into salvation (John 10:11,15),

4) **Irresistible grace:** God's call to someone for salvation that cannot be resisted,

5) **Perseverance of the saints:** that it is not possible to lose one's salvation (John 10:27-28).

Canon: The list of all the books that belong in the Bible (from the Greek karuin, "reed; measuring rod; standard of measure"). This is another word for scripture. The Canon consists of the 39 books of the Old Testament and the 27 books of the New. The Canon is closed which means there is no more revelation to become Scripture.

canonical: A term describing preserved writings that are deemed to have divine authorship and therefore which are to be included in the canon of Scripture as God's authoritative words in written form.

Capital sins: In Catholicism, the seven causes of all sin: pride, covetousness, lust, anger, gluttony, envy, sloth

Cartesianism: The philosophical outlook especially associated with Rene´ Descartes (1596–1650), particularly in relation to its emphasis on the separation of the knower from the known, and its insistence that the existence of the individual thinking self is the proper starting point for philosophical reflection.

catechism: A popular manual of Christian doctrine, usually in the form of question and answer, intended for religious instruction.

catharsis: The process of cleansing or purification by which the individual is freed from obstacles to spiritual growth and development.

catholic: Term used to describe the Universality of the entire Christian Church. Refers to the universality of the church in space and time, and also to a particular church body (sometime also known as the Roman Catholic Church) which lays emphasis upon this point.

Causality: The relationship between cause and effect. The principle that all events have sufficient causes.

certain knowledge: Knowledge that is established beyond doubt or question. Because God knows all the facts of the universe and never lies, the only absolutely certain knowledge we can have is found in God's words in Scripture.

cessationist: Someone who thinks that certain miraculous spiritual gifts ceased when the apostles died and Scripture was complete.

Chalcedonian definition: The formal declaration at the Council of Chalcedon that Jesus Christ was to be regarded as having two natures, one human and one divine.

charisma: A set of terms especially associated with the gifts of the Holy Spirit. In medieval theology, the term "charisma" is used to designate a spiritual gift, conferred upon individuals by the grace of God. Since the early twentieth century, the term "charismatic" has come to refer to styles of theology and worship which place particular emphasis upon the immediate presence and experience of the Holy Spirit.

charismatic: Term referring to any groups or people that trace their historical origin to the charismatic renewal movement of the 1960s and 1970s. Such groups seek to practice all the spiritual gifts mentioned in the New Testament but, unlike many Pentecostal denominations, allow differing viewpoints on whether baptism in the Holy Spirit is subsequent to conversion and whether tongues is a sign of baptism in the Holy Spirit.

Charismatic Gifts: Special spiritual gifts given to the church. They are for edifying and building up the church. They are mentioned in Rom. 12, 1 Cor. 12, and 1 Cor. 14: Word of wisdom, word of knowledge, faith, healing, miracles, prophecy, distinguishing of spirits, tongues, interpretation of tongues.

Charismatic Movement: Form of Christianity which places particular emphasis upon the personal experience of the Holy Spirit in the life of the individual and community, often associated with various "charismatic" phenomena, such as speaking in tongues.

cherubim: A class of created spiritual beings who, among other things, guarded the entrance to the Garden of Eden.

Chiliasm: Also known as millennialism. The belief that there is a future 1000 year reign of Christ where perfect peace will reign and the Lord Jesus will be King on earth.

Christ: New Testament equivalent of the Old Testament term "messiah" and means "anointed one." It is applied to Jesus as the anointed one who delivers from sin. Jesus alone is the Christ. As the Christ He has three offices: Prophet, Priest, and King. As Prophet He is the mouthpiece of God (Matt. 5:27-28) and represents God to man. As Priest He represents man to God and restores fellowship between them by offering Himself as the sacrifice that removed the sin of those saved. As King He rules over His kingdom. By virtue of Christ creating all things (John 1:3; Col. 1:16-17), He has the right to rule. Christ has come to do the will of the Father (John 6:38), to save sinners (Luke 19:10), to fulfill the O.T. (Matt. 5:17), to destroy the works of Satan (Heb. 2:14; 1 John 3:8), and to give life (John 10:10,28). Christ is holy (Luke 1:35), righteous (Isaiah 53:11), sinless (2 Cor. 5:21), humble (Phil. 2:5-8), and forgiving (Luke 5:20; 7:48; 23:34).

Christian: The word "Christian" comes from the Greek word christianos which is derived from the word christos, or Christ, which means "anointed one." A Christian, then, is someone who is a follower of Christ. The first use of the word "Christian" in the Bible is found in Acts 11:26, "And the disciples were called Christians first in Antioch." It is found only twice more in Acts 26:28 and 1 Pet. 4:16. However, it is important to note that it is the true Christ that makes someone a Christian, not the Mormon one (brother of the devil), or the JW one (Michael the Archangel), the New Age Jesus (a man in tune with the divine Christ Consciousness), etc.

Christian Demonology: Systematic study of demons or of beliefs about demons; supernatural reality of evil spirits, devils, an tricksters. Study of demons or of beliefs about demons based on teachings found in the Bible. Demonology is related to the larger theological Angelology and helps provide answers on what demons are, their activities, their identity power and final destination. Also deals with benevolent beings that have no circle of worshippers or so limited a circle as to be below the rank of the gods.

Christian ethics: Any study that answers the question, "What does God require us to do and what attitudes does he require us to have today?" with regard to any given situation.

Christology: The section of Christian theology dealing with the identity of Jesus Christ, particularly the question of the relation of his human and divine natures.From the Greek, [christos] meaning "anointed one," and [logos] meaning "word." By extension the words or discourse about the anointed one. This is the doctrine that deals with the person of Jesus Christ. It encompasses the theological study of both the divine and the human nature of the Saviour, and the roles they play in Christianity. Christology is the study of the Person and work of Jesus Christ as revealed in the Bible. Some of the issues studied are: 1) His deity, 2) His incarnation, 3) His offices (See Christ), 4) His sacrifice, 5) His resurrection, 6) His teaching, 7) His relation to God and man, and 8) His return to earth.

Church: The word is used in two senses: the visible and the invisible church. The visible church consists of all the people that claim to be Christians and go to church. The invisible church is the actual body of Christians; those who are truly saved. The true church of God is not an organization on earth consisting of people and buildings, but is really a supernatural entity comprised of those who are saved by Jesus. It spans the entire time of man's existence on earth as well as all people who are called into it. We become members of the church (body of Christ) by faith (Acts 2:41). We are edified by the Word (Eph. 4:15-16), disciplined by God (Matt. 18:15-17), unified in Christ (Gal. 3:28), and sanctified by the Spirit (Eph. 5:26-27). The community of all true believers for all time.

circular argument: An argument that seeks to prove its conclusion by appealing to a claim that depends on the truth of the conclusion.

Circumcision: An operation (note the shedding of blood) that entered one into the covenant in O.T. times. It was instituted by God (Gen. 17:10-14) and performed on the eighth day after birth (Luke 1:59). It was a sign of the covenant God made with Abraham (Gen. 17:12; Rom. 4:11). In the N.T. the physical operation is not practiced. Instead, a circumcision of the heart of the Christian is taught (Rom. 2:29; Col. 2:11-12). This is the true circumcision (Rom. 2:29).

clarity of Scripture: The idea that the Bible is written in such a way that its teachings are able to be understood by all who will read it seeking God's help and being willing to follow it.

classis: term for a regional governing body within the Christian Reformed Church (similar to a presbytery in a presbyterian system).

Codex: An early book form made from papyri leaves cut, folded, and sewn together in the middle to make a book. First used in the 2nd century.

Common Grace: The grace of God given to the creation as a whole. The grace of God by which he gives people innumerable blessings that are not part of salvation. God still allows the sun to shine upon the unsaved. He feeds them, allows them to work, and have joy. It is common grace that "restrains" the wrath of God until a later time. It is in special grace that salvation is given to the Christians.

Codex Sinaiticus: One of the most important books in the world. It is the earliest complete copy of the Christian New Testament. Handwritten well over 1600 years ago, the manuscript contains the Christian Bible hand-written text in Greek. The New Testament appears in the original vernacular language (koine) and the Old Testament in the version, known as the Septuagint, that was adopted by early Greek-speaking Christians. In the Codex, the text of both the Septuagint and the New Testament has been heavily annotated by a series of early correctors.

Codex Vaticamus: Most famous manuscript in the possession of the Vatican library, is generally believed to be from the fourth century, and is thought to be the oldest (nearly) complete copy of the Greek Bible in existence. It is written on 759 leaves of vellum in uncial letters and has been dated palaeographically to the 4th century.

communicable attributes: Aspects of God's character that he shares or "communicates" with us.

Communion: term commonly used to refer to the Lord's Supper (Matt. 26:26-30; Mark 14:22-26; Luke 22:14-20; 1 Cor. 1:23-26). It is the breaking of bread (Acts 2:42,46) and a time to give thanks (Luke 22:17,19). It was originally instituted by Jesus (Matt. 26:26-29) on the night of the Passover meal which was an annual occurrence celebrating the "passing over" of the angel of death that claimed the firstborn of every house in Egypt (Exodus 12). The Lord's Supper, or communion, replaces the Passover meal with the "body and blood" (Mark 14:22-24) of Jesus. It is to be taken only by believers (1 Cor. 11:23-28). (For further study see John 6:26-58 and 1 Cor. 11:27-34).

communion of saints: term in the Apostles' Creed referring to the fellowship that believers on earth have with believers in heaven by virtue of a common worship.

Compatibilism: The belief that God's unconditional sovereign election and human responsibility are both realities taught in Scripture that finite minds are unable to comprehend and must be held in tension.

Complementarianism: Position that the Bible teaches that men and women are of equal worth, dignity, responsibility before God (ontological equality). The Bible also teaches that men and women have different roles to play in society, the family, and the church. These roles do not compete but complement each other.

conciliarism: An understanding of ecclesiastical or theological authority which places an emphasis on the role of ecumenical councils.

Condemnation: Declaring an evildoer to be guilty; the punishment inflicted. Without Jesus we stand condemned before God not only because of the sin of Adam (Rom. 5:16-18) but also because of our own sin (Matt. 12:37). However, "There is therefore now no condemnation for those who are in Christ Jesus. For the law of the Spirit of life in Christ Jesus has set you free from the law of sin and of death" (Rom. 8:1-2). Christians have passed out of condemnation because they are forgiven in Christ.

Conditional Election: The belief that God's election is conditional, being based on his foreknowledge. God looks ahead into the future, sees who will make a free-will decision to place their faith in him, and then elects to save them. Or as contemporary Arminians would put it, God's elects Christ and all who are found in Him.

Conditional immortality: The view that immortality is given only to those Christians who believe in Christ. The rest are destroyed and do not exist. Some adherents to conditional immortality believe that the wicked will be punished in hell for a period proportional to their sins and then they are annihilated.

confession: The act of disclosing one's sins. In Catholicism, it is telling sins to a priest and the Lord forgives the person through the priest. Biblically, confession of sins is done to the one offended without the mediatorship of a priest. Although the term refers primarily to the admission to sin, it acquired a rather different technical sense in the sixteenth century – that of a document which embodies the principles of faith of a Protestant church, such as the Lutheran Augsburg Confession (1530), which embodies ideas of early Lutheranism, and Reformed First Helvetic Confession (1536).

Covenant: From the Hebrew [ber-eeth] meaning to cut, and by extension means an agreement (or more accurately a "promise" or pledge) to do something. In Theological terms, Covenants, an unchangeable, divinely imposed legal agreement between God and man that stipulates the conditions of their relationship. An agreement between two parties, according to Ancient Near East custom, consists of five parts: **1)** Identification of parties, **2)** Historical prologue where the deeds establishing the worthiness of the dominant party is established, **3)** Conditions of the agreement, **4)** Rewards and punishments in regard to keeping the conditions, and **5)** Disposition of the documents where each party receives a copy of the agreement (e.g. the two tablets of stone of the 10 Commandments). Ultimately, the covenants God has made with man result in our benefit. We receive eternal blessings from the covenant of grace.

covenant community: The community of God's people. Protestant proponents of infant baptism view baptism as a sign of entrance into the "covenant community" of God's people.

covenant of grace: The legal agreement between God and man, established by God after the fall of Adam, whereby man could be saved. Although the specific provisions of this covenant varied at different times during redemptive history, the essential condition of requiring faith in Christ the redeemer remained the same.

covenant of redemption: The agreement between the members of the Trinity in which each agreed to fulfill his respective role to accomplish the salvation of human beings.

covenant of works: The legal agreement between God and Adam and Eve in the Garden of Eden whereby participation in the blessings of the covenant depended on the obedience, or "works," of Adam and Eve.

Covenant Theology: A system of theology that views God's dealings with man in respect of covenants rather than dispensations (periods of time). It represents the whole of scripture as covenantal in structure and theme. Some believe there is one Covenant and others believe two and still others believe in more. The two main covenants are covenant of works in the O.T. made between God and Adam, and the Covenant of Grace between the Father and the Son where the Father promised to give the Son the elect and the Son must redeem them. Some consider these to be one and the same. The covenants have been made since before the world was made (Heb. 13:20).

Creation: The doctrine that God created the entire universe out of nothing. The universe was originally very good; and he created it to glorify himself. Everything that exists except God himself. This includes material as well as immaterial things and time. God is the creator, (Heb. 11:3) we are the creatures. The creator/creature distinction must be maintained to properly remain in humble relationship with God. We are not God, cannot create, nor can we help ourselves do good in order to be saved. Only God is God. Only He can create. And, only He has the ability to save man.

creationism: The view that God creates a new soul for each person and sends it to that person's body sometime between conception and birth.

creed: A formal definition or summary of the Christian faith, held in common by all Christians. The purpose of a creed is to provide a doctrinal statement of correct belief, or Orthodoxy. It was intended to be symbolic or the outward sign of belief. The creeds of Christianity have been drawn up at times of conflict about doctrine: acceptance or rejection of a creed served to distinguish believers and deniers of a particular doctrine or set of doctrines. The most important are those generally known as the "Apostles' Creed" and the "Nicene Creed."

Cult: From the Latin [cultus] meaning to cultivate, and by extension, any group or sect which cultivates, or 'promotes growth' through their beliefs to make proselytes. In modern Theological terms, the word is generally reserved for religious groups which (in contrast to classical Christianity, of having God's Word as their authority) blindly give authority to their leader. These leaders are often venerated, and manipulate and control the group through their charisma, deception, fear, and even perceived power. Anyone having a fanatical veneration of, or loyalty to, a human leader, animal, or thing. A religious group that follows a particular theological system. In the context of Christianity, and in particular, CARM, it is a group that uses the Bible but distorts the doctrines that affect salvation sufficiently to cause salvation to be unattainable. A few examples of cults are Mormonism, Jehovah's Witnesses, Christian Science, Christadelphians, Unity, Religious Science, The Way International, and the Moonies.

culture shock: The trauma and anxiety, the disorientation, caused by movement from one's familiar cultural surroundings to an alien one. Experienced by refugees and missionaries, or anyone who goes from one society to another.

Darwinism: The theory of how evolution might have come about which constitutes the major contribution to science made by Charles Darwin (1809-1882) The general theory of evolution (see also "macro-evolution") named after Charles Darwin, the British naturalist who expounded this theory in 1859 in his Origin of Species by Means of Natural Selection.

deacon: A translation of the Greek diakonos ("servant"). In certain contexts the term refers to a church officer whose responsibilities involves various forms of service, including financial oversight, administrative responsibilities, and caring for the physical needs of the congregation.

Death: The word "death" is used in two main ways in the Bible. First, it is used to describe the cessation of life. Second, death is used in reference to the lost. This refers to their eternal separation from God as a result of sin (Isaiah 59:2), in a conscious state of damnation without hope (1 Thess. 4:13; Rev. 20:10,14,15).   Death to humans is unnatural. When God created Adam and Eve, death was not part of the created order. It was not until they sinned that death entered the scene (Rom. 5:12; 6:23). Death will be destroyed when Christ returns and the believers receive their resurrected bodies.

Decalogue: The Ten Commandments found in Exodus 20. Deca means ten in Latin. Logue comes from "logos" which means "word."

Decrees, of God: Eternal plans of God whereby, before the creation of the world, he determined to bring about everything that happens.according to His will, whereby He has foreordained whatever comes to pass. His Decrees do not negate the responsibility of people for their sins nor does it mean that God is responsible for sin. But, it necessarily is true that God knows all things actual as well as potential, and that that which exists, exists due to His creative effort. It also follows that God has eternally known all events that have occurred, are occurring, and will occur in this creation including the fall, redemption, glorification, etc. Yet, God is not the one responsible for the sin in the world but has decreed, by His permission, that it be allowed to exist. Isaiah 46:9-10 says, "Remember the former things long past, for I am God, and there is no other; I am God, and there is no one like Me, 10Declaring the end from the beginning and from ancient times things which have not been done, saying, 'My purpose will be established, and I will accomplish all My good pleasure." God's efficacious decrees are those decrees which God has purposed and determined to occur, i.e., Acts 2:23 "this Man, delivered up by the predetermined plan and foreknowledge of God, you nailed to a cross by the hands of godless men and put Him to death." God's permissive decrees are those decrees where He permits things to occur such as evil.

Deduction: A system of logic, inference and conclusion drawn from examination of facts. Conclusions drawn from the general down to the specific.

Deism: Derived the latin word [deus], which means God, and has come to mean, "the belief in the existence of God strictly by the use of logic, common sense, and reason." This is as opposed to the historical belief in God's existence based upon revelation, scripture, and Church or congregational teachings. In general, Deists believe that God has not shown himself through scripture or any religious texts, but is revealed by logic and rational thought. They look at their philosophy as being a 'natural' belief, as opposed to what they see as religions which are artificially created by humans. In Deism, God is simply the initial creator, not one who is actively involved in His creation. Deism constitutes a secularization of religious thinking. The belief that God exists but is not involved in the world. The view that God created the universe but is no longer involved in the creation. It maintains that God created all things and set the universe in motion and left its operation. A term used to refer to the views of a group of English writers, especially during the seventeenth century, the rationalism of which anticipated many of the ideas of the Enlightenment. The term is often used to refer to a view of God which recognizes the divine creatorship, yet which rejects the notion of a continuing divine involvement with the world.

Demon: A fallen angel that assists Satan in the opposition of God. Demons are evil (Luke 10:17,18), powerful (Luke 8:29), and under the power of Satan (Matt. 12:24-30). They recognized Christ (Mark 1:23,24) and can possess non-Christians (Matt. 8:29).

demonized: To be under demonic influence (Greek daimonizomai). The term often suggests more extreme cases of demonic influence.

demons: Evil angels who sinned against God and who now continually work evil in the world.

Deontology: The study of moral obligation.

Depravity: Another term for inherited moral corruption, a state of corruption or sinfulness. Total depravity is the teaching that sin has touched all aspects of the human: body, soul, spirit, emotions, mind, etc.

design, argument by: One of the so-called proofs for the existence of God, which in reality is not a proof at all, but only evidence. Because the universe is complex and resembles a machine, and since machines clearly have an intelligent origin, the thought is that the universe too, should be assumed to be of intelligent origin.

detachment: The cultivation of a habit of mind in which the individual aims to abandon dependence upon worldly objects, passions, or concerns. This is not intended to imply that these worldly things are evil; rather, the point being made is that they have the ability to enslave individuals if they are not approached with the right attitude. Detachment is about fostering a sense of independence from the world, so that it may be enjoyed without becoming a barrier between the individual and God.

Determinism: The teaching that every event in the universe is caused and controlled by natural law; that there is no free will in humans and that all events are merely the result of natural and physical laws. The idea that acts, events, and decisions are the inevitable results of some condition or decision prior to them that is independent of the human will.

Devil: Greek is "diabolos," which means accuser. The greatest of all the fallen angels. He opposes God and is completely evil. He is often called Lucifer which is a Latin translation of "light bearer" found in Isaiah 14:12, and also the accuser of the brethren in (Rev. 12:10), dragon (Rev. 12:9), the devil (Matt. 4:1), the tempter (Matt. 4:3), the accuser (Rev. 12:10), the prince of demons (Luke 11:15), the ruler of this world (John 12:31), See Isaiah 14:12-15 for a description of the fall of the devil. Upon Jesus' return, the Devil will be vanquished -- depending on the eschatological position. His future is the eternal lake of fire.

Devotio Moderna: A school of thought which developed in the Netherlands in the fourteenth century, and is especially associated with Geert Groote (1340–84) and Thomas a` Kempis (1380–1471), which placed an emphasis on the imitation of the humanity of Christ. The Imitation of Christ is the best-known work emanating from this school.

Dialectic: The practice of examining ideas and beliefs using reason and logic. It is often accomplished by question and answer.

dialectical theology: A term used to refer to the early views of the Swiss theologian Karl Barth (1886–1968), which emphasized the tensions, paradoxes, and contradictions in the relationship between God and humanity and the absolute gulf fixed between the human and the divine.

Diatessaron text: The most prominent early Gospel harmony; created by Tatian, an early Christian Assyrian apologist and ascetic. Tatian sought to combine all the textual material he found in the four gospels (Matthew, Mark, Luke, and John) into a single coherent narrative of Jesus' life and death. However, unlike later gospel harmonists, the works were not aimed toward validating the four separate canonical gospel accounts; or to demonstrate that, as they stood, they could each be shown as being without inconsistency or error. Tatian's harmony follows the gospels closely in terms of text but he created his own narrative sequence, which is different from both the synoptic sequence and John's sequence; and occasionally creates intervening time periods that are found in none of the source accounts.

Dichotomy: The view or teaching that a human consists or is made up of two parts: body and soul. Sometimes the soul is also referred to as spirit. (See Trichotomy)

dictation: The idea that God expressly spoke every word of Scripture to the human authors.

Didactics: The branch of education dealing with teaching.

diocese: In Catholicism, an area of many parishes presided over by a bishop. In an episcopalian system of church government, the churches under the jurisdiction of a bishop.

Disciple: A pupil or follower of a religion, a person, or a movement. As Christians we are to be disciples of Jesus (Luke 14:26,27). We follow in the teaching and example of what He said and did. A disciple is a convert but not all converts are disciples. As disciples we are to bear our cross daily (Matt. 16:24). This means to live and die for Him if necessary (Matt. 16:25).

Dispensation: A period of time during which man is tested in respect of obedience to some specific revelation of the will of God. Dispensationalism says that God uses different means of administering His will and grace to His people. These different means coincide with different periods of time. There are seven dispensations: of innocence, of conscience, of civil government, of promise, of law, of grace, and of the kingdom. Dispensationalists interpret the scriptures in light of these (or other perceived) dispensations.

dispensational premillennialism: Another term for "pretribulational premillennialism." The term" dispensational" is used because most proponents of this view wish to maintain a clear distinction between the church and Israel, with whom God deals under different arrangements, or "dispensations."

dispensationalism: A theological system that began in the nineteenth century with the writings of J. N. Darby. Among the general doctrines of this system are the distinction between Israel and the church as two groups in God's overall plan, the pretribulational rapture of the church, a future literal fulfillment of Old Testament prophecies concerning Israel, and the dividing of biblical history into seven periods, or "dispensations," of God's ways of relating to his people.

distinguishing between spirits: A special ability to recognize the influence of the Holy Spirit or of demonic spirits in a person.

Divinity: The nature or quality of being God. It belongs to God alone. Jesus was divine in nature (Col. 2:9) as well as being a man.

Docetism: An early Christological heresy, which treated Jesus Christ as a purely divine being who only had the "appearance" of being human, not really a man but only seemed to be one (from the Greek verb dokeq"to seem, to appear to be"). Docetism was an error with several variations concerning the nature of Christ. Generally, it taught that Jesus only appeared to have a body, that he was not really incarnate, (Greek, "dokeo" = "to seem"). This error developed out of the dualistic philosophy which viewed matter as inherently evil, that God could not be associated with matter, and that God, being perfect and infinite, could not suffer.

Doctrine: set of accepted beliefs held by a group. In religion, it is the set of true beliefs that define the parameters of that belief system. Hence, there is true doctrine and false doctrine relative to each belief set. In Christianity, for example, a true biblical doctrine is that there is only one God in all existence (Isaiah 43:10; 44:6,8). A false doctrine is that there is more than one God in all existence.

Dogma: Another term for "doctrine" or a generally held set of formulated beliefs. The word is often used to refer more specifically to doctrines that have official church endorsement.

dogmatic theology: Another term for "systematic theology."

Donatism: A movement, centering upon Roman north Africa in the fourth century, which developed a rigid view of the church and sacraments. Donatism was the error taught by Donatus, bishop of Casae Nigrae that the effectiveness of the sacraments depends on the moral character of the minister. In other words, if a minister who was involved in a serious enough sin were to baptize a person, that baptism would be considered invalid.

Double Predestination: The belief that God predestines the elect to eternal life, and the rest are predestined to hell. God does this by actively hardening their hearts and preparing them for unbelief.

doxology: From the two Greek words [doxa] meaning glory, and [logos], meaning to speak. By implication the word logos can mean "word." These are the same Greek words found in your Bible that are translated "word" and "glory." So very literally, doxology means "words to glorify." A form of praise, usually especially associated with formal Christian worship. A "doxological" approach to theology stresses the importance of praise and worship in theological reflection.

Dualism: In theology, the concept that the world is controlled by two independent and opposing forces, i.e., good and bad, God and Satan in continual conflict. In Philosophy the idea that the world consists of two main components: thought and matter. The idea that both God and the material universe have eternally existed side by side as two ultimate forces in the universe. It implies that there is an eternal conflict between God and the evil aspects of the material universe. This theory is considered heresy by some because it denies the Omniscience and Sovereignty of God, over all things.

E

Eastern Orthodox: officially the Orthodox Catholic Church, also referred to as the Orthodox Church and Orthodoxy, is the second largest Christian Church in the world, with an estimated 225–300 million adherents.

Ebionitism: An early Christological heresy, which treated Jesus Christ as a purely human figure, although recognizing that he was endowed with particular charismatic gifts which distinguished him from other humans.

Ecclesiology: The study of the Christian church, its structure, order, practices, and hierarchy. The study of the nature and mission of the church. The word Ecclesiology comes from two Greek words meaning "assembly" and "word" - combining to mean "the study of the church." The church is the assembly of believers who belong to God. Ecclesiology is crucial to understand God's purpose for believers in the world today.

Ecumenicalism: (also ecumenical, ecumenicity, ecumenism) From the Latin [ecumenicus] meaning universal or of the whole. In theological terms it means promoting a universal or united Church. Any movement which fosters Christian unity or encourages cooperation between different faiths, denominations or churches, is called ecumenical. It is the beliefs or practices of those who want worldwide unity or cooperation between Churches.

Egalitarian Doctrine: Holds that all of mankind is equal, or that everyone (including men and women) are to be looked upon as equals. In some Theological circles Egalitarianism is also used to identify the doctrine of those who promote wealth redistribution or economic equality.

Edify: To build up. In the Christian context it means to strengthen someone, or be strengthened, in relationship to God, the Christian walk, and holiness. As Christians, we are to "let all things be done for edification" (1 Cor. 14:26). We are edified by the Word of God (Acts 20:32) and by love (1 Cor. 8:1). (See also Rom. 14:19; Eph. 4:29 and 1 Cor. 3:1-4; James 4:1-6).

effective calling: An act of God the Father, speaking through the human proclamation of the gospel, in which he summons people to himself in such a way that they respond in saving faith.

Efficacy: Producing a result. Christ's atonement was efficacious; it produced the result of forgiveness of sins for the elect. The atonement is efficacious grace in action.

Eisegesis: From the Greek [eicegesis] meaning 'a bringing in.' It's root is from the two Greek words [eis], meaning 'into,' and [hegeisthai], meaning 'to lead.' i.e., to lead into. In Christian Theology, by implication, it means the interpretation of a text by reading extraneous ideas into it. Eisegesis is when a person interprets and reads information into the text that is not there. An example would be in viewing 1 Cor. 8:5 which says, "For though there be that are called gods, whether in heaven or in earth, (as there be gods many, and lords many," (kjv). With this verse, Mormons, for example, bring their preconceived idea of the existence of many gods to this text and assert that it says there are many gods. But that is not what it says. It says that there are many that are called gods. Being called a god doesn't make it a god. Therefore, the text does not teach what the Mormons say and they are guilty of eisegesis; that is, reading into the text what it does not say. See also exegesis.

ekklesiai: Greek term translated "church" in the New Testament. The word literally means "assembly" and in the Bible indicates the assembly or congregation of the people of God.

elder: The main governing group in a church in the New Testament (Greek presbyteros).

election: The elect are those called by God to salvation. This election occurs before the foundation of the world (Eph. 1:4) and is according to God's will not man's (Rom. 8:29-30; 9:6-23) because God is sovereign (Rom. 9:11-16). The view of election is especially held by Calvinists who also hold to the doctrine of predestination. An act of God before creation in which he chooses some people to be saved, not on account of any foreseen merit in them, but only because of his sovereign good pleasure.

electromagnetism: One of the four fundamental forces in nature. Electricity and magnetism are two aspects of one force. Electric currents running along a wire produce magnetic forces, as in an electromagnet, and rotating magnets around a wire produce electricity.

Empiricism: The proposition that the only source of true knowledge is experience. It is the search for knowledge through experiment and observation. Denial that knowledge can be obtained a priori.

empowerment for service: A primary aspect of the work of the Holy Spirit to bring evidence of God's presence and to bless.

Enlightenment: A term used since the nineteenth century to refer to the emphasis upon human reason and autonomy, characteristic of much of western European and North American thought during the eighteenth century.

episcopalian government: A hierarchical form of church government in which bishops have governing authority over groups of churches (from the Greek episkopos, "overseer," "bishop").

Epistemology: The branch of philosophy that deals with the area of knowledge, its source, criteria, kinds, and the relationship between what is known and the one who is knowing it.

equality in personhood: The idea that men and women are created equally in God's image and therefore are equally important to God and equally valuable to him.

Eschatology: The study of the teachings in the Bible concerning the end times, last days, last things, or of the period of time dealing with the return of Christ and the events that follow. It is about what the Bible says is going to happen in the end times especially the ideas of resurrection, hell, the Last Judgment, and eternal life. Therefore the study of future events that will happen to individuals, such as death, the intermediate state, and glorification. Many treat Eschatology as an area of theology to be avoided. Eschatological subjects include the Resurrection, Resurrection, the Rapture, the Tribulation, the Millennium, the Binding of Satan, the Three witnesses, the Final Judgment, Armageddon, and The New Heavens and the New Earth. In the New Testament, eschatological chapters include Matt. 24, Mark 13, Luke 17, and 2 Thess. 2. In one form or another most of the books of the Bible deal with end times subjects. But some that are more prominently eschatological are Daniel, Ezekiel, Isaiah, Joel, Zechariah, Matthew, Mark, Luke, 2 Thessalonians, and of course Revelation. (See Amillennialism and Premillennialism for more information on views on the millennium.)

eternal conscious punishment: A description of the nature of punishment in hell, which will be unending and of which the unbeliever will be fully aware.

Eternal Security: The doctrine that salvation cannot be lost. Another term for "perseverance of the saints." However, this term can be misunderstood to mean that all who have once made a profession of faith are "eternally secure" in their salvation when they may not have been genuinely converted at all.   Since it is not gained by anything we do, it cannot be lost by anything we do. This does not mean that we can sin all we want (Rom. 6:1-2) because we have been freed from sin and are set apart for holy use (1 Thess. 4:7).

Eternal life: Life everlasting in the presence of God. "This is eternal life, that they may know Thee the only true God, and Jesus Christ, whom Thou has sent" (John 17:3). There are two senses in which this is used. First, as Christians we possess eternal life (1 John 5:13), yet we are not in heaven or in the immediate presence of God. Though we are still in mortal bodies and we still sin, by faith we are saved (Rom. 4:5; Eph. 2:8-9) and possess eternal life as a free gift from God (Rom. 6:23). Second, eternal life will reach its final state at the resurrection of the believers when Christ returns to earth to claim His church. It is then that eternal life will begin in its complete manifestation. We will no longer sin.

eternity: When used of God, the doctrine that God has no beginning, end, or succession of moments in his own being, and he sees all time equally vividly, yet God sees events in time and acts in time.

Ethics: See "Christian ethics." The study of right and wrong and wrong, good and bad, moral judgment, etc.

Eucharist: Another term for the Lord's Supper (from the Greek eucharistia, "giving of thanks").The elements of the communion supper in Christian Churches where the bread and wine are consumed as a representation the sacrifice of Christ. They correspond, representatively, as the body and blood of Christ. The term used in the present volume to refer to the sacrament variously known as "the mass," "the Lord's Supper," and "holy communion."

Eutychianism: Another term for monophysitism, named after the fifth-century monk Eutyches. It states that Christ's natures were so thoroughly combined -- in a sense scrambled together -- that the result was that Christ was not really truly able to relate to us as humans. The problem is this implies that Jesus was not truly God nor man.

Therefore, He would be unable to act as mediator and unable to truly atone for our sins. (See Hypostatic Union, which is the correct view of Christ's two natures, and also Nestorianism and Monophycitism which are the incorrect views of Christ's two natures.)

evangelical: A term initially used to refer to reforming movements, especially in Germany and Switzerland, in the 1510s and 1520s, but now used of a movement, especially in English language theology, which places especial emphasis upon the supreme authority of Scripture and the atoning death of Christ.

evangelism: The proclamation of the gospel to unbelievers (from the Greek euangelizd "to announce good news").

Evil: Moral rebellion against God. It is contrary to the will of God. There is natural evil (floods, storms, famines, etc.) and moral evil (adultery, murder, idolatry, etc.). Natural evil is a result of moral evil. Adam's sin resulted in sin entering the world allowing floods, storms, famines, etc. Evil originated with Satan (Isaiah 14:12-15) and is carried on by man (Matt. 15:18-19). (See Theodicy.)

Evolution: Process by which all existing organisms have developed from earlier forms through modification of characteristics in successive generations. Though you might not expect to find the subject of evolution in a dictionary of theology, it is appropriate if you consider that the theory of evolution requires faith. The evidence for evolution is actually quite weak. There are numerous difficulties facing it and, the theory has undergone many changes since its inception in the 1800's. It is the theory that over an incredible duration of time, life developed from random combinations of non-organic materials. This life was improved upon through mutations and the process of natural selection. The Scriptures do not speak about evolution but instead negate the theory by stating that God created all things (Gen. 1).

ex nihilo: A Latin phrase meaning "out of nothing," referring to God's creation of the universe without the use of any previously existing materials.

exaltation of Christ: One of the two "states" of Christ, the other being humiliation. The state of exaltation includes four aspects of his work: his resurrection, ascension into heaven, session at the right hand of God, and return in glory and power.

Excommunication: The final step of church discipline in which a person is put out of the fellowship, or "communion," of the church. The act of discipline where the Church breaks fellowship with a member who has refused to repent of sins. Matt. 18 is generally used as the model of procedures leading up to excommunication. Those excommunicated are not to partake in the Lord's supper. In the Bible, serious offends of God's law, who were supposed to be Christian, were "delivered over to Satan for the destruction of the flesh" (1 Cor. 15:5; 1 Tim. 1:20). However, upon repentance, the person is welcomed back into fellowship within the body of Christ.

Exegesis: From the Greek [exegsis] meaning 'lead out of.' It's root is from the two Greek words [ex], meaning 'out,' and [hegeisthai], meaning 'to lead.' In Christian theology, by implication, this term means gleaning a explanation from "out of" the pertinent text of scripture (as opposed to Eisegesis). It is the critical analysis and defense of an understanding of a text of scripture by getting the interpretation from 'out of' the scripture itself. The process of interpreting a text of Scripture; Exegesis is when a person interprets a text based solely on what it says. That is, he extracts out of the text what is there as opposed to reading into it what is not there (Eisegesis). There are rules to proper exegesis: read the immediate context, related themes, word definitions, etc., that all play a part in properly understand what something does say and not what it does not say. The science of textual interpretation, usually referring specifically to the Bible. The term "biblical exegesis" basically means "the process of interpreting the Bible." The specific techniques employed in the exegesis of Scripture are usually referred to as "hermeneutics."

exemplarism: A particular approach to the atonement, which stresses the moral or religious example set to believers by Jesus Christ. fathers An alternative term for "patristic writers."

Existentialism: A philosophical viewpoint that emphasis human freedom and abilities. Therefore, subjectivity and individual choice are elevated often above conceptual and moral absolutes.

exorcism: The action of driving out an evil spirit by a spoken command.

Expiation: The cancellation of sin. Expiation and propitiation are similar but expiation does not carry the implication of dealing with wrath, of appeasing it through a sacrifice. Generally speaking, propitiation cancels sin and deals with God's wrath. Expiation is simply the cancellation of sin. Jesus was our propitiation (1 John 2:2; 4:10 -- "atoning sacrifice" in the NIV).

external calling: The general gospel invitation offered to all people that comes through human proclamation of the gospel. Also referred to as "general calling" or "the gospel call," this call can be rejected by people.

extreme unction: One of the seven sacraments in Roman Catholic teaching, the anointing with oil that is administered to a dying person (also known as "last rites").

faith and practice: A term used by some people who, denying the inerrancy of the Bible, claim that the Bible's purpose is only to tell us about these two subjects. "Now faith is the assurance of things hoped for, the conviction of things not seen" (Heb. 11:1). It is synonymous with trust. It is a divine gift (Rom. 12:3) and comes by hearing the Word of God (Rom. 10:17). It is the means by which the grace of God is accounted to the believer who trusts in the work of Jesus on the cross (Eph. 2:8). Without faith it is impossible to please God (Heb. 11:6). It is by faith that we live our lives, "The righteous shall live by faith" (Hab. 2:4; Rom. 1:17). Trust or dependence on God based on the fact that we take him at his word and believe what he has said. (See also "saving faith.")

faithfulness: The doctrine that God will always do what he has said and fulfill what he has promised.

Fall, The: The fall is that event in the Garden of Eden where Adam and Eve disobeyed the command of God and ate of The Tree of the Knowledge of Good and Evil (Gen. 2 and 3). Since Adam represented all of mankind, when He sinned, all of mankind fell with Him (Rom. 5:12).

fallacy: A logically unsound argument.

False Prophet, (The): The second beast of Revelation (Rev. 13:11-18). He is a person who will manifest himself near the culmination of this epoch shortly before the physical return of Christ. He will be a miracle worker and during the Tribulation period will bring fire down from heaven and command that people worship the image of the Beast (Rev. 11:15). See also (13:16-17). Jesus warned about false prophets in Matt. 24:24

stating that in the last days many false prophets would arise and deceive, if possible, even the elect. False prophets teach false doctrine and lead people away from the true gospel message and teaching of God found in the Bible. Examples of modern day false prophets are Joseph Smith (Mormonism), Charles Taze Russell (Jehovah's Witnesses), Mary Baker Eddy (Christian Science), etc. Each of them distorts the truth sufficient to cause damnation.

Falsifiability: The ability of something to be proven false. A non falsifiable statement would be, "There is a green lizard sitting in a rocking chair on the fourth largest moon of Jupiter." This statement is not falsifiable in that it cannot be proven false because it cannot be verified or denied. Jesus' resurrection was falsifiable in that all the critics had to do was produce the body, but they did not. Falsifiability, generally, is a test of the validity of a belief or occurrence. Something that is not falsifiable can be said to be untrue since it cannot be confirmed or denied.

Fast, Fasting: The discipline of abstaining for a time from all or certain foods. In the Bible, fasting often accompanies prayer for the purpose of intensive intercession, repentance, worship, or the seeking of guidance. Depriving oneself of food for a period of time for a specific purpose, often spiritual. It is the "weakening" of the body in order to "strengthen" the spirit. It is interesting to note that sin entered the world through the disobedience of eating (Gen. 3:6). We are called to fast in the N.T. (Matt. 6:16). (See also 1 Kings 21:27; Psalm 35:13; Acts 13:3; 2 Cor. 6:5).

Fatalism: A system in which human choices and human decisions make no real difference because things will turn out as they have been previously ordained. This is in contrast to the doctrine of election, in which people make real choices that have real consequences and for which they will be held accountable. The idea that all things are predetermined to occur and that there is no ability of the person to alter the predetermined plan of God in any event. This is not the correct biblical view. The Bible teaches us that we can influence God with our prayers (James 5:16). How this influence is worked out by God who knows all things from eternity is something apparently unexplainable in Christianity.

Fellowship: There is no specific definition given in the N.T. But we are called into fellowship with one another (1 John 1:3, with Jesus (1 Cor. 1:9), with the Father (1 John 1:3), and with the Holy Spirit (2 Cor. 13:14). Fellowship implies sharing common interests, desires, and motivations. Fellowship requires that time be spent with another communicating, caring, etc. It carries with it a hint of intimacy. As Christians we fellowship with one another because of our position in Christ, because we are all redeemed and share an intimate personal knowledge of Jesus. We share a common belief (Acts 2:42), hope (Heb. 11:39-40), and need (2 Cor. 8:1-15). The Greek word for fellowship is koinonia. This word is also translated communion in 1 Cor. 10:16 in the KJV. This is where we get the term the communion supper.

Fideism: An understanding of Christian theology which refuses to accept the need for (or sometimes the possibility of) criticism or evaluation from sources outside the Christian faith itself; the position that religious doctrines rest not on reason, but only on faith.

Filioque: A Latin phrase, literally meaning "and from the Son," found in western versions of the Nicene Creed. On this view, the Holy Spirit originates and proceeds from both the Father and the Son, rather than (as in the Eastern church) from the Father alone. The phrase had its origins at the third council of Toledo (589). By the ninth century, it was regularly in use within the western church. After the 1054 schism, it became one of the major theological points of difference between the Orthodox and

Catholic churches, and a subject of intense debate and polemic on both sides. The doctrine that the Holy Spirit proceeds equally from both the Father and the Son.

filled with the Holy Spirit: An event subsequent to conversion in which a believer experiences a fresh infilling with the Holy Spirit that may result in a variety of consequences, including greater love for God, greater victory over sin, greater power for ministry, and sometimes the receiving of new spiritual gifts.

final judgment: The last and ultimate proclamation by Jesus Christ of the eternal destinies of all people which will take place after the millennium and the rebellion that occurs at the end of it

first cause argument: One of the so-called proofs for the existence of God, which in reality is not a proof at all, but only evidence. The argument proceeds as follows: All effects have a cause. The universe is an effect. Therefore the universe has a cause. That cause must be God.

Firstborn: The first of the mother's offspring. It stands figuratively for that which is most excellent. The firstborn male of the family carried certain familial rites and privileges (Gen. 27:1-29; 48:13-14) and was given a double portion of the inheritance (Deut. 21:17). The term is also applied to Christ as the pre-eminent one and the first one raised from the dead (Col. 1:15,18). It does not mean first created as Jehovah's Witnesses believe. In fact, the firstborn rites were transferable. Compare Jer. 31:9 with Gen. 41:50-52.

firstfruits: The first portion of a ripening harvest (Greek aparchei. In describing Christ in his resurrection as the "firstfruits" (1 Cor. 15 :20), the Bible indicates that our resurrection bodies will be like his when God raises us from the dead.

Five Ways, The: A standard term for the five "arguments for the existence of God" associated with Thomas Aquinas.

Fool: Hater of God. One who is morally weak, who misuses what God has given him for selfish purposes. He is lustful (Prov. 7:22), lazy (Ecc. 10:15), does not fear God (Prov. 14:1), hates knowledge (Prov. 1:22), and is self-righteous (Prov. 12:15). As Christians, we are to avoid foolishness (Eph. 5:4). (See Ecc. 7:25; Prov. 3:35, 10:8.)

Foreknowledge: It is God's knowledge about things that will happen. Past, present, and future are all "present" in the mind of God. He inhabits eternity (Isaiah 57:15). God has infinite knowledge (Isaiah 41:22,23) and knows all things in advance. In the N.T. it does not always mean "to know beforehand" but also to cause to be. See 1 Pet. 1:2,20. Relating to the doctrine of election, the persona!, relational knowledge by which God thought of certain people in a saving relationship to himself before creation.

forensic: A term that means "having to do with legal proceedings." This term is used to describe justification as being a legal declaration by God that in itself does not change our internal nature or character.

Forgiveness: There are seven words in Scripture that denote the idea of forgiveness: three in Hebrew and four in Greek. No book of religion except Christianity teaches that God completely forgives sins. God remembers our sins no more (Heb. 10:17). God is the initiator of forgiveness (Col. 2:13).

There is only one sin for which the Father does not promise forgiveness: blasphemy against the Holy Spirit (Mark 3:28; Matt. 12:32). The contexts suggest this to be the sin of attributing to unclean spirits the work of the Holy Spirit. For man to receive forgiveness, repentance is necessary (Luke 17:3-4). For the holy God to extend forgiveness, the shedding of blood is necessary (Heb. 9:22; Lev. 17:11). Forgiveness is based upon the sacrifice of Christ on the cross.

Fourth Gospel: A term used to refer to the Gospel according to John. The term highlights the distinctive literary and theological character of this gospel, which sets it apart from the common structures of the first three gospels, usually known as the "Synoptic Gospels."

Free Knowledge: The free act of God's will where, after His free act of creation, He knows all things that are going to happen and that this knowledge is contingent upon His free creative will. Therefore, the free knowledge of God would be different if He had chosen a different creative fiat. In other words, because God created one possible existence instead of another, the range of His knowledge regarding actual existence would have been different had He created something different in the first place. (See also Natural knowledge and Middle Knowledge.)

Free will: Freedom of self determination and action independent of external causes. All things that God decided to will but had no necessity to will other people define this in other ways, including the ability to make choices that are not determined by God).

Freethinker: A person who forms his opinions about religion and God without regard to revelation, scripture, tradition, or experience.

fundamentalism: A form of American Protestant Christianity, originating in America, which lays especial emphasis upon the authority of an inerrant Bible.

#

galaxy: A system of stars, their planetary systems (if any) dust, and gas held together by gravitation. They come in various shapes, and typically contain billions of stars and are thousands of lightyears across. There are billions of galaxies in the universe. The Milky Way is the galaxy in which our solar system is located. The Milky Way has a spiral shape, and our solar system is located in one of the spiral arms. The Milky Way contains approximately 100 billion stars and is about a hundred thousand light years across. It takes the Milky Way about 200 million years to rotate once on its axis, even though it is rotating at about 600,000 miles per hour (260 kilometers per second).

Gametria: a Kabbalistic method of interpreting the Hebrew scriptures by computing the numerical value of words, based on those of their constituent letters.

gap theory: The idea that between Genesis 1:1 and 1:2 is a gap of millions of years during which; God judged an earlier creation, making it "without form and void" and necessitating a second creation depicted in Genesis 1:3 -2:3.

Gehenna: Originally, a location southwest of Jerusalem where children were burned as sacrifices to the god Molech. It later became a garbage dump with an continuous burning of trash. Therefore, it was used biblically, to illustrate the abode of the damned in Christian and Jewish theology. Gehenna is mentioned in Mark 9:43ff and Matt. 10:28 as the place of punishment of unquenchable fire where both the body and soul of the wicked go after death. It is apparently the future abode of Satan and his angels (Matt. 25:41).

general assembly: In a presbyterian form of church government, the term for the national (or regional) governing body.

general eschatology: The study of future events that will affect the entire universe, such as the second coming of Christ, the millennium, and the final judgment.

general redemption: Another term for "unlimited atonement."

general revelation: The knowledge of God's existence, character, and moral law that comes through creation to all humanity.

Gentile: Those who are not Jews. Gentiles were used by God to punish apostate Judea (Deut. 28:49; 1 Kings 8:33) and often included in blessings by God upon the Jewish people. "Gentiles" is often used biblically in reference to nations.

geocentric: Sometimes called the Ptolemaic theory, it was commonly believed before Copernicus that the Earth was the center of the universe, and that the sun, moon, planets, and stars all revolved around the Earth.

gifts of the Holy Spirit: All abilities that are empowered by the Holy Spirit and used in any ministry of the church.

Gifts, Spiritual Gifts: Spiritual abilities given by God for the purpose of building up the church. Every Christian has at least one (1 Cor. 7:7). They are listed and discussed in different places in the N.T. (Rom. 12:6-8; 1 Cor. 12:4-11, 28-30; Eph. 4:7-12). Following is a list of the gifts arranged in two groups. The first are gifts that require supernatural intervention and are possessed only by true Christians. The second are gifts that do not require supernatural intervention. Even non-Christians can have the second group of gifts. A further issue is whether or not the gifts are still in use today. Some believe they ceased with the apostles and the closing of the Canon (the completion of the writings of the Bible) and they are no longer needed for the building up of the body of Christ (Eph. 4:12). Others believe the gifts are still in use but not in the pure apostolic sense. In other words, they are still in use but not in the same way possessed by the apostles. Instead, they are available to the believer if and when God decides it is beneficial to use them.

glorification: The final step in the application of redemption. It will happen when Christ returns and raises from the dead the bodies of all believers for all time who have died, and reunites them with their souls, and changes the bodies of all believers who remain alive, thereby givingall believers at the same time perfect resurrection bodies like his own.

glory: The created brightness that surrounds God's revelation of himself. In another sense of the term, it refers to God's honor.

Gnosticism: From the Greek [gnosis], meaning knowing or knowledge, and implies a esoteric knowledge of higher things. It is not a system, but more a school of thought, or philosophical ideas which are generally related to mystery religions. In first 3 centuries A.D., many different groups believed men (Gnostics) were saved through this transcendental higher knowledge, which came not through God, but through self awareness and understanding. Basically, salvation by knowledge. A theological error prevalent around the time of Christ. Generally speaking, Gnosticism taught that salvation is achieved through special knowledge (gnosis). This knowledge usually dealt with the individual's relationship to the transcendent Being. It denies the incarnation of God as the Son. In so doing, it denies the true efficacy of the atonement since, if Jesus is not God, He could not atone for all of mankind and we would still be lost in our sins. One of the most dangerous influences of Greek thought on Christianity concerned Greek beliefs about the physical and the spiritual realms. Greek philosophy taught that the earth was created not by the Most High God, but by an underling, several levels below, who imbued the physical nature of his creation with imperfection. The physical was seen as evil. Only the spirit was good. These beliefs manifested in several ways. If the physical is evil, then Jesus cannot be fully man and fully God; He either only appears to be physical, or He cannot be the Son of God. Similarly, if the physical is evil, there is no resurrection from the dead. Instead, "salvation" is reuniting in spirit with the High God.

God: The supreme being of the universe. He is the creator of all things (Isaiah 44:24). He alone is God (Isaiah 45:21,22; 46:9; 47:8). There have never been any Gods before Him nor will there be any after Him (Isaiah 43:10). God is God from all eternity (Psalm 90:2). In Exodus 3:14, God revealed His name to His people. The name commonly known in English is Jehovah. This comes from the four Hebrew consonants that spell the name of God. (See Tetragrammaton.) God is a Trinity, knows all things (1 John 3:20), can do all things (Jer. 32:17,27 - except those things against His nature like lie, break His word, cheat, steal, etc.), and is everywhere all the time (Psalm 119:7-12). In the New Testament, a translation of the Greek word theos, which is usually, but not always, used to refer to God the Father.

God-breathed: A translation of the Greek theopneustos (sometimes translated "inspired by God"), which the Bible (2 Tim. 3:16) uses metaphorically to describe the words of Scripture as being spoken by God.

Gods, False: Gods that are not real, but invented by men or inspired by demons the purpose of which is to deceive people so they do not believe in the true and living God. Some of the false gods listed in the Bible are Adrammelech and Anammelech (2 Kings 17:31), Asherah (1 Kings 15:13; 18:19), Ashtoreth (1 Kings 11:5,33), Baal (1 Kings 14:23; 2 Kings 23:7), Baalzebub (2 Kings 1:1-16); Luke 11:19-23), Dagon (Judges 16:23-30), Molech/Moloch (Lev. 18:21; 20:1-5), Rimmon (2 Kings 5:18, and Tammuz (Ezekiel 8:14).

gospel call: The general gospel invitation to all people that comes through human proclamation of the gospel. Also referred to as "external calling."The Gospel is the good news that we have forgiveness of sins though Jesus. Specifically, the gospel is defined by Paul in 1 Cor. 15:1-4: "Now I make known to you, brethren, the gospel which I preached to you, which also you received, in which also you stand, by which also you are saved, if you hold fast the word which I preached to you, unless you believed in vain. For I delivered to you as of first importance what I also received, that Christ died for our sins according to the Scriptures, and that He was buried, and that He was raised on the third day according to the Scriptures." The gospel comes from God (Gal. 1:10-12), is the power of God for salvation (Rom. 1:16), is a mystery (Eph. 6:19), and is a source of hope (Col. 1:23), faith (Acts 15:7), life (1 Cor. 4:15), and peace (Eph. 6:15).

government: An aspect of God's providence that indicates that God has a purpose in all that he does in the world and providentially governs or directs all things in order that they accomplish his purposes.

governmental theory of Atonement: The theory that Christ's death was not a payment for our sins but God's demonstration of the fact that, since he is the moral governor of the universe, some kind of penalty must be paid whenever his laws are broken ; Christ's death was a "nominal" substitute for the penalty of sin of man, which God graciously chose to accept, thereby upholding his moral government.

Grace: Unmerited favor; God's goodness toward those who deserve only punishment. It is God's free action for the benefit of His people. It is different than Justice and Mercy. Justice is getting what we deserve. Mercy is not getting what we deserve. Grace is getting what we do not deserve. In grace we get eternal life, something that, quite obviously, we do not deserve. But because of God's love and kindness manifested in Jesus on the Cross, we receive the great blessing of redemption. Grace rules out all human merit. It is the product of God, that is given by God, because of who He is not because of who we are. It is the means of our salvation (Eph. 2:8-9). We are no longer under the Law, but under grace (Rom. 6:14). (See 1 Cor. 15:11; Rom. 5:2, 15-20; 2 Cor. 12:9; and 2 Cor. 9:8).

gravity: One of the four fundamental forces of nature, it is the force that cause objects to move or tend to move toward the center of the earth, moon, or any planet. A writer in the New Yorker put it this way: "What is gravity? To begin with, let's simply call it a force that every mass in the universe exerts on every other mass in the universe."

Great Commission: The final commands 00 esus to the disciples, recorded in Matthew 28:18-20.

great tribulation: An expression from Matthew 24:21 referring to a period of great hardship and suffering prior to the return of Christ.

Greek: The primary language used in the Roman Empire during the time of Jesus Christ, it was used by the authors of the New Testament. About 200 BC the Old Testament had been translated into Greek, a translation called the Septuagint.

Guilt: Being responsible for and accountable for an offense. Biblically, it is the state of being under a present or pending consequence due to a sin against God's Law. It is also an emotional state as well as legal condition. Guilt feelings are used by the Holy Spirit to inform the sinner of broken fellowship with God (Isaiah 59:2; John 16:8). Because of our guilt before God, we need reconciliation (Rom. 5:6-9).

H

Hades: New Testament term for the Hebrew "sheol," which is the abode of the conscious dead. It is apparently a place (Acts 2:31). In Revelation it is referred to as a creature on a horse (Rev. 6:8). In Rev. 1:18, it says that Christ holds the keys to death and Hades.

Hamartiology: The study of the doctrine of sin, the nature and its effects. Hamartiology deals with how sin originated, how it affects humanity, and what it will result in after death. To sin essentially means to "miss the mark." We all miss God's mark of righteousness (Romans 3:23). Hamartiology, then, explains why we miss the mark, how we miss the mark, and the consequences of missing the mark. These are some important questions in Hamartiology.

healing: A gift of the Holy Spirit that functions to bring a restoration to health as a foretaste God's mercy; infirmity that Christ purchased for us by God most fully reveals his glory, and where angels, other heavenly creatures, and redeemed saints all worship him.

Heaven: Heaven is the dwelling place of God and for those who go there a place of everlasting bliss. Scripture implies three heavens, since "the third heaven" is revealed to exist (2 Cor. 12:2). It is logical that a third heaven cannot exist without a first and second. Scripture does not describe specifically the first and second heaven. The first, however, apparently refers to the atmospheric heavens of the fowl (Hosea 2:18) and clouds (Dan. 7:13). The second heaven may be the area of the stars and planets (Gen. 1:14-18). It is the abode of all supernatural angelic beings. The third heaven is the abode of the triune God. Its location is unrevealed. (See Matt. 23:34-37; Luke 10:20; and Rev. 22:2, 20-27).

Hebraica Veritas: Referred to as Jerome's truth of the Hebrew (Veritas Hebraica) doctrine. The superior one in the interpretation of the Old Testament. In the Middle Ages, the expression referred to the Latin translation of the Bible by St. Jerome (Vulgate). Following Jerome's Veritas Hebraica (truth of the Hebrew) doctrine, the Protestant Old Testament consists of the same books as the Hebrew Bible, but the order and division of the books are different. Protestants number the Old Testament books at 39, while Judaism numbers the same books as 24. Judaism considers Samuel, Kings, and Chronicles to form one book each, groups the 12 minor prophets into one book, and also considers Ezra and Nehemiah a single book. Also, the Bible for Judaism is specifically the Masoretic Text. Protestant translations of the Hebrew Bible often include other texts, such as the Septuagint.

Hebrew: A northwest Semitic language used by the people of Israel, used by most of the writers of the Old Testament (except for part of Daniel and Ezra).

Hedonism: The teaching that pleasure is the principle good and proper goal of all action. Self indulgence.

heliocentric: Baker, Astronomy writes "The heliocentric view, dating formally from the time of Copernicus, establishes the solar system on an approximately correct basis." That is, the Sun is the center of the solar system, around which the Earth and other planets revolve.

Hell: A place of eternal conscious punishment for the wicked.; the future place of eternal punishment of the damned including the devil and his fallen angels. There are several words rendered as Hell: Hades - A Greek word. It is the place of the dead, the location of the person between death and resurrection. (See Matt. 11:23; 16:18; Acts 11:27; 1 Cor. 15:55; Rev. 1:18; 6:8). Gehenna - A Greek word. It was the place where dead bodies were dumped and burned (2 Kings 23:13-14). Jesus used the word to designate the place of eternal torment (Matt. 5:22,29,30; Mark 9:43; Luke 12:5). Sheol - A Hebrew word. It is the place of the dead, not necessarily the grave, but the place the dead go to. It is used of both the righteous (Psalm 16:10; 30:3; Isaiah 38:10) and the wicked (Num. 16:33; Job. 24:19; Psalm 9:17). A place of eternal fire (Matt. 25:41; Rev. 19:20). It was prepared for the devil and his angels (Matt. 25:41) and will be the abode of the wicked (Rev. 22:8) and the fallen angels (2 Pet. 2:4).

Hellenism: term used to describe the influence of Greek culture on the people the Greek and Roman Empires interacted with conquered. The Jews tried to protect their national identity by following the law closely after their exile. This led to the rise of the hyper-conservative Pharisees and their added, unnecessary laws. About one hundred years after the Jews returned, Alexander the Great swept across western Asia, increasing his territory, down into Egypt, and east to the border of India. The influence of the Greek culture continued past the first century B.C., when the Roman Empire took control of Palestine. The Pharisees' rival sect, the Sadducees (wealthy, powerful Jewish aristocrats), welcomed the Greek influence and worked openly with these Gentile rulers to maintain peace and ensure a measure of political clout. All Jews were influenced by the Greek language. The Jewish leadership changed from a God-ordained priesthood to the Sadducee-controlled Sanhedrin, and the law of the land more closely reflected Grecian laws than those given through Moses. Some changed their names (i.e., Saul took the name Paul). Hellenism had a great influence whether direct or indirect (i.e., safe roads for the missionaries; theological synergism). Greek culture exerted influence on the spread, language, and culture of Christianity, and even spawned unbiblical cults but did not affect the orthodox theology. Hellenism did not infiltrate the Christian belief of monotheism, but it did reject it, and Christians (and Jews) paid a heavy price for their faithfulness.

Henotheism: The teaching that there are many gods but that only one of them must be honored and worshipped.

Heptadic structure: The recurrence of the number seven, or an exact multiple of seven, is found throughout the Bible and is widely recognized.

Heresy: from the Greek [hairesis] meaning, choose, and by extension in Theological terms, "doctrines of men who have chosen to follow their own views." In general, heresy is a self-chosen doctrine not emanating from God's word. Any doctrine or teaching which is contradictory to established Church doctrine based on the Holy Bible is called a heresy. A doctrinal view that deviates from the truth, a false teaching. We are warned against it in Acts 20:29-32 and Phil. 3:2. Heresies include teachings that Jesus is not God and that the Holy Spirit is not a person (Jehovah's Witnesses, Christadelphians, The Way International), that men may become gods (Mormonism), that there is more than one God (Mormonism), that Jesus lost His divinity in hell and finished the atonement there, and that good works are necessary for salvation (all cults say this), to name a few.

hermeneutics: From the Greek [hermeneutikos], which is derived from the name of the Greek god Hermes (the Roman god mercury also stems from hermes), who was said to be the interpreter and messenger of the gods. In Christianity, hermeneutics means the science or art of the structured biblical exegesis of scripture, and usually denotes certain principles or rules by which sound interpretation is measured. The study of correct methods of interpreting texts. The art or skill or theory of interpretation: the method of coming to an understanding of a text. The principles underlying the interpretation, or exegesis, of a text, particularly of Scripture, and particularly in relation to its present-day application.

Herodotus: A Greek historian (484?-425? BC) who was the author of The Histories.

Heterodoxy: See Orthodoxy. A set of beliefs or opinions that are not in agreement with accepted doctrinal beliefs of a church.

Hexaplaric: A set of beliefs or opinions that are not in agreement with accepted doctrinal beliefs of a church. of or relating to the edition of the Old Testament compiled by Origen in the 3d century a.d. and consisting of the Hebrew text, a transliteration in Greek, and the Greek versions of Aquila, Symmachus, the Septuagint, and Theodotion.

hierarchical government: Another term for an episcopalian form of church government in which final decision-making authority lies outside the local church.

historic premillennialism: The view that Christ will return to the earth after a period of great tribulation and then establish a millennial kingdom. At this time believers who have died will be raised from the dead and believers who are alive will receive glorified resurrection bodies, and both will reign with Christ on earth for a thousand years.

historical Jesus: term used, especially during the nineteenth century, to refer to the historical person of Jesus of Nazareth, as opposed to the Christian interpretation of that person, especially as presented in the New Testament and the creeds.

historical theology: The historical study of how Christians in different periods have understood various theological topics.

historical-grammatical interpretation: Sometimes mistakenly called the "literal" approach. Walter E. Kaiser, Jr. wrote: "The grand object of grammatical and historical interpretation is to ascertain...the specific usage of words as employed by an individual writer and/or as prevalent in a particular age. And the most fundamental principle in grammatico-historical exposition is that words and sentences can have only one signification in one and the same connection.

historico-critical method: An approach to historical texts, including the Bible, which argues that their proper meaning must be determined on the basis of the specific historical conditions under which they were written.

history of redemption: The series of events throughout history by which God acted to bring about the salvation of his people.

history of religions school: The approach to religious history, and Christian origins in particular, which treats Old and New Testament developments as responses to encounters with other religions, such as Gnosticism.

holiness: The doctrine that God is separated from sin and devoted to seeking his own honor.

Holy, Holiness: A quality of perfection, sinlessness, and inability to sin that is possessed by God alone. As Christians we are called to be holy (1 Pet. 1:16). But this does not refer to our nature. Instead, it is a command of our practice and thought. We are to be holy in obedience (1 Pet. 1:14). God has made us holy through His Son Jesus (Eph. 1:4; 1 Pet. 2:9).

Holy Orders: In Catholicism, one of the seven sacraments by which men, bishop, deacons, and priests, are given the power and authority by a bishop to offer sacrifice and forgive sins. One of the seven sacraments in Roman Catholic teaching, the ordination to the priesthood or diaconate.

Holy Spirit: One of the three persons of the Trinity whose work it is to manifest the active presence of God in the world, and especially in the church. He is the third person of the Godhead. He is completely God. He is called God (Acts 5:3-4), has a will (1 Cor. 12:11), speaks (Acts 8:29; 13:2), and knows all things (John 14:17). He is not an "active force" as the Jehovah's Witnesses mistakenly teach. The Holy Spirit is alive and is fully and completely God. He is called the Spirit of God (Gen. 1:2), Holy Spirit (Psalm 51:1), the Helper (John 14:16,26), and Eternal Spirit (Heb. 9:14). He knows all things (1 Cor. 2:10-11), is all powerful (Luke 1:35), and is everywhere (Psalm 139:7-13). (See Trinity and Holy Spirit.)

Holy Water: In Catholicism, special water that has been blessed by a priest, bishop, etc. or a liturgical ceremony. It is used to bring a blessing to a person when applied.

Holy Writ: The Bible, writings or sayings of unchallenged authority.

Homiletics: That branch of theology concerned with preaching and sermons and the proper way in which to deliver them.

homo sapiens: The scientific designation for an early form of man (lit., "wise man"), believed by many to have lived sometime between 300,000 B.C. and 40,000 B.C.
homoiousios : A Greek word meaning "of a similar nature," used by Arius in the fourth century to affirm that Christ was a supernatural heavenly being but to deny that he was of the same nature as God the Father. Greek word, meaning "of the same nature," which was included in the Nicene Creed to teach that Christ was of the exact same nature as God the Father and therefore was fully divine as well as fully human.

homoousion: Greek term, literally meaning "of the same substance," which came to be used extensively during the fourth century to designate the mainline Christological belief that Jesus Christ was of the same substance as God. The term was polemical, being directed against the Arian view that Christ was "of similar substance (homoiousios)" to God. See also "consubstantial."

Humanism: A philosophical system of thought that focuses on human value, thought, and actions. Humans are considered basically good and rationale creatures who can improve themselves and others through natural human abilities of reason and action. Secular Humanism is a late development emphasizing objectivity, human reason, and human standards, that govern art, economics, ethics, and belief. As such, no deity is acknowledged. In the strict sense of the word, an intellectual movement linked with the European Renaissance. At the heart of the movement lay, not (as the modern sense of the word might suggest) a set of secular or secularizing ideas, but a new interest in the cultural achievements of antiquity. These were seen as a major resource for the renewal of European culture and Christianity during the period of the Renaissance.

Hume: David Hume (1711-1776)was an empiricist philosopher, historian, economist, and essayist who conceived of philosophy as the inductive, experimental science of human nature.

humiliation of Christ: One of the two "states" of Christ, the other being exaltation. The state of humiliation includes four aspects of his work: his incarnation, suffering, death, and burial.

Humility: The attitude of the Christian that teaches us not to "...think more highly of himself than he ought to think; but to think so as to have sound judgment..." (Rom. 12:3). It teaches us to prefer others over ourselves (Rom. 12:10). It is knowing our true position before God. It is not self-abasement or demeaning one's self. "God is opposed to the proud, but gives grace to the humble" (James 4:6). Humility is necessary to be a disciple of Jesus (Matt. 18:3-4). The humility of Jesus is described in Philippians 2:5-8, "Your attitude should be the same as that of Christ Jesus: Who, being in very nature God, did not consider equality with God something to be grasped, but made himself nothing, taking the very nature of a servant, being made in human likeness. And being found in appearance as a man, he humbled himself and became obedient to death - even death on a cross!"

Hypostatic Union: The doctrine of the union of divine and human natures in Jesus Christ, without confusion of their respective substances, in one person (from the Greek hypostasis, "being"). Jesus is God in flesh (John 1:1,14; 10:30-33; 20:28; Phil. 2:5-8; Heb. 1:8). He is fully God and fully man (Col. 2:9); thus, He has two natures: God and man. He is not half God and half man. He is 100% God and 100% man. He never lost his divinity.1 He continued to exist as God when He became a man and added human nature to Himself (Phil. 2:5-11). Therefore, there is a "union in one person of a full human nature and a full divine nature." Right now in heaven there is a man, Jesus, who is our Mediator between us and God the Father (1 Tim. 2:5). (For related information on Jesus and His two natures, see Incarnation, and the errors concerning His natures known as Eutychianism, Monophycitism, and Nestorianism.)

hypothesis: an unproved or unverified assumption that can be either used or accepted as probable in the light of established facts. Theological proposals should be viewed as hypotheses, subject to verification.

I

Iconoclasts: From Middle Greek [eikonoklastEs], meaning image destroyer. It has come to refer to someone who destroys religious images, or who attacks established beliefs or institutions. In Christianity it means one who opposes any image or icon worship or reverence. Iconoclasts hold that such respect of graven images is contrary to biblical worship, and that the veneration thereof is strictly forbidden by the scriptures (Ex. 20:4), and a form of idolatry.

icons: Sacred pictures, particularly of Jesus, which play a significant role in Orthodox spirituality as "windows for the divine."

ideology: A group of beliefs and values, usually secular, which govern the actions and outlooks of a society or group of people.

idiom: Latin [idima], from Greek [idiousthai], meaning "to make one's own." It is a specific grammatical phrase or combination of words in a given dialect or language that has a figurative meaning that would have been naturally understood in its region by its native speakers (Linguistics). Expression whose meaning cannot be derived from its constituent elements. An example might be "to kick the bucket", meaning "to die."

Idol, Idolatry: An idol is a representation of something in the heavens or on the earth. It is used in worship and is often worshiped. It is an abomination to God (Exodus 20:4). Idolatry is bowing down before such an idol in adoration, prayer, or worship. In a loose sense, idolatry does not necessitate a material image nor a religious system. It can be anything that takes the place of God: a car, a job, money, a person, a desire, etc. Idolatry is denounced by God at the beginning of the Ten Commandments and is considered a form of spiritual fornication.

Ignatian spirituality: A loose term used to refer to the approach to spirituality associated with Ignatius Loyola (1491–1556), based on his Spiritual Exercises.

illumination: Spiritual ilumination in which "turning on the light" of understanding in some area occurs when studying the Word.

Image of God: Man was made in the image of God (Gen. 1:26). The image of God is generally held to mean that people contain within their nature elements that reflect God's nature: compassion, reason, love, hate, patience, kindness, self-awareness, etc. Though we have a physical image, it does not mean that God has one. Rather, God is spirit (John 4:24), not flesh and bones (Luke 24:39).

imago Dei: Latin phrase meaning "image of God."

Immaculate Conception: The teaching that Mary was conceived without original sin. Typically believed as true in Roman Catholicism.

immanent: Existing or remaining in. The term is used in theology to speak of God's involvement in creation

immersion: The mode of baptism in the New Testament in which the person is put completely under the water and then brought back up again.

imminent: A term referring to the fact that Christ could return and might return at any time

Immortality: Life without death anytime in the future. God is immortal. The souls of people are immortal though their bodies are not. All people can die in a physical sense but they continue on after death. Therefore, it is the soul that is immortal. However, after the return of Christ and the resurrection, the Christians' bodies will also become glorified and immortal (1 Cor. 15:50-58). The wicked will likewise be resurrected to immortality but they will be cast into hell for eternal.

Immutability: The divine attribute of unchangeableness. God said in Exodus 3:14, "I AM that I AM," signifying His eternal sameness and His sovereignty. He cannot change

His moral character, His love, His omniscience, omnipresence, omnipotence, etc. God is "From everlasting to everlasting," (Psalm 90:2). Immutability does not mean that God does not vary. The incarnation is just such an example of variation. Also, God's attitude toward a person is changed when the person becomes a Christian. For example, the enmity between God and man is removed (Rom. 5:10). Mormonism denies the immutability of God. It says that God was not always God, that He was a man on another planet who became a God (Mormon Doctrine, by Bruce McConkie, p. 321.).

impassibility: The doctrine, often based on a misunderstanding of Acts 14:15, that God does not have passions or emotions. Scripture instead teaches that God does have emotions, but he does not have sinful passions or emotions.

impeccability: The doctrine that Christ was not able to sin.

impute: To think of as belonging to someone, and therefore to cause it to belong to that person. God "thinks of" Adam's sin as belonging to us, and it therefore belongs to us, and in justification he thinks of Christ's righteousness as belonging to us and so relates to us on this basis.

Impute, Imputation: To reckon to someone the blessing, curse, debt, etc. of another. Adam's sin is imputed to all people (Rom. 5:12-21), therefore, we are all guilty before God. Our sins were put upon, imputed, to Jesus on the cross where He became sin on our behalf (2 Cor. 5:21) and died with them (Isaiah 53:4-6). Therefore, our sins are forgiven. Understanding imputation is very important. Imputation is the means of our salvation. Our sins were put upon, imputed, to Jesus on the cross. Our sins were "given" to Jesus. When He died on the cross, our sins, in a sense, died with Him. The righteousness that was His through His perfect obedience to the Father in His complete obedience to the Law is imputed, given, to us. In short, our sins were given to Jesus. His righteousness was given to us. Technically speaking our sins were imputed to Jesus. His righteousness was imputed to us.

Imputed Sin: Specifically refers to the guilt or condemnation of the first sin which was imputed to humanity. (Also: original guilt.)

in Christ: A term referring to a variety of relationships between believers and Christ through which Christians receive the benefits of salvation.

In facto: Something that exists and is complete.

In fieri: Beginning to be, but not yet complete.

in the Holy Spirit: The state of consciously dwelling in an atmosphere of God's manifested presence.

incarnation: A term used to refer to the assumption of human nature by God, in the person of Jesus Christ. The term "incarnationalism" is often used to refer to theological approaches which lay especial emphasis upon God becoming human. The act of God the Son whereby he took to himself a human nature. The addition of human nature to the nature of God the second person of the Trinity. It is where God became a man (John 1:1,14; Phil. 2:5-8). It was the voluntary act of Jesus to humble Himself so that He might die for our sins (1 Pet. 3:18). Thus, Jesus has two natures: Divine and human. This is known as the Hypostatic Union.

Incarnation doctrine: Teaching of the human nature of God, ensures accuracy concerning the knowledge that God died on the cross to atone for sin and that the God-man (Jesus) is now in heaven as a mediator (1 Tim. 2:5) between us and God. Jesus came to reveal the Father (Matt. 11:27; Luke 10:22), to do His will (Heb. 10:5-9), to fulfill prophecy (Luke 4:17-21), to reconcile the world (2 Cor. 5:18-21), and to become our High Priest (Heb. 7:24-28). (Contrast with Kenosis.) The doctrine is of vital importance to the Christian. By it we understand the true nature of God, the atonement, forgiveness, grace, etc. It is only God who could pay for sins. Therefore, God became man (John 1:1,14) to die for our sins (1 Pet. 2:24) which is the atonement. Through Jesus we have forgiveness of sins. Since we are saved by grace through faith (Eph. 2:8-9) it is essential that our object of faith be accurate.

incommunicable attributes: Aspects of God's character that God does not share with us.

incomprehensible: Not able to be fully understood. As this applies to God, it means that God cannot be understood fully or exhaustively, although we can know true things about God.

incorruptible: The nature of our future resurrection bodies, which will be like Christ's resurrection body and therefore will not wear out, grow old, or be subject to any kind of sickness or disease.

Induction: A system of logic where specific facts are used to draw a general conclusion.

Indulgence: In Catholicism, a means by which the Catholic church takes away some of the punishment due the Christian in this life and/or purgatory because of his sin.

Inerrancy: Without error, non-errant. In Christianity, inerrancy states that the Bible, in its original documents, is without error regarding facts, names, dates, and any other revealed information. Inerrancy does not extend to the copies of the biblical manuscripts.

infallibility: The idea that Scripture is not able to lead us astray in matters of faith and practice.

Infant baptism: See "paedobaptisrn."
The practice of baptizing infant children of believing parents. In the Catholic Church infant baptism washes away original sin and is regenerative. In Reformed circles, infant baptism is not regenerative but covenantal and validated through the believing parent(s). There are no explicit accounts of infant baptism in the Bible. However, it cannot be completely excluded as a possibility given that entire households were baptized Acts 16:15, 33; 18:8.

Infidel: A person who does not believe in any particular religious system.

infinite: When used of God, a term referring to the fact that he is not subject to any of the limitations of humanity or of creation in general.

Infinity: The state or quality of being infinite, unlimited by space or time, without end, without beginning or end. God is infinite in that He is not limited by space or time. He is without beginning and without end (Psalm 90:2).

infinity with respect to space: Another term for God's omnipresence.

infinity with respect to time: Another term for God's eternity.

Infra-lapsarianism: From the Latin term [infra] meaning after and [lapsus] meaning fall (after fall), is the doctrine that God created the world first, and then after foreseeing that His creation would fall into sin, he then declared the Election. As opposed to Supra-lapsarianism which is the doctrine that God chose the election solely for His own glory "prior" to the decision to let sin enter that there be a fall. In other words, infra-lapsarianism means that God first foresaw His people as fallen and after foreseeing, ordained that some of them, according to His will alone, would be Saved An issue within Reformed theology dealing with what may have happened in God's mind regarding the logical order of His considering whom to elect into salvation before the foundation of the world. The word means "after the fall." The position is that God first decided he would allow sin into the world and second that he would then save people from it. By contrast, the supralapsarian ("before the fall") position holds that God first decided that he would save some people and then second that he would allow sin into the world.

By this order:

- God decreed to create man in the image of God.
- God decreed to permit the Fall of mankind in Adam.
- After the Fall, God decreed to elect some of the fallen souls to salvation and to leave others in a natural state of condemnation.
- God decreed to provide a Redeemer for the elect whose work of redemption would be sufficient for all.
- God decreed to secure the application of this salvation to the elect by means of the Holy Spirit.

infused righteousness: Righteousness that God actually puts into us and that changes us internally. The Roman Catholic Church understands justification to involve such an infusion, which differs from Protestantism's view that justification is a legal declaration by God.

inherited corruption: The sinful nature, or the tendency to sin, which all people inherit because of Adam's sin (often referred to as "original pollution"). This idea entails that (1) in our natures we totally lack spiritual good before God; and (2) in our actions we are totally unable to do spiritual good before God.

inherited guilt: The idea that God counts all people guilty because of Adam's sin (often referred to as "original guilt").

inherited sin: The guilt and the tendency to sin that all people inherit because of Adam's sin (often referred to as "original sin"). Specifically refers to the transferring of the sinful nature. (Also: original corruption, original pollution, sinful nature.)

Inspiration: doctrine that the Bible was written by the influence of God. It is, therefore, without error. It is accurate and authoritatively represents God's teachings (2 Tim. 3:16). As such it is a revelation from God which implies direct knowledge about God, creation, man, salvation, the future, etc. It is an illumination in that it shows us what we could not know apart from it. One of the ways to prove that the Bible is inspired is to examine the O.T. prophecies fulfilled in the N.T. concerning Jesus (Luke 24:27-45). Because the Bible is inspired, its words are unbreakable (John 10:34-36), eternal (Matt. 24:35), trustworthy (Psalm 119:160), and able to pierce the heart of man (Heb. 4:12). Additionally, the inspired Word of God will not go forth without accomplishing what God wishes it to (Isaiah 55:11).

intelligent design: the view that God directly created the world and its many life forms, which stands against the view that new species came about through an evolutionary process of random mutation.

intercession: Jesus' ongoing act of standing in God's presence and making petitions before him on our behalf as our great high priest. (29B.3) The term is also used to refer to prayers of request for ourselves or others.

Intermediate state: The condition or mode of being of a person between the time of one's death and the time that Christ returns to give believers new resurrection bodies or the period between death and resurrection. The condition of the person in the intermediate state is debated. One theory is that the person is without a body, yet is conscious, and that he will receive his body at the resurrection. Another theory states that the person has a different sort of spiritual body that will be lost at the resurrection when body and soul are reunited (2 Cor. 5:1-4).

International Council on Biblical Inerrancy: This organization drafted the "Chicago Statement on Biblical Inerrancy" in 1978 that affirmed the inerrancy of Scripture and defined what most evangelicals understand by the term inerrancy

interpretation: The explanation or elucidation of a creative work, a political event, or other activity.

interpretation of tongues: The gift of the Holy Spirit by which the general meaning of something spoken in tongues is reported to the church.

invisible church: The church as God sees it.

irresistible grace: term that refers to the fact that God effectively calls people and also gives them regeneration, both of which guarantee that we will respond in saving faith. This term is subject to misunderstanding since it seems to imply that people do not make a voluntary, willing choice in responding to the gospel.

J

jealousy: The doctrine that God continually seeks to protect his own honor.

Jehovah: An anglicized pronunciation of the Hebrew tetragrammaton, YHWH, which are the four consonant letters used to spell God's name in the Old Testament (Exodus 3:14). The Hebrews considered the name of God too holy to pronounce and substituted the word "Lord" (adonai) when the text was read. The vowels of the word "adonai" was combined with YHWH to get the word "Jehovah" which was first used in the 12th century. A more accurate pronunciation of YHWH would be "Yahweh." Howver, the exact and proper pronunciation has been lost.

Jerome: Saint Jerome also known as the Doctor of the Church, the first Latin-speaking Christian writer who started research into the Hebrew Bible; also the person who achieved such mastery in Hebrew that no other Christian writer, before and a few thousand years after him, could compete with him. Known most of all from the biblical commentaries as well as from the Vulgate, the Latin translation of the Bible.

Jesus Only Movement: This is a movement in some Pentecostal circles. It is an error in the understanding of the nature of the Trinity. The biblical Trinity consists of three persons simultaneously and eternally existing in one God. The Jesus Only Movement maintains that there is only one person in the Godhead: Jesus. It teaches that the person of the Father became the person of the Son who then became the person of the Holy Spirit and that the persons are consecutive not simultaneous. This movement is incorrect in its Trinitarian interpretation. Additionally, they mistakenly believe that baptism is necessary for salvation and that tongues are evidence of true conversion.
Son of God, God in flesh (John 1:1,14). He is fully God and fully man (Col. 2:9) thus, He has two natures: God and man. He is not half God and half man. He is 100% God and 100% man. He never lost his divinity. He existed in the form of God and when He became a man, He added human nature1 to Himself (Phil. 2:5-11). Therefore, there is a "union in one person of a full human nature and a full divine nature."2 Right now in heaven there is a man, Jesus, who is Mediator between us and God the Father (1 Tim. 2:5). Our advocate with the Father (1 John 2:1). He is our Savior (Titus 2:13). He is

our Lord (Rom. 10:9-10). He is not, as some cults teach, an angel who became a man (Jehovah's Witnesses) or the brother of the devil (Mormonism). He is wholly God and wholly man, the Creator, the Redeemer.

NOTE: Jesus' adding to Himself the nature of man by becoming one of us is known as the Hypostatic Union. Errors dealing with the relationship of Jesus' two natures are: 1) Monophycitism which states that Jesus' two natures combined into one new one; the problem here is that neither God nor man was represented in Christ. **2)** Nestorianism which states that the two natures of Christ were so separated from each other that they were "not in contact;" the problem here is that worship of the human Jesus would then not be allowed. **3)** Eutychianism is similar to Monophycitism. It states that Christ's natures were so thoroughly combined -- in a sense scrambled together -- that a new third thing emerged; the problem is this implies that Jesus was not truly God nor man, therefore unable to act as mediator.

Jews: Originally, a Jew was a member of the state of Judah during the period of the division of Israel into two nations: Judah and Israel. It became a common reference from the 8th century B.C. Today it is used of adherents of the Jewish religion.

Judgment: Condemnation. There are several judgments: the judgment of the believer's sins (John 5:24), the judgment of the believer's self (1 Cor. 11:31-32), the judgment of the believer's works (2 Cor. 5:10), the judgment of the nations (Matt. 25:31-46), and the judgment of the wicked (Rev. 20:11-15). There is no judgment for the Christian in respect to salvation (Rom. 8:1). We were judged in Christ on the cross 2000 years ago. However, as Christians we will be judged according to our works (2 Cor. 5:10) with, most probably, varying degrees of rewards. But, remember, the judgment of our works does not affect our salvation.

judgment of the nations: In the dispensational premillennial view, a judgment that will come between the tribulation and the beginning of the millennium, during which time nations are judged according to how they have treated the Jewish people during the tribulation.

Justice: The due reward or punishment for an act. Justice is getting what is deserved. God is merciful but He is also just (Deut. 32:4 - righteous) and must punish sin. In the grace of God, justice fell upon His Son so that mercy would fall upon us. (See also Prov. 8:15; Gen. 18:19; Heb. 10:38). Another term for God's righteousness.

justification: An instantaneous legal act of God in which he (1) thinks of our sins as forgiven and Christ's righteousness as belonging to us, and (2) declares us to be righteous in his sight.

justification by faith: doctrine of The section of Christian theology dealing with how the individual sinner is able to enter into fellowship with God. The doctrine was to prove to be of major significance at the time of the Reformation.

Justify: To be justified is to be made righteous. It is a divine act where God declares the sinner to be innocent of his sins. It is not that the sinner is now sinless, but that he is "declared" sinless. This justification is based on the shed blood of Jesus, "...having now been justified by His blood..." (Rom. 5:9). When God sees the Christian, He sees him through the sacrifice of Jesus and "sees" him without sin. This declaration of innocence is not without cost for it required the satisfaction of God's Law, "...without shedding of blood there is no forgiveness" (Heb. 9:22). By the sacrifice of Jesus, in the "one act of righteousness there resulted justification of life to all men" (Rom. 5:18, NASB). In justification, the justice of God fell upon Himself--Jesus. We receive mercy--we are not judged according to our sins. And grace is shed upon us--we receive eternal life. This justification is a gift of grace (Rom. 3:24), by faith (Rom. 3:28) because Jesus bore our guilt (Isaiah 53:12).

K

Kabbalistic: a student of Kabbalah; practicing or active in traditional, esoteric, occult, secret matters.

Kabbalah: A medieval and modern system of Jewish theosophy, mysticism, and thaumaturgy marked by belief in creation through emanation and a cipher method of interpreting Scripture. This is an esoteric doctrine or mysterious art. Traditional, esoteric, occult, or secret matter. Often referred to as the "soul" of the Torah, the Kabbalah is an ancient Jewish tradition which teaches the deepest insights into the essence of God, His interaction with the world, and the purpose of Creation. Teaches the essential Jewish cosmology, integral to all other Torah disciplines. Sometimes called "the Inner Torah" or the "Wisdom of Truth", it offers a comprehensive overall structure and plan for the universe, as well as a detailed understanding of the particulars of our lives.

Karma: In Hinduism, the total compilation of all a person's past lives and actions that result in the present condition of that person. Normally, it is associated with reincarnation.

Kenotic Theology: From the Greek [Kenosis] meaning to empty (Philippians 2:7). In this theory it is hypothesized that Jesus was not both on earth as man and in heaven as God simultaneously. The contention is that Jesus was divine before He came to earth as man, but gave up His divine properties, (excluding His moral attributes) and became a mere man.

kenosis theory: Teaching concerning Jesus' incarnation. The Kenosis attempts to solve some paradoxes between the nature of God and of man as united in Jesus. For example, how could an all knowing God become a baby, or how could God be tempted? The Kenosis maintains that God, when becoming a man, divested Himself of some qualities of being a man. In a sense, the Kenosis is God minus something; God subtracting some qualities of deity to become a man. The Hypostatic Union is God plus something; God adding human nature to Himself. The Kenosis, then, jeopardizes the true incarnation because it puts in doubt the full indwelling of God among men in the person of Jesus. (Compare with Hypostatic Union.)

Koine Greek: Common Hellenistic Koiné dialect also known as Alexadrian dialect, common Hellenistic Greek (Modern Greek). The language of the Christian New Testament, of the Septuagint (the 3rd-century BC Greek translation of the Hebrew Bible and of most early Christian theological writing. In this context, Koine Greek is also known as "Biblical", "New Testament", "ecclesiastical" or "patristic" Greek. Common supra-regional form of Greek spoken and written during Hellenistic and Roman antiquity. Developed through the spread of Greek following the conquests of Alexander the Great in the 4th century BC, and served as the common language of much of the Mediterranean region and the Middle East during the following centuries. Based mainly on Attic and related Ionic speech forms, with various mixtures brought about through dialect leveling with other varieties. The liturgical language of services in the Greek Orthodox Church.

L

Law of non-contradiction: The Law of non-contradiction is the law that something cannot be both true and not true at the same time when dealing with the same context. For example, the chair in my living room, right now, cannot be made of wood and not made of wood at the same time. In the law of non-contradiction, where we have a set of statements about a subject, we cannot have any of the statements in that set negate the truth of any other statement in that same set. For example, we have a set of two statements about Judas. 1) Judas hung himself. 2) Judas fell down and his bowels spilled out. Neither statement about Judas contradicts the other. That is, neither statement makes the other impossible because neither excludes the possibility of the other. The statements can be harmonized by stating: Judas hung himself and then his body fell down and his bowels spilled out. In order to make the set of statements contradictory, we would have something like: 1) Judas hung himself. 2) Judas did not hang himself. Since either statement excludes the possibility of the other, we would then have a contradiction.

Laying on of hands: A practice that often accompanied prayer in the New Testament as a means of personal ministry to individuals. Physical contact by touching of the hands. In the OT and NT it was sometimes used in reference to doing physical harm (Gen. 22:12; Luke 20:19). In the NT it is also used to signify an attempt at healing (Acts 9:12) and commissioning of Holy Work (1 Tim. 4:14). Usually, during the ordination of an elder, hands are layed on him as symbolic of a transfer of authority and power.

liberal Protestantism: A movement, especially associated with nineteenth-century Germany, which stressed the continuity between religion and culture, flourishing between the time of F. D. E. Schleiermacher and Paul Tillich.

Liberalism: In Christianity, the movement away from traditional orthodoxy often in an attempt to harmonize biblical teachings with science, humanism, or other secular fields. The result is often a denial of essential biblical doctrines such as the Trinity, the deity of Christ, His virgin birth, His resurrection, and salvation by grace.

Libertarianis: Belief that a person's actions are uncaused by any coercion whatsoever. The agent is the "first cause" in the effect of his action.

liberation theology: A theological movement, popular in the Third World, which interprets salvation, particularly as seen in the Exodus, in political terms. Therefore, the tendency is to believe the church's primary purpose is to assist in changing oppressive social, economic, and political structures. Although this term designates any theological movement laying emphasis upon the liberating impact of the gospel, the term has come to refer to a movement which developed in Latin America in the late 1960s, which stressed the role of political action and orientated itself towards the goal of political liberation from poverty and oppression.

Life without death in the future: God is immortal. The souls of people are immortal though their bodies are not. All people can die in a physical sense but they continue on after death. Therefore, it is the soul that is immortal. However, after the return of Christ and the resurrection, the Christians' bodies will also become glorified and immortal (1 Cor. 15:50-58). The wicked will likewise be resurrected to immortality but they will be cast into hell for eternal. The heretical view that Jesus was "adopted" as the Son of God at some point during his ministry (usually his baptism), as opposed to the orthodox teaching that Jesus was Son of God by nature from the moment of his conception.

likeness: A term referring to something that is similar but not identical to the thing it represents.

limbo: According to a view common in Roman Catholic theology, the place where the souls of believers who died before Christ's resurrection went to wait for his work of redemption to be complete (from the Latin limbus, "border").

limited atonement: The Reformed view that Christ's death actually paid for the sins of those whom he knew would ultimately be saved. A preferable term for this view is "particular redemption" in that the power of the atonement is not limited, but rather it is fully effective for particular people. The teaching held in Reformed (Calvinist) circles of Christianity that Jesus bore only the sins of the elect, and not that of the entire world. It maintains that the sacrifice was sufficient for all, but intended for the elect.

Lindisfarne: An illuminated manuscript gospel book produced around the year 700 in a monastery off the coast of Northumberland at Lindisfarne and which is now on display in the British Library in London. One of the most magnificent manuscripts of the early Middle Ages, presumed to be the work of a monk named Eadfrith, who became Bishop of Lindisfarne in 698 and died in 721. Written and decorated at the end of the 7th century, the manuscript is one of the finest works in the unique style of Hiberno-Saxon or Insular art, combining Mediterranean, Anglo-Saxon and Celtic elements.

literary framework theory: An "old earth" theory of creation that views the six days of Genesis 1, not as a chronological sequence of events, but as a literary "framework" that the author uses to teach about God's creative activity.

liturgy: written text and set forms of public services, especially of the Eucharist. In the Greek Orthodox church, the word "liturgy" often means "the (liturgy of the) Eucharist."

living creatures: class of created spiritual beings with appearances like a lion, an ox, a man, and an eagle who are said to worship around the throne of God.

Logic: branch of philosophy concerned with the rules of valid inference and reasoning. From the Greek "logos" meaning "word." Logic is study of the principles of reasoning. A set of premises that are examined and arranged so as to bring a conclusion. If A = B and B = C, then A = C. Deductive logic is the method of validating a claim by means of supportive information where both the claim and the information are necessarily true. For example, People exist. All people breath. Therefore, all people breath. Inductive logic is the method of drawing a conclusion from a set of supportive information, yet the conclusion has not yet been verified. For example, each night I get tired at 10 PM. Therefore, I conclude that tonight, I will be tired at 10 PM.

Logos: The Greek word for "word" by which the apostle John refers to Jesus in John 1: 1. As applied to Jesus, the term implies both the Old Testament concept of the powerful, creative word of God and the Greek idea of the organizing and unifying principle of the universe. Mentioned only in the writings of John. John 1:1 says, "In the beginning was the Word [logos] and the Word [logos] was with God and the Word [logos] was God." The Logos is sometimes used to refer to the second person of the Trinity as the Son in preincarnate form. Jesus is the word [logos] made flesh (John 1:1,14). This played a crucial role in the development of patristic Christology. Jesus Christ was recognized as the "word of God"; the question concerned the implications of this recognition, and especially the way in which the divine "logos" in Jesus Christ related to his human nature.

Lord: In the New Testament, a translation of the Greek word kyrios that is usually, but not always, used to refer to Christ. In the Greek translation of the Old Testament, this word is used to translate the Hebrew yhwh, the personal name of the omnipotent God.

Lord's Supper: *See Communion*
One of the two ordinances that Jesus commanded his church to observe. This is an ordinance to be observed repeatedly throughout our Christian lives as a sign of continuing in fellowship with Christ.

Lutheranism: The religious ideas associated with Martin Luther, particularly as expressed in the Lesser Catechism (1529) and the Augsburg Confession (1530).

M

macro-evolution: The "general theory of evolution," or the view that all organisms emerged from nonliving substance.

major doctrine: A doctrine that has a significant impact on our thinking about other doctrines, or that has a significant impact on how we live the Christian life.
Man : Man is the creation of God. It is man alone who reflects God. The first man, Adam, was made in God's image (Gen. 1:2627), and placed in the Garden of Eden for the purpose of enjoying the fellowship of the Lord and fulfilling the purpose of God's creation. He was told to "be fruitful and multiply, and fill the earth, and subdue it; and rule over the fish of the sea and over the birds of the sky, and over every living thing that moves on the earth" (Gen. 1:28). When Adam and Eve sinned, all of humanity fell with them (Rom. 5:12-21). Adam represented all humanity: "In Adam all die..." (1 Cor. 15:22). As a result of Adam's disobedience, condemnation resulted to all men (Rom. 5:18). Therefore we are by nature children of wrath (Eph. 2:3). We do not seek God (Rom. 3:11) nor can we understand the spiritual things of God (1 Cor. 2:14). Since this is the condition of man in his natural state, salvation is then impossible for us to achieve (Matt. 19:26). That is why we need the free gift of salvation (Rom. 6:23) given by God to Christians through faith in Jesus' sacrifice on the cross.

Manicheism: A strongly fatalist position associated with the Manichees, to which Augustine of Hippo attached himself during his early period. A distinction is drawn between two different divinities, one of which is regarded as evil, and the other good. Evil is thus seen as the direct result of the influence of the evil god.

Manuscript: A document or a copy of an original writing. There are thousands of existing manuscripts of the biblical documents ranging from vellum (animal skins) to papyri (plant material) upon which the original and copies of the original writings were made.

maranatha: An Aramaic term used in 1 Corinthians 16:22, meaning "Our Lord, come," expressing eager longing for Christ's return.

Marcion: Second century originator of the heretical idea that there were two Gods, a judgmental, harsh, tyrannical God of the Old Testament, and a loving Father as revealed by Jesus in the New Testament.

Martyr: Someone who dies for a belief or cause. A Christian martyr would be a person who dies because of his or her faith in Christian principles.

Masoretic text: The authoritative Hebrew and Aramaic text of the Tanakh for Rabbinic Judaism. However, contemporary scholars seeking to understand the history of the Hebrew Bible's text use a range of other sources.

Mass: In Catholicism, a reenactment of the sacrifice of Christ cross in a ceremony performed by a priest. This ceremony is symbolically carried out by the priest and involves Consecration where the bread and wine are changed into the body and blood of Jesus.

Materialism: The position that only material things exist and that all other things can be explained in terms of matter and the physical properties of matter. The view that the material universe is all that exists.

mature creationism: A "young earth" theory of creation which holds that the original creation had an "appearance of age" from the very beginning. Also called the "ideal time" theory, in that the appearance of age does not in fact indicate any actual time.

Means of Grace: This is associated with sacramental theology; any activities within the fellowship of the church that God uses to give more grace to Christians. A means of grace is a manner in which the Lord imparts grace to a believer as he partakes in the sacrament. A sacrament is a visible manifestation of the word. The bread and wine in the Lord's Supper are considered sacraments in that they are visible manifestations of the covenant promise of our Lord: "In the same way, after the supper he took the cup, saying, 'This cup is the new covenant in my blood, which is poured out for you.'" (Luke 22:20). Generally, the means of grace are considered to be the Gospel, baptism, and the Lord's Supper. The Catholic church has seven total: baptism, confirmation, communion, penance, extreme unction, holy orders, and matrimony.

Mediator: someone who intervenes, someone who conveys and conciliates. The word "mediator" is not found in the O.T., but its principle is. God gave the Law to the people through a mediator, Moses (Gal. 3:19), who was a type of the true mediator, Jesus. The word occurs only a few times in the N.T.: 1 Tim. 2:5; Heb. 8:6; 9:15; 12:24. It is in the N.T. that the true nature of mediation is understood in the person of Jesus Christ. The role that Jesus plays in coming between God and us, enabling us to come into the presence of God. He is the mediator of a better covenant (Heb. 8:6). He was able to become our mediator by becoming man (John 1:1,14) and dying as our substitute (1 Pet. 1:18,19; 2:24). He reconciled us to God (Eph. 2:16).

meditation: form of prayer, distinguished from contemplation, in which the mind uses images (such as those provided by Scripture) as a means for focusing on God.

mental attributes: Aspects of God's character that describe the nature of his knowing and reasoning.

Mercy: act of not administering justice when that justice is punitive. Because of our sinfulness we deserve death and eternal separation from God (Rom. 6:23; Isaiah 59:2), but God provided an atonement for sin and through it shows us mercy. That is, He does not deliver to the Christian the natural consequence of his sin which is damnation. That is why Jesus became sin on our behalf (2 Cor. 5:21) and bore the punishment due to us (Isaiah 5345). It was to deliver us from damnation. (Compare with justice and grace). God saved us according to His mercy (Titus 3:5) and we can practice mercy as a gift (Rom. 12:8). "Let us therefore draw near with confidence to the throne of grace, that we may receive mercy and may find grace to help in time of need" (Heb. 4:16).

Messiah: Messiah is a Hebrew word. It means "anointed one." It is the equivalent of the N.T. word "Christ" which also means "anointed." Jesus, as the messiah, was anointed by God (Matt. 3:16) to carry out His three-fold ministry of Prophet, Priest, and King. As the messiah He has delivered the Christian from the bonds of sin and given to him eternal life. In that sense, messiah means deliverer, for He has delivered us. The Messiah was promised in the O.T. in the seed of the woman (Gen. 3:15).

Metaphysics: Branch of philosophy involved with examining and discussing the ultimate nature of reality. The term comes from "meta" which means "after" and "phusika" which means "physics." Around A.D. 70 Andronicus applied to the section of Aristotelian writings that came after the physics section; hence, metaphysics.

micro-evolution: view that small developments occur within one species without creating new species.

Middle Knowledge: That knowledge of God dealing with what individuals will do in a given set of circumstances. God has an infinite set of potential circumstances that could exist and knows all actual choices that would be made by individuals in each set. (See also Free Knowledge and Natural knowledge.)

midtribulation rapture: variation of the pretribulational premillennial view in which Christ returns in the middle of the seven year tribulation to rescue believers, and then again after the tribulation to reign on earth for 1,000 years.

mighty work: A biblical term for miracles (translating the Hebrew geburcfh and the Greek dynamis), indicating an act displaying great or divine power.

Millennial: From the Latin words [mille] meaning thousand, and [annum] meaning years. It is not a biblical term, other than it is used by many Christian Theologians to identify the thousand year reign spoken of in Revelation Chapter 20. The Word Millennial is referring to that period of time when God says Satan is bound and the Kingdom of Christ goes forth. For all practical purposes, in theology the words Millennium or Millennial is synonymous with the "one thousand years."

Millennium: term that refers to the period of 1,000 years mentioned in Revelation 20:4-5 as the time of the reign of Christ and believers over the earth (from Latin millennium, "thousand years"). iterally, this word means 1000 years. In the study of end times doctrines (eschatology) the millennium is the duration of Christ's rule over the earth. The debate has been over when the millennium will take place and what it actually is. The terms that have arisen out of this debate are premillennialism, amillennialism, and postmillennialism. Premillennialism teaches that the millennium is yet future and that upon Christ's return He will set up His earthly kingdom. Amillennialism teaches that the millennium is a figurative period and that Christ's rule began when He first became man. Postmillennialism teaches that through the preaching of the Word of God, the world will be converted and will then usher in Christ and the kingdom of God. There are good arguments for each position.

minor doctrine: doctrine that has very little impact on how we think about other doctrines, and that has very little impact on how we live the Christian life. (lC.2.c)

Minuscule: The Greek characters of lower case: abgde, etc. Different copies of Greek manuscripts appear in minuscule form. By contrast, uncials are the Greek characters in upper case.

Miracle: miracle is an out-of-the-ordinary direct and divine intervention in the world. A less common kind of God's activity in which he arouses people's awe and wonder and bears witness to himself. Examples would be the parting of the Red Sea, Jesus walking on water, the resurrection of Lazarus, etc. Some hold that it is a violation of the natural order of physical laws. Others maintain that there is no such violation upon God's part but only a natural manifestation of His work. They are also known as powers and signs (Mark 9:39; Acts 2:22, 19:11) and mighty works (John 10:25-28). They are a manifestation of the power of God over nature (Joshua 10:121-14), animals (Num. 22:28), people (Gen. 19:26), and illness (2 Kings 5:1014). They are produced by God's power (Acts 15:12), Christ's power (Matt. 10:1), and the Holy Spirit's power (Matt. 12:28).

miraculous gifts: Gifts given by the Holy Spirit that are less common, and that arouse people's awe and wonder and bear witness to God.

modalism: The heretical teaching that holds that God is not really three distinct persons, but only one person who appears to people in different "modes" at different times. The error that there is only one person in the Godhead who manifests himself in three forms or manners: Father, Son, and Holy Spirit. It is a trinitarian heresy, which treats the three persons of the Trinity as different "modes" of the Godhead. A typical modalist approach is to regard God as active as Father in creation, as Son in redemption, and as Spirit in sanctification.

Monarchianism: Monarchianism (mono - "one"; arche - "rule") was an error concerning the nature of God that developed in the second century A.D. It arose as an attempt to maintain Monotheism and refute tritheism. Unfortunately, it also contradicts the orthodox doctrine of the Trinity. Monarchianism teaches that there is one God as one person: the Father. See Heresies for more information. From the Greek [monarchia] meaning "uniqueness of one." It was a heretical doctrine of the second and third centuries which grew out of an attempt to explain the person of Jesus so that it preserved the unity of God. Unfortunately what it actually did was effectively teach against the Christian doctrine of the Trinity. there were basically three types.
Adoptionist: They believed that Christ was originally just a man (born of Mary and the Holy Spirit) but was adopted by God, and was only deified after his resurrection.
Modalistic or Sabellianism: They believed the Father, Son, and Holy Spirit were simply three ways in which God revealed himself, and not the three persons of the trinity.
Patripassianism: They believed that there was no difference between God the Father, and God the Son, and that it was God the father who was born of Mary and went to the cross. Monarchianism in general is simply the belief that the Godhead was singular, consisting of one (monarchia). Though the name has faded, there are many today who hold to a similar Oneness theology, denying the three persons of the Godhead.

Monergism: teaching that God alone is the one who saves. It is opposed to synergism which teaches that God and man work together in salvation. Cults are synergistic. Christianity is monergistic.

Moniker or Monicker: Derived from the Irish word [munnik], which is actually the modified form the word ainm. Moniker means a title, name or a nickname. When used in Christianity it is usually referring to titles such as Calvinists, Monotheists or Paedobaptists, signifying that people are of that particular family of beliefs.

Monism: The view that there is only one basic and fundamental reality, that all existence is this one reality even though we perceive different aspects of this reality. The holds that man is only one element, and that his body is the person.

Monolatry: belief that there is more than one God, but only one is served and worshiped. Mormonism is an excellent example of monolatry. Mormonism teaches the existence of many Gods of many worlds, yet worships only the one of this planet. Therefore, monolatry is a division of polytheism, the belief in many gods. It is a false teaching contrary to Scripture. See Isaiah 43:10; 44:6,8; 45:5-6.

monophysitism: The doctrine that there is only one nature in Christ, which is divine (from the Greek words monos, "only one," and physis, "nature"). This view differed from the orthodox view, upheld by the Council of Chalcedon (451), that Christ had two natures, one divine and one human. The fifth-century heresy which held that Christ had only one nature, that being a mixture of divine and human natures (from the Greek monos, "one," and physis, "nature"). This is an error regarding the two natures of Jesus (See Hypostatic Union). It states that Jesus' two natures are combined into one new one; the problem here is that neither God nor man was represented in Christ but a new third thing. (Other errors regarding the two natures of Christ are Nestorianism and Eutychianism.)

Monotheism: From the Greek [mono] meaning one and [theos] meaning God. It is the doctrine applied particularly to religions like Judaism or Christianity which believe in only one God. The belief that there is only one God in all places at all times. There were none before God and there will be none after Him. Monotheism is the teaching of the Bible (Isaiah 43:10; 44:6,8; 45:5,14,18,21,22; 46:9; 47:8; John 17:3; 1 Cor. 8:5-6; Gal. 4:89). The Christian-Judeo belief in one God was foreign to the Greeks who were fairly accepting of other religions, however, wishing not to destroy nations, like the Assyrians did, but incorporate them. The Jewish, and later Christian, insistence on keeping their religion pure amused and sometimes angered the Greeks. It was the cause of the Maccabean Revolts, the destruction of Jerusalem in A.D. 70, and the martyrdom of many Christians. Hellenism did not infiltrate the Christian belief of monotheism, but it did reject it, and Christians (and Jews) paid a heavy price for their faithfulness.

Moral Example Theory of the Atonement: Belief that Christ came to show people how to live so that they would turn to him in love. His death was not required and has no atoning value, but only serves as a moral example for people to follow.

N

natural selection: The idea, assumed in evolutionary theory, that living organisms that are most fitted to their environment survive and multiply while others perish (also called "survival of the fittest").

Naturalism: The belief that all of human experience can be described through natural law. It asserts that biological evolution is true and that there are no supernatural realities.

necessity of Scripture: The idea that the Bible is necessary for knowing the gospel, for maintaining spiritual life, and for knowing God's will, but is not necessary for knowing that God exists or for knowing something about God's character and moral laws.

neo-catastrophism: Another term for the flood geology view of the geological status of the earth.

Neo-orthodoxy: term used to designate the general position of Karl Barth (1886–1968), especially the manner in which he drew upon the theological concerns of the period of Reformed Orthodoxy. A focus on existential and psychological aspects of religious experience and denounces the literalism of the Bible. Experience with the divine is what makes scripture real, not biblical revelation, not reason. Neo orthodoxy is subjective and selective in its "orthodox" positions. A twentieth -century theological movement represented by the teachings of Karl Barth. Instead of the orthodox position that all the words of Scripture were spoken by God, Barth taught that the words of Scripture become God's words to us as we encounter them.

Nestorianism: A fifth-century heresy that taught that there were two separate persons in Christ, a human person and a divine person. States that the two natures of Christ were so separated from each other that they were "not in contact"; the problem here is that worship of the human Jesus would then not be allowed. (See Hypostatic Union Nestorianism and Eutychianism.)

new covenant: The administration of the covenant of grace established after the death and resurrection of Christ, a covenant in which Christ's atoning death covers all of the believer's sins and the Holy Spirit empowers the believer to fulfill the righteous demands of the law. The more powerful work of the Holy Spirit in people's lives that began at Pentecost for the disciples and now happens at conversion for believers.

New Covenant Theology: From the Hebrew [ber-eeth] meaning to cut, and by extension means a promise or pledge to do something. New Covenant theology declares that the New Covenant (testament) clearly characterizes itself as superior to the old, and therefore this means that the law of Christ stands in contrast to the law of Moses. As opposed to "Covenant Theology" which declares that the old Covenant and New Covenant are particular aspects of a single covenant relationship, and that there is continuity between the Old and the New Covenant.

New Testament theology: A description of the entirely renewed creation in which believers will dwell after the final judgment. The study of the teaching of the individual authors and sections of the New Testament, and of the place of each teaching in the historical development of the New Testament.

Nicaea: Ancient city in northwestern Anatolia, and is primarily known as the site of the First and Second Councils of Nicaea (the first and seventh Ecumenical councils in the early history of the Christian Church), the Nicene Creed (which comes from the First Council), and as the capital city of the Empire of Nicaea following the Fourth Crusade in 1204, until the recapture of Constantinople by the Byzantines in 1261.

Nicaean, First Council: The first ecumenical council of the Church. Most significantly, it resulted in the first uniform Christian doctrine. Its main accomplishments were settlement of the Christological issue of the nature of the Son of God and his relationship to God the Father, the construction of the first part of the Creed of Nicaea, establishing uniform observance of the date of Easter, and promulgation of early canon law.

Nicene Creed: Profession of faith widely used in Christian liturgy. Originally adopted in the face of Arian controversey in the city of Nicaea (present day Iznik, Turkey) by the First Council of Nicaea in 325. Amended (381) at the First Council of Constantinople, to the Nicene or the Niceno-Constantinopolitan Creed. Churches of Oriental Orthodoxy use it with the verbs in the original plural ("we believe") form. The Eastern Orthodox Church and the Roman Catholic Church use it in the singular ("I believe") form. The Anglican Communion and many Protestant denominations also use it, sometimes with the verbs of believing in the plural form but generally in the singular. The Apostles' Creed is also used in the Latin West, but not in the Eastern liturgies. The Nicene Creed of 325 explicitly affirms the co-essential divinity of the Son, applying to him the term "consubstantial" therefore "one in Being" with the Father, sharing the same divine nature; that He is begotten, not made or created; and that Mary conceived by the power of the Holy Spirit, and through her, Jesus Christ, true God, became also true man. The 381 version speaks of the Holy Spirit as worshipped and glorified with the Father and the Son. The Athanasian Creed (not used in Eastern Christianity) describes in much greater detail the relationship between Father, Son and Holy Spirit. The Apostles' Creed makes no explicit statements about the divinity of the Son and the Holy Spirit, but, in the view of many who use it, the doctrine is implicit in it. Without question, the basis for the Nicene Creed was the Apostles Creed and the profession of faith administered at Baptism. One or other of these two creeds is recited in the Roman Rite Mass after the homily. The Nicene Creed is also part of the profession of faith required of those undertaking important functions within the Catholic Church.

Nietzsche, Friedrich: German philosopher whose Beyond Good and Evil sought to refute traditional notions of morality. Nietzsche penned a memorable secular statement of the Doctrine of Eternal Recurrence in Thus Spoke Zarathustra and is forever associated with the phrase, "God is dead" (first seen in his book, The Gay Science). Key ideas include perspectivism, the will to power, master-slave morality, the death of God, and eternal recurrence. Key tenet of his philosophy is "life-affirmation", which embraces the realities of the world in which we live over the idea of a world beyond. It further champions the creative powers of the individual to strive beyond social, cultural, and moral contexts. Attitude towards religion and morality was marked with atheism, psychologism and historism: he considered them to be human creations ultimately produced by insecurities and flaws rather than effective means to alleviate those flaws. Considered godfather of fascism, had strong influence on Hitler, German militarism and Nazism; suffered a collapse and a complete loss of his mental faculties at age 44.

non-miraculous gifts: Gifts given by the Holy Spirit that are more common and appear to be more ordinary, such as serving, teaching, encouraging, and doing acts of mercy.

not discerning the body: A phrase used in 1 Corinthians 11 :29 of the Corinthians' abuse of the Lord's Supper. In their selfish, inconsiderate conduct toward each other during the Lord's Supper, they were not understanding the unity and interdependence of people in the church, which is the body of Christ.

Nun: Especially in the Roman Catholic Church, those women who consecrate their lives to spiritual service and various religious orders. They do not marry and are normally virgins.

Objectivism: A branch of philosophy that asserts that reality exists apart from the human mind and that the knowability of this reality based upon observation.

Occult: "Hidden". It covers practices that are not approved of by God e.g., astrology (Isaiah 47:13), casting spells (Deut. 18:11), consulting with spirits (Deut. 18:11), magic (Gen. 41:8), sorcery (Exodus. 22:8), witchcraft (Deut. 18:10), and spiritism (Deut. 18:11). Occult practices such as Ouija boards, tarot cards, astrology charts, contacting the dead, séances, etc. are to be avoided by the Christian and Jews alike.

old covenant: term referring specifically to the Mosaic covenant established at Mount Sinai, which was an administration of detailed written laws given for a time to restrain the sins of man.

old earth theory: theory of creation that views earth as very old, perhaps as old as 4.5 billion years.

Old English literature: English literature of the period from 750 until the time of the invasion of the Normans in 1066.

Old Testament theology: study of the teaching of the individual authors and sections of the Old Testament, and of the place of each teaching in the historical development of the Old Testament.

Omnipotence: doctrine that God is able to do all his holy will (from Latin omni, "all," and patens, "powerful"). An attribute of God alone. It is the quality of having all power (Psalm 115:3). He can do all things that do not conflict with His holy nature. God has the power to do anything He wants to.

Omnipresence: doctrine that God does not have size or spatial dimensions and is present at every point of space with his whole being, yet God acts differently in different places.An attribute of God alone. It is the quality of being present in all places at all times (Jer. 23:23.4). He is not bound by time and space. This does not mean that nature is a part of God and is, therefore, to be worshiped. Creation is separate from God, but not independent of Him.

Omniscience: The doctrine that God fully knows himself and all things actual and possible in one simple and eternal act. An attribute of God alone. It is the quality of having all knowledge (Isaiah 40:14). Omnipotence, Omnipresence, and Omniscience represent the nature of God concerning His relation to the creation.

Ontological Argument: An attempt to prove God's existence first postulated by Anselm. In brief, it states that God is a being of which no greater thing exists or can be thought of. Therefore, since we can conceive of God as the greatest of all things that exist, then God must exist. An argument for the existence of God that begins with the idea of God as the greatest of beings that can be imagined. As such, the characteristic of existence must belong to such a being, since it is greater to exist than not to exist. A term used to refer to the type of argument for the existence of God especially associated with the scholastic theologian Anselm of Canterbury. It claims that as God is greater than any other being that is conceivable, God must be greater than any being who exists only as an idea, so God must necessarily exist in reality.

ontological equality: phrase that describes the members of the Trinity as eternally equal in being or existence.

Ontology: The study of the nature of being, reality, and substance.

Oracles: Oracles are the divine revelations given to God's people. God's method of communicating these oracles varied from dreams and visions (Num. 12:6-8), to wisdom (Prov. 30:1), and even the Urim and Thummim (Num. 27:21; 1 Sam. 14:337).

Oracles of God: The mouthpiece of God; the revelation or utterance supposed to issue from a divinity usually through, a priest or priestess, thought to be inspired. The term refers both to divine responses to a question asked of God and to pronouncements made by God without His being asked. Oracle occurs only 21 times in the King James Version. In 2 Samuel 16:23 it means the Word of God. A man inquired "at the oracle of God" by means of the Urim and Thummim in the breastplate on the high priest's ephod. In the New Testament it is used only in the plural, and always denotes the Word of God (Romans 3:2 ; Hebrews 5:12 , etc.). The Scriptures are called "living oracles" (Compare Hebrews 4:12) because of their quickening power (Acts 7:38).

Ordo Salutis: Refers to the logical order in which the process of salvation takes place.

Original Sin: A broad term that refers to the effects that the first sin had on humanity; the "origin" of sin.

Orthodox: From the Latin [ortho] meaning right, and [doxus] meaning doctrine or belief. In Theological terms it means sound theological doctrine as represented by the strict adherence to the law of God's Word, the Bible. Many Orthodox Churches still use forms of worship that were practiced in the first centuries, as they were based to a great degree on passages of Scripture.

Paedobaptism: From the Greek [paidos] meaning child, and [baptisma] meaning Baptism. It is the doctrine of baptizing infants or children in the Church.

Parable: An illustrative discourse or story that uses common events and culture and is meant to convey a meaning or lesson. Jesus used parables extensively. Some of the OT parables are Trees Making a King (2 Sam. 12:1-4); The Thistle and the Cedar (2 Kings 14:9); Israel, a Vine Planted by Water (Ezek. 24:1014), etc. Some NT parables are The Sower (Luke 8:5-8); the Ten Virgins (Matt. 25:1-13); The Good Samaritan (Luke 10:25-37); The Prodigal Son (Luke 15:11-32), etc.

Paraclete: Advocate or helper. In Christianity, the term paraclete most commonly refers to the Holy Spirit.

Paradise: Biblically, paradise is the place of uninterrupted bliss. The Garden of Eden was considered a paradise. Jesus mentioned paradise while on the cross (Luke 23:43) and Paul also mentioned Paradise (2 Cor. 12:1-4). Some consider paradise to be the abode of people in the intermediate state while others believe it is the permanent location of the saved.

paradox: A seemingly contradictory statement that may nonetheless be true; an apparent but not real contradiction.

parallelism: In Hebrew (and other Ancient Near Eastern) poetry, the primary element which distinguishes poetry from prose is a rhyming of ideas rather than a rhyming of sounds or rhythm.

Parapsychology: The study of things not generally explainable by the scientific method. Examples of subjects studied by parapsychologists would be telepathy, clairvoyance, ghosts, etc.

Parousia: A Greek term (par-ooo-see'-a)that means "arrival" or "coming." The term is often referred to as the time of Christ's return; hence, the Parousia, i.e., 2 Thess. 2:1. The second coming of Christ (from the Greek parousia, "coming") which literally means "coming" or "arrival," used to refer to the second coming of Christ. The notion of the parousia is an important aspect of Christian understandings of the "last things."

Pascal's Wager: The argument that believing in God is the most logical thing to do since if there is a God and you deny him, then you are in trouble. If there is no god and you accept him, there is no problem because it doesn't matter. Logically, it is better to not deny that God exists than to deny he does. There is truth to this argument, but the problem is that it does not define which "god" to believe in since in many religions, believing in a different god brings a punishing judgment. Nevertheless, this does not excuse a person from at least trying to discover if there is a God or not and who He might be.

passover: Passover or Pesach, is an important, biblically derived Jewish festival. The Jewish people celebrate Passover as a commemoration of their liberation by God from slavery in Egypt and their freedom as a nation under the leadership of Moses.

pastor: term used interchangeably with "elder," "overseer," and "bishop" to refer to the main governing office of a local church in the New Testament. Translating the Greek poirnen, the term identifies the shepherding task with the office of elder.

patripassianism: theological heresy, which arose during the third century, associated with writers such as Noetus, Praxeas, and Sabellius, focusing on the belief that the Father suffered as the Son. In other words, the suffering of Christ on the cross is to be regarded as the suffering of the Father. According to these writers, the only distinction within the Godhead was a succession of modes or operations, so that Father, Son, and Spirit were just different modes of being, or expressions, of the same basic divine entity.

patristic: adjective used to refer to the first centuries in the history of the church, following the writing of the New Testament (the "patristic period"), or thinkers writing during this period (the "patristic writers"). For many writers, the period thus designated seems to be c.100–451 (in other words, the period between the completion of the last of the New Testament writings and the landmark Council of Chalcedon).

peace: doctrine that God is separate from all confusion and disorder in his being and in his actions, yet he is continually active in innumerable well-ordered, fully controlled, simultaneous actions

Pedobaptism: The practice of infant baptism.

Pelagianism: The teaching of a monk named Pelagius in the fifth Century. He taught that man's will was and still is free to choose good or evil and there is no inherited sin (through Adam). Every infant born into the world is in the same condition as Adam before the fall and becomes a sinner because he sins. This is opposed to the Biblical teaching that we are by nature children of wrath (Eph. 2:3) and that we sin because we are sinners. Pelagius said we are able to keep the commandments of God because God has given us the ability. Therefore, there is no need of redemption and the crucifixion of Jesus is merely a supreme example of love, humility, obedience, and sacrifice. This heresy has its relatives in the form of the cults that deny the total dependence upon God and maintain that salvation is obtainable through our own efforts. (Compare to Arminianism and Calvinism). An understanding of how humans are able to merit their salvation which is diametrically opposed to that of Augustine of Hippo, placing considerable emphasis upon the role of human works and playing down the idea of divine grace.

Pelagianism, Semi or Simi: Later, John Cassian's doctrine in a compromise between the Pelagius view and the Augustine view surfaced. This doctrine taught man was not dead in tresspass and sin, just sick. That man was only weakened by the fall and that man had the ability to save himself by accepting or rejecting of his own will, Christ's offer. Pelagius himself was excommunicated, and his theology condemned by a series of church councils, though the issues of the doctrine of free will have remained a sore point for the Church even to our day. The Church looks on the three positions as, St. Augustine regarding natural man as dead, Pelagius regarding him as alive and well, and Cassian regarding him as being merely sick. Augustine's position being the only one that leans entirely on the Sovereign mercies of God.

Pelagius: A fifth-century monk who taught (Pelagianism) that man has the ability to obey God's commands and can take the first and most important steps toward salvation on his own.

penal substitution: The view that Christ in his death bore the just penalty of God for our sins as a substitute for us.

Penance: In Catholicism, a means by which all sins committed after baptism are removed. The means are assigned by a priest and usually consist of special prayers or deeds performed by the sinner.

Pentateuch: This word is from the Greek penta, "five" and teuchos, "a tool". It refers to the first five books of the Bible known as Genesis, Exodus, Leviticus, Numbers, and Deuteronomy. All five were authored by Moses and are also known as "the Law".

Pentecost: word comes from the Greek which means fifty. A Jewish feast during which, following the ascension of Jesus, the Holy Spirit was poured out in new covenant fullness and power on the disciples. This day marked the point of transition between the old covenant work and ministry of the Holy Spirit and the new covenant work and ministry of the Holy Spirit. So, the Pentecost was a celebration on the fiftieth day after Passover. It was a culmination of the feast of weeks (Exodus 34:22,23). Pentecost in the NT is the arrival of the Holy Spirit for the church (Acts 2). At Pentecost the disciples of Jesus were gathered and upon the filling of the Holy Spirit, they heard a great wind and spoke in tongues as tongues of fire that settled upon them. The significance of the fire can be found in recognizing it as a symbol of the dwelling of the Spirit of God (Exodus 19:18; 1 Pet. 4:14). Any denomination or group that traces its historical origin to the Pentecostal revival that began in the United States in 1901 and that holds to the doctrinal positions **(a)** that baptism in the Holy Spirit is ordinarily an event subsequent to conversion, **(b)** that baptism in the Holy Spirit is made evident by the sign of speaking in tongues, and **(c)** that all the spiritual gifts mentioned in the New Testament are to be sought and used today.

perdition: State of eternal punishment and damnation into which a sinful and unpenitent person passes after death.

perfection: The doctrine that God completely possesses all excellent qualities and lacks no part of any qualities that would be desirable for him.

perfectionism: The view that sinless perfection, or freedom from conscious sin, is possible in this life for the Christian.

perichoresis: A term relating to the doctrine of the Trinity, often also referred to by the Latin term circumincessio. The basic notion is that all three persons of the Trinity mutually share in the life of the others, so that none is isolated or detached from the actions of the others.

Piety: From the Latin [pietas] meaning dutifulness. In Theological terms it means dutifulness to God, as in being devout in having reverential commitment to the Lord, which is expressed in the Christian life. The virtue of acting in devotion, duty, and worship to God, is called Piety.

Pneumatology: From the Greek [numa] meaning breath (and by extension Spirit), and [logos] meaning word or discourse. In Theological terms, it is the discourse or study of the Holy Spirit of God. It encompasses the study of His person, work, gifts, and ministry. The Spirit of God being manifested in many ways including teaching (John. 14:26), restraining sin (Genesis 6:3, 20:6), Revelation (Matthew 11:27), and interceding (Romans 8:26). The study of the Holy Spirit, His person, works, relation to the Father and Son, relation to man, ministry in salvation and sanctification, conviction, and indwelling. The study of the Holy Spirit, comes from two Greek words which mean "wind, air, spirit" and "word" - combining to mean "the study of the Holy Spirit." Pneumatology is the study of God the Holy Spirit, the "third Person" of the Trinity.

Polemics: From the Greek [polemikos], meaning of war. In Theological terms by implication it has come to mean an aggressive attack on (or refutation of) the opinions or principles of another. As in the disputation or argument with another over a controversial issue in the Church.

Polytheism: The teaching that there are many gods. In the Ancient Near East the nation of Israel was faced with the problem of the gods of other nations creeping into the theology of Judaism and corrupting the true revelation of God. Baal was the god of rain and exercised a powerful influence over the religion of many pagan cultures and even into the Jewish community. This is so because rain was essential to survival. Rain meant the crops would grow, the animals would have water, and the people would be able to eat. If there was no rain, death prevailed. Such visible realities as rain, drought, crops, and death often carried the spiritual character of the nation of Israel into spiritual adultery: worshiping other gods. The Bible does recognize the existence of other gods, but only as false gods (1 Cor. 8:5-6; Gal. 4:8-9) and clearly teaches that there is only one true God (Isaiah 43:10; 44:6,8; 45:5,14,18,21,22; 46:9; 47:8;). (See Monotheism.)

Pope: In Catholicism, the Pope is supposed to be Christ's representative on earth. He is the alleged, visible successor of Peter.

Post-Enlightenment: A transition from an Enlightenment confidence in human reason to a post-Enlightenment view that recognizes the challenge of reasonable pluralism. The post-Enlightenment view still aspires to show that our diverse reasoning can lead us to converge on public principles that protect human freedom, but its aspirations are chastened. The fact of reasonable pluralism explains why many liberals have become public reason liberals, because treating others as free and equal requires admitting that the free use of practical reason leads in many different directions.

postliberalism: A theological movement, especially associated with Duke University and Yale Divinity School in the 1980s, which criticized the liberal reliance upon human experience, and reclaimed the notion of community tradition as a controlling influence in theology.

postmillennialism: The view that Christ will return to the earth after the millennium. In this view, the millennium is an age of peace and righteousness on the earth, brought about by the orozress of the zosnel and the growth of the church.   Belief that through the preaching of the word of God, the entire world will be converted to Christianity and this will usher in the kingdom of Christ. This is when Christ will return.

Postmodernism: A relativistic system of observation and thought that denies absolutes and objectivity. Postmodernism has influenced theology, art, culture, architecture, society, film, technology, and economics. A cultural development, starting n the late twentieth century, which resulted from the general collapse in confidence of the universal rational principles of the Enlightenment. It is characterized by a rejection of absolutes and of objective and rational attempts to define reality.Traditional social, art, social, and cultural, constructs are discarded and reinterpreted in relativistic terms. An example of postmodern thought would be the validation of homosexuality as an equally legitimate sexual expression over and against the Judeo-Christian ethic of heterosexual monogamy. In other words, previously taboo practices and beliefs are given equal validity to traditional values and norms often to the point of displacing the latter. This equalization and displacement are not restricted to religious realms, but affect all circles of human interaction.

posttribulational rapture: The "taking up" of believers after the great tribulation to be with Christ just a few moments prior to his coming to earth with them to reign during the millennial kingdom (or, on the amillennial view, during the eternal state).

power: Another term for God's omnipotence.

Predestination: (as a doctrine in Christian theology) the divine foreordaining of all that will happen, especially with regard to the salvation of some and not others. It has been particularly associated with the teachings of St. Augustine of Hippo and of Calvin. Also see Single predestination; Double predestination

power of the church: The church's God-given authority to carryon spiritual warfare, proclaim the gospel, and exercise church discipline.

Premillennialism: From the Latin [pre] meaning before, [mille] meaning thousand, and [annum] meaning years. This is a doctrine very similar to the Messianic expectations of the first-century Judaizers in that it teaches that sometime in the future Christ will return to establish a literal political and earthly Kingdom in Jerusalem and will reign 1000 years on earth. Pre-millennial, meaning that Christ comes to establish this Kingdom pre or "before" the millennium.

Preterism: (Praeterist, preterist) Identifies Christians who believe that most or all of Bible Prophecy has already been fulfilled in Christ, by 70 A.D., or the on-going expansion of His Kingdom. The word Preterit is Latin and means Pre (before) in fulfillment. i.e., [L. praeteritus, gone by]. It is expressing time fulfilled. It is the doctrine of Past-fulfillment of most of the prophesy of scripture.

Preterition: The act of passing over something, or neglecting it. In theology, it is the Reformed doctrine that God passed over people by not electing them into salvation. Instead, only those elected to salvation will be saved and passed over all others.

pretribulational premillennialism: The view that Christ will return secretly before the great tribulation to call believers to himself, and then again after the tribulation to reign on earth for 1,000 years.

pretribulational rapture: The "taking up" of believers into heaven secretly during Christ's first return prior to the great tribulation.

Priest: A person appointed by God in the Old Testament to offer sacrifices, prayers, and praises to God on behalf of the people. This office was fulfilled by Christ, who has become the great high priest for all believers. The term can also refer to a category of church officers in both Roman Catholic and Anglican churches, though they each attach different meanings to the word "priest." A person having the ability to perform certain religious rites, sacraments. Generally, a priest stands between God and Man and administers the ceremonial rites on behalf of the individuals as an offering to God. In many churches (Catholic), the priest is below the Bishop in ecclesiastical order and rank.

primogeniture: The Old Testament practice in which the firstborn in any generation in a human family has leadership in the family for that generation.

principalities and powers: In every place where the phrase appears in the Bible in the King James version, the contexts make it clear that it refers to the vast array of evil and malicious spirits who make war against the people of God. The principalities and powers of Satan are in view here, beings that wield power in the unseen realms to oppose everything and everyone that is of God. Other versions translate it variously as "rulers and authorities," "forces and authorities," and "rulers and powers." It refers to demonic powers in some verses of the Bible.

Process Theology: A modern theological movement based on the view of reality in which process, change and evolution are as fundamental as substance, permanence, and stability. God is undergoing a process of growth and development. He is not omnipotent or omniscient.

progressive creationism: An "old earth" theory which holds that God created new types of plant and animal creatures at several different points of time in the earth's history, and between those points, plant and animal life developed more diversity on its own.

prophecy: The New Testament gift of the Holy Spirit that involves telling something that God has spontaneously brought to mind. It is listed among the gifts of the Spirit in 1 Corinthians 12:10 and Romans 12:6. The Greek word translated "prophesying" or "prophecy" in both passages properly means to "speak forth" or declare the divine will, to interpret the purposes of God, or to make known in any way the truth of God which is designed to influence people. Many people misunderstand the gift of prophecy to be the ability to predict the future. While knowing something about the future may sometimes have been an aspect of the gift of prophecy, it was primarily a gift of proclamation ("forth-telling"), not prediction ("fore-telling").

Prophet: One who is the mouthpiece of God, standing between God and man to communicate to man the word of God, inspired and without error. Not a puppet or a mindless repeater of what he hears. Instead, he retains his own will, mind, and thoughts as he speaks for God. God would put His words in their mouths (Deut. 18:18; Jer. 1:9). God's servant (Zech. 1:6) and messenger (2 Chron. 36:15). In OT, the prophecies fell into three categories: concerning the destiny of Israel, the messianic prophecies, and eschatological prophecies. The term Law and Prophets refers to the writings of the OT divided into two categories. The Law is the Pentateuch, or Genesis, Exodus, Leviticus, Numbers, and Deuteronomy. The Prophets are all the rest of the OT books. This is one of the offices fulfilled by Christ, (He was prophet, priest, and King); it is the office by which he most fully reveals God to us.

Propitiation: A sacrifice that bears God's wrath to the end and in so doing changes God's wrath toward us into favor.; it is a turning away of wrath by an offering. It is similar to expiation but expiation does not carry the nuances involving wrath. For the Christian the propitiation was the shed blood of Jesus on the cross. It turned away the wrath of God so that He could pass "over the sins previously committed" (Rom. 3:25). It was the Father who sent the Son to be the propitiation (1 John 4:10) for all (1 John 2:2). The act whereby God's righteous wrath is satisfied by the atonement of Christ.

R

ransom to Satan theory of the Atonement: The theory or view that in the atonement Christ paid a ransom to Satan to redeem us out of his kingdom; Belief that by virtue of Adam's sin, all humanity was sold into bondage to Satan who had "legal" rights to them. Christ, by his death, made a payment to Satan, buying them back and making salvation possible.

Rapture: An eschatological (end times) event whereupon the return of Christ the true believers who are "alive and remain shall be caught up together with them [those who already died as Christians] in the clouds to meet the Lord in the air..." (1 Thess. 4:17). This "taking up" or snatching up (from Latin rapio, "seize, snatch, carry away") of believers to be with Christ when he returns to the earth represents the time of the resurrection where the Christian receives his resurrected body. First to receive their new bodies are those who have died as Christians, and then "those who are alive and remain." There is much debate over the time of the rapture. Does it occur at the beginning, in the middle, or at the end of the tribulation period? (See Tribulation.)

Rationalism: A branch of philosophy where truth is determined by reason.

Lit. "to be purchased." This is the scriptural teaching that God paid a price for man's salvation, redeeming us from sin.

Reconciliation: Changing for the better a relationship between two or more persons. Theologically it refers to the change of relationship between God and man. We are naturally children of wrath (Eph. 2:3), and are at enmity with God (Eph. 2:11-15); but, "...we were reconciled to God through the death of His Son..." (Rom. 5:10). Because of the death of Jesus, the Christian's relationship with God is changed for the better.

We are now able to have fellowship with Him (1 John 1:3) whereas before we could not. So, we are reconciled to Him (Rom. 5:10-11). The problem of sin that separates us from God (Isaiah 59:2) has been addressed and removed in the cross. It was accomplished by God in Christ (2 Cor. 5:18).

Redemption: The saving work of Christ viewed as an act of "buying back" sinners out of their bondage to sin and to Satan through the payment of a ransom (though the analogy should not be pressed to specify anyone to whom a ransom was paid). It means to free someone from bondage. It often involves the paying of a ransom, a price that makes redemption possible. The Israelites were redeemed from Egypt. We were redeemed from the power of sin and the curse of the Law (Gal. 3:13) through Jesus (Rom. 3:24; Col. 1:14). We were bought with a price (1 Cor. 6:20; 7:23).

Reformation: The Protestant Reformation, often referred to simply as the Reformation, was the schism within Western Christianity initiated by Martin Luther, John Calvin, Huldrych Zwingli and other early Protestant Reformers. This 16th-century religious, political, intellectual and cultural upheaval splintered Catholic Europe, setting in place the structures and beliefs that would define the continent in the modern era. The Reformation came about because of the Roman Catholic Church claim of a unique authority over all other churches and denominations because of the line of Roman Catholic Popes throughout the centuries, all the way to the Apostle Peter. In their view, this "apostolic succession" gives them a unique authority superseding all other denominations or churches. According to the Catholic Encyclopedia, this apostolic succession is only "found in the Catholic Church" and no "separate Churches have any valid claim to it."

Reformed: Another term for the theological tradition known as Calvinism and used to refer to a tradition of theology which draws inspiration from the writings of John Calvin (1510–64) and his successors. The term is now generally used in preference to "Calvinist."

Regeneration: The secret act of God whereby He renews the spiritual condition of a sinner. He imparts new spiritual life to us; sometimes called "being born again." It is a spiritual change brought about by the work of the Holy Spirit so that the person then possesses new life, eternal life. Regeneration is a change in our moral and spiritual nature where justification is a change in our relationship with God. Also, sanctification is the work of God in us to make us more like Jesus. Regeneration is the beginning of that change. It means to be born again.

Reincarnation: The belief in the birth and rebirth of a person's soul over and over again in different human bodies throughout history. Some forms of reincarnation include incarnations into animals, plants, or inanimate objects. The purpose of reincarnation is to allow the individual to learn spiritual lessons through life so that he/she may return to God from whence the soul came. Reincarnation is closely tied to Karma.

Reprobate: Refers to those individuals that are destined for hell.

Rosary: In Catholicism, a string of beads containing five sets with ten small beads. Each set of ten is separated by another bead. It also contains a crucifix. It is used in saying special prayers, usually to Mary where the rosary is used to count the prayers.

Sabellianism: An early trinitarian heresy, which treated the three persons of the Trinity as different historical manifestations of the one God. It is generally regarded as a form of modalism. Another name for modalism, a term derived from the third-century teacher Sabellius, who propagated this doctrine.

Sacrament: In Protestant teaching, a ceremony or rite that the church observes as a sign of God's grace and as one means by those justified continue to receive God's grace; a visible manifestation of the word. The bread and wine in the Lord's Supper are considered sacraments in that they are visible manifestations of the covenant promise of our Lord: "In the same way, after the supper he took the cup, saying, 'This cup is the new covenant in my blood, which is poured out for you.'" (Luke 22:20). God, in the OT, used visible signs along with His spoken word. These visible signs, then, were considered to have significance. "Among the OT sacraments the rites of circumcision and the Passover were stressed as being the OT counterparts of baptism (Col. 1:10-12) and the Lord's Supper (1 Cor. 5:7)." Also a church service or rite which was held to have been instituted by Jesus Christ himself. Although Roman Catholic theology and church practice recognize seven such sacraments (baptism, confirmation, Eucharist, marriage, ordination, penance, and unction), Protestant theologians generally argue that only two (baptism and Eucharist) were to be found in the New Testament itself.

Sadducee: A group of religious leaders in the Jewish religion from the second century B.C. to the first century A.D. In Hebrew their names mean "the righteous ones." They were smaller in size than the group of the Pharisees. The Sadducees were generally on the upper class, often in a priestly line, and the Pharisees in the middle class, usually merchants and tradesmen. The Sadducees accepted only the Torah, the first five books of the old Testament, as authoritative. They held rigidly to the old Testament law and a denying the life after death, reward and punishment after death, the resurrection, and the existence of angels and demons. They controlled the temple and its services and were unpopular with the majority of the Jewish population.

Salvation: Salvation is the "saving" of a sinner from the righteous judgment of God. When someone appeals to God and seeks forgiveness in Jesus, his sins are forgiven. He is cleansed. His relationship with God is restored, and he is made a new creature (2 Cor. 5:17). All of this is the work of God, not man. Salvation is a free gift (Rom. 6:23). We are saved from damnation. When anyone sins, and we all have (Rom. 3:23; 6:23), he deserves eternal separation from God (Isaiah 59:2). Yet, because of His love and mercy, God became a man (John 1:1,14) and bore the sins of the world in His body on the cross (1 Pet. 2:24; 1 John 2:2). We are forgiven when we realize that there is nothing we can do to earn the favor of God and we put our trust in what Jesus did for us on the cross (Eph. 2:8-9; 1 Cor. 15:1-4). Only God saves. The only thing we bring to the cross is our sin. Both God the Father (Isaiah 14:21) and Jesus (John 4:42) are called Savior; that is, deliverer from sin. Remember, it was the Father who sent the Son (1 John 4:10) to be the Savior.

Sanctification: To sanctify means to be set apart for a holy use. God has set us apart for the purpose of sanctification not impurity (1 Thess. 4:7) and being such we are called to do good works (Eph. 2:10). Christians are to sanctify Christ as Lord in their hearts (1 Pet. 3:15). God sanctified Israel as His own special nation (Ezek. 27:28). People can be sanctified (Exodus 19:10,14) and so can a mountain (Exodus 19:23), as can the Sabbath day (Gen. 2:3), and every created thing is sanctified through the word of God and prayer (1 Tim. 4:4). Sanctification follows justification and is the process by which the Holy Spirit makes us more like Christ in all that we do, think, and desire. True sanctification is impossible apart from the atoning work of Christ on the cross because only after our sins are forgiven can we begin to lead a holy life. In justification our sins are completely forgiven in Christ. A progressive work of God and man that makes us more and more free from sin and more like Christ in our actual lives.

Sanhedrin: Name given in the mishna to the council of seventy-one Jewish sages who formed a "sitting together," hence "assembly" or "council"). The assembly of twenty-three to seventy-one men (usually 71) was appointed in every city in the Land of Israel. These individuals (71), around the time of Christ that was comprised of Pharisees and Sadducees who governed the Jewish nation while under the rule of Rome. It often served as a court to settle legal and religious matters.

Satan: The personal name of the head of the demons.

saving faith: Trust in Jesus Christ as a living person for forgiveness of sins and for eternal life with God.

schism: A deliberate break with the unity of the church, condemned vigorously by influential writers of the early church, such as Cyprian and Augustine.

scholasticism: The method of study in the Middle Ages which was used to support the doctrines of the church through reason and logic; a particular approach to Christian theology, associated especially with the Middle Ages, which lays emphasis upon the rational justification and systematic presentation of Christian theology.

Scripture: The writings (Greek graphe; rendered in Latin by scriptural of the Old and New Testaments, which have historically been recognized as God's words in written form. Another term for the Bible. The scriptures are, quite simply, the Bible which consists of 39 books in the Old Testament and 27 in the New Testament. Each one is inspired, without error, and is completely accurate in all things it addresses. The entire Bible, though written by many people over thousands of years is harmonious in all its teachings. This is because each book of the Bible is inspired.

Scripture principle: The theory, especially associated with Reformed theologians, that the practices and beliefs of the church should be grounded in Scripture. Nothing that could not be demonstrated to be grounded in Scripture could be regarded as binding upon the believer. The phrase sola scriptura, "by Scripture alone," summarizes this principle.

Second Coming: Term applied to the return of Christ in which there will be a sudden, personal, visible, bodily return of Christ from heaven to earth. If there is a second coming, it follows that there must have been a first. The first coming of Christ was His incarnation when He was born. At the Second Coming of Christ every eye will see Him (Rev. 1:7) as He descends from heavens in the clouds (Matt. 24:30; Mark 14:6).

self-existence: Another term for God's independence.

Septuagint, The (LXX): The Greek translation of the Old Testament. The Old Testament was originally written in Hebrew. It was during the reign of Ptolemy Philadelphus (285-246 B.C.) that the Pentateuch, the first five books of the Bible, were translated into Greek. Shortly afterwards the rest of the Old Testament was also translated. This translation was done by approximately 70 translators. Therefore, the Septuagint is known by the letters LXX, the Roman numerals for seventy.

seraphim: A class of created spiritual beings that are said to continually worship God.

Sin: Sin is anything that is contrary to the law or will of God or any failure to conform to the moral law of God in act, attitude, or nature. For example: if you lie, you have sinned. Why? Because God has said not to lie (Exodus 20:16). If you do what God has forbidden, then you have sinned. In addition, if you do not do what God has commanded, you sin (James 4:17). Either way, the result is eternal separation from God (Isaiah 59:2). Sin is lawlessness (1 John 1:3) and unrighteousness (1 John 5:17). Sin leads to bondage (Rom. 6:14-20) and death (Rom. 6:23). Paul, in the book of Romans, discusses sin. He shows that everyone, both Jew and Greek, is under sin (Rom. 3:9). He shows that sin is not simply something that is done, but a condition of the heart (Rom. 3:10-12). In Ephesians Paul says that we are "by nature children of wrath" (Eph. 2:3). Yet, "while we were still helpless, at the right time Christ died for the ungodly" (Rom. 5:6).

Single Predestination: God predestines the elect to eternal life, and passively destines the non-elect by "passing over" them, choosing not to elect them, leaving them in their sins, destined to eternal punishment.

sinless perfection: The state of being totally free from sin; some hold that such a state is possible in this life. (See also "perfectionism."

Skepticism: Skepticism is the philosophical approach that denies that the world can be objectively known in any absolute sense. It further denies the true knowability of God social darwinism: The application of the concept of evolution to the historical development of human societies, placing special emphasis on the idea of "struggle for survival." Hitler picked up these ideas and incorporated them into Nazism.

Socinianism: A form of Christian heterodoxy especially associated with the Italian writer Socinus (Fausto Paolo Sozzini, 1539–1604). Although Socinus was noted for his specific criticisms of the doctrine of the Trinity and the incarnation, the term "Socinian" has come to refer particularly to the idea that Christ's death on the cross did not have any supernatural or transcendent implications. On this view, Christ died as an outstanding moral example, to encourage humanity to avoid sin, not to make satisfaction for human sin.

Socratic: The word is of Greek origin, meaning [of socrates]. It pertains to the methodology of the Greek Scholar and Philosopher Socrates, who often attempted to elicit truth by question and answer. In Christian circles it is used in the same fashion, defining a method of debate or discussion wherein one would try to elicit truth by means of question and answer.

Sola Fide: The teaching that faith alone saves a person when he places his faith and trust in the sacrificial work of Christ.

Sola Gratia: The teaching that God pardons believers without any merit of their own based solely on the sacrificial work of Christ.

Sola Scriptura: The teaching that the Scriptures contain all that is necessary for salvation and proper living before God.

solar system: The sun and its attendant planets, their moons, asteroids, dust, and comets, bound to the sun by gravitation.

Son of God: A title of Jesus, often used of Jesus to designate him as the heavenly, eternal Son who is equal in nature to God himself. It implies His deity (John 5:18) because the title is one of equality with God. In the OT it was figuratively applied to Israel (Exo 4:22). In the NT it is applied to Christ (Luke 1:35). It has many facets, for example: It shows that He is to be honored equally with the Father (John 5:22-23). That He is to be worshiped (Matt. 2:2,11; 14:33; John 9:35-38; Heb. 1:6); called God (John 20:28; Col. 2:9; Heb. 1:8); prayed to (Acts 7:55-60; 1 Cor. 1:1-2).

Son of Man: The term by which Jesus referred to himself most often, which had an Old Testament background, especially in the heavenly figure who was given eternal rule over the world in the vision in Daniel 7:13.

Soteriology: Derived from the Greek word(sote¯ria) soterious which means salvation, it is the study of the doctrine of salvation through Christ. Soteriology discusses how Christ's death secures the salvation of those who believe. It helps us to understand the doctrines of redemption, justification, sanctification, propitiation, and the substitutionary atonement. From two Greek words [sozo] meaning Save, and [logos] meaning word. By extension the word or discourse of Salvation. It is the doctrine of the study of God's work in Salvation. How through the passion, death, resurrection, and ascension of Christ, man's redemption is accomplished. It is the Theology of salvation. Theological reflection on the meaning of salvation in Christ and how we may share salvation by faith. Salvation is eternal life in the fullness of God's love. In Christ, we are redeemed from sin and death and restored to right relationship with God. We are made righteous and justified in Christ, despite the inadequacy of our works for salvation. Salvation is deliverance from anything that threatens to prevent fulfillment and enjoyment of our relationship with God. Through the Spirit, especially in the life and sacraments of the church, we may share in Christ's life, death, and resurrection. We may participate in a saving process of sanctification by which the saving life of Christ becomes increasingly our own reality. This process is completed and revealed in Christ, and it is begun in us through faith in him. Completed union with God is the end of this saving process. In Christ, we come to be at one with God. Although this saving process is not yet completed, we look with hope for its fulfillment in the final coming of the kingdom of God. The Episcopal theologian William Porcher DuBose wrote The Soteriology of the New Testament (1892), which is a significant presentation of soteriology. See Atonement; see Heaven; see Redeemer; see Righteousness.

Soul Sleep: The teaching that when a person dies his soul ceases to exist. On the final judgment day he is brought back to life and judged. This is not a heresy, only an error of interpretation. The Bible is not specific on the condition of the person between death and resurrection. However, there are scriptures that strongly suggest man's continued self-awareness and continued existence after death (Luke 16:19-31; 2 Cor. 5:1-10; Phil. 1:21-23).

Sovereignty: The right of God to exercise power over his creation and do as He wishes (Psalm 50:1; Isaiah 40:15; 1 Tim. 6:15) with His creation. This implies that there is no external influence upon Him and that He also has the ability to exercise His power and control according to His will.

spacetime: The mathematical construct representing the arena of events. Since the theory of relativity it has been recognized that space and time cannot be separated, with time then becoming the fourth dimension of our Universe.

speaking in tongues: Prayer or praise spoken in syllables not understood by the speaker.

special revelation: God's words addressed to specific people, including the words of the Bible. This is to be distinguished from general revelation, which is given to all people generally. God has told people about himself in the Bible, a specific and detailed revelation of himself, which gives us details regarding his person and what he expects of people. It is not complete revelation, though: natural revelation is complementary and completes his revelation of himself.

spirit: The immaterial part of man, a term used interchangeably with "soul."

spiritual body: The type of body we will receive at our future resurrection, which will not be "immaterial" but rather suited to and responsive to the guidance of the Holy

Spirit.

Spiritual Gifts: Spiritual gifts are gifts given by Jesus to His church. Spiritual gifts are discussed in 1 Cor. 12 - 14 and Rom. 12. They vary in degree and nature. There are some that are obviously supernatural in the usage: speaking in tongues, discerning of spirits, healing, etc. There are others that are not so supernatural: administrations, help, admonition, etc. There is debate over the continuance of the gifts. Some say that the gifts have ceased because we now have the Bible and that the gifts were used to build of the body of Christ during the beginning of the Christian church stating no further need for the revelatory gifts like speaking in and the interpretation of tongues. Others maintain that the gifts are all for today though to a lesser degree. There are good arguments on both sides.

spiritual presence: A phrase descriptive of the Reformed view of the Lord's Supper that regards Christ as spiritually present in a special way as we partake of the bread and wine.

spirituality: The doctrine that God exists as a being that is not made of any matter, has no parts or dimensions, is unable to be perceived by our bodily senses, and is more excellent than any other kind of existence.

strong force: The attraction acting over extremely short distances between nucleons and thus enabling the atomic nucleus to resist the electrostatic mutual repulsion of its protons.

Subjectivism: The teaching that the individual is the source and judge of all religious knowledge based upon his own knowledge and experience.

sufficiency of Scripture: The idea that Scripture contained all the words of God he intended his people to have at each stage of redemptive history, and that it now contains all the words of God we need for salvation, for trusting him perfectly, and for obeying him perfectly.

Sumerians: An Ancient Near Eastern people living in Mesopotamia during the third and second millenniums BC, speaking an agglutinative, ergative language unrelated to any other known language. The writing system they developed (cuneiform) was later borrowed by the Babylonians and Assyrians.

supernatural: Used sometimes in the sense of make-believe, it originally referred to that which had been done by a being other than natural (human or animal) - though no less real.

Supralapsarianism: From a Latin term, [supra] meaning before and [lapsum] meaning fall, is the doctrine that God chose the election for his own glory prior to the decision to let sin enter into creation. An issue within Reformed theology dealing with what may have happened in God's mind regarding the logical order of His considering whom to elect into salvation before the foundation of the world. The word means "before the fall." This position holds that God first decided that he would save some people and then second that he would allow sin into the world. By contrast, the infralapsarian ("after the fall") position is the reverse in that it holds that God first decided he would allow sin into the world and second that he would then save people from it.

The order of effects would be as follows.

- In eternity past God proposed to elect some of mankind to eternal life and to condemn others.
- God proposed to create man.

- God proposed to permit the Fall.
- God proposed to send Christ to redeem the elect.
- God proposed to send the Holy Spirit to apply salvation to the elect

Synagogue: A Jewish house of worship. Traditionally the first synagogues were established during the Babylonian exile. The early synagogues had a place in the center of the room where the sacred scrolls were kept and from where they were read. It is from the worship order established in synagogues that our modern church patterns of reading and expounding upon scripture from the pulpit are derived.

Synergism: From the Greek word [synergia], meaning, to cooperate with, or to work together. In Christian theology it is the teaching that man's will works together or cooperates with God to accomplish our Salvation. It is based upon one or more of the theories of prevenient grace, all of which are deficient and biblically unsound. The teaching that we cooperate with God in our efforts of salvation. This is opposed to monergism which is the teaching that God is the sole agent involved in salvation. Cults are synergistic in that they teach that God's grace combined with our efforts are what makes forgiveness of sins possible.

Synoptic Gospels: A term used to refer to the first three gospels (Matthew, Mark, and Luke). The term (derived from the Greek word synopsis, "summary") refers to the way in which the three gospels can be seen as providing similar "summaries" of the life, death, and resurrection of Jesus Christ. They are referred to as the synoptic gospels because of their great similarity.

Synoptic problem: The scholarly question of how the three Synoptic Gospels relate to each other. Perhaps the most common approach to the relation of the three Synoptic Gospels is the "two source" theory, which claims that Matthew and Luke used Mark as a source, while also drawing upon a second source (usually known as "Q"). Other possibilities exist: for example, the Griesbach hypothesis, which treats Matthew as having been written first, followed by Luke and then Mark.

Syriac: Encompasses the multiple Churches of Eastern Christianity whose services tend to feature liturgical use of ancient Syriac, a dialect of Middle Aramaic that emerged in Edessa in the early 1st century AD, and is closely related to the Aramaic of Jesus.

systematic theology: A discipline of Christian theology that formulates an orderly, rational, and coherent account of the Christian faith and beliefs. Subdisciplines are dogmatics, ethics and philosophy of religion. It is a study that answers the question, "What does the whole Bible teach us today?" about any given topic. Systematic theology is, therefore, the division of theology into systems that explain its various areas. For example, many books of the Bible give information about the angels. No one book gives all the information about the angels. Systematic theology organizes the teachings of the Bible into categorical systems taking into consideration all the information about a given topic from all books within the Bible.

T

Tabernacle: The structure ordered built by God so that He might dwell among His people (Exodus 25:8). It was to be mobile and constructed to exacting specifications. It is referred to in Exodus 25-27, 30-31, 35-40; Num. 3:25ff.; 4:4 ff.; 7:1ff. In all of scripture more space is devoted to the tabernacle than any other topic. Many books have been written on the spiritual significance of the tabernacle, how it represented Christ, and how it foretold the gospel. The tabernacle consisted of the outer court and the tabernacle. The outer court was entered from the East. The outer court contained the altar of burnt offering (Exodus 27:1-8) and the bronze laver (Exodus 30:17-21). The tabernacle stood within the court (Exodus 26:1ff.). It was divided into two main divisions: the holy place and the holy of holies which were separated by a veil (Exodus 26:31 ff.), the same veil that was torn from top to bottom at the crucifixion of Jesus (Matt. 27:51). Where the veil had represented the barrier separating sinful man from a holy God (Heb. 9:8), its destruction represented the free access sinners have to God through the blood of Christ (Heb. 10:19ff.). The tabernacle was a place of sacrifice. The holy place contained three things: first, a table on which was placed the shewbread, the bread of the presence (Exodus 25:23-30), second, a golden lampstand (Exodus 25:31-40) and third, an altar of incense (Exodus 30:1-7). In the Holy of Holies was the ark of the covenant which contained the Ten Commandments (Exodus 25:16). The holy of holies was entered only once a year by the high priest who offered sacrifice for the nation of Israel.

Tanakh: Also known as the Mikra is the canon of the Hebrew Bible. The traditional Hebrew text is known as the Masoretic Text.

Targums: Spoken paraphrases, explanations and expansions of the Jewish scriptures that a Rabbi would give in the common language of the listeners, which during the time of this practice was commonly, but not exclusively, Aramaic. This had become necessary near the end of the last century before the Christian era, as the common language was in transition and Hebrew was used for little more than schooling and worship. Eventually it became necessary to give explanations and paraphrases in the common language after the Hebrew scripture was read. The noun Targum is derived from early semitic quadriliteral root 'trgm', and the Akkadian term 'targummanu' refers to "translator, interpreter".

Teleological argument: An argument for the existence of God which reasons that, since the universe exhibits evidence of order and design, there must be an intelligent and purposeful God who created it to function in this way; an attempted proof of God's existence based upon the premise that the universe is designed and therefore needs a designer: God.

Teleology: The study of final causes, results. Having a definite purpose, goal, or design.

Temptation: That which moves us to sin. God cannot be tempted (James 1:13). But we can be tempted by our lusts (James 1:13-15), money (1 Tim. 6:9), lack of self examination (Gal. 6:1), and the boastful pride of life (1 John 2:16), to name a few. We are commanded to pray to be delivered from temptation (Matt. 6:13) for the Lord is capable of delivering us from it (2 Pet. 2:9).

Testament: A derivation of the Latin word testamentum, which was used in Jerome's Vulgate to translate the Hebrew word b'rith, covenant. The Greek equivalent is diatheke, which also means covenant. The word used in describing the two main divisions of the Bible: The Old Testament and The New Testament. It should be understood then, that the Bible is generally to be looked at as a covenant between God and man.

Tetragrammaton (YHWH): Term applied to the four Hebrew letters that make up the name of God as revealed to Moses in Exodus 3:14. God said to Moses, "And God said to Moses, "I AM WHO I AM"; and He said, "Thus you shall say to the sons of Israel, 'I AM has sent me to you.'" YHWH makes up the base of the verb "to be" from which God designated His own name as "I AM." In English the letters are basically equivalent to YHWH. It is from these four letters that the name of God is derived and has been rendered as Yahweh and Jehovah. The true pronunciation of God's name has been lost through lack of use, because the Jews, who were first given the name of God, would not pronounce it out of their awe and respect for God.

Theism: The teaching that there is a God and that He is actively involved in the affairs of the world. This does not necessitate the Christian concept of God, but includes it. (Compare to Deism)

Theodicy: A term coined by the German philosopher Gottfried Wilhelm Leibnitz (1646–1716) to refer to a theoretical justification of the goodness of God in the face of the presence of evil in the world. It is the study of the problem of evil in the world. The issue is raised in light of the sovereignty of God. How could a holy and loving God who is in control of all things allow evil to exist? The answer has been debated for as long as the church has existed. We still do not have a definitive answer and the Bible does not seek to justify God's actions. It is clear that God is sovereign, and that He has willed the existence of both good and evil, and that all of this is for His own glory. Prov. 16:4 says, "The LORD works out everything for his own ends -- even the wicked for a day of disaster"; Isaiah 45:7 says, "I form the light and create darkness, I bring prosperity and create disaster; I, the LORD, do all these things."

Theology: From the Greek [theos] meaning God, and [logos] meaning word or discourse. It is is the discourse or study of God and the revelation of His omni-perfect attributes, such as His Word, omnipresence, mercy, justice and purposes. The study of God, His nature, attributes, character, abilities, revelation, etc. True theology is found in the Bible which is the self-revelation of God.

theopaschitism: A disputed teaching, regarded by some as a heresy, which arose during the sixth century, associated with writers such as John Maxentius and the slogan "one of the Trinity was crucified." The formula can be interpreted in a perfectly orthodox sense and was defended as such by Leontius of Byzantium. However, it was regarded as potentially misleading and confusing by more cautious writers, including Pope Hormisdas (died 523), and the formula gradually fell into disuse.

Theophany: From the Greek words [theos] meaning God, and [phaninomai], meaning manifestation or appearance. A Theophany is the Pre-Incarnate appearance of the God of heaven on earth in the likeness of a human, a angel, a messenger or some other form. That is to say, God appears to man in a form which he can visibly see. A visible appearance or manifestation of God (usually restricted to the Old Testament) in which he takes on a visible form to show himself to people. God has appeared in dreams (Gen. 20:3-7; Gen. 28:12-17), visions (Gen. 15:1-21; Isaiah 6:1-13), as an angel (Gen. 16:7-13; 18:1-33), etc. There is a manifestation known as the Angel of the Lord (Judges 6:20f.) and seems to have characteristics of God Himself (Gen. 16:7-9; 18:1-2; Exodus 3:2-6; Joshua 5:14; Judges 2:1-5; 6:11). Such characteristics as having the name of God, being worshiped, and recognized as God has led many scholars to conclude that the angel of the Lord is really Jesus manifested in the Old Testament. This does not mean that Jesus is an angel. The word "angel" means messenger. Other scriptures that describe more vivid manifestations of God are Gen. 17:1; 18:1; Ex. 6:2-3; 24:9-11; 33:20; Num. 12:6-8; Acts 7:2.

Theorem: A proposition that can be deduced from the premises of a system.

Theotokos: Literally, "the bearer of God." A Greek term used to refer to Mary, the mother of Jesus Christ, with the intention of reinforcing the central insight of the doctrine of the incarnation – that is, that Jesus Christ is none other than God. The term was extensively used by writers of the eastern church, especially around the time of the Nestorian controversy, to articulate both the divinity of Christ and the reality of the incarnation.

Thummim: *See Urim and Thummim.*

Time dilation: The resulting fluidity of time because of speed and/or gravitational conditions. Time is not an absolute.

Tithe: A portion of one's earnings, usually one tenth, that are given to those who perform the work of the Lord since it belongs to the Lord (Lev. 27:30-33). Those who received tithes the OT consisted of priests (Num. 18:21-32). Further OT references are Gen. 14:20; 28:22; 2 Chron. 31:5f; Mal. 3:7-12). In the NT there is no command to tithe a tenth (since we are not under law but grace). But the tithe is mentioned in Luke 18:9-14; 1 Cor. 16:1; 2 Cor. 8).

total depravity: The traditional term for the doctrine referred to in this text as "total inability." The doctrine that fallen man is completely touched by sin and that he is completely a sinner. He is not as bad as he could be, but in all areas of his being, body, soul, spirit, mind, emotions, etc., he is touched by sin. In that sense he is totally depraved. Because man is depraved, nothing good can come out of him (Rom. 3:10-12) and God must account the righteousness of Christ to him. This righteousness is obtainable only through faith in Christ and what He did on the cross. Total depravity is generally believed by the Calvinist groups and rejected by the Arminian groups.

tradition: Ideas or beliefs handed down from the past. Opinion with the force of history behind it.

Transcendence: A theological term referring to the relation of God to creation. God is "other," "different" from His creation. He is independent and different from His creatures (Isaiah 55:8-9). He transcends His creation. He is beyond it and not limited by it or to it. The term describes God as being greater than the creation and independent of it.

Transfiguration: Refers to the mysterious change that occurred to Jesus on the mount: "Six days later, Jesus took with him Peter and James and his brother John and led them up a high mountain, by themselves. And he was transfigured before them, and his face shone like the sun, and his clothes became dazzling white." (Matt. 17:1-2). Preceded Jesus' time on the cross and may have been the Father's preparatory provision to strengthen Jesus as He prepared to bear the sins of the world.

Transliteration: The conversion of a text from one script to another. Transliteration is not concerned with representing the sounds of the original, only the characters, ideally accurately and unambiguously.

Transubstantiation: From the two Latin words [trans], being the intensifying prefix meaning "across," or by extension, "through," and [substantia], which means substance. Thus in the communion service it means the bread actually transforms through the substance of the body. Mainly recognized by Roman Catholicism and Eastern Orthodox Churches. The doctrine according to which the bread and the wine are transformed into the body and blood of Christ in the Eucharist, while retaining their outward appearance. The Roman Catholic theory accepted and taught by Catholicsm in which the elements of bread and wine of the Lord's Supper (often referred to as "the eucharist") actually become the body and blood of Christ. However, there is no perceptible or measurable change in the elements. The transformation occurs during the Mass at the elevation of the elements by the priest.

Tribulation, The: According to premillennialism, this is a seven year period that immediately precedes the return of Christ and the millennial kingdom of His rule which lasts for 1000 years. It will be a time of great peace (the first 3 ½ years) and great war (the second 3 ½ years) when the Antichrist rules over many nations. At the midpoint of the tribulation (at the end of the first 3 ½ years) the Antichrist will proclaim himself worthy of worship. Many will bow down and worship the Antichrist and many will refuse. Those who refuse to worship the Antichrist will be killed. The second half of the tribulation is called the Great Tribulation. It will involve the whole world (Rev. 3:10). There will be catastrophes all over the world. (See Matt. 24; Mark 13; Luke 17.)

Trichotomy: The teaching that the human consists or is made of three parts: body, soul, and spirit. (Compare with Dichotomy.)

Trinitarian theology: Though the word "trinity" is not found in the Bible, it is used to describe one fact the Bible teaches about God: Our God is a Trinity. This means there are three persons in one God, not three Gods. The persons are known as the Father, the Son, and the Holy Spirit and they have all always existed as three separate persons. The person of the Father is not the same person as the Son. The person of the Son is not the same person as the Holy Spirit. The person of the Holy Spirit is not the same person as the Father. If you take away any one, there is no God. God has always been a trinity from all eternity: "From everlasting to everlasting, Thou art God" (Psalm 90:2). God is not one person who took three forms, i.e., the Father who became the Son, who then became the Holy Spirit. This belief is known today as the "Jesus Only Movement". It is taught by the United Apostolic and United Pentecostal churches, and is an incorrect teaching. Nor is God only one person as the Jehovah's Witnesses, the Way International, and the Christadelphians teach (These groups are classified as non-Christian cults). The Bible says there is only one God. Yet, it says Jesus is God (John 1:1,14); it says the Father is God (Phil. 1:2); and it says the Holy Spirit is God (Acts 5:3-4). Since the Son speaks to the Father, they are separate persons. Since the Holy Spirit speaks also (Acts 13:2), He is a separate person. There is one God who exists in three persons.

Trinity: The distinctively Christian doctrine of God, which reflects the complexity of the Christian experience of God as Father, Son, and Holy Spirit. The doctrine is usually summarized in maxims such as "three persons, one God" in which God eternally exists as three persons-Father, Son, and Holy Spirit and each person is fully God, and there is one God.

Tritheism: From the Greek [theis] meaning three and [theos] meaning God. It is the Heretical doctrine that there are three Gods, or that the Father, the Son and the Holy Spirit are three different or distinct Gods. Tritheism is the teaching that the Godhead is really three separate beings forming three separate gods. This erring view is often misplaced for the doctrine of the Trinity which states that there is but one God in three persons: Father, Son, and Holy Spirit.

trust: An aspect of biblical faith or belief in which we not only know and agree with facts about Jesus, but also place personal trust in him as a living person.

two natures, doctrine of: A term generally used to refer to the doctrine of the two natures, human and divine, of Jesus Christ. Related terms include "Chalcedonian definition" and "hypostatic union."

Type, Typology: A type is a representation by one thing of another. Adam was a type of Christ (Rom. 5:14) and so was Isaac (Heb. 11:19). The Passover was a type of Christ (1 Cor. 5:7). There are many types in the Bible and most of them are too extensive and

deep to be listed. An example of a typology follows: Isaac a type of Jesus.
A way of interpreting the Bible which sees certain Old Testament figures and events as anticipating aspects of the gospel. Thus Noah's ark is seen as a "type" (Greek typos, "figure") of the church. From the Latin [typos] meaning a figure of, or image of, and [logos] meaning word or discourse. Typology is thus the discourse of figures, and the true things they represent. In Theology, typology is the discourse of the types in scripture which were (or are) fulfilled in the realities they typify. For example, Old Testament ceremonial laws God gave Israel, apart fro m the obvious moral implications, were symbols which prefigured coming dispensation, activity, grace, and the suffering of Christ. The old Testament ceremonial laws (The types now fulfilled), are no longer physically observed, but the substance of them are forever observed by us in Jesus Christ, in whom they have their completion.

U

Unchangeableness: *See Immutability*
The doctrine that God is unchanging in his being, perfections, purposes, and promises, yet he does act and feel emotions, and he acts and feels differently in response to different situations. God stands above His creation, unchanged and unchanging. An often overlooked and insufficiently pondered attribute of God that sets Him apart from creation is His immutability, His unchangeableness.

Uncia: The Greek characters of upper case: ABGDE, etc. Different copies of Greek manuscripts appear in Uncial form. Minuscules are the lower case letters of the Greek alphabet order and rank.

Unconditional Election: The belief that God predestined people for salvation before the beginning of time. God's election is not conditioned by anything in man, good or evil, foreseen or present, but upon God's sovereign choice.

Unction: From the Greek [chrisma] meaning an ointment or unguent. An unction is thus a type of oil, salve or balm used for example as a medicine or to relieve pain or discomfort. In Theology, an unction from God is a spiritual anointing or healing.

Unitarianism: A theological error that holds to the unity of God by denying the Trinity, the deity of Jesus, and the deity of the Holy Spirit. Unitarians teach the unity of God and hold to a common system of believing as you will about God, salvation, sin, etc. They often profess to have no dogma. Unitarians also hold to the universal redemption of all humankind.

unity: The doctrine that God is not divided into parts, yet we see different attributes of God emphasized at different times.

Universalism: The teaching that all people will eventually be saved through the universal redemption of Jesus. Some universalists teach that even the devil, after a time of punishment, will be redeemed.

Universe: The entire cosmos, made of everything that is. Spacetime.

Unlimited atonement: The view that Christ's death actually paid for the sins of all people who ever lived.

Urim and Thummim: Associated with the hoshen (High Priest's breastplate), divination in general, and cleromancy in particular. Most scholars suspect that the phrase refers to specific objects involved in the divination. Thummim is widely considered to be derived from a root word meaning innocent, while Urim has traditionally been taken to derive from a root meaning lights; these derivations are reflected in the Neqqudot of the Masoretic Text. In consequence, Urim and Thummim has traditionally been translated as lights and perfections, or, by taking the phrase allegorically, as meaning revelation and truth, or doctrine and truth (it appears in this form in the Vulgate, in the writing of Jerome, and in the Hexapla).

NOTE: The Urim and Thummim were placed in the breastplate of the high priest (Exodus 28:30) and were used as a means of communication with God. They mean "light" and "perfection". Unfortunately, they are not described anywhere in the Bible. Some theories maintain that they were twelve stones that made up part of the High Priest's garments. The process of the communication with God is not given either.

Utopian: Term used to describe both intentional communities that attempt to create an ideal society and imagined societies. Comes from a Greek word meaning "no-place", and strictly describes in considerable detail, any non-existent society. In standard usage, its meaning has narrowed to simply describe a non-existent society that is intended to be viewed as considerably better than contemporary society or community having highly desirable or near perfect qualities. The word was coined by Sir Thomas More in Greek for his 1516 book Utopia (in Latin), describing a fictional island society in the Atlantic Ocean.

V

Vellum: A material used for writing, like paper. It was made from animal skins, usually from cattle, sheep, goats, and antelope. The hair was scraped off of the skins, then they were washed, smoothed, and dressed with chalk. Vellum was used until the late Middle Ages until paper was introduced into Europe from China via Arab traders. Vellum lasted longer than papyrus and was tougher, but the edges sometimes became torn and tattered. The two oldest parchment manuscripts are the Codex Vaticanus (from Egypt) and the Codex Sinaiticus.

Venial Sin: In Catholicism, a sin but not as bad as mortal Sin. It lessens the grace of God within a person's soul.

Vicarious Substituionary View of the Atonement: The theory of the atonement which states that Christ's death was "legal." It satisfied the legal justice of God. Jesus bore the penalty of sin when he died on the cross. His death was a substitution for the believers. In other words, he substituted himself for them upon the cross. Jesus hung in our place as He bore our sin in his body on the cross. (See 1 Pet. 2:24).

Virgin birth: The biblical teaching that Jesus was conceived in the womb of his mother Mary by a miraculous work of the Holy Spirit and without a human father.

Visible church: The church as Christians on earth see it. Because only God sees our hearts, the visible church will always include some unbelievers.

Vulgate: The Latin translation of the Bible, largely deriving from Jerome, upon which medieval theology was largely based.

W

weak force: The force which causes the unstable elementary particles to decay.

Wisdom: The doctrine that God always chooses the best goals and the best means to those goals.

Word of God: A phrase that refers to several different things in the Bible, including the Son of God, the decrees of God, God's words of personal address, God's words spoken through human lips, and God's words in written form, the Bible. It is this last form of the Word of God that is the focus of systematic theology, since it is the form that is available for study, for public inspection, for repeated examination, and as a basis for mutual discussion.

Word of knowledge: The ability to speak with knowledge about a situation.

Word of wisdom: The ability to speak a wise word in various situations.

Word, The: In Greek the word for "word" is logos. It is used in many places, but of special interest is how it is used of Jesus. In John 1:1 it says, "In the beginning was the Word and the Word was with God and the Word was God." The Word is divine and the word "became flesh and dwelt among us" (John 1:14). In other words, Jesus is the Word of God who represents God to us and us to God. The term is also used to describe the Scriptures (Rom. 9:6; Heb. 4:12), Christ's teaching (Luke 5:1), and the gospel message (Acts 4:31). The Word of God is inspired: "All scripture is inspired by God and profitable for teaching, for reproof, for correction, for training in righteousness" (2 Tim. 3:16). The Word of God is truth: "all thy commandments are truth" (Psalm 119:151). The Word of God makes free: "...If you abide in My word, then you are truly disciples of mine; and you shall know the truth, and the truth shall make you free" (John 8:32). The Word of God produces faith: "So faith comes from hearing, and hearing by the word of Christ" (Rom. 10:17, NASB). The Word of God judges: "For the word of God is living and active and sharper than any two-edged sword, and piercing as far as the division of soul and spirit, of both joints and marrow, and able to judge the thoughts and intentions of the heart" (Heb. 4:12).

Worship: The activity of glorifying God in his presence with our voices and hearts. The obligation of God's creation to give to Him all honor, praise, adoration, and glory due Him because He is the holy and divine creator. Worship is to be given to God only (Exodus 20:3; Matt. 4:10). Jesus, being God in flesh (John 1:1,14 ; Col. 2:9), was worshipped (Matt. 2:2,11; 14:33; John 9:35-38; Heb. 1:6).

Wrath: Biblically, it is the divine judgment upon sin and sinners. It does not merely mean that it is a casual response by God to ungodliness, but carries the meaning of hatred, revulsion, and indignation. God is by nature love (1 John 4:16), however, in His justice He must punish sin. The punishment is called the wrath of God. It will occur on the final Day of Judgment when those who are unsaved will incur the wrath of God. It is, though, presently being released upon the ungodly (Rom. 1:18-32) in the hardening of their hearts. Wrath is described as God's anger (Num. 32:10-13), as stored up (Rom. 2:5-8), and as great (Zech. 7:12). The believer's deliverance from God's wrath is through the atonement (Rom. 5:8-10). "For God has not destined us for wrath, but for obtaining salvation through our Lord Jesus Christ" (1 Thess. 5:9).

#

Yoga: A philosophical as well as physical way of life emphasizing harmony of body and mind. The philosophy of yoga is based in Eastern Metaphysical beliefs. The goal of the philosophy is to help a person become balanced in mind and body and attain self-enlightenment. Yoga, apart from its metaphysical teachings, is beneficial to the body.

Young earth theory: A theory of creation that views the earth as relatively young, perhaps as young as 10,000 to 20,000 years old.

Key Salvation Glossary Terms

◆ ◆ ◆

Atonement	To make amends and to be at one with God.
Call, Effectual	The call of the Holy Spirit goes out to the elect, effectually calling them to repent and believe the Gospel (internal call).
Call, General	The call of God's message that goes out to many people, elect and non-elect, ultimately calling them to repent and believe in the Gospel (external call).
Compatiblism	The belief that God's unconditional sovereign election and human responsibility are both realities taught in Scripture that finite minds cannot comprehend and must be held in tension.
Complementarianism	Position that the Bible teaches that men and women are of equal worth, dignity, responsibility before God (ontological equality). The Bible also teaches that men and women have different roles to play in society, the family, and the church. These roles do not compete but complement each other.
Egalitarianism	Position that the Bible does not teach that women are in any sense, functionally or ontologically, subservient to men. Women and men hold ministry positions according to their gifts, not their gender. The principle of mutual submission teaches that husbands and wives are to submit to each other equally.
Election, Conditional	The belief that God's election is conditional, being based on his foreknowledge. God looks ahead into the future, sees who will make a free-will decision to place their faith in him, and then elects to save them. Or as contemporary Arminians would put it, God's elects Christ and all who are found in Him.

Election, Unconditional	The belief that God predestined people for salvation before the beginning of time. God's election is not conditioned by anything in man, good or evil, foreseen or present, but upon God's sovereign choice.
Election, Unconditional	God's free choice before creation, not based on foreseen faith, to whom he will grant faith and repentance, pardoning them, and adopting them into his everlasting family of joy.
ex opere operato	Belief accepted by Roman Catholics and rejected by Protestants that the sacraments administer grace to the recipient by virtue of the act itself through the power given to the Church, regardless of the faith of the individual.
Exclusivism	The belief that Christ is the only way to God.
Extra ecclesiam nulla salus	Belief that since the Church held the "keys to heaven" through the administration of the sacraments, there was no possibility of salvation outside the institution of the Church. This was the belief of many in the medieval church, but was rejected by the Reformers and later rejected by Roman Catholics at Vatican II (1962-1965).
Fatalism	Belief that a person's life and choices are totally and unalterably the result of an endless series of cause and effects.
Flesh	The principle force of human nature that is bent toward sin.
Free Grace Salvation	The belief that salvation is by faith alone. Repentance and submitting to Christ's Lordship is something that only a born again believer can do.
Imputation	Refers to the transferal of the sin of man to Christ while He was on the Cross. The understanding that God justifies sinners by reckoning Christ's righteousness to their account through a legal declaration.
Inclusivism	The belief that Christ's atonement is the only way that anyone can be saved, but that one does not necessarily need to have knowledge of Christ to have the atonement applied to them.
Irresistible Grace	The belief that God's call to the elect will always be effectual in bringing about their salvation.

Justification	A forensic declaration in which a sinner is declared righteous while still in a sinning state; to make right or even, to make right or even with God.
Liberation	To be freed from oppression or bondage.
Libertarianism	Belief that a person's actions are uncaused by any coercion whatsoever. The agent is the "first cause" in the effect of his action.
Lordship Salvation	The belief that salvation includes both faith and repentance, which are two sides of the same coin. In repentance, the believer is committing to give up all known sin, thereby making Christ Lord of his or her life.
New Man	The new way of life that is energized by the power of the Spirit.
Old Man	The former way of life that is energized by the power of the flesh.
Ordo Salutis	Refers to the logical order in which the process of salvation takes place.
Pelagianism	The belief that man is inherently good. The Fall did not bring condemnation upon any but Adam. As well, the disposition of the will is unaffected. Man sins as a result of bad examples that began with Adam.
Perseverance of the Saints	The belief that true believers will persevere in their faith and cannot ever be lost.
Pluralism	The belief that all belief systems ultimately point in the same direction and to the same God, even if the belief systems themselves are contradictory.
Predestination, Double	The belief that God predestines the elect to eternal life, and the rest are predestined to hell. God does this by actively hardening their hearts and preparing them for unbelief.
Predestination, Single	God predestines the elect to eternal life, and passively destines the non-elect by "passing over" them, choosing not to elect them, leaving them in their sins, destined to eternal punishment.
Propitiation	The act whereby God's righteous wrath is satisfied by the atonement of Christ.

Reconciliation	To restore/repair/reform a relationship
Redemption	Lit. "to be purchased." This is the scriptural teaching that God paid a price for man's salvation, redeeming us from sin.
Regeneration	The act whereby God awakens or regenerates the dead spirit of a person, restoring the ability to respond to and have a relationship with Him.
Regeneration, Monogistic	The belief that regeneration is an act of God alone.
Regeneration, Synergistic	The belief that regeneration is a cooperative act between God and man.
Repentance	To change one's thinking and way of life as a result of a change of attitude with regard to sin and righteousness.
Reprobate	Refers to those that are destined for hell.
Restrictivism	The belief that knowledge of and trust in the Gospel is necessary for anyone to be saved.
Salvation	Latin "salv"- to save or heal; An event and a process in which people are brought into a right relationship with God.
Sanctification	A lifelong process in which believers become conformed to the image of Christ, relying on the power of God to mortify sin in their lives.
simul iustus et peccator	Luther's paradoxical dictum explaining that a Christian has a legal or forensic righteous standing before God according to the work of Christ, while at the same time lives as a sinner according to his own merits.
Sin, Imputed	Specifically refers to the guilt or condemnation of the first sin which was imputed to humanity. (Also: original guilt.)
Sin, Inherited	Specifically refers to the transferal of the sinful nature. (Also: original corruption, original pollution, sinful nature.)
Sin, Mortal	Sins against God's Law that destroy the grace of God in the heart of the sinner thereby cutting of his or her relationship with God.

Sin, Original	A broad term that refers to the effects that the first sin had on humanity; the "origin" of sin.
Sin, Personal	Specifically refers to the sins that are committed by individuals.
Soteriology	The study of salvation.
Theory of Atonement, *Governmental*	Christ's death was a "nominal" substitute for the penalty of sin of man, which God graciously chose to accept, thereby upholding his moral government.
Theory of Atonement, *Moral Example*	Belief that Christ came to show people how to live so that they would turn to him in love. His death was not required and has no atoning value, but only serves as a moral example for people to follow.
Theory of Atonement, *Ransom to Satan*	Belief that by virtue of Adam's sin, all humanity was sold into bondage to Satan who had "legal" rights to them. Christ, by his death, made a payment to Satan, buying them back and making salvation possible.
Theory of Atonement, *Recapitulation*	Belief that Christ lived a perfect life that Adam could not live. Christ recapitulated all stages of the human life; birth, infancy, childhood, teenage, manhood--and obeyed the Law perfectly. Salvation is made possible by virtue of his perfect life.
Venial sin	Sins against God's Law that do not destroy the grace of God.
Vicarious Substitutionary, *View of the Atonement*	The atonement is made on the Cross when Christ vicariously bore the exact penalty of his people, thereby placating the wrath of God and satisfying his righteousness.

Bibliography

◆ ◆ ◆

1.0 | Bibliology

Allender Dan B., Leading with a Limp: Take Full Advantage of Your *Most Powerful Weakness*

Anderson, Lynn, They Smell Like Sheep (*Pastoral Book*)

Bavinck, Herman, *The Doctrine of God.* Trans. by William Hendriksen. Grand Rapids: Eerdmans, 1951.

Berkhof, Louis, Systematic Theology, *New Combined Edition containing the full text of Systematic Theology and the original.* Williams B. Eerdmans Publishing Company, 255 Jefferson Ave., S.E., Grand Rapids, MI 49503, 1996.

Boreham, Frank, Life Verses,The Best of Life Texts, *The Bible's Impact on Famous Lives,* Volume Five (Great Text Series), Kregel Publications, P.O. Box 2607, Grand Rapids, MI 49501, 1004.

Brake, Donald L. Ph.D, "World's Best-Selling Book", Washington Times Communities Paper, Thursday, July 28, 2011, Dean Emeritus of Multnomah Biblical Seminary, President of Jerusalem University College, Israel; A Visual History of the English Bible: *The Tumultuous Tale of The World's Bestselling Book;* Baker Books, 2008. Retrieved from http://communities.washingtontimes.com/neighborhood/worlds-best-selling-book/2012/feb/27/bible-collectors-unexpected-discovery-unlikely-pla/

E.W. Bullinger, Numerology in Scripture, *It's Supernatural Design and Spiritual Significance,* Mansfield Centre, CT. Martino Publishing Company, P.O. Box 373 06250. 2011

Cramer, Steven A., Putting on the Armor of God, *How to Win Your Battles with Satan,* Cedar Fort, Incorporated., 925 North Main Street, Springville, UT 84663.

Bruce A. Demarest, General Revelation: *Historical Views and Contemporary Issues,* Grand Rapids: Zondervan, 1982.

Dockery, David, Editor. Holman Bible Handbook, Holman Bible Publishing Company, Nashville, TN, 1992.

Flavius Josephus, Against Apion, book 1, chapter 8. https://answersingenesis.org/archaeology/dead-sea-scrolls-timeless-treasures/

Gaussen, L. D.D. *Oratoire, Geneva,* Theopneustia - The Plenary *Of The Holy Scriptures Deduced From Internal Evidence, And The Testimonies Of Nature, History And Science.*

Geisler, Norman, Ph.D, Christian Apologetics, PO Box 6287 Grand Rapids MI 49516-6287 Baker Publishing Group (1988)

Goldberg, M. Hirsh, "Jewish Connection," Maryland: Scarborough House, 1993.
Grudem, Wayne. Christian Beliefs: Twenty Basics Every Christian Should Know, Zondervan Publishing House, 5300 Patterson Ave., Grand Rapids, MI 60515.

Grudem, Wayne. Systematic Theology Laminated Sheet (Zondervan Get an A! Study Guides) Pamphlet, Zondervan Publishing House, 5300 Patterson Ave., Grand Rapids, MI 60515.

Grudem, Wayne. Systematic Theology, An Introduction to Biblical Doctrine. Inter-Varsity Press, 38 De Montfort Street Leicester LE1 7GP Great Britain, Zondervan Publishing House, 5300 Patterson Ave., Grand Rapids, MI 60515.

Halley, Henry. Halley's Bible Handbook with the New International Version---Deluxe Edition - Henry H. Halley (for Archeology), Grand Rapids, MI: Zondervan Publishing House, 5300 Patterson Ave., 60515.

Hodge, Charles. Hodge's Systematic Theology Collection (3 Volumes), Hendrickson Publishers, Peabody, MA 01961-3473, 1999.

Hughes, R. Kent. The Coming Evangelical Crisis: Current Challenges to Authority of Scripture and the Gospel (The most important aspects and issues confronting the church are thoughtfully presented by various credible authors). Pp 17-22

Kennedy, D. James and Jerry Newcombe. What if the Bible Had Never Been Written, published in association with the literary agency of Alive Communications, Nelson Books 1465 Kelly Johnson Blvd., Suite 320, Colorado Springs, CO 80920.

Lutzer, Erwin W., B.Th. Seven Reasons Why You Can Trust the Bible, Winnipeg Bible College; Th.M., Dallas Theological Seminary; M.A., Loyola University, 1998.

MacArthur, John. Ephesians: New Testament Commentary, Thomas Nelson Publishing, Nashville, TN.

MacArthur, John, Jr. Why I Trust the Bible, [Formerly Focus on Fact], A Pastor-Teacher Shares how confidence in the Word of God can lead you to greater spiritual growth, SP Publications, Wheaton, IL 60184,1983.

Murphy, Mark C. Cornell Studies in the Philosophy of Religion, Cornell University Press, Sage House, 512 East State Street, Ithaca, NY 14850, 2002.

Pearlman, Myer. Knowing the Doctrines of the Bible, Gospel Publishing House, Springfield, MI 65802, 2002.

Peterson Eugene. Eat This Book: A Conversation in the Art of Spiritual Reading (for Illumination), Eerdmans Publishing Company, 255 Jefferson Ave, S.E. Grand Rapids, MI 49503, 2006.

Qimron, E. and J. Strugnell. Discoveries in the Judean Desert, vol. 10 "Qumran Cave 4, 5: Miqsat Ma'ase ha-Torah." (Oxford: Clarendon Press, 1994). https://answersingenesis.org/archaeology/dead-sea-scrolls-timeless-treasures/

Ridderbos, Herman. Paul: An Outline of His Theology, The Self-Disclosure of Jesus, Eerdmans Publishing Company, 255 Jefferson Ave, S.E. Grand Rapids, MI 49503, 1953.

Ridderbos, Herman. Commentary on Galatians for the New International Commentary on the New Testament series, Eerdmans Publishing Company, 255 Jefferson Ave, S.E. Grand Rapids, MI 49503, 1958.

Sproul, R.C. The Mystery of the Holy Spirit, Thomas Nelson Publishers, Nashville, TN, 1982.

Strong, James. LL.D. The Strongest Strong's Exhaustive Concordance of the Bible, *the only Strong compiled and verified by computer technology with Nave's Topical Bible Reference; most up-to-date Hebrew and Greek dictionaries for precise word studies, corrects all others.*

Swinburne, Richard. Revelation, Oxford University Press. Great Clarendon Street, New York, NY 1992.

Tenney, Merrill C. and Alexander Cruden, The Handy Bible Dictionary, Zondervan Publishing Company, Grand Rapids, MI 49530, 1983.

Tozer A.W. Mystery of the Holy Spirit, Cedar Fort, Inc. 925 N.Main St., Springfield, IL 84663

Vine, W.E., Merrill Unger, and William White, Jr. Vine's Complete Expository Dictionary, *of Old and New Testament Words*, Thomas Nelson Publishers, Nashville, TN, 2001.

Warfield, Benjamin Breckinridge. The Inspiration and Authority of the Bible, Philadelphia, PA: The Presbyterian and Reformed Publishing House, 1948.

Warren, Rick. Rick Warren's Bible Study Methods: *Twelve Ways You Can Unlock God's Word*, Zondervan Publishing House, 5300 Patterson Ave., Grand Rapids, MI 2006.

Wilmington, Harold L. Wilmington's Guide to the Bible, Tyndale House Publishers, Inc, Wheaton, Illinois, 1984.

Zondervan Comparative Study Bible, NIV, Amplified, KJV, NASB, Zondervan, Grand Rapids, MI 1999.

Mel Gibson, Director. *The Passion for Christ, American epic biblical drama film directed by Mel Gibson and starring Jim Caviezel, 2004.*

Keathley III, J. Hampton. *A Study of the Bible,* www.http://bible.org/seriespage/bible-understanding-its-message

http://www.neverthirsty.org/pp/corner/read/r00054.html

http://www.adherents.com/largecom/fam_chrsci.html

http://en.wikipedia.org/wiki/Studies_in_the_Scriptures

http://www.rapidnet.com/~jbeard/bdm/Psychology/neoe.htm

http://www.bibletruths.net/Archives/BTAR125.htm, Ex. 17: 14; 24: 4; 34: 27, 28; Num. 33: 2; Deut. 31: 9, 24; 32: 1-43, cp. 31: 22)

http://www.theologue.org/THEOPNEUSTIA.htm, Theopneustia: The Christian Doctrine Of Divine Inspiration (page 61)

Richardson, Alan. Christian Apologetics [New York: Harper, 1948], http://www.newadvent.org/cathen/03267a.htm (page 83)

Pastore, Frank. Introduction to Bibliology, http://www.ntslibrary.com/Introduction%20to%20Bibliology.pdf

http://www.why-the-bible.com/bible.htm

http://www.gallup.com/poll/1690/Religion.aspx

http://www.biblebelievers.org.au/panin1.htm

How Do We Know the Bible is True? Christian Answers Network, PO Box 200 Gilbert AZ 85299, Nov 2011. http://www.christiananswers.net/q-eden/edn-t003.html

Henry Morris and Martin Clark, The Bible Has the Answer, New Leaf Publishing, Master Book Group, 3142 Hwy 103 N, Green Forest, AR 72638, 1985.

McDowell, Josh. Evidence That Demands A Verdict, Here's Life Publishers, San Bernadino, CA, 1990

F.F. Bruce observation, http://www.angelfire.com/sc3/myredeemer/Evidencep4.html (page 114)

Augustine, "On the Merits and Forgiveness of Sins, and on the Baptism of Infants," Book 1, Chapter 53, "The Utility of the Books of the Old Testament."; http://www.kneillfoster.com/ClassicChristianity/cc26.html

Davis, Stephen T. The Debate about the Bible [Philadelphia: Westminster Press, 1977].

E. J. Young, *Thy Word Is Truth,* p. 119.

William R. Eichhorst, The Issue of Biblical Inerrancy: *In Definition and Defence,* Winnipeg, Man.: Winnipeg Bible College, n.d., p. 9.

http://www.yutopian.com/religion/theology/Inerrancy.html

http://www.victorious.org/churchbook/chur49.htm

Nida, Eugene Albert. *The Book of a Thousand Tongues,* 2d ed. (New York: United Bible Societies, 1972), viii. (page 134)

Edited by Roberts, Alexander. Irenaeus: Against Heresies. *From:* Ante-Nicene Fathers, Vol. 1. 3.21.2 (apud Eusebius, Ecclesiastical History 5.8.11-15). For an account of still further elaborations in the third and fourth centuries, see Sidney Jellicoe, *The and Modern Study,* 44-47, and Hadas, *Aristeas to Philocrates,* 73-80. For these several points on which there is general agreement among scholars, see W. F. Howard's succinct account in *The Bible in Its Ancient and English Versions* (Oxford: *Masechet Soferim,* ed. Joel Miller (Leipzig: Hinrichs, 1878), i. 8.

http://www.allabouttruth.org/history-of-bible-translation-faq.htm

2.0 | Christology

Barclay, William. The Parables of Jesus, William Barclay Library, Westminster John Knox Press, 100 Witherspoon Street, Louisville, KY 40202-1396, 1999.

Bevere, John. The Bait of Satan, *Living Free from the Deadly Trap of Offense,* Charisma House A Strang Company, 600 Rhinehart Road, Lake Mary, FL 32746, 2004.

Booker, Richard. The Miracle of the Scarlet Thread, *for new believers and seasoned Christians-this practical book helps the Bible come alive with fresh insights,* Destiny Image Publishers, P.O. Box 310, Shippensburg, PA 17257, 1981.

Buechner, Frederick. The Faces of Jesus, *A Life Story,* Paraclete Press, Brewster, MA 2005

Chapman, Colin. The Cross and the Crescent: *Responding to the Challenge of Islam (for Christians encountering Muslims for the first time),* 2nd Edition, InterVarsity Press, P.O. Box 1400, Downer's Grove, IL 60515-1428, 2007.

Cerullo, Morris. Marked for God's Commanded Blessing "*I am a Child of God*", Morris Cerullo World Wide Evangelism, P., Box 86277, San Diego, CA 92186, 2009.

Copeland, Kenneth. The Image of God in You, Kenneth Copeland Publications, Ft. Worth, TX 76192, 1989.

Demarest, Dr. Bruce, Soul Guide, *Following Jesus as Spiritual Director,* NAV Press, P.O. Box 35001, Colorado Springs, CO 90835

Dickow, Gregory. Precious Promises of the Blood of Jesus, *30 Day Devotional,* Gregory Dickow Ministries, P.O. Box 7000, Chicago, IL 60680.

Dirks, Jerald F. The Cross and the Crescent, *Parallelling Christianity and with Islamic / Muslim worship,* Bethany House Publishers, 11400 Hampshire Ave South Bloomington, MN 55438, 2003.

Duplantis, Jesse. Leave It in the Hands of a Specialist, Duplantis Ministries, P.O. Box 20149, New Orleans, LA 79141, 2003.

Fitzmyer, Joseph A. Scripture and Christology: *a statement of the Biblical Commission with a commentary,* English translation, and Catholic Church. Pontificia Commissio Biblica, Paulist Press, 1986. http://www.bc.edu/dam/files/research_sites/cjl/texts/cjrelations/resources/documents/catholic/pbc_christology.htm

Forest, Jim. The Ladder of the Beatitudes, Orbis Books, P.O. Box 308, Mary Knoll, NY 10545-0308, 1999.

Hagin, Jr. Kenneth. Jesus, Name Above All Names, *Prophets, and Pastors,* Faith Library Publications, RHEMA Bible Church AKA Kenneth Hagin Ministries, Inc., Tulsa, OK, 2000.

Hagin, Kenneth E. In Him, RHEMA Bible Church AKA Kenneth Hagin Ministries, Inc., P.O. Box 40126, Tulsa, OK 74150-0126, 1980.

Hagin, Kenneth E. The Precious Blood of Jesus, RHEMA Bible Church AKA Kenneth Hagin Ministries, Inc., P.O. Box 40126, Tulsa, OK 74150-0126, 2000.

Hagin, Kenneth. A Better Covenant, RHEMA Bible Church AKA Kenneth Hagin Ministries, Inc., P.O. Box 40126, Tulsa, OK 74150-0126, 2000.

Hickey, Marilyn. Speak the Word, *Revised 1983 Edition,* P.O. Box 17340, Denver, CO 80217.

Hodge, Charles. Systematic Theology. 3 vols. Reprint edition: Grand Rapids: Eerdmans, 1970. First published 1871-73.

Kereszty, Roch. Jesus: Fundamentals of Christology, Published by A. O. H. Stetzephandt, St Paul, 2010.

Kennedy, D. James and James Newcombe, What if Jesus Had Never Been Born, *the Positive Impact of Christianity on History,* Thomas Nelson Publishers, Nashville, TN, 1994.

Klein, Robert Lassalle. Jesus of Galilee: *Contextual Christology for the 21st Century,* Orbis Books, Maryknoll, New York, New York. 2001.

Lewis, C.S. Mere Christianity, HarperOne, of Harper Collins, 10 East 53rd St, New York, NY 10022, 1952.

Loyd-Jones, Martyn D. Commentary on Matthew 5 – The Sermon on the Mount, William B. Eerdmans Publishing Company, 2140 Oak Industrial Drive, N.E. Grand Rapids, MI 49505, Cambridge, U.K., 1959.

MacArthur, John. Slave, The Hidden Truth About Your Identity, Thomas Nelson Publishers, Nashville, TN 2010.

Ramachandra, Vinoth. The Scandal of Jesus, InterVarsity Press, P.O. Box 1400 Downer's Grove, ILL, 60515, 2001.

Relton, Herbert M.D.D. Christ: A Study in Christology: The Problem of Relations between of the Two Natures in the Person of Christ, The MacMillan Company, Society for Promoting Christian Knowledge, New York, New York. 1934.

Rogers, Adrian. Believe in Miracles but Trust in Jesus (), Crossway Books, a Division of Good News Publishers, 1300 Crescent Street, Wheaton, IL 60187, 1997.

Sheman, Doug. Keeping Your Ethical Edge Sharp: *How to Cultivate a personal character that is honest, faithful, just and morally clean*, NavPress Publications, P.O. Box 35001, Colorado Springs, CO 80935, 1990.

Stalker, James D. The Life of Jesus Christ, (Volume 3), General Books, Memphis, TN, 2010.

Straughan, Walt. By Jesus' 39 Stripes We Were Healed, Walt Straughan Ministries, Staunton, VA 2004

Swindoll, Charles R. Jesus, Our Lord, *Bible Study Guide*, Insight for Living, 1604 Pacific Center Drive, Suite 400, Anaheim, CT 92806-2126, 1987.

Swindoll, Charles R. Jesus, the Greatest Life of All, *Great Lives from God's Word*, Bible Companion, Insight for Living, 1604 Pacific Center Drive, Suite 400, Anaheim, CT 92806-2126, 1987.

Swindoll, Charles R. Mission Possible: *A 40-Day Adventure With Jesus*, Thomas Nelson Publishers, Nashville, TN, 2009.

Swindoll, Charles R. Jesus: When God Became a Man, Insight for Living, 1604 Pacific Center Drive, Suite 400, Anaheim, CT 92806-2126, 1993.

Tenney, Merrill C. New Testament Survey, Revised by Walter M. Dunnett, Wm. B. Eerdmans Publishing Company, Inter Varsity Press, Leister, LEI 7GP England, 255 Jefferson, S.E., Grand Rapids, MI 49503

Thiessen, Henry Clarence. Introductory Lectures in Systematic Theology. Rev. by Vernon D. Doerksen. Grand Rapids: Eerdmans, 1977. First published 1949.

Wiersbe, Warren. Classic Sermons on the Cross of Christ, Hendrickson Publishers, by special arrangements with Kregel Publications, a division of Kregel, P.O. Box 2607, Grand Rapids, MI 49501, 1990.

What the Bible is All About, Bible Handbook - Clear Concise Overviews of Every book of the Bible, Regal, From Gospel Light Worldwide, P.O. Box 3875, Ventura, CA, 43006, 1973.

Yancey, Philip. The Jesus I Never Knew, Zondervan, Grand Rapids, MI, 49503,1995.

3.0 | Pneumatology

Arrington , French L, Encountering the Holy Spirit: *Paths of Christian Growth and Service*, 105-7691749-8689055 SouthernBookhounds

Berkhoff's Systematic Theology, Wm. B. Eerdmans Publishing Company, Grand Rapids, Michigan, 1988.

Cairns, Earle E., Church History Through the Centuries, A History of the Christian Church, Revised and Expanded, Third Edition , Zondervan PublishingGrand Rapids, MI, 1996

Cairns, Earle E. Christianity Through the Centuries. Grand Rapids: Zondervan, 1981.

Copeland, Gloria, God's Will is the Holy Spirit, Kenneth Copeland Publications Ft. Worth, TX 76192, 1995

Edwards, David L. Christian England, Grand Rapids: Eerdman's Publishing Co., 1983.

Estep, William R. Renaissance Reformation. Grand Rapids: Eerdman's Publishing Co., 1986.

Erickson, Millard J., Introducing Christian Doctrine, edited by L. Arnold Hustad , Baker Academic, A Division of Baker House Co., P.O. Box 6287, Grand Rapids, MI, 49516-6287, 1992

Evans, Tony, The Promise - *Experiencing God's Greatest Gift:* The Holy Spirit, 105-2799292-7449850 Redux_books

Finis Jennings, Dake Finis Jennings, Dake's Annotated Reference Bible, Dake Bible Sales, Inc., P.O. Box 1050, Lawrenceville, GA 30246 1981, 2001

Gillies, George and Harriet, The Power of the Holy Spirit, *But You shall receive power when the Holy Spirit comes upon you,* Acts 1:8, Whitaker House, 30 Hunt Valley Circle, New Kensington, PA 15068, 1979.

Grudem, Wayne, Grudem's Systematic Theology, An Introduction to Biblical Doctrine, InterVarsity Press, 38 De Montfort Street Leicester LE1 7GP Great Britain , Zondervan Publishing House, 5300 Patterson Ave., Grand Rapids, MI 60515

Guthrie, Shirley C., Christian Doctrine, Revised Edition, Westminster/John Knox Press, 100 Witherspoon Street, Louisville, KY, 40202.

Hagin, Kenneth E., The Holy Spirit and His Gifts (Study Guide) Hagin, RHEMA Bible Church AKA Kenneth Hagin Ministries, Inc., Tulsa, OK, 1991.

Halley, Henry, Halley's Bible Handbook with the New International Version---Deluxe Edition - Henry H. Halley (for Archeology).

Hayford, Jack, God's Way to Wholeness Divine Healing by the Power of the Holy Spirit, *Spirit-Field Life Kingdom Dynamics Study Guides,* Thomas Nelson Publishers, Nashville, TN 1993.

Harrison, Everett. Baker's Dictionary of Theology, ed. Baker Book House, Grand Rapids, Michigan, 1960.

Hinn, Benny, Good Morning, Holy Spirit, Thomas Nelson Publishers, Nashville, TN, 1990.

Hodge's Systematic Theology, Wm. B. Eerdmans Publishing Company, 255 Jefferson, S.E., Grand Rapids, MI 49503, 1981.

Jernigan, Kenneth. Blindness: *Concepts And Misconceptions,* National Federation of the Blind, 1969.

Lockyer, Herbert, All the Doctrines of the Bible, *A Study and Analysis of Major Bible Doctrines,* Zondervan, Grand Rapids, MI, 49530, 1964.

Pearlman, Myer, Knowing the Doctrines of the Bible.

Plantinga, Richard, Thomas Thompson and Matthew D. Lundberg , An Introduction to Christian Theology, Cambridge University Press , New York ,The Edinburgh Building, Cambridge CB2 8RU, UK, 2008

Rea, John, The Holy Spirit in the Bible, *All the Major Passages About the Spirit,* A commentary, Creation House, Strang Communications Company,600 Rhinehart Road, Lake Mary, FL,32746.

Schaff, Philip. *History of the Christian Church* Volume 7. Grand Rapids: Eerdman's Publishing Co., 1950.

Shults, F. LeRon and Andrea Hollingsworth, The Holy Spirit, Guides to Theology, William B. Eerdmans Publishing Company, 255 Jefferson S.E. Grand Rapids, MI

49505, 2008

Spitz, Lewis W. *The Protestant Reformation.* Harper and Row: New York, 1984

Sproul, R.C., The Mystery of the Holy Spirit, Christian Focus Publications, Ligonier Ministries, 400 technology Park, Lake Mary, FL37426-6229, 1990

Charles, and Robert Hall, What the Holy Spirit Does in a Believer's Life, Christian Living Classics, Emerald Books, P.O. Box 625, Lynnwood, Washington 98046, 1993.

Stott, John, The Beatitudes, *Developing Spiritural Character*, IVP Connect, An imprint of InterVarsity Press, P.O. Box 1400 Downers Grove, IL 60515-1426, 1998

Strong, James, LL.D,The New Strong's Expanded Dictionary of Bible Words, most complete and accurate and up-to-date Hebrew and Greek dictionaries-now with the best of Vine's Complete Expository Dictionary, Thomas Nelson Publishers, Nashville, TN, 2001

Sumrall, Lester, The Gifts and Ministries of the Holy Spirit, Whitaker House 1030 Hunt Valley Circle, New Kensington, PA 15068, 1982.

Swindoll, Charles, R., Flying Closer to the Flame: *A Passion For The Holy Spirit -* Bible Study Guide, 105-3638259-9030634

Thiessen, Henry C., Lectures in Systematic Theology, Revised by Vernon D. Doerksen, William B. Eerdmans Publishing Company, 255 Jefferson S.E., Grand Rapids, MI 49530, 1998.

Torrey, R.A., What the Bible Teaches, *The Truths of the Bible Made Plain, Simple and Understandable*, Hendrickson Publishers, Inc. P.O. Box 3473, Peabody, MA, 01961, 1998.

Torrey, R.A., The Person and Work of the Holy Spirit, Whitaker House, 30 Hunt Valley Circle, New Kensington, PA 15068, 1996.

Tozer, A.W., Mystery of the Holy Spirit, Cedar Fort, Inc. 925 N. Main St., Springfield, IL 84663, 2007.

Tozer, A.W., Divine Conquest, *Settle for Nothing Less than the Power of God*, Wingspread Publishers, Inc. 3825 Hartzdale Dr., Camp Hill PA 17011, 1978.

Wigglesworth, Smith, Smith Wigglesworth on Spiritual Gifts, Whitaker House, 30 Hunt Valley Circle, New Kensington, PA 15068, 1998.

Wilmington, Harold L., Wilmington's Guide to the Bible (from Jerry Falwell's Church), Tyndale House Publishers, Inc, Carol Stream, Illinois: 105-0430140-6660227.

4.0 | Soteriology

Badger, Anthony. Confronting Calvinism: *A Free Grace Refutation and Biblical Resolution of Radical Reformed Soteriology,* Lockman Foundation (www.Lockman.org), 1995.

Berkhof, Louis. Introductory Volume to Systematic Theology, Revised and Enlarged Edition., Williams B. Eerdmans Publishing Company, 255 Jefferson Ave., S.E., Grand Rapids, MI 49503, 1996.

Boa, Kenneth D. and Robert M. Bowman Jr. Faith Has its Reasons, An Integrative Approach to Defending Christianity, An Apologetics Handbook, NAVPress, Bringing truth to Life, P.O. Box 35001, Colorado Springs, 80935, 20001.

Cairns, Earle E. Christianity Through the Centuries. Grand Rapids: Zondervan,

1981.

Chafer, Lewis Sperry. *Systematic Theology.* 7 vols. plus index vol. Dallas: Dallas Seminary Press, 1947-48.

Demarest, Bruce, Soul Guide, *Following Jesus As A Spiritual Director.* 2003 NAV-PRESS, Bringing Truth to Life, Colorado Springs, CO 80935.

Erickson, Millard J. Introducing Christian Doctrine, edited by L. Arnold Hustad, Baker Academic, A Division of Baker House Co., P.O. Box 6287, Grand Rapids, MI, 49516-6287, 1992.

Erickson, Millard J. The Word Became Flesh, *A Contemporary Incarnational Christology,* Baker Books, A Division of Baker House Co., P.O. Box 6287, Grand Rapids, MI, 49516-6287, 1991.

Erickson, Millard. ChristianTheology. Grand Rapids: Baker, 1985.

Estep, William R. Renaissance Reformation. Grand Rapids: Eerdman's Publishing Co., 1986.

Geisler, Norman L. Baker Encyclopedia of Christian Apologetics, Baker Books, A Division of Baker House Co., P.O. Box 6287, Grand Rapids, MI, 49516-6287, 1992.

Gill, John. Complete Body of Doctrinal and Practical Divinity. 2 vols. Grand Rapids: Baker, 1978.

Grudem, Wayne. Christian Beliefs: *Twenty Basics Every Christian Should Know,* Zondervan Publishing House, 5300 Patterson Ave., Grand Rapids, MI 60515

Grudem, Wayne. Systematic Theology, *An Introduction to Biblical Doctrine.* Inter-Varsity Press 38 De Montfort Street Leicester LE1 7GP Great Britain, Grand Rapids, MI:Zondervan Publishing House, 5300 Patterson Ave., 60515.

Hill, Andrew E. and John H. Walton. A Survey of the Old Testament, 2nd Edition, Zondervan, Grand Rapids, MI 49530, 2011.

Hodges, Charles. Hodge's Systematic Theology Collection (3 Volumes), Hendrickson Publishers (June 1999).

Horton, Michael. For Calvinism, Zondervan, Grand Rapids, MI, 49530, 2011.

Lucado, Max. Grace: *More Than We Deserve, Greater Than We Imagine,* Thomas Nelson Publishers, Nashville, TN, 2012.

Mather G.A. & L.A. Nichols. Dictionary of Cults, Sects, Religions and the Occult, Zondervan, Grand Rapids, MI, (1993).

Olson, Roger. Against Calvinism, Zondervan, Grand Rapids, MI, 49530, 2011.

Pentecost, J. Dwight. The Words & Works of Jesus Christ, A Study of the Life of Christ, Zondervan, Grand Rapids, MI, 49530, 1981.

Porterfield, Amanda. Religion in American History, edited by, and John Corrigan, Wiley-Blackwell, A John Wiley & Sons, Ltd. Publication, 350 Main Street, Malden, MA 02148-, 2010.

Radmacher, Earl D. Salvation, Word Publishing, A Thomas Nelson Publishing Co., P.O. Box 14100, Nashville, TN 37214, 2000.

Schaff, Philip. History of the Christian Church. Volume 7. Grand Rapids: Eerdman's Publishing Co., 1950.

Spitz, Lewis W. *The Protestant Reformation.* Harper and Row: New York, 1984.

Spurgeon, C.H. A Defence of Calvinism, The Banner of Truth Trust, # Murrayfield

Road, Edinburgh, EH 124 6EL UK, P.O Box 621, Carlisle, PA 17013, 2008.

Steele, David N. and Curtis Thomas. The Five Points of Calvinism: *Defined, Defended, and Documented*, R&R Publishing P.O. Box 817, Phillipsburg, NJ 08865-0817, 2004.

Strong, James. LL.D., The Strongest Strong's Exhaustive Concordance of the Bible, *the only Strong compiled and verified by computer technology with Nave's Topical Bible Reference; most up-to-date Hebrew and Greek dictionaries for precise word studies, corrects all others.*

Tenney, Merrill C. New Testament Survey, Revised by Walter M. Dunnett, Wm. B. Eerdmans Publishing Company, Inter Varsity Press, Leister, LEI 7GP England, 255 Jefferson, S.E., Grand Rapids, MI 49503.

Thiessen, Henry C. Lectures in Systematic Theology, Revised by Vernon D. Doerksen, William B. Eerdmans Publishing Company, 255 Jefferson S.E., Grand Rapids, MI 49530, 1998.

John F. Walvoord, Systematic Theology: *Abridged edition.* 2 vols. Ed. By Donald K. Campbell, and Roy B. Zuck. Wheaton: Victor, 1988.

Wilhoit, James C., John H. Westerhoff reference), III Spiritual Formation as if the Church Mattered, Growing in Christ through Community 2008. Baker Academic. Grand Rapids, MI 49516.

Yancey, Philip, What's So Amazing About Grace?, Zondervan, Grand Rapids, MI, 49530, 1997.

Index of Hymns and Songs

◆ ◆ ◆

Index of Textual Illustrations

◆ ◆ ◆

Index of Salvation Scriptures

◆ ◆ ◆

Genesis 49:18	I have waited for thy **salvation**, O LORD.
Exodus 14:13	And Moses said unto the people, Fear ye not, stand still, and see the **salvation** of the LORD, which he will shew to you to day: for the Egyptians whom ye have seen to day, ye shall see them again no more for ever.
Exodus 15:2	The LORD is my strength and song, and he is become my **salvation**: he is my God, and I will prepare him an habitation; my father's God, and I will exalt him.
Deuteronomy 32:15	But Jeshurun waxed fat, and kicked: thou art waxen fat, thou art grown thick, thou art covered with fatness; then he forsook God which made him, and lightly esteemed the Rock of his **salvation**.
1 Samuel 2:1	And Hannah prayed, and said, My heart rejoiceth in theLORD, mine horn is exalted in the LORD: my mouth is enlarged over mine enemies; because I rejoice in thy **salvation**.
1 Samuel 11:13	And Saul said, There shall not a man be put to death this day: for to day the LORD hath wrought **salvation** in Israel.
1 Samuel 14:45	And the people said unto Saul, Shall Jonathan die, who hath wrought this great **salvation** in Israel? God forbid: as the LORD liveth, there shall not one hair of his head fall to the ground; for he hath wrought with God this day. So the people rescued Jonathan, that he died not.
1 Samuel 19:5	For he did put his life in his hand, and slew the Philistine, and the LORD wrought a great **salvation** for all Israel: thou sawest it, and didst rejoice: where-

fore then wilt thou sin against innocent blood, to slay David without a cause?

2 Samuel 22:3	The God of my rock; in him will I trust: he is my shield, and the horn of my **salvation**, my high tower, and my refuge, my saviour; thou savest me from violence.
2 Samuel 22:36	Thou hast also given me the shield of thy **salvation**: and thy gentleness hath made me great.
2 Samuel 22:47	The LORD liveth; and blessed be my rock; and exalted be the God of the rock of my **salvation**.
2 Samuel 22:51	He is the tower of **salvation** for his king: and sheweth mercy to his anointed, unto David, and to his seed for evermore.
2 Samuel 23:5	Although my house be not so with God; yet he hath made with me an everlasting covenant, ordered in all things, and sure: for this is all my **salvation**, and all my desire, although he make it not to grow.
1 Chronicles 16:23	Sing unto the LORD, all the earth; shew forth from day to day his **salvation**.
1 Chronicles 16:35	And say ye, Save us, O God of our **salvation**, and gather us together, and deliver us from the heathen, that we may give thanks to thy holy name, and glory in thy praise.
2 Chronicles 6:41	Now therefore arise, O LORD God, into thy resting place, thou, and the ark of thy strength: let thy priests, O LORD God, be clothed with **salvation**, and let thy saints rejoice in goodness.
2 Chronicles 20:17	Ye shall not need to fight in this battle: set yourselves, stand ye still, and see the **salvation** of the LORD with you, O Judah and Jerusalem: fear not, nor be dismayed; tomorrow go out against them: for the LORD will be with you.
Job 13:16	He also shall be my **salvation**: for an hypocrite shall not come before him.
Psalm 3:8	**Salvation** belongeth unto the LORD: thy blessing is upon thy people. Selah.
Psalm 9:14	That I may shew forth all thy praise in the gates of the daughter of Zion: I will rejoice in thy **salvation**.

Psalm 13:5	But I have trusted in thy mercy; my heart shall rejoice in thy **salvation**.
Psalm 14:7	Oh that the **salvation** of Israel were come out of Zion! when the LORD bringeth back the captivity of his people, Jacob shall rejoice, and Israel shall be glad.
Psalm 18:2	The LORD is my rock, and my fortress, and my deliverer; my God, my strength, in whom I will trust; my buckler, and the horn of my **salvation**, and my high tower.
Psalm 18:35	Thou hast also given me the shield of thy **salvation**: and thy right hand hath holden me up, and thy gentleness hath made me great.
Psalm 18:46	The LORD liveth; and blessed be my rock; and let the God of my **salvation** be exalted.
Psalm 20:5	We will rejoice in thy **salvation**, and in the name of our God we will set up our banners: the LORD fulfill all thy petitions.
Psalm 21:1	The king shall joy in thy strength, O LORD; and in thy **salvation** how greatly shall he rejoice!
Psalm 21:5	His glory is great in thy **salvation**: honour and majesty hast thou laid upon him.
Psalm 24:5	He shall receive the blessing from the LORD, and righteousness from the God of his **salvation**.
Psalm 25:5	Lead me in thy truth, and teach me: for thou art the God of my **salvation**; on thee do I wait all the day.
Psalm 27:1	The LORD is my light and my **salvation**; whom shall I fear? the LORD is the strength of my life; of whom shall I be afraid?
Psalm 27:9	Hide not thy face far from me; put not thy servant away in anger: thou hast been my help; leave me not, neither forsake me, O God of my **salvation**.
Psalm 35:3	Draw out also the spear, and stop the way against them that persecute me: say unto my soul, I am thy **salvation**.
Psalm 35:9	And my soul shall be joyful in the LORD: it shall rejoice in his **salvation**.

Psalm 37:39	But the **salvation** of the righteous is of the LORD: he is their strength in the time of trouble.
Psalm 38:22	Make haste to help me, O Lord my **salvation**.
Psalm 40:10	I have not hid thy righteousness within my heart; I have declared thy faithfulness and thy **salvation**: I have not concealed thy lovingkindness and thy truth from the great congregation.
Psalm 40:16	Let all those that seek thee rejoice and be glad in thee: let such as love thy **salvation** say continually, The LORD be magnified.
Psalm 50:23	Whoso offereth praise glorifieth me: and to him that ordereth his conversation aright will I shew the **salvation** of God.
Psalm 51:12	Restore unto me the joy of thy **salvation**; and uphold me with thy free spirit.
Psalm 51:14	Deliver me from bloodguiltiness, O God, thou God of my **salvation**: and my tongue shall sing aloud of thy righteousness.
Psalm 53:6	Oh that the **salvation** of Israel were come out of Zion! When God bringeth back the captivity of his people, Jacob shall rejoice, and Israel shall be glad.
Psalm 62:1	Truly my soul waiteth upon God: from him cometh my **salvation**.
Psalm 62:2	He only is my rock and my **salvation**; he is my defence; I shall not be greatly moved.
Psalm 62:6	He only is my rock and my **salvation**: he is my defence; I shall not be moved.
Psalm 62:7	In God is my **salvation** and my glory: the rock of my strength, and my refuge, is in God.
Psalm 65:5	By terrible things in righteousness wilt thou answer us, O God of our **salvation**; who art the confidence of all the ends of the earth, and of them that are afar off upon the sea:
Psalm 68:19	Blessed be the Lord, who daily loadeth us with benefits, even the God of our **salvation**. Selah.

Psalm 68:20	He that is our God is the God of **salvation**; and unto GOD the Lord belong the issues from death.
Psalm 69:13	But as for me, my prayer is unto thee, O LORD, in an acceptable time: O God, in the multitude of thy mercy hear me, in the truth of thy **salvation**.
Psalm 69:29	But I am poor and sorrowful: let thy **salvation**, O God, set me up on high.
Psalm 70:4	Let all those that seek thee rejoice and be glad in thee: and let such as love thy **salvation** say continually, Let God be magnified.
Psalm 71:15	My mouth shall shew forth thy righteousness and thy **salvation** all the day; for I know not the numbers thereof.
Psalm 74:12	For God is my King of old, working **salvation** in the midst of the earth.
Psalm 78:22	Because they believed not in God, and trusted not in his **salvation**:
Psalm 79:9	Help us, O God of our **salvation**, for the glory of thy name: and deliver us, and purge away our sins, for thy name's sake.
Psalm 85:4	Turn us, O God of our **salvation**, and cause thine anger toward us to cease.
Psalm 85:7	Shew us thy mercy, O LORD, and grant us thy **salvation**.
Psalm 85:9	Surely his **salvation** is nigh them that fear him; that glory may dwell in our land.
Psalm 88:1	O lord God of my **salvation**, I have cried day and night before thee:
Psalm 89:26	He shall cry unto me, Thou art my father, my God, and the rock of my **salvation**.
Psalm 91:16	With long life will I satisfy him, and shew him my **salvation**.
Psalm 95:1	O come, let us sing unto the LORD: let us make a joyful noise to the rock of our **salvation**.

Psalm 96:2	Sing unto the LORD, bless his name; shew forth his **salvation** from day to day.
Psalm 98:2	The LORD hath made known his **salvation**: his righteousness hath he openly shewed in the sight of the heathen.
Psalm 98:3	He hath remembered his mercy and his truth toward the house of Israel: all the ends of the earth have seen the **salvation** of our God.
Psalm 106:4	Remember me, O LORD, with the favour that thou bearest unto thy people: O visit me with thy **salvation**;
Psalm 116:13	I will take the cup of **salvation**, and call upon the name of the LORD.
Psalm 118:14	The LORD is my strength and song, and is become my **salvation**.
Psalm 118:15	The voice of rejoicing and **salvation** is in the tabernacles of the righteous: the right hand of the LORD doeth valiantly.
Psalm 118:21	I will praise thee: for thou hast heard me, and art become my **salvation**.
Psalm 119:41	Let thy mercies come also unto me, O LORD, even thy **salvation**, according to thy word.
Psalm 119:81	My soul fainteth for thy **salvation**: but I hope in thy word.
Psalm 119:123	Mine eyes fail for thy **salvation**, and for the word of thy righteousness.
Psalm 119:155	**salvation** is far from the wicked: for they seek not thy statutes.
Psalm 119:166	LORD, I have hoped for thy **salvation**, and done thy commandments.
Psalm 119:174	I have longed for thy **salvation**, O LORD; and thy law is my delight.
Psalm 132:16	I will also clothe her priests with **salvation**: and her saints shall shout aloud for joy.
Psalm 140:7	O GOD the Lord, the strength of my **salvation**, thou hast covered my head in the day of battle.

Psalm 144:10	It is he that giveth **salvation** unto kings: who delivereth David his servant from the hurtful sword.
Psalm 149:4	For the LORD taketh pleasure in his people: he will beautify the meek with **salvation**.
Isaiah 12:2	Behold, God is my **salvation**; I will trust, and not be afraid: for the LORD JEHOVAH is my strength and my song; he also is become my **salvation**.
Isaiah 12:3	Therefore with joy shall ye draw water out of the wells of **salvation**.
Isaiah 17:10	Because thou hast forgotten the God of thy **salvation**, and hast not been mindful of the rock of thy strength, therefore shalt thou plant pleasant plants, and shalt set it with strange slips:
Isaiah 25:9	And it shall be said in that day, Lo, this is our God; we have waited for him, and he will save us: this is the LORD; we have waited for him, we will be glad and rejoice in his **salvation**.
Isaiah 26:1	In that day shall this song be sung in the land of Judah; We have a strong city; **salvation** will God appoint for walls and bulwarks.
Isaiah 33:2	O LORD, be gracious unto us; we have waited for thee: be thou their arm every morning, our **salvation** also in the time of trouble.
Isaiah 33:6	And wisdom and knowledge shall be the stability of thy times, and strength of **salvation**: the fear of the LORD is his treasure.
Isaiah 45:8	Drop down, ye heavens, from above, and let the skies pour down righteousness: let the earth open, and let them bring forth **salvation**, and let righteousness spring up together; I the LORD have created it.
Isaiah 45:17	But Israel shall be saved in the LORD with an everlasting **salvation**: ye shall not be ashamed nor confounded world without end.
Isaiah 46:13	I bring near my righteousness; it shall not be far off, and my **salvation** shall not tarry: and I will place **salvation** in Zion for Israel my glory.

Isaiah 49:6	And he said, It is a light thing that thou shouldest be my servant to raise up the tribes of Jacob, and to restore the preserved of Israel: I will also give thee for a light to the Gentiles, that thou mayest be my **salvation** unto the end of the earth.
Isaiah 49:8	Thus saith the LORD, In an acceptable time have I heard thee, and in a day of **salvation** have I helped thee: and I will preserve thee, and give thee for a covenant of the people, to establish the earth, to cause to inherit the desolate heritages;
Isaiah 51:5	My righteousness is near; my **salvation** is gone forth, and mine arms shall judge the people; the isles shall wait upon me, and on mine arm shall they trust.
Isaiah 51:6	Lift up your eyes to the heavens, and look upon the earth beneath: for the heavens shall vanish away like smoke, and the earth shall wax old like a garment, and they that dwell therein shall die in like manner: but my **salvation** shall be forever, and my righteousness shall not be abolished.
Isaiah 51:8	For the moth shall eat them up like a garment, and the worm shall eat them like wool: but my righteousness shall be forever, and my **salvation** from generation to generation.
Isaiah 52:7	How beautiful upon the mountains are the feet of him that bringeth good tidings, that publisheth peace; that bringeth good tidings of good, that publisheth **salvation**; that saith unto Zion, Thy God reigneth!
Isaiah 52:10	The LORD hath made bare his holy arm in the eyes of all the nations; and all the ends of the earth shall see the **salvation** of our God.
Isaiah 56:1	Thus saith the LORD, Keep ye judgment, and do justice: for my **salvation** is near to come, and my righteousness to be revealed.
Isaiah 59:11	We roar all like bears, and mourn sore like doves: we look for judgment, but there is none; for **salvation**, but it is far off from us.
Isaiah 59:16	And he saw that there was no man, and wondered that there was no intercessor: therefore his arm brought **salvation** unto him; and his righteousness, it sustained him.

Isaiah 59:17	For he put on righteousness as a breastplate, and an helmet of **salvation** upon his head; and he put on the garments of vengeance for clothing, and was clad with zeal as a cloak.
Isaiah 60:18	Violence shall no more be heard in thy land, wasting nor destruction within thy borders; but thou shalt call thy walls **Salvation**, and thy gates Praise.
Isaiah 61:10	I will greatly rejoice in the LORD, my soul shall be joyful in my God; for he hath clothed me with the garments of **salvation**, he hath covered me with the robe of righteousness, as a bridegroom decketh himself with ornaments, and as a bride adorneth herself with her jewels.
Isaiah 62:1	For Zion's sake will I not hold my peace, and for Jerusalem's sake I will not rest, until the righteousness thereof go forth as brightness, and the **salvation** thereof as a lamp that burneth.
Isaiah 62:11	Behold, the LORD hath proclaimed unto the end of the world, Say ye to the daughter of Zion, Behold, thy **salvation** cometh; behold, his reward is with him, and his work before him.
Isaiah 63:5	And I looked, and there was none to help; and I wondered that there was none to uphold: therefore mine own arm brought **salvation** unto me; and my fury, it upheld me.
Jeremiah 3:23	Truly in vain is **salvation** hoped for from the hills, and from the multitude of mountains: truly in the LORD our God is the salvation of Israel.
Lamentations 3:26	It is good that a man should both hope and quietly wait for the **salvation** of the LORD.
Jonah 2:9	But I will sacrifice unto thee with the voice of thanksgiving; I will pay that that I have vowed. **Salvation** is of the LORD.
Micah 7:7	Therefore I will look unto the LORD; I will wait for the God of my **salvation**: my God will hear me.
Habakkuk 3:8	Was the LORD displeased against the rivers? was thine anger against the rivers? was thy wrath against the sea, that thou didst ride upon thine horses and thy chariots of **salvation**?

Habakkuk 3:13	Thou wentest forth for the salvation of thy people, even for **salvation** with thine anointed; thou woundedst the head out of the house of the wicked, by discovering the foundation unto the neck. Selah.
Habakkuk 3:18	Yet I will rejoice in the LORD, I will joy in the God of my **salvation**.
Zechariah 9:9	Rejoice greatly, O daughter of Zion; shout, O daughter of Jerusalem: behold, thy King cometh unto thee: he is just, and having **salvation**; lowly, and riding upon an ass, and upon a colt the foal of an ass.
Luke 1:69	And hath raised up an horn of **salvation** for us in the house of his servant David;
Luke 1:77	To give knowledge of **salvation** unto his people by the remission of their sins,
Luke 2:30	For mine eyes have seen thy **salvation**,
Luke 3:6	And all flesh shall see the **salvation** of God.
Luke 19:9	And Jesus said unto him, This day is **salvation** come to this house, forsomuch as he also is a son of Abraham.
John 4:22	Ye worship ye know not what: we know what we worship: for **salvation** is of the Jews.
Acts 4:12	Neither is there **salvation** in any other: for there is none other name under heaven given among men, whereby we must be saved.
Acts 13:26	Men and brethren, children of the stock of Abraham, and whosoever among you feareth God, to you is the word of this **salvation** sent.
Acts 13:47	For so hath the Lord commanded us, saying, I have set thee to be a light of the Gentiles, that thou shouldest be for **salvation** unto the ends of the earth.
Acts 16:17	The same followed Paul and us, and cried, saying, These men are the servants of the most high God, which shew unto us the way of **salvation**.
Acts 28:28	Be it known therefore unto you, that the **salvation** of God is sent unto the Gentiles, and that they will hear it.

Romans 1:16	For I am not ashamed of the gospel of Christ: for it is the power of God unto **salvation** to every one that believeth; to the Jew first, and also to the Greek.
Romans 10:10	For with the heart man believeth unto righteousness; and with the mouth confession is made unto **salvation**.
Romans 11:11	I say then, Have they stumbled that they should fall? God forbid: but rather through their fall **salvation** is come unto the Gentiles, for to provoke them to jealousy.
Romans 13:11	And that, knowing the time, that now it is high time to awake out of sleep: for now is our **salvation** nearer than when we believed.
2 Corinthians 1:6	And whether we be afflicted, it is for your consolation and **salvation**, which is effectual in the enduring of the same sufferings which we also suffer: or whether we be comforted, it is for your consolation and **salvation**.
2 Corinthians 6:2	(For he saith, I have heard thee in a time accepted, and in the day of **salvation** have I succoured thee: behold, now is the accepted time; behold, now is the day of salvation.)
2 Corinthians 7:10	For godly sorrow worketh repentance to **salvation** not to be repented of: but the sorrow of the world worketh death.
Ephesians 1:13	In whom ye also trusted, after that ye heard the word of truth, the gospel of your **salvation**: in whom also after that ye believed, ye were sealed with that holy Spirit of promise,
Ephesians 6:17	And take the helmet of **salvation**, and the sword of the Spirit, which is the word of God:
Philippians 1:19	For I know that this shall turn to my **salvation** through your prayer, and the supply of the Spirit of Jesus Christ,
Philippians 1:28	And in nothing terrified by your adversaries: which is to them an evident token of perdition, but to you of **salvation**, and that of God.

Philippians 2:12	Wherefore, my beloved, as ye have always obeyed, not as in my presence only, but now much more in my absence, work out your own **salvation** with fear and trembling.
1 Thessalonians 5:8	But let us, who are of the day, be sober, putting on the breastplate of faith and love; and for an helmet, the hope of **salvation**.
1 Thessalonians 5:9	For God hath not appointed us to wrath, but to obtain **salvation** by our Lord Jesus Christ,
2 Thessalonians 2:13	But we are bound to give thanks alway to God for you, brethren beloved of the Lord, because God hath from the beginning chosen you to **salvation** through sanctification of the Spirit and belief of the truth:
2 Timothy 2:10	Therefore I endure all things for the elect's sakes, that they may also obtain the **salvation** which is in Christ Jesus with eternal glory.
2 Timothy 3:15	And that from a child thou hast known the holy scriptures, which are able to make thee wise unto **salvation** through faith which is in Christ Jesus.
Titus 2:11	For the grace of God that bringeth **salvation** hath appeared to all men,
Hebrews 1:14	Are they not all ministering spirits, sent forth to minister for them who shall be heirs of **salvation**?
Hebrews 2:3	How shall we escape, if we neglect so great **salvation**; which at the first began to be spoken by the Lord, and was confirmed unto us by them that heard him;
Hebrews 2:10	For it became him, for whom are all things, and by whom are all things, in bringing many sons unto glory, to make the captain of their **salvation** perfect through sufferings.
Hebrews 5:9	And being made perfect, he became the author of eternal **salvation** unto all them that obey him;
Hebrews 6:9	But, beloved, we are persuaded better things of you, and things that accompany **salvation**, though we thus speak.
Hebrews 9:28	So Christ was once offered to bear the sins of many; and unto them that look for him shall he appear the second time without sin unto **salvation**.

1 Peter 1:5	Who are kept by the power of God through faith unto **salvation** ready to be revealed in the last time.
1 Peter 1:9	Receiving the end of your faith, even the **salvation** of your souls.
1 Peter 1:10	Of which **salvation** the prophets have enquired and searched diligently, who prophesied of the grace that should come unto you:
2 Peter 3:15	And account that the longsuffering of our Lord is **salvation**; even as our beloved brother Paul also according to the wisdom given unto him hath written unto you;
Jude 1:3	Beloved, when I gave all diligence to write unto you of the common **salvation**, it was needful for me to write unto you, and exhort you that ye should earnestly contend for the faith which was once delivered unto the saints.
Revelation 7:10	And cried with a loud voice, saying, **salvation** to our God which sitteth upon the throne, and unto the Lamb.
Revelation 12:10	And I heard a loud voice saying in heaven, Now is come **salvation**, and strength, and the kingdom of our God, and the power of his Christ: for the accuser of our brethren is cast down, which accused them before our God day and night.
Revelation 19:1	And after these things I heard a great voice of much people in heaven, saying, Alleluia; **Salvation**, and glory, and honour, and power, unto the Lord our God:

Index of
Deliverance Scriptures

◆ ◆ ◆

Genesis 45:7	And God sent me before you to preserve you a posterity in the earth, and to save your lives by a great **deliverance**.
Judges 15:18	And he was sore athirst, and called on the LORD, and said, Thou hast given this great **deliverance** into the hand of thy servant: and now shall I die for thirst, and fall into the hand of the uncircumcised?
2 Kings 5:1	Now Naaman, captain of the host of the king of Syria, was a great man with his master, and honourable, because by him the LORD had given **deliverance** unto Syria: he was also a mighty man in valour, but he was a leper.
2 Kings 13:17	And he said, Open the window eastward. And he opened it. Then Elisha said, Shoot. And he shot. And he said, The arrow of the LORD's **deliverance**, and the arrow of **deliverance** from Syria: for thou shalt smite the Syrians in Aphek, till thou have consumed them.
1 Chronicles 11:14	And they set themselves in the midst of that parcel, and delivered it, and slew the Philistines; and the LORD saved them by a great **deliverance**.
2 Chronicles 12:7	And when the LORD saw that they humbled themselves, the word of the LORD came to Shemaiah, saying, They have humbled themselves; therefore I will not destroy them, but I will grant them some **deliverance**; and my wrath shall not be poured out upon Jerusalem by the hand of Shishak.
Ezra 9:13	And after all that is come upon us for our evil deeds, and for our great trespass, seeing that thou our God

	hast punished us less than our iniquities deserve, and hast given us such **deliverance** as this;
Esther 4:14	For if thou altogether holdest thy peace at this time, then shall there enlargement and **deliverance** arise to the Jews from another place; but thou and thy father's house shall be destroyed: and who knoweth whether thou art come to the kingdom for such a time as this?
Psalm 18:50	Great **deliverance** giveth he to his king; and sheweth mercy to his anointed, to David, and to his seed for evermore.
Psalm 32:7	Thou art my hiding place; thou shalt preserve me from trouble; thou shalt compass me about with songs of **deliverance**. Selah.
Psalm 44:4	Thou art my King, O God: command **deliverances** for Jacob.
Isaiah 26:18	We have been with child, we have been in pain, we have as it were brought forth wind; we have not wrought any **deliverance** in the earth; neither have the inhabitants of the world fallen.
Joel 2:32	And it shall come to pass, that whosoever shall call on the name of the LORD shall be delivered: for in mount Zion and in Jerusalem shall be **deliverance**, as the LORD hath said, and in the remnant whom the LORD shall call.
Obadiah 1:17	But upon mount Zion shall be **deliverance**, and there shall be holiness; and the house of Jacob shall possess their possessions.
Luke 4:18	The Spirit of the Lord is upon me, because he hath anointed me to preach the gospel to the poor; he hath sent me to heal the brokenhearted, to preach **deliverance** to the captives, and recovering of sight to the blind, to set at liberty them that are bruised,
Hebrews 11:35	Women received their dead raised to life again: and others were tortured, not accepting **deliverance**; that they might obtain a better resurrection:

Index of Subjects

◆ ◆ ◆

Made in the USA
Middletown, DE
11 May 2022

65656057R00235